MOHAWK FRONTIER

MOHAWK FRONTIER

The Dutch Community of Schenectady, New York, 1661–1710

Thomas E. Burke, Jr.

Cornell University Press

Ithaca and London

OCLC: 23868727

WITHDRAWN

For Terry and for my parents

Contents

Maps and Tables   ix

Preface   xi

Abbreviations   xv

1. The Founding of Schenectady   1

2. "The most beautiful land"   33

3. A "sad and deplorable massacre"   68

4. White, Black, and Red at Schenectady   109

5. A Divided Community   157

6. To "gain some little profit"   196

Bibliography   223

Index   239

Maps

The lands of the Iroquois 5
Initial land grants at Schenectady 34
Detail of Schenectady from the 1698 Romer map 37
Albany, Schenectady, Rensselaerswyck, and vicinity 45
The 1698 Romer map of Albany 167

Tables

1. Farms at Rensselaerswyck in 1651 35
2. Comparison of four Schenectady farms 41
3. Comparison of livestock holdings on Schenectady farms 49
4. An inventory of William Teller's farm at Schenectady, 1664 and 1679 54
5. Slaves at Schenectady on February 8, 1690 62
6. The 1690 attack on Schenectady compared with other French and Iroquois raids, 1689–1704, by casualties 107
7. Schenectady's estimated population on February 8, 1690 110
8. Number of slaves killed or captured at Schenectady, February 8, 1690, by owner 123
9. Evidence of slave ownership at Schenectady before 1690 126

10. Slave ownership at Schenectady, 1690 compared with
    1697   136
11. White and slave populations of Albany, Schenectady, and
    Rensselaerswyck in 1714, by sex and age group   138
12. Schenectady church records documenting ceremonies for
    Indians and slaves, 1694–1760   140
13. Opponents and supporters of Jacob Leisler at Schenectady   160
14. Schenectady officeholders, 1669–1690   163
15. Schenectady signers of 1701 address to King William III   178
16. Supporters of Reyer Schermerhorn at Schenectady   179
17. Opponents of Reyer Schermerhorn at Schenectady   192
18. Number of marriages performed in the New York
    Reformed Dutch church in which at least one member of
    the couple was from Albany County, 1680–1699   197
19. Return of captives to Schenectady   202
20. Englishmen at Schenectady, 1690–1705   207

Preface

This book is an examination of the Dutch community at Schenectady, a village founded on the Mohawk River—the northern frontier of New Netherland—three years before that colony's conquest by the English. Schenectady was a small community, but in many aspects its history mirrors much of the contemporary history of New Netherland and New York, so that to delineate the details of its political, social, and economic life is to illuminate a larger picture as well.

A village at Schenectady had been proposed by Arent van Curler as early as the 1640s, but almost two decades elapsed before the community's establishment. For many years, the inhabitants of the Hudson River communities at Beverwyck and Rensselaerswyck could depend on the annual arrival of Mohawks and other Indians bearing furs overland from the Mohawk River to trade for clothing, food, drink, and weapons. This profitable relationship collapsed at the end of the 1650s. Suddenly furs were scarce. Moreover, at this same moment the Dutch trade received the unwelcome attention of prominent New Englanders such as John Pynchon who were eager to expand English trade and settlement into the region. Incentive for a settlement on the Mohawk thus ultimately derived from both the designs of members of the nearby trading communities at Beverwyck and Rensselaerswyck (individuals seeking to repair their damaged fortunes) and those of the Dutch governor, Petrus Stuyvesant, who sanctioned the village's creation at this moment of crisis in the fur trade with the Iroquois and in relations with the English.

In this work I explore Schenectady's origins and its destruction in

1690, placing both in a broad context of Anglo-Dutch, Dutch-French, and Anglo-French relations throughout the period. I have paid particular attention to Dutch-Indian relations, but Schenectady is also revealed to have been a more ethnically and culturally diverse community than has previously been realized. Members of the Iroquois tribes were present at the village during summer trading months and as they readied themselves for war, and Indian men, women, and children played a vital role in the community's daily life. French *coureurs de bois*, African slaves, and, from the 1690s on, English soldiers and settlers all visited, resided, or were garrisoned at the village. This is their story as well.

Situated on the banks of the Mohawk River, less than twenty miles by land from Beverwyck (Albany) and midway between that community and the first "castle" of the Mohawks, Schenectady was ideally located for participation in the fur trade. The plans of Schenectady's founders were frustrated, however, by Albany's monopoly of that trade and by the reduced number of furs available after 1660. Instead, a rising demand for grain, especially wheat for export, enhanced the value of the rich alluvial land at Schenectady and along the Mohawk River, making it the community's most sought-after and profitable resource. But land was a commodity unequally divided among Schenectady's settlers. By the first decade of the eighteenth century, if not earlier, the distribution of the village's common lands emerged as a fundamental point of dispute between two groups at the village, factions that corresponded closely to the Leislerian and anti-Leislerian parties that had existed there a decade earlier.

In 1690 the Schenectady community was paralyzed by dissension and unable to attend to even the most basic considerations of defense. As a result, the attack by some two hundred French and Indians on the night of February 8 succeeded in the destruction of the village and the killing or capturing of many of its inhabitants. Rebuilt and repopulated in the years afterward, Schenectady remained a divided community. Indeed, the dispute centering on the village's common lands resisted resolution for almost a century. That this should be so may be explained in part by the mores and motivations of the village's founders and settlers. From its earliest origins, Schenectady was an individualistic, pluralistic community. No ethos of otherworldly communalism ever joined the inhabitants together. The settlers were bound by no point of common origin or moment of arrival. For some, the village was only one of a series of residences and not necessarily the last. Perhaps for all, Schenectady was at least as much an investment as a home. Its founding and settlement had been and remained a starkly economic venture.

The publication of Oliver A. Rink's *Holland on the Hudson: An Economic and Social History of Dutch New York* (1986) has provided scholars with the text that must be considered the definitive starting point for all future New Netherland studies. But Rink's perspective, focused as it is on the commercial and mercantile history of New Netherland, needs to be complemented by a close examination of the internal life of the communities that made up the Dutch colony. Schenectady was one of the last settlements established during the era of Dutch rule, and its history straddles both the Dutch and the English periods. Yet standard works such as Robert Ritchie's *The Duke's Province: A Study of New York Politics and Society* (1977) hardly mention the Mohawk Valley settlement.

Of modern historians, only Donna Merwick and the late Alice Kenney have used, in any comprehensive sense, many of the community history records cited in this book. Readers familiar with the growing body of scholarship on Dutch New Netherland and Anglo-Dutch New York, however, will recognize that my understanding of the concerns that motivated and divided Schenectady's inhabitants stems ultimately from the community's Mohawk Valley setting and the immediacy of events within New Netherland and New York— the impact of developments focused by ethnic diversity, economic transformation, and imperial rivalry—rather than the replication of traditions derived from the Dutch homeland.

The present work is a product of several years' effort to comprehend the history of the settlements of the upper Hudson and Mohawk region. My being able to continue research and writing on this subject was one result of my association with the Colonial Albany Social History Project, located at the New York State Museum. The work undertaken by the project and its director, Stefan Bielinski, will recast our understanding of life in early American communities. I hope that this book will mark one step in that larger effort.

I must reserve a special thanks for Sung Bok Kim, at the State University of New York at Albany, who has supported this work since its inception. Peter Agree at Cornell University Press has provided much encouragement, and Carol Betsch's copyediting improved the book's organization and expression. I also extend my gratitude to the New Netherland Project for the selection of this work as the winner of the 1988 Hendricks manuscript award.

An earlier version of Chapter 1 appeared as "The New Netherland Fur Trade, 1657–1661: Response to Crisis," *De Halve Maen*, 59 (March 1986). Portions of Chapters 2, 3, and 5 were previously published in "Leisler's Rebellion at Schenectady, New York, 1689–1710," *New York History*, 70 (October 1989), and "Arent van Curler and the Fur Trade at Early Schenectady," Dutch Settlers Society of Albany *Yearbook*, 49 (1984–1987). The material has been reworked and appears here by permission of the Holland Society of New York, the Dutch Settlers Society of Albany, and the New York State Historical Association.

Where possible, I have sought to use the most recent and authoritative translations and documentary editions. Many important documents remain untranslated, however, or exist only in flawed nineteenth-century texts. I am particularly grateful for the efforts of Charles Gehring and Peter Christoph of the New Netherland Project and the New York State Library, who are making many relevant seventeenth-century Dutch and English documents available for the first time. Except for minor alterations, placed in brackets, I have not changed or expanded quoted material; all superscripts, however, have been brought down to the line.

THOMAS E. BURKE, JR.

Albany, New York

Abbreviations

AP   *The Andros Papers: Files of the Provincial Secretary of New York during the Administration of Governor Sir Edmund Andros, 1674–1680.* Ed. Peter R. and Florence A. Christoph. 3 vols. Trans. Charles T. Gehring. Syracuse: Syracuse University Press, 1989–1991.

ARS   *Minutes of the Court of Albany, Rensselaerswyck, and Schenectady, 1668–1685.* Ed. A. J. F. van Laer. 3 vols. Albany: University of the State of New York, 1926–1932.

AVDD   Van der Donck, Adriaen. *A Description of New Netherland.* Ed. Thomas F. O'Donnell. Syracuse: Syracuse University Press, 1968.

BGE   *Books of General Entries of the Colony of New York, 1664–1688.* Ed. Peter R. and Florence A. Christoph. 2 vols. Baltimore: Genealogical Publishing, 1982.

CHMD   *Calendar of Historical Manuscripts in the Office of the Secretary of State, Albany, N.Y. Dutch Manuscripts, 1630–1664.* Ed. Edmund B. O'Callaghan. Albany: Weed, Parsons, 1865.

CHME   *Calendar of Historical Manuscripts in the Office of the Secretary of State, Albany, N.Y. English Manuscripts, 1664–1776.* Ed. Edmund B. O'Callaghan. Albany: Weed, Parsons, 1866.

CHR   *Canadian Historical Review.*

CJVR   *Correspondence of Jeremias van Rensselaer, 1651–1674.* Ed. A. J. F. van Laer. Albany: University of the State of New York, 1932.

CMVR   *Correspondence of Maria van Rensselaer, 1669–1689.* Ed. A. J. F. van Laer. Albany: University of the State of New York, 1935.

DCB   *Dictionary of Canadian Biography.* 11 vols. Toronto: University of Toronto Press, 1966–1982.

DHNY   *Documentary History of the State of New York.* Ed. Edmund B. O'Callaghan. 4 vols. Albany: Weed, Parsons, 1849–1851.

DSSAY   Dutch Settlers Society of Albany, *Yearbook.*

ER   *Ecclesiastical Records of the State of New York.* Ed. Edward T. Corwin. 7 vols. Albany: James B. Lyon, 1901–1916.

ERAR   *Early Records of the City and County of Albany and Colony of Rensse-*
            laerswyck. Ed. A. J. F. van Laer. Trans. Jonathan Pearson. 4 vols.
            Albany: University of the State of New York, 1869–1919.
FOB   *Minutes of the Court of Fort Orange and Beverwyck, 1652–1660.* Ed.
            A. J. F. van Laer. 2 vols. Albany: University of the State of New
            York, 1920–1923.
FS   Pearson, Jonathan. *Contributions for the Genealogies of the Descendants of*
            the First Settlers of the Patent and City of Schenectady. Albany, 1873;
            reprint, Baltimore: Genealogical Publishing, 1976.
HMVDB   Van den Bogaert, Harmen Meyndertsz. *A Journey into Mohawk and*
            Oneida Country, 1634–1635: The Journal of Harmen Meyndertsz van den
            Bogaert. Ed. Charles T. Gehring and William A. Starna. Syracuse:
            Syracuse University Press, 1988.
HNAIN   *Handbook of North American Indians.* William C. Sturtevant, gen. ed.
            Vol. XV, *Northeast.* Ed. Bruce G. Trigger. Washington, D.C.:
            Smithsonian Institution, 1978.
JAH   *Journal of American History.*
JD   Danckaerts, Jasper. *Journal of Jasper Danckaerts, 1679–1680.* Ed. Bart-
            lett Burleigh James and J. Franklin Jameson. New York: Charles
            Scribner's Sons, 1913.
JR   *The Jesuit Relations and Allied Documents: Travels and Explorations of*
            the Jesuit Missionaries in New France, 1619–1791. Ed. Reuben G.
            Thwaites. 73 vols. Cleveland, 1896–1901; reprint, New York: Pag-
            eant Book, 1959.
LIR   *The Livingston Indian Records, 1666–1723.* Ed. Lawrence H. Leder.
            Gettysburg, Pa., 1956.
LONN   *Laws and Ordinances of New Netherlands, 1636–1674.* Ed. Edmund B.
            O'Callaghan. Albany: Weed, Parsons, 1868.
MVHR   *Mississippi Valley Historical Review.*
NL   *Administrative Papers of Governors Richard Nicolls and Francis Lovelace,*
            1664–1673. Ed. Peter R. Christoph. Baltimore: Genealogical
            Publishing, 1980.
NNN   *Narratives of New Netherland, 1609–1664.* Ed. J. Franklin Jameson.
            New York: Charles Scribner's Sons, 1909.
NYCD   *Documents Relative to the Colonial History of the State of New York.* Ed.
            Edmund B. O'Callaghan and Berthold Fernow. 15 vols. Albany:
            Weed, Parsons, 1856–1887.
NYH   *New York History.*
NYHSC   New-York Historical Society, *Collections.*
NYHSQ   *New-York Historical Society Quarterly.*
PA   *Pennsylvania Archives.* Ed. Samuel Hazard et al. 138 vols.
            Philadelphia: Joseph Severens et al., 1852–1949.
SP   Pearson, Jonathan. *A History of the Schenectady Patent in the Dutch and*
            English Times. Ed. J. W. MacMurray. Albany: Joel Munsell's Sons,
            1883.

VRBM   *Van Rensselaer Bowier Manuscripts.* Ed. A. J. F. van Laer. Albany: University of the State of New York, 1908.
WMQ   *William and Mary Quarterly.*

MOHAWK FRONTIER

I

The Founding of Schenectady

During the sixteenth century, the seven provinces that became the United Provinces of the Netherlands were only one part of the extensive empire of Charles V and Philip II. Armed resistance against Habsburg rule began in 1566, but not before 1648 would the Netherlands achieve political and religious independence from the Spanish crown and the Roman Church. These eighty years of conflict witnessed both the reduction of Spanish power and the expansion of Dutch worldwide commerce.[1]

In the 1590s, Jan Huighen van Linschoten published an *Itinerario*, a geography of the world including his own observations of the East derived from several years of service at the Portuguese colony of Goa on the west coast of India. The first Dutch fleet to use van Linschoten's directions sailed in 1595. Others followed, and by 1598 at least thirteen Dutch ships representing several companies of merchants were trafficking in the region. Four years later, in 1602, the Dutch States General determined to combine these companies into one national concern, the Dutch East India Company. The Company was given a monopoly of trade extending from the Cape of Africa to Magellan's Strait. It could make war or peace, capture foreign vessels, found colonies, establish forts, and coin money.[2]

Initially, Dutch experience in the Americas was as limited as it had been in the East. The success of the East India Company, however, suggested a pattern for profit in the Western territories claimed by

1. Pieter Geyl, *The Revolt of the Netherlands, 1555–1609* (New York, 1958), 79–99; Charles R. Boxer, *The Dutch Seaborne Empire, 1600–1800* (New York, 1965), chap. 1; Violet Barbour, *Capitalism in Amsterdam in the 17th Century* (Ann Arbor, 1966).

2. J. H. Parry, *The Establishment of European Hegemony: 1415–1715* (New York, 1961), 87–89.

Spain and Portugal. The sugar region of northern Brazil, the natural salt pans at Curaçao in the West Indies, and the fur trade of the North (Hudson), South (Delaware), and Fresh (Connecticut) rivers, all attracted Dutch merchants and ship owners, especially during the years of truce with Spain between 1609 and 1621.[3]

Apprehension of renewed conflict after 1621 served as a catalyst for the creation of a Dutch West India Company during that year. As its first large-scale undertaking in the Americas, the Company wrested control of the sugar-producing region of northeast Brazil from the Portuguese. Elsewhere, in 1634, a Dutch fleet seized Curaçao off the coast of Venezuela. This island soon became the focus of Dutch commerce in the West Indies. At the same time, a third center of Dutch trade emerged on the North American mainland between the Connecticut and Delaware rivers.[4]

Brazil, Curaçao, and New Netherland—these holdings constituted the extended domain of the Dutch West India Company in the Western hemisphere. Although commercially important because of its fur trade, New Netherland attracted only a fraction of the Company's efforts and resources. In 1647, when Petrus Stuyvesant arrived as the colony's director-general, its population stood at no more than 1,200 persons. New Netherland continued to survive until 1664, but Indian hostilities, expansive pressures from both Maryland and Massachusetts, and the declining state of the fur trade all suggested the tenuous hold of the Dutch West India Company on its North American colony. It was at the end of this period of Dutch rule, however, and as a direct response to the troubled condition of the colony's fur trade, that a community was founded at Schenectady on the Mohawk River.[5]

The beginnings of the fur trade in New Netherland extended back at least as far as 1609. When Henry Hudson's *Halve Maen* entered New York Bay in September 1609, Robert Juet, an English crew member, recorded that local Indians who boarded the vessel were clothed in "divers sort of good Furres." Hudson himself traded for

3. Ibid., 110–114; Thomas J. Condon, *New York Beginnings: The Commercial Origins of New Netherland* (New York, 1968), 39–51.
4. Oliver A. Rink, *Holland on the Hudson: An Economic and Social History of Dutch New York* (Ithaca, 1986), chap. 2 and 3; Condon, *New York Beginnings*, 52–55; Parry, *Establishment of European Hegemony*, 112–113.
5. Rink, *Holland on the Hudson*, 156–171; Parry, *Establishment of European Hegemony*, 116–119; Ronald D. Cohen, "The Hartford Treaty of 1650: Anglo-Dutch Cooperation in the Seventeenth Century," *NYHSQ*, 53 (1969), 311–332.

beaver and otter pelts in the region of present-day Albany and was presented with "stropes of Beades," possibly a belt or belts of wampum.[6]

Hudson's voyage demonstrated the existence of a readily available source of fine quality furs and of native peoples who were eager to exchange such peltry for European-made goods. This knowledge figured prominently in the commercial calculations of Dutch merchants who previously had depended on Russia as a source for furs. The Russian trade was burdened by a 5-percent tax imposed by the czarist government on all imports and exports. Offered an opportunity to acquire duty-free furs, Dutch merchants responded immediately. Each year after 1609 one or more Dutch ships were trading on the Hudson River. Hendrick Christiaensen, Adriaen Block, and others plied the waterway, and in 1614 a fortified trading post, Fort Nassau, was constructed on an island with Hendrick Christiaensen in command. This structure, near present-day Albany, was subject to yearly flooding, however, and was soon abandoned. In 1624 the newly established Dutch West India Company erected a more permanent post, Fort Orange, on the west bank of the river to the north of the now derelict Fort Nassau.[7]

By accident, the Dutch had located their trading operations on the Hudson River at the juncture of two similar, if conflicting, native cultures. At least three Mahican villages were situated north and south of Fort Orange between Catskill and Cohoes. During his brief stay upriver in 1609, Hudson had traded with these Algonquian-speaking people. The nearest Iroquoian-speaking group, the Mohawks, had settled some thirty or more miles to the west, near modern Canajoharie. Although Johannes de Laet recorded in his *Nieuwe*

6. *NNN*, 18, 22–23; Lynn Ceci, "The Effect of European Contact and Trade on the Settlement Patterns of Indians in Coastal New York, 1524–1665: The Archeological and Documentary Evidence" (Ph.D. diss., City University of New York, 1977), 170–176. See also Christopher L. Miller and George R. Hamell, "A New Perspective on Indian-White Contact: Cultural Symbols and Colonial Trade," *JAH*, 73 (1986), 311–328; Elizabeth Shapiro Peña, "Wampum Production in New Netherland and Colonial New York: The Historical and Archaeological Context" (Ph.D. diss., Boston University, 1990).

7. Donald Lenig, "Of Dutchmen, Beaver Hats, and Iroquois," in Robert E. Funk and Charles F. Hayes, III, eds., *Current Perspectives in Northeastern Archeology* (Albany, 1977), 77. For the role of the private traders and for the formation of the Dutch West India Company, see Rink, *Holland on the Hudson*, chap. 1 and 2. For Fort Orange, see Paul Huey, "Archaeological Excavations in the Site of Fort Orange, a Dutch West India Company Trading Fort Built in 1624," in Boudewijn Bakker, ed., *New Netherland Studies: An Inventory of Current Research and Approaches* (Utrecht, 1985), 68–79.

Wereldt ofte beschrijvinghe van West-Indien (New World or Descriptions of the West Indies) that the Mohawks lived west of the Hudson River and their enemies, the Mahicans, lived to the east, in fact, not until 1628 or 1629 were the Mohawks able to force the Mahicans to vacate land to the west of the river. Perhaps the clearest indication of the Mahicans' diminished power was the agreement, concluded on August 13, 1630, between the tribe and the director and council of New Netherland by which a substantial body of land to the west of the Hudson River was purchased for the benefit of the patroon, Kiliaen van Rensselaer.[8]

Until the events of 1628–1629, the position of the Dutch at Fort Orange was analogous to that of the French under Champlain at Quebec. Like the French, the Dutch were in contact with local Algonquian-speaking tribes with whom they carried on the bulk of their trade in furs. The Iroquois, in particular the Mohawks, were a peripheral and disruptive element in that trade. At Quebec, Champlain eventually assented to Algonquian requests that he join their war parties against the Mohawks. So too did the Dutch commander at Fort Orange, though with more tragic results. In 1625 Nicolaes van Wassenaer reported that Daniel van Krieckenbeeck, together with six of his men and a party of Mahicans, were ambushed near Fort Orange by the Mohawks, "who peppered them . . . with a discharge of arrows . . . leaving many slain among whom were the Commander and three of his men."[9]

With the exception of the unfortunate van Krieckenbeeck, the Dutch refused to become enmeshed in local Indian rivalries. Unlike their French competitors on the St. Lawrence, the Dutch at Fort Orange found that they could have ready access to, and maintain trading relations with, both Algonquian and Iroquoian groups. That

---

8. Lenig, "Of Dutchmen, Beaver Hats, and Iroquois," 78; Allen Trelease, *Indian Affairs in Colonial New York: The Seventeenth Century* (Ithaca, 1960), 14–15; T. J. Brasser, "Mahican," *HNAIN*, 198; T. J. Brasser, *Riding on the Frontier's Crest: Mahican Indian Culture and Culture Change* (Ottawa, 1974). For Johannes de Laet, see Rink, *Holland on the Hudson*, 30. For the Indian war, see Bruce G. Trigger, "The Mohawk-Mahican War (1624–1628): The Establishment of a Pattern," *CHR*, 52 (1971), 276–286. For the land acquisition of 1630, see Trelease, *Indian Affairs*, 48–49; *VRBM*, 29, 166–169.

9. For Champlain's 1610 and 1615 forays against the Iroquois, see Samuel E. Morison, *Samuel de Champlain, Father of New France* (Boston, 1972), 117–120, 153–161. For Champlain and the French in Canada at this time, see Samuel de Champlain, *The Works of Samuel de Champlain*, ed. H. P. Biggar, 6 vols. (Toronto, 1922–1936), II and III. For Wassenaer, see Rink, *Holland on the Hudson*, 70; concerning van Krieckenbeeck, see *DHNY*, III, 43–44.

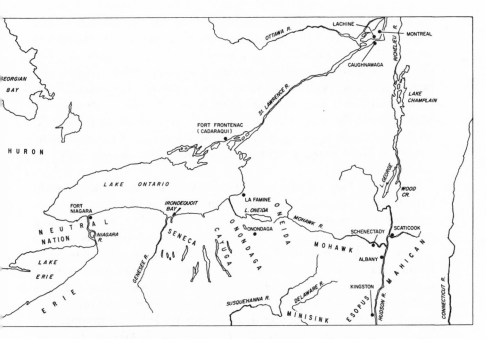

The lands of the Iroquois. From Trelease, *Indian Affairs*

the Mohawks were as willing to trade as to fight was made clear in the aftermath of the van Krieckenbeeck affair. When visited by Pieter Barentsz, a local trader, the Mohawks complained "that they had never injured the whites and asked the reason why the latter had meddled with them." Realizing that little else could be done, Barentsz accepted the protest as an apology. As of yet, however, the Mohawks enjoyed no favored status as trading partners. According to Wassenaer, "this Pieter Barentsz . . . [was] conversant with all the Tribes thereabout; he traded with . . . the Sinnekox, Wappenox, Maquaes and Maikans, so that he visited all the Tribes . . . and traded in a friendly manner . . . for peltries."[10]

During the 1620s and 1630s, the Dutch West India Company sought to control the New Netherland fur trade and to prohibit private traders at Fort Orange and throughout the colony. Kiliaen van

---

10. *DHNY*, III 44, 46. In the wake of the events at Fort Orange there was a new focus on settlement at Manhattan. Rink, *Holland on the Hudson*, 86–87. This early period of settlement and trade sponsored by the Dutch West India Company is examined in A. J. F. van Laer, ed., *Documents Relating to New Netherland, 1624–1626, in the Henry E. Huntington Library* (San Marino, Calif., 1924).

Rensselaer also instructed his settlers at Rensselaerswyck that no one employed by him or living in his colony "shall presume to barter any peltries with the savages or seek to obtain them as a present." But official prohibitions, whether by the Company or by the patroon, proved fruitless. New Netherland's inhabitants quickly became competitors for both furs and wampum (seawan). Indeed, as early as 1626, Isaac de Rasiere, the Company secretary, admitted that he was buying wampum from the inhabitants at Manhattan. That same year, settlers at Fort Orange sought to outbid each other and the Company for furs.[11]

Until 1639 Fort Orange was officially the exclusive trading post of the Dutch West India Company. Yet the Company was forced to contend with smuggling by its servants and settlers, the increasing sophistication of native traders, and the efforts of patroons such as Kiliaen van Rensselaer who sought to exploit the fur trade in order to finance the operation of their domains. In that year the Company opened its upriver trade to private individuals provided that they pay a duty on all goods imported to or exported from the province. Soon van Rensselaer was bragging that "the fur trade begins gradually to get into our hands." Finally, in 1644, the Dutch West India Company closed its trading house at Fort Orange. The fort continued to be maintained as a Company outpost, but it became increasingly a place of rendezvous and settlement for private traders who congregated in the village of Beverwyck located to the north of the wooden structure.[12]

Father Isaac Jogues, the Jesuit missionary to the Mohawks who was at Beverwyck and Rensselaerswyck in 1643, has provided one of the earliest accounts of those settlements in the period immediately after the opening of the fur trade to private individuals. According to

---

11. *VRBM*, 209. For the Dutch West India Company's efforts to control trade, see *LONN*, 10–12; Oliver A. Rink, "Company Management or Private Trade: The Two Patroonship Plans for New Netherland," *NYH*, 59 (1978), 5–26. The commercial history of New Netherland is treated in Rink, *Holland on the Hudson*; Condon, *New York Beginnings*; and Van Cleaf Bachman, *Peltries or Plantations: The Economic Policies of the Dutch West India Company in New Netherland, 1623–1639* (Baltimore, 1969). For the illegal trade in furs, see Ceci, "Effect of European Contact and Trade," 195–196; Trelease, *Indian Affairs*, 50.

12. *VRBM*, 520. For Company developments during the 1630s and for the transformation of Fort Orange into a center for private traders, see *VRBM.*, 247–248; Rink, *Holland on the Hudson*, 134–135; Ceci, "Effect of European Contact and Trade," 188; Trelease, *Indian Affairs*, 49, 60–61, 112–113; Donna Merwick, "Dutch Townsmen and Land Use: A Spatial Perspective on Seventeenth-Century Albany, New York," *WMQ*, 3d ser., 37 (1980), 57.

Jogues, trade was "free to all; this gives the Indians all things cheap, each of the Hollanders outbidding his neighbor, and being satisfied provided he can gain some little profit." Adriaen Van der Donck, a resident at Rensselaerswyck during the 1640s, concurred, complaining that New Netherland suffered from a "superabundance of Petty Traders and . . . a want of Farmers and Farm servants." For the local inhabitants, the easiest way to "gain some little profit" was through bartering with the Indians. The result, however, was an economy severely sensitive to the state of that trade.[13]

During the same year that Father Jogues visited Beverwyck and Rensselaerswyck, Arent van Curler reported to the patroon on the success of the annual fur trade: "The residents have shipped fully 3,000 to 4,000 skins from above. There has never been such a big trade as this year." Contemporary records suggest a steady increase in volume in New Netherland's fur trade during the three decades after 1624. In that year, 4,700 beaver and otter skins were exported from the province. Between 1625 and 1640 Fort Orange alone may have returned over 5,000 skins each year. At a later date, Adriaen Van der Donck estimated that 80,000 beavers were killed annually between 1644 and 1653 in the whole of New Netherland. The high point of the trade at Beverwyck came in 1656 and 1657, when as many as 40,000 beaver and otter skins were shipped to New Amsterdam each year. Within two years, however, the situation had altered dramatically. In 1659 Governor-General Stuyvesant reported to the directors of the Dutch West India Company that at Beverwyck neighbor complained against neighbor "because of the decline of the trade, which grows worse from year to year." Stuyvesant noted the high prices that now had to be paid for skins as well as the extravagant quantity of presents demanded by the natives.[14]

13. *NNN*, 262; *NYCD*, I, 259. See also, Rink, *Holland on the Hudson*, 87–88. Jogues's description of Fort Orange and Rensselaerswyck should be contrasted with that provided by Arent van Curler during the same year in his correspondence with Kiliaen van Rensselaer. See A. J. F. van Laer, ed., "Arent van Curler and His Historic Letter to the Patroon," *DSSAY*, 3 (1927–1928), 18–29.

14. Van Laer, ed., "Van Curler and His Historic Letter," 29; *NYCD*, XIV, 444. For a brief biographical entry on Arent van Curler, see *VRBM*, 817. In 1628 two ships reached Holland with 10,000 pelts from New Netherland. Lenig, "Of Dutchmen, Beaver Hats, and Iroquois," 80. For additional information on the early fur trade in New Netherland, see *NNN*, 76–83. For the yearly return from Fort Orange for the period 1625–1640 and for a list that includes most of the years between 1624 and 1635, see *VRBM*, 483; *Historical Collections: Consisting of State Papers and Other Authentic Documents*, ed. Ebenezer Hazard, 2 vols. (Philadelphia, 1792–1794), I, 397 (hereafter

Obvious explanations for the decline of the fur trade after 1657 include exhaustion of the supply of fur-bearing animals within native hunting territories as well as intertribal warfare, which disrupted the trade in furs from regions not yet depleted to the west. Overhunting and -trapping may have contributed to the record volume of furs traded at Beverwyck during the 1650s. If so, a decline in the population of beaver, otter, and other pelt-producing species could have followed. Additionally, in July 1660, the Senecas admitted to Director-General Stuyvesant that warfare had indeed interrupted their trade for furs with other, more distant, tribes. This meeting, the first formal diplomatic appearance of the Senecas at Beverwyck, was itself a signal that, of necessity, the trade in furs was exploiting ever more westerly sources of supply.[15]

In 1657 some 37,000 beaver skins were shipped from Beverwyck to New Amsterdam between June 20 and September 27. For the community's Dutch traders, a year's profits had to be made within the three- or four-month period between June and September by the exchange of merchandise, clothing, food, and liquor for skins. Increasing competition among the traders led to a greater dependence on Indian and white "brokers." Such persons were Dutchmen or natives hired for a fee by the local traders. Their job was to intercept Indians bringing furs overland from the Mohawk River to Beverwyck and to offer presents (often shirts or coats) in the name of the trader for whom they worked. If the gifts were accepted, it was expected that the Indians would stop at that trader's house on reaching Beverwyck.

Not surprisingly, it was a system open to abuse and difficult to

---

cited as *State Papers*). For Van der Donck's estimate, see *AVDD*, 111. In 1688 Symon Groot of Schenectady testified that as a youth, "in one year ye Deponent hath help to Trade & Pact up 37 thousand Bever." *LIR*, 143–144. For the fur trade in the 1650s, see Trelease, *Indian Affairs*, 131; Edmund B. O'Callaghan, *History of New Netherland*, 2 vols. (Spartanburg, S.C., 1966), II, 310n; *NYCD*, XIII, 27n.

15. For the July 1660 Indian conference, see *FOB*, II, 284; Trelease, *Indian Affairs*, 127–128. There is disagreement as to how rapidly the Mohawks and other Iroquois depleted the peltry resources within their own territories. George T. Hunt argued that the depletion had occurred by 1640, but Thomas Norton is not convinced that it was this early. Bruce Trigger concludes that 1670 was the date by which beaver had been hunted to extinction within the Iroquois heartland. He suggests that as early as 1640 the number of furs that could be taken from this territory was insufficient to meet the Iroquois demand for European trade goods. George T. Hunt, *The Wars of the Iroquois: A Study in Intertribal Trade Relations* (Madison, Wisc., 1940), 33; Thomas E. Norton, *The Fur Trade in Colonial New York, 1686–1776* (Madison, Wisc., 1974), 9–11; Bruce G. Trigger, "Ontario Native People and the Epidemics of 1634–1640," in Shepard Krech, ed., *Indians, Animals, and the Fur Trade* (Athens, Ga., 1981), 27–28.

control. Any disruption of the trade, however momentary, could lead to distrust and dissatisfaction on both sides. Because of the first Anglo-Dutch war, between 1652 and 1654 a smaller than usual amount of merchandise was shipped to New Netherland. As a result, the price of goods available for trade was inflated. Dutch explanations of the law of supply and demand failed to relieve Mohawk suspicions that they were being cheated, and members of the tribe responded by killing cattle at Rensselaerswyck. In an effort to prevent the further destruction of livestock and to renew the now strained alliance with the Iroquois, the Beverwyck court determined "to send a present to the Maquas" and to promise that "when the ships come here . . . to let them have the goods cheaper, on the old basis."[16]

The reduction of trade also escalated the pressures of competition among the local traders. In July 1655, after the court issued an "ordinance against going into the woods to trade," the magistrates were accused "in scandalous, villanous and contemptuous terms . . . of . . . trying to reserve the entire trade to themselves." The court members swiftly handled this challenge to their authority, their accuser being forced to beg forgiveness on his knees. After 1657, however, the use of brokers gained added significance as each trader sought to improve his advantage in the competition for a declining number of furs. In the face of such acquisitive pressures, the ability of the court to regulate the use of brokers eroded rapidly.[17]

By 1659 the troubled state of the fur trade was creating division and dissension within the community at Beverwyck. In June, as in previous years, the court granted permission to employ Indian brokers, but with the added restriction that they be sent "into the woods without any presents." Almost immediately, charges were made against traders who continued to violate the ordinance. One individual, Philip Pietersen Schuyler, admitted "that he gave a present to the Indians and if he did wrong in that, he says that not a single beaver is bartered in the Fuyck [Beverwyck] but it is done contrary to the ordinance." Other defendants were equally unrepentant, one declaring "that the magistrates were a lot of perjurers and that he did not care a thing about the magistrates."[18]

In seeking to enforce its ordinances, the court and its members were becoming an object of abuse within the Dutch community. The

16. *FOB*, I, 170.
17. Ibid., 223–224; *LONN*, 190.
18. *FOB*, II, 189, 191.

strained state of Dutch-Mohawk relations only added to the troubles of the local authorities. Between September and October of 1659, a series of meetings were held at Beverwyck and the first Mohawk village, Caughnawaga. The Mohawks complained of beatings received at the hands of Dutch traders, and the court members were forced to acknowledge that they had received complaints "about the insolent treatment of the savages in beating them and throwing things at them." In response, they forbade "all residents of this jurisdiction to molest any savage . . . on pain of arbitrary correction."[19]

The passage from one trading season to the next failed to abate either dissension within the Dutch community or disputes between the Dutch and Mohawks. In May 1660, twenty-five persons (later identified as the community's "principal traders") petitioned the court, announcing that they awaited the start of another trading season and warning "that the Christians are again about to run into the woods as brokers in order by . . . improper ways to get the trade entirely into their hands." The petitioners claimed that this would result in the "decline and utter ruination of Fort Orange and the village of Beverwyck." They urged instead "that every one may be free to employ Indian brokers." In response, on May 31, the magistrates voted four to two that "no brokers whether Christians or Indians, shall be employed, but that the Indians without being . . . solicited shall be allowed to trade their beaver where they please." Permission was granted, however, "to every one to go on the hill, as far up as the houses stand, to inquire where the Indians wish to go."[20]

The most complete explanation of the state of affairs at Beverwyck was presented in a June 1660 letter from Vice-Director Johannes La Montagne to Director-General Stuyvesant. According to La Montagne, Beverwyck was divided into "two directly opposite parties, one asking to be allowed to employ Indian brokers and no Christians, and the other Christians and no Indians." Subsequently, at the court's request, the entire community of traders assembled in the fort. Heard individually, they "expressed a different opinion [from that of the May petition] . . . that it would be better, to give the enormous amount of brokerage, which went now yearly into the pockets of the Indian brokers . . . to Dutchmen." The use of Indian

19. Ibid., 218–219. For the September and October meetings, see 211–223. During the fall of 1659, for the first time, a defensive plank wall was erected around the community at Beverwyck. Ibid., 226.

20. Ibid., 255–256.

brokers was expensive. La Montagne estimated that each year fifty thousand guilders in fees were funneled into their hands. By urging the use of only Indian brokers, the "principal traders" must have realized that at a time of declining profits from the fur trade many small traders would be hard pressed to afford the fees demanded by the native woods runners.[21]

Eighty of the small traders made the clearest statement of their situation in an appeal to the court in late June. They claimed that the May petition had been presented by persons "who, being moved by excessive greed . . . make themselves believe . . . that they thereby increase the trade." In reply the small traders charged that this was only "a pretext invented for no other purpose than to divert the trade to themselves." The petitioners declared that they were not a "rabble" and urged the magistrates not to "tolerate that the community be oppressed, considering that the least [of the citizens] has as much right as the most [important one]."[22]

The continuing complaints of the Mohawks to the local court at this time provide further testimony to the fierce competition for furs at Beverwyck and to the abuses that could result. The Mohawks requested that no Dutchmen on horseback or on foot be allowed to roam in the woods. They would surround an Indian with skins and "drag him along saying: 'Come with me, so and so has no goods,' thus interfering with one another," which the Mohawks feared would "end badly." Such self-interested pursuit of profit violated the natives' concern for communal well-being. In conference with Governor-General Stuyvesant at Beverwyck during the summer of 1660, members of the tribe urged instead that "each house ought to have something. . . . The brokers, pull one hither and thither. . . . That should not be tolerated, but each house ought to have something."[23]

The court's May ruling reduced neither the number of petitions nor the bitter divisions within the community of traders. It also proved difficult to enforce, as Vice-Director La Montagne frankly admitted: "Since that time I have been obliged to go into the woods with soldiers to prevent mishaps and to see that the ordinances are observed. It comes very hard upon me . . . and . . . I must frequently

---

21. Ibid.; *NYCD*, XIII, 175. The standard account of the events at Beverwyck at this time provided by Allen Trelease is incorrect. Trelease confuses the positions of the two groups of traders, claiming that it was the principal traders who urged the use of Dutch brokers. Trelease, *Indian Affairs*, 134.

22. *FOB*, II, 266–268.

23. Ibid, 269, 285.

remain over night in the woods." Recognizing that its resources of enforcement were limited, the court soon abandoned the effort to regulate the use of brokers and acceded to the request that both Dutchmen and Indians be allowed to enter the woods. This was a victory for the small traders, but the court members warned of the "dangerous consequence" and the magistrates protested "their innocence of all mischief that may result therefrom."[24]

Divisions within the Dutch community were expressed not only by petitions presented to the court but also in complaints of slander and defamation of character. During June, Cornelis Teunissen Bos and Jacob Tyssen Van der Heyden brought suit against William Teller, charging that he had "called them a rabble and injured their reputation." In his defense, Teller claimed that he had stated "that it would be a miserable thing if I or the common people or rabble should rebel against the law of the public authorities." Testimony was presented, however, which suggested that Teller's remarks had been more candid, that he had actually declared, "If the principals of this place listened to this rabble, they would be crazy." One of Beverwyck's "principal traders," Teller had signed the May 25 petition urging the sole use of Indian brokers; his opponents, Bos and Van der Heyden, were among those who signed the subsequent appeal of the "small traders." Both men were vocal opponents of the large traders, and each seems to have been an individual whose status had fallen with the decay in trade.[25]

For the small traders, the decline of the fur trade after 1657 proved increasingly troublesome. During July 1658, Jeremias van Rensselaer (then patroon at Rensselaerswyck) wrote his mother in the Netherlands that "the common traders get no beavers . . . which is a great loss." By fall 1659, little improvement had been recorded and van

24. Ibid., 268; *NYCD*, XIII, 175. For additional ordinances against trading in the woods issued at Beverwyck and Rensselaerswyck in 1660 and 1661, see *LONN*, 381, 394.

25. *FOB*, II, 260; *CHMD*, XVI, 159. The suit against William Teller was initiated June 8, 1660, only two weeks after presentation of the May 25 petition and nine days before the petition of the small traders. The charges and countercharges continued throughout the summer. On September 28, Teller brought suit against both Bos and Van der Heyden, asking "of the defendants reparation of honor." *FOB*, II, 267–268, 300. Although included among the small traders in 1660, six years earlier, both Bos and Van der Heyden had been counted among "the most prosperous and loyal citizens" at Beverwyck. Bos had served as a community magistrate during 1653–1654. *FOB*., I, 126, 162–163.

Rensselaer reported, "Many persons here are now so deeply in debt that I would rather keep my goods than to extend credit to them."[26]

What did it mean to be a large or a small trader? In 1657 almost 40,000 beaver and otter pelts were shipped from Beverwyck between June and September. During that year, Abraham Staats, one of the large traders, shipped 4,200 skins; Jan van Bremen, one of the small traders, shipped only 300. Taken together, the May 1660 petition of the "principal traders" and the June petition of the "small traders" provide the best picture of the fur-trading community at Beverwyck at this moment of crisis. In all, sixty names can be identified from the two lists—twenty of the principal traders and forty of the small. As a group, the latter individuals had resided in the community for a shorter period of time. Over half had not been at Beverwyck before 1655. They were less likely to be property holders or heads of families, and within another half decade, many (over one-third) would no longer be found in the community. In contrast, the principal traders were more established and less transient. Almost all were heads of families, most were property owners who had been in the community for over a half decade. Moreover, many would remain at Beverwyck (Albany) after the English conquest. Finally, fully half of those who can be identified as principal traders had acted as magistrates at one point or another during the 1650s. The small traders were rarely chosen as magistrates.[27]

For the Dutch, the depressed state of the fur trade was further complicated by the threat of English competition and intervention in that trade. As early as 1640, Kiliaen van Rensselaer expressed his fear that the English on the Connecticut River would employ Mahican Indians living below Fort Orange as emissaries to the Mohawks and in this manner "draw everything away from us over land." In fact, the English had a long-standing interest in the New Netherland fur trade. As early as 1634, John Winthrop estimated that the Dutch trade amounted to nine or ten thousand skins a year. Thomas Mor-

26. *CJVR*, 104, 175.
27. *ERAR*, I, 244. It is likely that Staats and van Bremen dispatched both their own furs and those received from other community traders. Additional work on this subject is being done by Martha Shattuck of the New Netherland Project at the New York State Library. For the 1660 petitions, see *FOB*, II, 255, 266–268. Information on community residence, family relations, office holding, and property ownership can be found in *ERAR*, *VRBM*, *FOB*, and *FS*, as well as in *New York Historical Manuscripts: Dutch, Land Papers*, ed. Charles T. Gehring, vols. GG, HH, II (Baltimore, 1980) (hereafter cited as *Land Papers*).

ton, in his *New English Canaan*, calculated the annual value of the Dutch beaver trade at twenty thousand pounds, and urged that the English waste no time in seizing this profitable commerce.[28]

During the 1630s, the Dutch competed unsuccessfully with traders from Plymouth Colony and settlers from Massachusetts for control of the fur resources of the Connecticut River region. After 1636 William Pynchon's settlement at Springfield cut off supplies from above and effected a near monopoly of trade on the river. Plans to tap the western fur trade by an overland route from the Connecticut River to the Hudson were soon proposed, and in 1645 a company of adventurers organized for that purpose. Although granted a twenty-year monopoly of trade by the General Court of Massachusetts, the group accomplished nothing. In 1659, however, two of the original members, William Hawthorne and William Paine, joined John Pynchon, the son of Springfield's founder, to form a new company devoted to the development of the western trade.[29]

All three were men of influence. William Paine of Ipswich was one of the wealthiest individuals in the Massachusetts Bay Colony. William Hawthorne served as a commissioner of the Confederation of New England. Meanwhile, John Pynchon had taken over his father's affairs at Springfield after the elder Pynchon's return to England in 1652. By this date, the trade in furs on the Connecticut River had been so reduced that there was hardly any profit to be made. For this reason, the designs of the previous decade were given new consideration. The journey of both Hawthorne and Pynchon to the Hudson River in the summer of 1659 indicated that this was to be a more serious attempt against the Dutch trade. At Beverwyck on August 4, the two Englishmen explained their visit as an attempt "to supply the place with cattle." For this purpose, they asked permission to settle a

---

28. *VRBM*, 483–484; John Winthrop, *Winthrop's Journal, 1630–1649*, ed. James K. Hosmer, 2 vols. (New York, 1908), I, 131. Thomas Morton wrote: "And, therefore it would be adjudged an irreparable oversight to protract time, and suffer the Dutch (who are but intruders upon his Majesties most hopefull Country of New England,) to possess themselves of that so plesant and commodious Country of Erocoise [Iroquois] before us." Thomas Morton, *The New English Canaan*, ed. Charles Francis Adams, Jr. (Boston, 1883), 240.

29. Arthur H. Buffington, "New England and the Western Fur Trade, 1629–1675," Publications of the Colonial Society of Massachusetts, *Transactions*, 18 (1915–1916), 160–192. John Pynchon, *Letters of John Pynchon, 1654–1700*, ed. Carl Bridenbaugh, Publications of the Colonial Society of Massachusetts, *Collections*, 60 (1982), 30.

village to the south, near the Hudson River, "east of the Wappengers' kill."[30]

Upon receiving notice of Pynchon's and Hawthorne's arrival, Governor-General Stuyvesant wrote to the directors of the Dutch West India Company, warning that English settlers near Fort Orange would "ruin and cut off our beaver trade, as they have done . . . on the Fresh river." The governor's suspicions were further aroused by the official correspondence he soon received from the New England authorities. The Commissioners for the United Colonies offered no apology for the recent English transgression into Dutch territory: "Wee presume you have heard from . . . Orania That some of our English have bin lately in those partes . . . the Government of the Massachusetts have granted libertie to some of theire people to erect a plantation in those partes . . . yett without entrenchment of the Dutch Rights."[31]

Stuyvesant had in fact long feared that the fur trade at Fort Orange

30. *FOB*, II, 208. For the commissioners of the Confederation of New England and for William Hawthorne, see *State Papers*, II, 26, 145, 174, 203, 227; Herbert L. Osgood, *The American Colonies in the Seventeenth Century*, 3 vols. (New York, 1904–1907; reprint, Gloucester, Mass., 1957), I, 399–403. For John Pynchon, see Pynchon, *Letters*, xv, xxxii–xxxv. For the fur trade on the Connecticut River as well as for information about William Paine, see Pynchon, *Letters.*, xxxviii–xxxix; David Grayson Allen, *In English Ways: The Movement of Societies and the Transferal of English Local Law and Custom to Massachusetts Bay in the Seventeenth Century* (Chapel Hill, N.C., 1981), 119, 133; Buffington, "New England and the Western Fur Trade," 177n; Ruth McIntyre, "John Pynchon and the New England Fur Trade, 1652–1676," in John Pynchon, *Selections from the Account Books of John Pynchon, 1651–1697*, ed. Carl Bridenbaugh and Juliette Tomlinson, Publications of the Colonial Society of Massachusetts, *Collections*, 61 (1985), 3–70, especially 55–60. For Pynchon's previous trade with the Dutch at Fort Orange, and for his continued dealings with William Hawthorne in an effort to exploit the western fur trade, see Pynchon, *Account Books*, 139, 140, 142–144. The most recent work on the Pynchon family and the community at Springfield includes only a brief reference to Pynchon's interest in the western fur trade. Stephen Innes, *Labor in a New Land: Economy and Society in Seventeenth-Century Springfield* (Princeton, 1983), 31–32.

31. *NYCD*, XIII, 126; *State Papers*, II, 408. In November 1659, Stuyvesant received the following statement of English territorial rights from the General Court of Massachusetts: "The patent granted to the Colony of Massachusetts by the late King Charles . . . is to extend . . . from Sea to Sea; and we are very well assured that some part of Hudsons River . . . is within our patent granted . . . and although the Dutch may have intruded within the said Limits . . . we conceive no Reason can be imagined why we should not improve and make use of our Just Rights . . . and should our enjoying our Right be some damage to your trade and profit, we would suppose that argument so unbecoming the professors of Christianity that those that do but pretend to common Justice and Honesty could never allege it seriously without blushing." *PA*, XXX, 281–282.

would be seized by a foreign power. As early as 1649, he accused Swedish settlers on the Delaware River of designs against the Dutch trade similar to those of which he now suspected the English. In 1655 the director-general dispatched a force to the Delaware to remove the threat posed by the Swedish colony. This military action was followed by the creation of New Amstel, a community sponsored by the city of Amsterdam. These steps to reassert Dutch control over the region had barely been taken, however, before the Delaware settlements were placed at risk by the nearby Maryland colony. In September 1659, at the same moment that Stuyvesant sought to alert the directors of the Dutch West India Company to the danger at Fort Orange, he also dispatched an embassy headed by Augustine Heerman to treat with the English of Maryland.[32]

Facing encroachments on both the Hudson and the Delaware rivers, Stuyvesant perceived his colony to be the victim of an enveloping movement of English population and military power. That he did not isolate his troubles geographically but treated them as part of an overall larger concern is clear. In a letter to the directors of the Dutch West India Company written in April 1660, Stuyvesant formulated his response to the English threat then confronting New Netherland: "Experience has taught . . . in regard to the invasions . . . of the English, that the forts . . . erected formerly on the South and Freshwater rivers, did not prevent the usurpations . . . of this nation . . . it is certainly beyond question, that, if . . . New Amstel, had not been erected there, that country and with it the whole Southriver would have been stolen." Stuyvesant concluded by praying, "God grant, that such means may be adopted, as will preserve not only the Southriver, but also this Northriver against . . . the English." To protect the economically and strategically vital Hudson River, the governor proposed that "the best and safest plan would be to forestall the English, by peopling and settling the lands with some good and clever farmers."[33]

32. For the geographic extent of New Netherland, the relations of the Dutch and Swedes on the Delaware, and the difficulties of the Dutch with the English of Maryland, see Trelease, *Indian Affairs*, 54–59, 108–111; Christopher Ward, *The Dutch and Swedes on the Delaware, 1609–1664* (Philadelphia, 1930); C. A. Weslager, *The English on the Delaware, 1610–1682* (New Brunswick, N.J., 1967), 154–175; *PA*, XIX, 495–497, 533–543, 571–572, 574, 579–581, 597–598, 623, 626–628; *New York Historical Manuscripts: Dutch, Delaware Papers, 1648–1664*, ed. Charles T. Gehring, XVIII–XIX (Baltimore, 1981), XVIII, 37–47, 84–97, 143–161, 211–222, 273–274 (hereafter cited as *Delaware Papers*).

33. *PA*, XIX, 631–632; *NYCD*, XIII, 107–108. In 1657 Philip Pietersen Schuyler

Stuyvesant may already have been approached by a group of proprietors headed by Arent van Curler who were seeking permission to establish a new community on the Mohawk River on property then controlled by the Iroquois. During the period 1659–1661, van Curler had several opportunities to introduce the project to both the Mohawks and the director-general. Not only was he among those persons who met with the Mohawks at Beverwyck and Caughnawaga in the fall of 1659, but when Stuyvesant journeyed to Beverwyck for a conference with the Iroquois in July 1660, it is likely that van Curler also was in attendance. Subsequently, in April 1661, he was at Manhattan where he met with the director-general on at least one occasion.[34]

The strategic requirements discerned by Petrus Stuyvesant coincided with a growing demand for agricultural lands outside the bounds of Rensselaerswyck. Years before, Father Isaac Jogues had remarked on the poor quality of the terrain at Rensselaerswyck, where there was "little land fit for tillage, being crowded by hills which are bad soil." In addition, the colony suffered from winter ice flows and periodic inundations of high water. During June 1660, the current patroon, Jeremias van Rensselaer, admitted, "Daily I must listen . . . to the murmuring of many people who request to buy of the Indians this or that island or small piece of land, for which they will pay rent."[35]

---

of Beverwyck was granted permission to acquire Half Moon (now Waterford, N.Y.) from the Indians to prevent "those of Connecticut" purchasing it. *ERAR*, I, 2n; George W. Schuyler, *Colonial New York: Philip Schuyler and His Family*, 2 vols. (New York, 1885), I, 152. The need to promote population growth and settlement as a deterrent against the English had been emphasized by Adriaen Van der Donck. *AVDD*, 11. During the 1650s, both the directors of the Dutch West India Company and the government of New Netherland sought to further the establishment of new agricultural villages. In 1654 the directors wrote to Stuyvesant of "our zeal in increasing the population" and urged him to "think of promoting the cultivation of the soil." Ordinances were passed for the formation of such communities in 1656 and 1660. *NYCD*, XIV, 264; *CHMD*, VIII, 56, IX, 53; *LONN*, 368–370.

34. For van Curler's status within New Netherland and his influence with the Iroquois and other tribes, see Van Laer, ed., "Van Curler and His Historic Letter," 15–16. For van Curler's influence with the Indians, see Trelease, *Indian Affairs*, 115. Concerning the fall 1659 meetings between the Dutch and Mohawks, see *FOB*, II, 211–219, 222–223. For Stuyvesant's July 1660 visit to Beverwyck and van Curler's April 1661 meeting with the director-general, see *FOB*, II, 281–287; *CJVR*, 251.

35. *CJVR.*, 225; *NNN*, 262. For the problems that plagued Rensselaerswyck, see Samuel G. Nissenson, *The Patroon's Domain* (New York, 1937), 46, 47; *CJVR*, 156–157, 321; *CMVR*, 27–30. In 1661 heavy rains that flooded the countryside and made travel difficult delayed the Mohawk grant of land at Schenectady to Arent van Curler

The attractiveness of a settlement at Schenectady was further enhanced by the increasing demand for produce within New Netherland as a whole. The soils were of excellent quality and the village
was to be located "upon a good flat, high enough to be free from the
overflowing of the water of the river." Not only would a community
at Schenectady forestall the English and secure the beaver trade for
the Dutch, it would provide a badly needed expansion of the colony's
agricultural production. In 1659 Director-General Stuyvesant wrote
to Jeremias van Rensselaer, informing the patroon of the shortage "of
bread and grain to help ourselves and others." Stuyvesant also included a request that van Rensselaer "accommodate us with as much
bread grain and pease as can possibly be obtained before the winter."
Although the community at New Amstel protected Dutch possession
of the Delaware Valley, it placed additional burdens on the colony's
agricultural resources. Everything was "scarce and in short supply"
and the authorities at New Amsterdam were urged to forward "grain,
peas and bacon."[36]

Finally, it is possible that by the late 1650s the growth of population at Beverwyck also created pressure for outward expansion. As
early as 1654 the local court proposed to Governor-General Stuyvesant that new ground be allowed for construction "as all the formerly
allotted ground has been built on." Whether similar demographic factors influenced events at Rensselaerswyck is less certain. In 1643 Father Jogues had estimated that there were about 100 persons in the
colony. A decade later there were at least 230. Only four farms were
under cultivation in 1640, but by 1651 there were eighteen, although
the number may have declined after this. Certainly for the province
as a whole, the 1650s marked a significant period of population expansion. In 1647 New Netherland's population approached 1,200 inhabitants. Within a decade this figure tripled as the result of immigration. Most newcomers settled on Long Island, but in 1652 Esopus

---

by a month, from June to July. George R. Howell and Joel Munsell, *History of the
County of Schenectady, N.Y., from* 1662 *to* 1886 (New York, 1886), 3.

36. *JD*, 213; *CJVR*, 187; *Delaware Papers*, XVIII, 134. In response to the director-general's request, van Rensselaer sent Stuyvesant 200 schepels of wheat. *CJVR*,
188–189. On occasion, Stuyvesant also sought to acquire supplies from New England, *NYCD*, II, 373. In later years, in defense of his administration, Stuyvesant
wrote: "Admitting, however, that the fertility of the country was such as never to
necessitate us to import provisions . . . which abundance, however, the Province
frequently could never attain, in consequence of the so numerous invasions and mas-
sacres on the part of the Indians within, and the continual vexation of the neighbors
without." *PA*, XVII, 811.

(modern Kingston) was founded and in 1661 another community (Wiltwyck) was established nearby, suggesting that the increase in population also had an impact on the Hudson Valley.[37]

On July 27, 1661, Arent van Curler and three Mohawk sachems signed a deed signaling the formal transfer of land at Schenectady from the Mohawks to a group of fourteen proprietors, individuals drawn from the communities at Beverwyck and Rensselaerswyck. One month before, van Curler had written Petrus Stuyvesant, reminding the director-general, "When last at Manhatans I informed your honor that there were some . . . who were well inclined . . . to take possession of and till the *Groote Vlackte* (Great Flats)." According to van Curler, "six or eight families" were ready to remove to the Mohawk River flats. Unfortunately, there exist no records of the negotiations that must have occurred between van Curler and Governor-General Stuyvesant, van Curler and the Mohawks, and among those individuals and families interested in the venture. Arent van Curler, however, was the ideal person to achieve consent for his proposal. His political and familial connections within New Netherland were impeccable, and his influence with the Iroquois has been compared to that of Sir William Johnson in the 1700s.[38]

In his June 1661 letter, van Curler addressed the director-general as a "lover of agriculture," and it was in this context that permission was granted for the establishment of the new community: "The letter of Arent Van Curler being presented and read . . . containing . . . a request . . . for the large plain situated to the back of Fort Orange . . . for the purpose of cultivation . . . the Director General and Council resolved to consent to it." Although this document makes clear that farming was expected to be a primary activity at the village, it makes no mention either of the extension or prohibition of the right

---

37. *NYCD*, XIV, 299. For the growth of population at Beverwyck, see Merwick, "Dutch Townsmen and Land Use," 60. For Rensselaerswyck, see Nissenson, *Patroon's Domain*, 80; *NNN*, 261–262; *VRBM*, 732–743; *CJVR*, 461–462. For the growth of New Netherland's population after 1647, see Oliver A. Rink, "The People of New Netherland: Notes on Non-English Immigration to New York in the Seventeenth Century," *NYH*, 62 (1981), 34–39; Trelease, *Indian Affairs*, 86. For Esopus, see Marius Schoonmaker, *The History of Kingston, New York, from Its Early Settlement to the Year 1820* (New York, 1888), 5–6, 31.

38. *SP*, 9–10. Besides van Curler, only one of these earliest settlers can be identified, Philip Hendricksen Brouwer. Brouwer transmitted van Curler's June 1661 letter to Governor-General Stuyvesant. *SP.*, 10. Six of the fourteen proprietors could not write and used marks to sign their names. *ARS*, III, 494; *ERAR*, I, 26. For van Curler's significance, see Trelease, *Indian Affairs*, 115; Van Laer, ed., "Van Curler and His Historic Letter," 15–16.

to trade. There is evidence, however, that Stuyvesant did grant trading rights to several of the original Schenectady proprietors. This privilege may not have been extended to the rest and, in any event, the liberty was soon withdrawn. Within a year, Stuyvesant had determined that Schenectady would not become a center for the fur trade. The settlers were ordered to sell no liquor to the Indians and their lands could not be surveyed until the proprietors promised to avoid all "trade with the savages." Indian troubles at Esopus and elsewhere during this period may have caused Stuyvesant to reconsider his initial grant of trading privileges to the Schenectady settlers. Certainly, the Beverwyck authorities were quick to protest that the new village's remoteness made it an unfit site for trade.[39]

To enforce the prohibition on trade, Stuyvesant ordered the provincial surveyor, Jacques Cortelyou, to depart for Schenectady in the spring of 1663 but to refuse to measure off any lands until the residents signed a bond promising that they would "not carry on, nor cause to be carried on, on the said Flat . . . any trade . . . with any of the savages." In response, on May 18, 1663, the "proprietors of Shinnechtady" addressed a lengthy petition to Stuyvesant protesting their willingness to obey his authority but noting that "the land was bought out of our own purse, . . . taken possession of, built upon and stocked with horses and cattle at great expense." Having invested so much in the new community, they deemed it injurious to be "treated differently . . . than other subjects, all their work would be in vain and they would be totally ruined."[40]

Arent van Curler also wrote to Stuyvesant, informing the director-general that the settlers were discouraged "and I have much trouble with them on that account." Van Curler still hoped to alter the governor's decision and placed the onus for the prohibition of trade not on Stuyvesant but on those persons who sought to maintain a monopoly of trade at Beverwyck: "As far as I can see, it seems that the honorable general and council in proposing the aforesaid resolution and bond were induced thereto by some jealous persons . . . under pretext that they fear that a few beavers be traded there [Schenectady] and that therefore they would have less." Van Curler denied that

39. *SP*, 10, 13. For the possibility that Stuyvesant granted trading privileges that were later withdrawn, see *SP*., 14; *ARS*, III, 493–494; Ruth L. Higgins, *Expansion in New York with Especial Reference to the Eighteenth Century* (Columbus, Ohio, 1931), 15. For the 1662 prohibition and the 1663 ordinance against trade, see *SP*, 12–14; *LONN*, 442–443.

40. *ARS*, III, 492–494.

trade with the Indians could be carried on at Schenectady as advantageously as at Beverwyck, "for all the goods must from here be transported thither." He also sought to appeal to Stuyvesant's sense of fairness: "It seems to me that those who support themselves by agriculture ought not to have less than those who entirely support themselves by trade." In the end, neither the proprietors' petition nor van Curler's letter were of avail, and the prohibition against trade at Schenectady remained in effect.[41]

During April 1664, a final petition was presented to Stuyvesant by the proprietors urging that the surveyor return to lay out the farm lands and house lots. Significantly, no mention was made of trading rights and, having failed to secure such a privilege, Arent van Curler was not included among those who signed the appeal. After two years of delay, on May 20, 1664, Stuyvesant again commanded the surveyor "to proceed . . . on the first Sailing Vessel to Fort Orange to lay out the aforesaid lands in the best manner possible and for the best accommodation of those interested therein."[42]

Although Director-General Stuyvesant intended that Schenectady would become a village of farmers, the community's proprietors were united by their desire to engage in the trading of furs. For two years the settlers protested to Stuyvesant against its prohibition, and even a decade later the village's magistrates continued to seek the right to trade from the colony's English governors. Meanwhile the inhabitants carried on an illicit commerce in violation of the orders of both Dutch and English governors. Attempts by the Beverwyck (Albany) magistrates to suppress the trade were met with evasion and, occasionally, violence.

Of Schenectady's fourteen original proprietors, eight, including Arent van Curler, are known to have participated in the fur trade at Beverwyck or Rensselaerswyck during the 1640s and 1650s. In addition, five of the proprietors were among those persons who signed the petitions in 1660 to the court at Beverwyck regarding the state of the community's fur trade and the use of Indian or Dutch brokers. Of the five, four were "small traders," the group most hurt by the decline in the trade. Philip Hendricksen Brouwer, for example, was a brewer and a small trader who in 1661 owed over three thousand guilders. Brouwer also was an early associate of Arent van Curler in

41. Ibid., 495–496.
42. *SP*, 16. Those persons who signed the April 17, 1664, petition were Sander Leendertsen Glen, William Teller, and Harmen Vedder.

the Schenectady settlement. At Schenectady, Brouwer mortgaged his
house and farm as a guarantee for repayment of his debt.[43]

Not only for small traders like Brouwer, but for several large
traders the establishment of a village at Schenectady offered new
hope for rescuing fortunes damaged by the decline in trade. Two of
Schenectady's most prominent founders, Arent van Curler and
Sander Leendertsen Glen, were seriously in debt by the early 1660s.
Van Curler owed nearly two thousand guilders and Glen more than
nine thousand. Together van Curler and Glen became the largest
landowners at Schenectady. Having acquired a farm and a house lot
at Schenectady, Glen recouped his fortunes by selling property that
he owned at Beverwyck and Rensselaerswyck. Even a decade later,
however, he was still making payments on his initial debt.[44]

Sander Leendertsen Glen and William Teller had both arrived in
New Netherland during the 1630s as servants of the Dutch West
India Company. Glen married the sister of Teller's first wife, and the
two men cooperated in trade and other ventures. Together they acquired adjacent properties at New Amstel on the Delaware. Although difficult to document, a variety of such personal and economic considerations may have united the Schenectady proprietors
and their families. Gerrit Bancker and Harmen Vedder, for example,
shared ownership of a bouwery on the Mohawk Flats. They both also
acted as upriver factors for the de Wolff family of Amsterdam merchants.[45]

43. The eight proprietors who engaged in the fur trade during the 1640s and 1650s
were Arent van Curler, Pieter Adriaensen van Woggelum, William Teller, Gerrit
Bancker, Sander Leendertsen Glen, Symon Volkertsen Veeder, Teunis Cornelissen
Swart, and Philip Hendricksen Brouwer. A ninth proprietor, Jacques Cornelissen van
Slyck, was probably too young to be active in the fur trade at this time, although he
later traded with the Indians at Schenectady. Finally, there is no evidence that Pieter
Jacobsen Borsboom was trading during these years, but he did so at Schenectady. For
the proprietors and the fur trade, see *ERAR*, III, 33, 237; *FOB*, II, 255, 267–268;
ARS, II, 468–469; *JD*, 206. The four small traders were Symon Volkertsen Veeder,
Teunis Cornelissen Swart, Pieter Adriaensen van Woggelum, and Philip Hendricksen
Brouwer. *FOB*, II, 267–268. A fifth proprietor, William Teller, was listed among the
principal traders. *FOB*, II 255. In 1660 Philip Hendricksen Brouwer owed 3,144
guilders for the purchase of a house and brewery. By May 1662 he had repaid almost
700 guilders and to guarantee payment of the remainder of the debt he mortgaged "his
estate . . . nothing excepted, specially his bouwery on the Great Flat." *ERAR*, I, 301.

44. *ERAR*, I, 313–314, 336, 505, III, 110–113, 221.

45. For Glen and Teller, see *FS*, 76, 188; *Land Papers*, HH, 81a, 81b; *New York
Historical Manuscripts: Dutch, Register of the Provincial Secretary, 1638–1660*, ed. Ken-
neth Scott and Ken Stryker-Rodda, 3 vols. (Baltimore, 1974), II, 403, III, 117–119;
ERAR, I, 61n, III, 221, IV, 26–27. For Gerrit Bancker and Harmen Vedder, see

Seven of the fourteen proprietors had ties to Rensselaerswyck. Of those more closely associated with the Beverwyck community, several had clashed with the local court during the previous decade, perhaps generating an element of estrangement with both the constituted authority and the community as a whole. For members of the Bradt family, for example, who were Lutherans from Scandinavia, or for the van Slycks (who were of mixed European-Indian descent), the decision to remove to Schenectady may have resulted from a desire to distance themselves from the established Dutch communities on the Hudson River. Yet many of the Schenectady proprietors continued to possess property at Beverwyck and elsewhere. At least two, William Teller and Gerrit Bancker, never took up permanent residence at Schenectady, apparently regarding the community as an additional investment rather than as a new home. Indeed, by accident or design, as a group the proprietors provided the community with little leadership or direction. Arent van Curler and three other proprietors died during the decade of the 1660s. Of those who remained, half either never resided at Schenectady or subsequently removed themselves from the community. But others, including Sander Leendertsen Glen, Jacques Cornelissen van Slyck, and Pieter Danielsen van Olinda, did make Schenectady their home, and they would be joined by a growing number of inhabitants in the years after 1661.[46]

The document signed by Arent van Curler and the Mohawk sachems marked the formal assent of the tribe to the establishment of a Dutch community at the Mohawk Flats. Indeed, Schenectady's location placed the community squarely across the overland route between the Dutch settlements on the Hudson River and the villages of the Iroquois. The trail headed west from Beverwyck through the sandy pine barrens to the Mohawk Flats, in this manner avoiding the lower Mohawk River and the falls at Cohoes. From Schenectady, the route followed the river to present-day Rome, New York, and beyond. Contemporary accounts indicate that during the seventeenth century the Mohawks had as many as eight villages. These included three

---

ERAR, III, 242–243; Rink, *Holland on the Hudson*, 187–190.

46. For the differences between several of the proprietors and the court at Beverwyck, see *FOB*, I, 231–232, 234, 266–267, II, 91, 93, 95–96, 290–291. The proprietors who died during the 1660s included Arent van Curler, Jan Barentsen Wemp, Arent Andriesen Bradt, and Philip Hendricksen Brouwer. Gerrit Bancker and William Teller remained inhabitants of Albany; Martin Cornelissen van Ysselsteyn, Simon Volkertsen Veeder, and Pieter Adriaensen van Woggelum soon departed Schenectady for other communities. *FS*; *SP*, 82–230.

principal "castles" and several smaller satellite communities. In 1666 the easternmost village, Caughnawaga, was destroyed by the French but was rebuilt to the west, near today's Fonda. A second Mohawk settlement, Kanagaro, was located two leagues from the first. A third, Tionnontoguen, the most westerly, was the principal village in population and influence. These were the Mohawk communities best known to the Dutch of Beverwyck, Rensselaerswyck, and Schenectady.[47]

By tradition, the Mohawk chief Hiawatha had played a significant role in founding the Iroquois Confederacy. This, coupled with tribe's close proximity to the Dutch traders at Beverwyck, conferred considerable influence on the Mohawks among the other Iroquois peoples. Although scholars have estimated that at the end of the sixteenth century the Mohawks had between six and eight hundred warriors, it is uncertain how this figure translated into actual military power. Both George T. Hunt and Allen Trelease have argued that during the first decades of the seventeenth century the Mohawks were on the defensive and were too weak to oppose the aggression of the neighboring Mahican tribe. In 1626, for example, the Mahicans may have destroyed a Mohawk village to the west of Fort Orange. Yet both the historical and the archeological evidence suggest that the Mohawks were indeed powerful enough to avail themselves of the early Dutch trade at Fort Orange.[48]

Archeological data provide the most emphatic evidence for Mohawk participation in the early fur trade, a commerce that centered initially on the St. Lawrence before shifting to the Hudson River during the seventeenth century. Significantly, the exchange of European-made goods for furs does not appear to have been an important part of the first recorded European-Indian contacts along the coastal regions of New York and New England. Giovanni da Verrazzano's description of the Indians at "Refugio" (Narragansett Bay) in the 1520s provides little evidence that he sought to acquire skins or that any were offered to him in barter. In 1534, however, the French

---

47. For the trail westward from Albany and for the Mohawk villages, see Lewis Henry Morgan, *League of the Iroquois* (Rochester, 1851; reprint, Secaucus, N.J., 1962), 414–429; William N. Fenton and Elisabeth Tooker, "Mohawk," in *HNAIN*, 466–467.

48. For the position of the Mohawks within the Iroquois Confederacy, see Fenton and Tooker, "Mohawk." For the debate over the strength of the Mohawks, see Lenig, "Of Dutchmen, Beaver Hats, and Iroquois," 73, 78, 80–81; Trigger, "Mohawk-Mahican War," 276–286; Hunt, *Wars of the Iroquois*, 23–24. For the attack against a Mohawk village in the 1620s, see *HMVDB*, 22.

explorer Jacques Cartier met upwards of three hundred Indians in Chaleur Bay near the mouth of the St. Lawrence River, and furs were exchanged for hatchets, knives, and beads. Cartier also participated in a similar barter of furs for trade goods at Hochelaga, the present site of Montreal.[49]

Verrazzano's and Cartier's voyages occurred within ten years of each other. During the former passage, no exchange for furs was reported, whereas on the latter voyage there was such trade. This result may have been more than coincidence, for Cartier's journey took him into northern waters frequented by Europeans since the late 1400s. The fur trade began as an offshoot of the fishing and whaling enterprises that were established in the region during the first half of the sixteenth century. This early Indian-European trade was a complex affair involving the exchange of beaver and other skins, wampum (seawan), and European-made goods. In an archeological context, evidence for any one or a combination of these material elements can serve to designate the onset of trade.[50]

Beaver skeletal remains make up little more than 2 percent of the faunal samples that have been collected from Iroquois village sites for the period before the mid-sixteenth century, suggesting that this animal was not an important source of food for the prehistoric peoples of New York. At the Mohawk village of Garoga, however, a significant alteration is apparent during the period 1550–1570. Beaver remains account for 10 percent of the faunal samples from this village site,

49. Reverend Thomas Grassmann, *The Mohawk Indians and Their Valley, Being a Chronological Documentary Record to the End of 1693* (Schenectady, 1969), 5; David B. Quinn, *North America from Earliest Discovery to First Settlements* (New York, 1977), 154–159, 169–183; Bruce G. Trigger and James F. Pendergast, *Cartier's Hochelaga and the Dawson Site* (Montreal, 1972); Ceci, "Effect of European Contact and Trade," 143–145, 157; David B. Quinn, *New American World: A Documentary History of North America to 1612*, 5 vols. (New York, 1979), I, 280–289, 293–328. Although Verrazzano did not engage in trade with the natives, he distributed "little bells, blue crystals, and other trinkets." Susan Tarrow, "Translation of the Cèllere Codex," in Lawrence C. Wroth, ed., *The Voyages of Giovanni da Verrazzano, 1524–1528* (New Haven, 1970), 138. It was to the north, at Casco Bay, that Verrazzano first encountered Indians who had experience in trading with Europeans. Neal Salisbury, *Manitou and Providence: Indians, Europeans, and the Making of New England, 1500–1643* (New York, 1982), 52–56. The development of the Hudson River trade is also noted in Salisbury, 78–82.

50. Lenig, "Of Dutchmen, Beaver Hats, and Iroquois," 73–76. Bruce J. Bourque and Ruth Holmes Whitehead question the direct involvement of Europeans in the trade and distribution of European-made goods in the Gulf of St. Lawrence and suggest a more extensive participation by native middlemen than previously realized in "Tarrentines and the Introduction of European Trade Goods in the Gulf of Maine," *Ethnohistory*, 32 (1985), 327–341.

and at this time too a small number of European-made goods make their first appearance. That the only contemporary source of European trade goods was several hundred miles to the north at Tadoussac does not seem to have been an impediment to trade.[51]

The Iroquois culture present in the Mohawk Valley at the onset of the historic period resulted from an in situ development extending back at least to A.D. 1100. Until the sixteenth century, however, the majority of known village sites were located at varying distances from the river, some up to seven miles away. Subsequently, a change in settlement pattern occurred during the late 1500s and early 1600s. By the third decade of the seventeenth century, "the majority of components [were] located on valley terraces overlooking the Mohawk River." Not only were the Mohawk villages now positioned along the principal water route leading to Fort Orange, but by 1628–1629 the tribe had also cleared the region bordering on the west bank of the Hudson River of their long-standing enemies, the Mahicans. During the course of the seventeenth century, the Mohawks continued to react to circumstances as needed. With the depression in the fur trade during the 1650s, the tribe consented to the founding of a new Dutch village at Schenectady.[52]

The arrival of the Dutch had signaled an advance in Mohawk military fortunes as first metal hatchets and knives and later guns, powder, and lead were acquired through trade or given as presents. Although during the 1620s the tribe was only one of several native

51. Bourque and Whitehead, "Tarrentines," 73. Archeological evidence of an increase in beaver remains has also been found at Onondaga village sites of the late 1500s. James W. Bradley, *Evolution of the Onondaga Iroquois: Accommodating Change, 1500–1655* (Syracuse, 1987), 54. By the first decade of the 1600s a geographically extensive trade in furs may already have existed throughout much of the northeast. In 1608 John Smith encountered Indians on Chesapeake Bay who possessed "many hatchets, knives, and peeces of yron, and brasse." These Indians informed Smith that the items had been gained from "Sasquesahanockes" who had originally obtained them from other Indians inhabiting "the river of Cannida." John Smith, *The Complete Works of Captain John Smith (1580–1631)*, ed. Philip L. Barbour, 3 vols. (Chapel Hill, N.C., 1986), I, 231–232.

52. For the shift in Mohawk settlement patterns, see Lenig, "Of Dutchmen, Beaver Hats, and Iroquois," 71–73. For the development of Iroquois culture before the historic period, see James A. Tuck, *Onondaga Iroquois Prehistory: A Study in Settlement Archaeology* (Syracuse, 1971); William A. Ritchie, *The Archeology of New York State* (Harrison, N.Y., 1980), 300–302. Other works on the Iroquois include Michael K. Foster, Jack Campisi, and Marianne Mithun, eds., *Extending the Rafters: Interdisciplinary Approaches to Iroquois Studies* (Albany, 1984); Daniel K. Richter and James H. Merrell, eds., *Beyond the Covenant Chain: The Iroquois and Their Neighbors in Indian North America, 1600–1800* (Syracuse, 1987); and Bradley, *Evolution of the Onondaga Iroquois*.

groups with whom the Dutch had contact and trade, all indications are that by the 1640s the situation was much altered. In the years after 1628–1629, the Mohawks achieved undisputed dominance over the region of the upper Hudson. Economically and diplomatically, Dutch-Mohawk relations became more formal and intimate during this period.

A treaty may have been concluded between the Dutch and Mohawks as early as the 1620s, but more substantial evidence exists that the first negotiations occurred in 1642 or 1643. The altered state of affairs is suggested by the special privilege extended to the Mohawks at this time in the acquisition of firearms, powder, and lead. In December 1634, when Harmen Meyndertsz van den Bogaert and several companions from Fort Orange were at the village of Tenotoge, twenty Mohawks executed a mock battle for the entertainment of the visitors. Clubs, axes, and sticks served for weapons. Some of the men were also protected by helmets and armor made of "thin reeds and cord woven together so that no arrow or axe could penetrate to cause serious injury." Although the Mohawks exhibited a ready interest in his pistols, Van den Bogaert's account gives no indication that at this time they possessed any other weapons than those mentioned above.[53]

The Dutch initally hesitated to distribute European weapons among the tribes. Ordinances were passed prohibiting the sale of firearms to the Indians in both 1639 and 1645. Director-General Stuyvesant even went so far as to arrest the armorer of Fort Amsterdam for secretly selling guns to private dealers. His imprisonment was followed by that of several of his clients, including Jacob Jansen Schermerhorn of Beverwyck. But in 1650 Cornelis van Tienhoven, the governor's assistant, explained to the directors of the Dutch West India Company that Stuyvesant had now "resolved to barter sparingly a few guns and a little powder through the Commissary at Fort Orange on the Company's account." While attempting to control and limit the trade in arms and ammunition, the Dutch singled out the Mohawks for special favor. As a result, the number of firearms

---

53. *HMVDB*, 9–10. Evidence for negotiations between the Dutch and Mohawks during the 1620s rests on the 1688 testimony of eighty-three-year-old Catelyn Trico, who was one of the first settlers at Fort Orange. Grassmann, *Mohawk Indians*, 210. For a treaty in the 1640s, see Grassmann, *Mohawk Indians*, 210. Historians must exercise caution in their use of early seventeenth-century documents relating to the Iroquois. See Charles T. Gehring and William A. Starna, "A Case of Fraud: The Dela Croix Letter and Map of 1634," *NYH*, 66 (1985), 249–261, and Charles T. Gehring, William A. Starna, and William N. Fenton, "The Tawagonshi Treaty of 1613: The Final Chapter," *NYH*, 68 (1987), 373–393.

among the tribe increased dramatically. During the 1640s, Dutch accounts indicate that the Mohawks possessed some 400 arms, enough
(if each was in working order) to equip almost every warrior with
such a weapon.[54]

Several factors accounted for this position of privilege. Most important was the role of the Mohawks as middlemen in the interior fur
trade. Also significant was Dutch desire to ally themselves militarily
and diplomatically with a native people powerful enough to overawe
other tribal groups throughout New Netherland. In addition, the
Dutch feared that the Mohawks, if not provided with arms and ammunition, would turn to English suppliers of these goods.[55]

Whatever their diplomatic or military ramifications, the crux of
Dutch-Mohawk relations was economic. The source of the tribe's
special position was their ability to supply the Dutch with furs. In
September 1659, at a moment of crisis in the fur trade, the Mohawks
pointedly reminded the Dutch of this fundamental fact: "The Dutch,
indeed, say we are brothers and are joined together with chains, but
that lasts only as long as we have beavers."[56]

Trade between the Dutch and Mohawks was a mutual exchange
with Dutch desire for furs matched by Mohawk demand for European-made goods, clothing, and arms. Only a particularly pressing
appetite for such goods and weaponry could have led the Mohawks to
tolerate the litany of abuses they received at the hands of the Dutch
traders. The tribe thus had a vested interest in maintaining its position as supplier of furs to the Dutch whether the peltry was obtained
directly from its own territory or indirectly from other more distant
tribal groups.[57]

54. *NYCD*, I, 427. For the 1639 and 1645 ordinances, see *LONN*, 18, 47. For the
arrest of Schermerhorn and the others, see *NNN*, 345; *NYCD*, I, 345, 428. Schermerhorn was the father of two future Schenectady settlers, Reyer and Symon Schermerhorn. *FS*, 158–159. For an estimate of the number of weapons among the Mohawks, see *NYCD*, I, 150. Donald Lenig suggested that the Mohawks had 600 to 800
warriors at the end of the 1500s. Lenig, "Of Dutchmen, Beaver Hats, and Iroquois,"
73. By the 1630s smallpox already was reducing the Mohawk population. *HMVDB*, 4.
55. *NYCD*, XIII, 35–36; Rink, *Holland on the Hudson*, 222.
56. *FOB*, II, 211.
57. Recent scholarship has highlighted the noneconomic aspects of Indian-white
exchange in early America. Neal Salisbury, for example, notes the importance to the
natives of New England of reciprocity between humankind and nature and among
human beings. The exchange of goods was a mechanism for keeping one's world in
balance. Salisbury, *Manitou and Providence*, 34–35, 43–44, 49. See also Miller and
Hamell, "New Perspective on Indian-White Contact." Many documents relating to
Dutch-Iroquois relations, however, do emphasize the economic connection and strategic position of the Mohawks in the trade with the Dutch (and the English). Among

As described by Francis Jennings, Indian-European trade involved "a process of exchange between two industries." The pelts supplied to European traders were garnered as a result of each native hunter acting as "a self-employed craftsman who purchased his own tools and sold semifinished products." The escalating demand for furs, however, placed mounting pressure on animal populations. Ancient taboos that promoted a religious respect for animals and helped to maintain a minimal breeding population crumbled. Moreover, conflict, which had been chronic among the tribes of the eastern woodlands in the pre-contact period, now intensified. To acquire the furs needed to satisfy their demand for Dutch and English trade goods, the Iroquois increasingly engaged in economic rivalries with tribes such as the Huron and the Illinois.[58]

The Mohawks especially were alert to any threat to their position in the fur trade. Indeed, as early as 1654, a diplomatic and economic alliance arranged between the French and the other Iroquois (the Senecas, Cayugas, Onondagas, and Oneidas) offered a serious challenge to their already established trading interests. The *Jesuit Relation* for that year reported that the Mohawks were "jealous of the upper Iroquois, because of the treaty of peace which the latter were the first to conclude with the French." The *Relation* also predicted that the tribe would "not lightly suffer these upper nations to come and trade with our French people; for they would no longer be compelled to pass through their Villages, which their route obliges them to do when they carry their merchandise to the Dutch." The writer noted "two great inconveniences" of the latter route: "The first is that they are compelled to perform the greater part of the journey by land and on foot, and to be their own beasts of burden. . . . The second arises from the insolence of the Anniehronons [Mohawks], who, being the Masters, so to speak, of this trade, do not always treat the upper Iroquois with civility."[59]

---

historians of early New York who have studied such records, Allen Trelease most clearly reflects this perspective in his work: "Peace was maintained because both sides had everything to lose and nothing to gain by hostilities. . . . The two races regarded each other less often as corn thieves, trespassers, or Indian givers than as sources of economic prosperity; what they thought of each other personally was beside the point." Trelease, *Indian Affairs*, 115.

58. Francis Jennings, *The Invasion of America: Indians, Colonialism, and the Cant of Conquest* (New York, 1976), 88–89; Bruce G. Trigger, *The Children of Aataentsic*, 2 vols. (Montreal, 1976); James Axtell, *The European and the Indian: Essays in the Ethnohistory of Colonial North America* (New York, 1981), 260–262. Salisbury, *Manitou and Providence*, chap. 2.

59. *JR*, XLI, 201, 203; Grassmann, *Mohawk Indians*, 157. In 1653 it was proposed

In July 1654 Father Simon Le Moyne left New France to confirm the peace with the Onondagas. The Mohawks were alerted to this development, and a tribal emissary soon arrived at Quebec to complain to the French that they "ought . . . to enter a house by the door, and not by the chimney. . . . It is with us Mohawks, that you should begin." The Mohawks, however, could anticipate little redress from their protest and must have realized that they exercised scant control over the designs of the French and other Iroquois. To their advantage was the fact that during both the Dutch and English periods better quality and cheaper goods could be obtained at Beverwyck (Albany) than at Montreal or Quebec. Yet the declining number of furs available for trade after 1657 made it imperative that the Mohawks, too, take some action to support their economically strategic position.[60]

Before 1661 the Dutch had purchased land only "from the Mahican and other River Indians who were in the process of extinction." The Mohawks could and did block expansion westward. For this reason, the Schenectady purchase was precedent-setting. The deed signed by Arent van Curler and the Mohawk sachems marked the first acquisition of land by the Dutch from the Iroquois. That the sale of the flats at Schenectady by the tribe was directly related to the current state of the fur trade was suggested by van Curler in a June 1661 letter to Governor Stuyvesant. He noted that the Mohawks were "quite willing to give it up for a small price, especially on account of the poor trade."[61]

In selling the land at Schenectady, the Mohawks were giving away little and potentially gaining much. Similar treaties in the coastal region of New Netherland often referred to the "inhabitants . . . of the land" and resulted in the removal of the original Indian owners. At

"to establish a trading-house, 18 or 20 leagues above Fort Orange." Such a post would attract the "Canadian Savages" who otherwise were "constantly molested by . . . the Maquas." *NYCD*, XIII, 35.

60. Grassmann, *Mohawk Indians*, 154. For a list indicating the cost of trade goods at Montreal in the 1680s as compared with Albany, see *NYCD*, IX, 408. For a list of typical trade goods, see *ERAR*, III, 554.

61. Trelease, *Indian Affairs*, 215; *NYCD*, XIII, 203. For the significance of the Schenectady purchase, see Grassmann, *Mohawk Indians*, 236. Jonathan Pearson's translation of the June 1661 letter reads, "as trade is so slack and meagre." For this document and for a translation of the 1661 grant to van Curler, see *SP*, 9–12. The Mohawks not only conveyed the land but promised "to free it from all pretensions which other Indians may have." *SP*, 12. Presumably, this was a reference to the Mahicans. In some later deeds between the Mohawks and the Dutch, the Mahicans received a token compensation in recognition of their former status as owners of the land being conveyed. *ERAR*, II, 197.

the Mohawk Flats, no village or population had to be resettled. Not only was the tribe selling land that was not then in use for settlement or agriculture (although the territory was, most likely, used for hunting and fishing and was part of the trail that passed from the Hudson River through the Mohawk Valley), they were turning to advantage property that only recently had been acquired as a result of their dispersal of the Mahicans to the east of the Hudson River during the 1620s.[62]

The Mohawks could expect to profit from the establishment of a Dutch community at Schenectady in several ways. As a site for the fur trade, it would eliminate the final overland passage required to reach Fort Orange and Beverwyck. In effect, the water route advantage would shift from the Dutch to the Mohawks. From their location on the Hudson River, the Dutch were easily able to bring merchandise to and carry furs away from Beverwyck, while the Indians had "to be their own beasts of burden for carrying their baggage and merchandise." Just the reverse would be the situation at Schenectady. With the convenience of water transport, the Mohawks could bring down more furs (if available) and demand and carry away more trade goods. Moreover, with their own villages located only a day's journey away, they could arrive and depart more easily and would be less dependent on the hospitality of their Dutch "brothers."[63]

At a time when fewer furs were available to trade, the Mohawks realized that the attractive property they controlled at the flats on the Mohawk River could be exploited as a resource to secure the merchandise they desired. Additionally, Arent van Curler occupied a crucial position in Dutch-Indian relations on the upper Hudson. In selling the lands at the Great Flats to a group of settlers and investors headed by van Curler, the Mohawks were cementing both their trade and their diplomatic relations with the Dutch. With the exchange of furs centered at Schenectady and van Curler in residence, the Mohawks may have hoped to avoid in the future many of the abuses to which they recently had been subjected.[64]

For all involved, the founding of a settlement at Schenectady was a

---

62. Ceci, "Effect of European Contact and Trade," 256.

63. *JR*, XLI, 201.

64. For van Curler's significance, see Trelease, *Indian Affairs*, 115; Van Laer, ed., "Van Curler and His Historic Letter," 15. For the Mohawks, the merchandise acquired by their sale of the flats may have been the least important consideration. The 1661 grant stated only that they were to receive "a certain number of cargoes." *SP*, 12. For comparison, one might note the quantity of goods given the Mahicans for their sale of a parcel of land that same year. *NYCD*, XIII, 193.

solution to problems that centered around the trade in furs. For Petrus Stuyvesant, it provided additional protection against English
usurpation of the Dutch trade. For at least some of the local traders at
Beverwyck and vicinity, the new community offered hope for relief
from their present economic distress, while for the Mohawks, it reaf-
firmed their position as key partners of the Dutch in the fur trade.[65]

The restriction on trade instituted by Petrus Stuyvesant and maintained by a succession of English governors after 1664 forced Schenectady's inhabitants into the unhappy position of occupying a locale
ideally suited for the trade in furs but having their economic activities
circumscribed by governmental prohibition. As would-be traders, in
the years before 1690, the members of the Schenectady community
were placed at the hub of Anglo-French rivalry for control of the fur
trade and influence with the Iroquois and surrounding tribes. Ultimately, the villagers would suffer severely as a result of their community's strategic position along the western trading route promoted by
New York governors such as Thomas Dongan. Yet, in spite of long-
standing attempts to engage in trade (efforts which will be detailed in
a later chapter), a majority of Schenectady's householders spent their
day-to-day lives not as merchants or traders but as husbandmen and
craftsmen. This daily effort is the subject to which we now turn.

65. For a brief review of the evidence presented in this chapter, see Thomas E.
Burke, Jr., "The New Netherland Fur Trade, 1657–1661: Response to Crisis," *De
Halve Maen*, 59 (March 1986), 1–4, 21.

2

"The most beautiful land"

A major attraction for settlement at Schenectady was, of course, the fine soil of the adjacent farmlands. It was in 1643 that Arent van Curler first reconnoitered the Mohawk River flats. Later observers echoed his description of "the most beautiful land." The community at Albany rested on "a barren sandy spot of Land," while Schenectady was "very commodiously seated on the Mohack's river, and much more pleasantly than Albany."[1]

For more than a century, farmers at the village concentrated their agricultural endeavors on the naturally fertile river flatlands and avoided the less easily tilled hills. The arable lowland was originally divided into twenty-three parcels assigned to fifteen individuals.

1. Van Laer, ed., "Van Curler and His Historic Letter," 28; *NYCD*, III, 411, IV, 410. In 1680 Jasper Danckaerts found the flats along the Mohawk River to be "exceedingly rich land." Danckaerts wrote, "Their cultivated lands are . . . large flats between the hills, on the margin or along the side of the rivers . . . very flat and level, without a single tree or bush upon them, of a black sandy soil which . . . can hardly be exhausted." *JD*, 201, 213. In the eighteenth century, William Smith, Jr., wrote of Schenectady: "This village is . . . on a rich flat of low land, surrounded with hills. . . . The windings of the river through the town, and the fields (which are often overflowed in the spring) form, about harvest, a most beautiful prospect." William Smith, Jr., *The History of the Province of New York*, ed. Michael Kammen, 2 vols. (Cambridge, Mass., 1972), I, 212. Other observers also noted the rich and fertile land surrounding Schenectady: Richard Smith, *A Tour of Four Great Rivers. The Hudson, Mohawk, Susquehanna, and Delaware in 1769, Being the Journal of Richard Smith*, ed. Francis W. Halsey (Port Washington, N.Y., 1964), 21. For descriptions of the community and estimates of the distance between Albany and Schenectady, see Van Laer, ed., "Van Curler and His Historic Letter," 28; *ER*, III, 1867; *LIR*, 175; Edward Randolph, *His Letters and Official Papers, 1676–1703*, ed. Robert N. Toppan and Alfred T. S. Goodrick, 7 vols. (Boston, 1898–1909), IV, 299; William Strickland, *Journal of a Tour in the United States of America, 1794–1795*, ed. J. E. Strickland, *NYHSC*, LXXXIII (New York, 1971), 135.

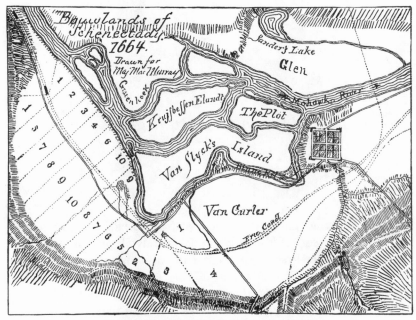

MAP, CONSTRUCTED FROM ACTUAL SURVEY AND THE ANCIENT DEED.

Initial land grants at Schenectady. From *SP*

Most properties lay to the west of the village along the south bank of
the Mohawk River. Arent van Curler's was the largest and most valuable farm and embraced approximately one hundred fourteen acres.
Property to the west of van Curler's bouwery was divided into two
ranges of land numbered one to ten with each plot containing about
twenty-five morgens, a total of fifty acres per holding (a Dutch mor-
gen equaling about two English acres). On the north bank of the
Mohawk, separated from the village by the river, Sander Leendertsen
Glen owned an additional fifty morgens. Glen was the only proprietor to possess land both on the flats and across the river. With the
exception of van Curler and Glen, no single proprietor held more
than twenty-five morgens. Jan Barentsen Wemp and Martin Cornelissen van Slyck, for example, acquired an island adjacent to the
community which consisted of forty-four morgens total.[2]

Although several bouweries such as van Curler's were self-con-
tained properties, the majority were strip farms laid out to the south

2. *SP*, 58–81. For the use of flatlands for farming during the eighteenth century,
see Smith, *Tour of Four Rivers*, 21.

Table 1. Farms at Rensselaerswyck in 1651

Used by	Size (morgens)	Value (guilders)	Number of horses/ cows		Comments
Thomas Chambers	30	500	9	8	
Evert Pels	20	400	7	8	
Cornelis van Nes	9	225	3	–	"poor"
t'heunis dirckse	30	500	11	14	"one of the best"
Jurriaen Westvael	28	560	10	5	"one of the best"
Claes Segerts	28	460	7	10	"one of the best"
Cornelis van Bruckelen	27	360	7	11	"a fine farm"
Jan Helms	40	300	6	11	
Aert Jacobsz	16	250	5	12	
Jan Barentse Wemp	14	275	8	9	"a stately farm"
Cornelis segers	70	1210	13	22	"a good farm"
t'homas jansen	6	130	1	8	
Arion Huijberts	14	300	9	10	
Cornelis teunesse van Bruckelen	25.5	600	10	9	
Arent van Curler	44	1,000	10	18	"the best farm"
TOTAL	401.5	7,070	116	155	
AVERAGE (MEAN):	26.8	471.3	7.7	10.3	

Source: *VRBM*, 740–743.

of the river. Philip Hendricksen Brouwer's farm Number Two, for example, consisted of property in two detached parcels. Most fortunate was Teunis Cornelissen Swart, who acquired the double farm Number Ten. During this period, the allotment of property in a numbered sequence was employed not only at Schenectady but at Beverwyck and Esopus as well. The distribution of land in separated bands, however, may have been less common. Such properties could be found in the Netherlands during the sixteenth and seventeenth centuries, but do not appear to have been the norm at Rensselaerswyck, the only agricultural community in the region prior to Schenectady.[3]

3. For the holdings of van Curler, Brouwer, and Swart, see *SP*, 60–61, 63, 67. Unfortunately, it is uncertain what impact such a pattern of property holding had on the villagers' labor routines or shared agricultural responsibilities. With a proprietor's lands divided among those of his neighbors, were fields plowed, planted, and harvested in common, or did each family guard and work its own property? At present, we do not know. For the allotment of land at Beverwyck and Esopus as well as for a proposed settlement at Saratoga, see *FOB*, I, 212; *ERAR*, II, 195–197, 347–349, III, 158–159, 189–190. For land use in the Netherlands, see Audrey M. Lambert, *The*

As notable as the distribution of the arable land at Schenectady was the size of the individual holdings. Arent van Curler and Sander Leendertsen Glen both owned properties of fifty morgens or more. Most parcels, however, were much smaller. The sale of Philip Hendricksen Brouwer's estate in 1664 included his "lot of about twenty-five morgens, or so much as shall be allotted to each of the other inhabitants." Although such plots may seem small, they approximated the size of farmsteads at Rensselaerswyck. In 1651 the van Rensselaer lands accommodated fifteen bouweries, the largest containing seventy morgens and the smallest six (Table 1). The average (mean) size was just under twenty-seven morgens, or approximately fifty-four acres. At that date, the "best farm," known as the patroon's farm or *de Vlackte*, was operated by Arent van Curler and contained forty-four morgens.[4]

The pattern of narrow, divided farmlands was maintained at Schenectady for many years. A map of the community drawn in 1698 shows the village surrounded by cultivated land divided into rectangular bands. Two years later, in 1700, the property conveyed by William Teller to his son Johannes comprised "two lots of arable land . . . each lot being accounted twelve morgens." Whatever the size or configuration of such property, settlement at Schenectady offered the possibility of owning one's own farm as opposed to leasing land from the patroon or someone else. In 1651 Cornelis van Ness operated a poor nine-morgen plot at Rensselaerswyck. A decade later, van Ness acquired twenty-five morgens at Schenectady through purchase of Philip Hendricksen Brouwer's estate.[5]

As previously noted, the initial distribution of land at Schenectady

---

Making of the Dutch Landscape: An Historical Geography of the Netherlands (New York, 1971), chap. 3. For a recent article on Dutch agriculture, see David Steven Cohen, "Dutch-American Farming: Crops, Livestock, and Equipment, 1623–1900," in Roderic H. Blackburn and Nancy A. Kelley, eds., *New World Dutch Studies: Dutch Arts and Culture in Colonial America, 1609–1776* (Albany, 1987), 185–200.

4. *ERAR*, I, 347. Fifteen farms and one tobacco plantation were located at Rensselaerswyck proper and two other farms were at Catskill. *VRBM*, 732–743; Nissenson, *Patroon's Domain*, 80. These properties approximated the size of agricultural properties elsewhere in New York during the seventeenth and early eighteenth centuries. Vivienne L. Kruger, "Born to Run: The Slave Family in Early New York, 1626 to 1827" (Ph.D. diss., Columbia University, 1985), 94. For agricultural property in the Netherlands, see Jan de Vries, *The Dutch Rural Economy in the Golden Age, 1500–1700* (New Haven, 1974), 56.

5. *ERAR*, II, 383–384. For van Ness, see *ERAR*, I, 347; *VRBM*, 741.

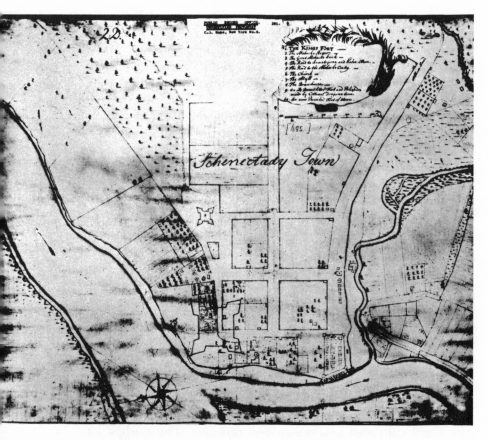

Detail of Schenectady from the 1698 Romer map. From Grassmann,
Mohawk Indians

had been complicated by Director-General Stuyvesant's order that
the provincial surveyor refuse to proceed with the laying out of lots
until the proprietors agreed to limit themselves strictly to agriculture.
Not until 1664 were the individual plots staked out and formally surveyed. As a result, for over two years, the designation and delinea-
tion of property holdings was in a state of confusion, a situation that
produced dissension among the proprietors and contributed to the
one murder recorded at the village during the seventeenth century.
With the survey completed, however, each landowner received a
ground brief as a record of his holdings and a document that could be

referred to at any later date to establish the extent or limits of individual property holdings.[6]

The surveying procedures followed at Schenectady were, presumably, typical of those employed elsewhere during this period. In 1661 Petrus Stuyvesant ordered the inhabitants of Wiltwyck near Esopus "to have their cultivated and uncultivated land surveyed by the sworn surveyor . . . also to have it marked and divided by proper signs and to ask and receive upon showing a certificate of survey, signed by the surveyor, a proper deed and proof of ownership under penalty of confiscation." Both at Wiltwyck and at Schenectady, the properties measured off included land intended for cultivation as well as that designated for a variety of domestic or agricultural purposes. According to the most authoritative nineteenth-century history of the community, Jonathan Pearson's *History of the Schenectady Patent*, several allotments were made to each of the first settlers: a house lot in the village, a farm on the flats or nearby islands, a pasture ground east of the village, and a garden lot in the lowland adjacent to the arm of the Mohawk River known as the Binne Kill.[7]

For almost two decades, Schenectady remained an unpalisaded settlement with the village proper adjoining the community's arable land. Pearson's fourfold division may be too exclusive, however, for pasture lands were located not only east of the village but also to the north, on the opposite bank of the Mohawk River. Indeed, by the early 1670s nearly three miles of land surrounding Schenectady was reserved for this purpose. Moreover, the distinction between settled and cultivated land was not so precise as Pearson has drawn it. In 1669, when Bent Bagge leased his Schenectady property to Jan Rinckhout of Albany, the agreement included "a certain house and barn and all the land that the lessor has sown on the south side of the house at Schanechtade, at present sown with eight skipples of oats and a half skipple of maize." The location of Bagge's property cannot be determined, but the close approximation of dwelling house with

6. In September 1663, Claes Cornelissen Swits was shot by Philip Hendricksen Brouwer while plowing land claimed by both Brouwer and William Teller. Swits had been head farmer on Teller's lands at Schenectady. *ERAR*, III, 200–201, 267–269. For surveying practices at Beverwyck and the disputes that could surround the laying out of lots, see *FOB*, I, 117, 146, 150, 187, 266–267, 272–273. In 1671 Teller was ordered by the court of Albany to "exhibit his groundbrief before the honorable court, as he occupies more ground at Schaenhechtede than belongs to him." *ARS*, I, 217.

7. *NYCD*, XIII, 195–196. For Pearson's discussion of land distribution at Schenectady, see *SP*, 58.

sown land suggests either that Bagge used his house lot within the village for this purpose or that the house and barn were located at some point removed from the community.[8]

Arent van Curler had calculated that the trip to the Mohawk Flats was a half day's journey at a time when the only available path was an Indian trail between the Hudson and the Mohawk rivers. A road was first constructed during the summer of 1661. Two decades later, in April 1680, in good weather Jasper Danckaerts made the journey on horseback in about four hours. Danckaerts, a Dutch Labadist then touring the former colony of New Netherland, left the following account of his trip: "We rode over a fine, sandy cart road through woods of nothing but beautiful evergreens or fir trees, but a light and barren soil." The route apparently changed little during the next century. In 1802 the Reverend John Taylor journeyed from Albany to Schenectady and found that his path traversed "a barren sandy plain . . . but 3 or 4 houses in the whole 17 miles." Throughout the colonial period this cart road marked the main course of passage between Albany and Schenectady.[9]

Preparations for removing to Schenectady began soon after the initial grant of land in July 1661. As early as May 1662, Philip Hendricksen Brouwer made reference to his bouwery at Schenectady, property he proposed "to take possession of this summer, with horses and cattle." Writing in the 1650s, Cornelis van Tienhoven observed that during a community's first years it was not necessary for a husbandman to acquire many animals, "since clearing the land and other necessary labor do not permit him to save much hay and to build barns for stabling." Were Brouwer and the other Schenectady settlers to heed van Tienhoven's advice, they would "employ the whole summer in clearing land and building cottages." This and more was accomplished. In 1663 Arent van Curler informed Petrus Stuyvesant that the settlers were proceeding "with plowing and seeding in order

---

8. *ERAR*, III, 313–314. In 1670, before removing to Schenectady, Hendrick Vrooman leased a farm on the east bank of the Hudson River which included land designated for a variety of purposes. This also was the case in 1681 when Reyer Schermerhorn acquired two parcels of land at Schenectady. *ERAR.*, II, 118–119, III, 370–372. For Bent Bagge's property, see *SP*, 85. The number of houses outside the village proper is uncertain. In 1684 Hilletie van Olinda petitioned the Schenectady court to exchange her house for another house and lot "in the village." Schenectady Court Minutes, 1684, Caldwell Family Papers, Albany Institute of History and Art, trans. Charles T. Gehring. These records also include some material from the 1690s.

9. *JD*, 201; *DHNY*, III, 1128; Van Laer, ed., "Van Curler and His Historic Letter," 28. For the building of a road to Schenectady in 1661, see *SP*, 10.

to have feed for the next winter for their horses and cattle." According to van Curler, they had "already invested the little they had in
building houses, barns and barracks and in horses and cattle."[10]

Three documents from 1663 and 1664 allow insight into these
initial efforts at settlement and cultivation. In August 1663 Gerrit
Bancker and Harmen Vedder leased their farm to Symon Groot for
six years. The agreement stipulated that Groot would receive "a
dwelling, barn and rick in proper condition, and 6 draft horses, 3 of
which mares, 6 milch cows, two sows . . . furthermore the lessors
shall deliver for the use of the lessee, carts, plows, harrows, and the
harness needful thereto." The following year, in April, Cornelis van
Ness acquired Philip Hendricksen Brouwer's estate, including "the
bouwery, house, lot, and garden." The farm consisted "of about
twenty-five morgens . . . all being broken up land, a part sowed with
nine and a half schepels of winter wheat and two and a half schepels
of summer wheat; furthermore, the house lot is two hundred feet
square, and the garden as it lies in fence, on which is a barn thirty by
twenty-four feet, besides the gangway, two ricks . . . a passable cart,
a stretcher (*span-touwen*), and an after plough (*achter ploegh*)." Also sold
at auction were Brouwer's farm animals, including three horses (a
mare, a gelding, and a yearling colt), two cows, three heifers, and
five sows.[11]

The most detailed account of any of the early Schenectady farmsteads is provided by a June 1664 contract in which William Teller
leased his farm to Claes Fredericksen van Petten and Isaac Cornelissen Swits. The twenty-three-year-old van Petten and twenty-
two-year-old Swits

> jointly hired of him a certain farm . . . lying at Schanechtede, consist-
> ing of dwelling house, barn, rick and arable land in two parcels. . . .
> The lessor delivers . . . for use on the farm six draft horses, namely,
> three geldings and three mares, with a one-year old stallion colt and
> another of this year, five milch cows, two heifers and two bull calves of
> this year, one heifer in her third year, two sows with five pigs four
> months old and a hog one year old. . . . The lessor has also delivered
> . . . two plows with their appurtenances and a wagon, while another
> wagon shall be delivered next harvest time; also a pot, kettles, churn,
> milk tubs, two sleds, three Flemish scythes with two scythe blades, and
> a grain winnow. . . . Moreover, the land is now sown with twenty-two

10. *DHNY*, IV, 30, 31; *ARS*, III, 495–496; *ERAR*, I, 301–302.
11. *ERAR*, I, 347–348, III, 242.

Table 2. Comparison of four Schenectady farms

Bancker/Vedder (August 1663)	Brouwer (April 1664)	Teller (June 1664)	Van Ysselsteyn (October 1668)
house	house	house	house
barn	barn	barn	barn
1 rick	2 ricks	1 rick	3 ricks
carts	cart	2 wagons	cart
harrows	stretcher		harrow
	after plow	2 plows	plow
		pot and kettles	
		churn and milk tub	
		2 sleds	
		3 Flemish scythes	
		grain winnow	
6 horses	3 horses	6 horses and 2 colts	4 horses
6 cows	3 cows and 2 heifers	5 cows and 3 heifers	5 cows
		2 bull calves	
2 sows	5 sows	2 sows, 3 pigs, 1 hog	8 hogs
	9.5 sch.[a] winter wheat	22 sch. winter wheat	
	2.5 sch. summer wheat	4 sch. summer wheat	
		3 sch. white peas	
		3 sch. buckwheat	
		49 sch. oats	

Source: ERAR, I, 347–348, 450–451, III, 242–243, 285–287.
[a]A schepel (sch.) equalled slightly more than three-quarters of an English bushel.

skipples of winter wheat, four skipples of summer wheat, three skipples of white peas, three skipples of buckwheat, and also forty-nine skipples of oats.

Evidently, even from the first years of settlement, the farms at Schenectady incorporated a variety of lands, buildings, animals, implements and crops. Although it is difficult to determine the makeup of a "typical" bouwery, we can describe the structures, implements, animals, and crops found on four of the earliest community properties (Table 2).[12]

A house and barn were among the most essential first structures raised on each of the Schenectady properties. An ordinance at Albany in 1676 required that "all new buildings fronting on the street shall be substantial dwelling houses, not less than 2 rooms deep and not less than 18 feet wide, being built in front on the street of brick or quarry stone and covered with tiles." Few of the early residences

12. Ibid., III, 286.

at Schenectady were this elaborate. In 1669 William Teller complained that several dwellings near his lacked chimneys and were fire
hazards. For some years the houses at Schenectady must have resembled those which Father Isaac Jogues described at Rensselaerswyck in
the 1640s: "All their houses are merely of boards and thatched, with
no mason work except the chimneys. The forest furnishing many
large pines, they make boards by means of their mills, which they
have here for the purpose."[13]

Unfortunately, there are no structures existing at Schenectady today which originate from its earliest period of occupation. The majority of dwellings found within the so-called Stockade Area as well
as at nearby Scotia date from the eighteenth century. The only extant
building that may, in part, derive from the late seventeenth century
is the Mabie house at Rotterdam Junction. This residence, built of
stone with a steep sloping roof, originally belonged to Daniel Jansen
van Antwerpen, who resided on the flats about eight miles above
Schenectady as early as 1670. The degree to which the home today
approximates its original appearance is uncertain, however, as it may
have been rebuilt by an eighteenth-century owner, Jan Pietersen
Mabie.[14]

Often such houses did not stand alone but were one of a combination of structures with varied uses which could be found on a dwelling site. At Beverwyck in 1657 a house was sold "of two planks
length, with a kitchen (*koockhuys*) of sixteen feet square attached to
said house, with a chimney and an oven therein, and the whole lot, in
which are contained . . . two gardens together with a well and
hogsty." Houses were, of course, as much worksites and storage facilities as they were dwelling places. Cellars were convenient places to
keep beer, wine, and vegetables, while lofts could hold thatching

---

13. *NNN*, 262; *ARS*, II, 136. For Teller's complaint, see *ARS*, I, 106. For details of
a seventeenth-century dwelling at Rensselaerswyck, see Robert G. Wheeler, "The
House of Jeremias van Rensselaer, 1658–1666," *NYHSQ*, 45 (1961), 75–88. During
the eighteenth century, brick seems to have been a more typical construction material.
The Dutch form of architecture was followed at Schenectady into the late 1700s.
Smith, Jr., *History*, I, 212; Strickland, *Journal*, 136. For a nineteenth-century photo-
graph illustrating the combined wood and brick structure of an eighteenth-century
Schenectady house (in the process of being demolished), see Larry Hart, *Tales of Old
Schenectady*, Vol. I: *The Formative Years* (Scotia, N.Y., 1975), 35.

14. For the van Antwerpen/Mabie house, see *SP*, 159–160. For Dutch structures
that are still extant, see Kammen, *Colonial New York*, 146–147; Hart, *Tales of Old
Schenectady*, 33, 46–50; Maud Esther Dillard, *An Album of New Netherland* (New York,
1963); Rosalie Fellows Bailey, *Pre-Revolutionary Dutch Houses and Families in Northern
New Jersey and Southern New York* (New York, 1936).

straw, hay, grains such as wheat and oats, and even gunpowder. Perhaps the best example of the multipurpose nature of Dutch dwellings comes from Albany, where in 1676 Elias van Ravesteyn, a maker of gunstocks, negotiated a lease for use of part of the house of Hendrick Roseboom. The agreement clearly illustrates the variety of domestic and occupational pursuits that could be carried on in a Dutch dwelling. Van Ravesteyn,

> hired said Rooseboom's front room of the house . . . on the express condition that said Ravelsteyn shall make therein a workbench for . . . gunstock making . . . and when any gunstocks are to be made for the Indians, Ravesteyn and Rooseboom's son shall make the same. . . . And Rooseboom expressly stipulates that during the summertime no fire shall be made in said front room and that he, Rooseboom, may trade there with the Indians . . . without disturbing thereby said Ravesteyn in his work, who may sleep in the garret or in the room and in wintertime burn his own wood in the room and eat and cook there.[15]

In the Netherlands, during the seventeenth century, farmers often erected dwellings that consisted of an attached house and barn. Archeological evidence suggests that Arent van Curler owned such a structure during the 1640s at the flats along the Hudson River above Beverwyck. Whether such buildings were replicated at Schenectady is not certain, but likely. Apparently, there was often a close approximation of house and barn, all enclosed within a fence, either post and rail or made "tight" by weaving branches between the rails. At his death, Philip Hendricksen Brouwer's estate included not only his bouwery lands but also "the house lot . . . two hundred feet square, and the garden as it lies in fence, on which is a barn thirty by twenty-four feet." Although the inventory of Brouwer's estate listed only the rough dimensions of his barn, a 1675 contract from Kinderhook called for the construction of a structure "fifty feet long and twenty-six feet wide, with an extension on each side, ten feet deep and running the full length of the barn, and at each end a gable with sloping peak; furthermore to make in said barn five bents with five loft beams . . . a double door at the front end of the barn and one

---

15. *ERAR*, I, 12–13, III, 353–354. For the use of Dutch homes as storage facilities, see *FOB*, I, 127; *ARS*, I, 96, 180, II, 120–121, 175. See also, Henk J. Zantkuyl, "The Netherlands Town House: How and Why It Works," in Blackburn and Kelley, eds., *Dutch Arts and Culture*, 143–160. For van Ravesteyn, see *ARS*, I, 22; *ERAR*, III, 399–400; William Vanderpoel Hannay, comp., "Burial Records, First Dutch Reformed Church, Albany, N.Y., 1654–1862," *DSSAY*, 8–9 (1932–1934), 18.

door in each of the extensions, a horse manger forty feet long and all
the inside work that belongs to a barn." Similarly, a barn built near
Catskill in 1677 included "an opening (*uytlaeting*) on both sides; the
barn shall be sixty feet long and thirty feet broad, with a floor of
timber (*balke*), horse crib, cow stall and loft (*solder*) therein."[16]

Obviously, each barn had its own dimensions, and there was room
for a variety of construction techniques—a floor of clay might serve
just as well as one of timber. However, as a shelter for horses, cattle,
and other animals, especially during the colder months of the year, a
typical Dutch barn, whether at Schenectady or elsewhere, must have
rung with familiar barnyard sounds. Jasper Danckaerts, for example,
described a night he and a traveling companion spent in a barn on
Long Island during the fall of 1679: "After supper, we went to sleep
in the barn, upon some straw spread with sheep-skins, in the midst of
the continual grunting of hogs, squealing of pigs, bleating and cough-
ing of sheep, barking of dogs, crowing of cocks, cackling of hens, and
especially, a good quantity of fleas and vermin." Such barns and
dwelling houses must have lent an Old World appearance to the community at Schenectady. So too would the final structure found on
most Dutch properties, the hay rick. The two ricks on Philip
Hendricksen Brouwer's bouwery were described as "one of four and
the other of five rods [square]." Still in use in the Netherlands today,
the hay rick consists of a wooden roof that can be jacked up on its
support posts to protect the grain stacked beneath.[17]

If Schenectady's appearance was that of the Old World, its setting
was the New, and the abundance of certain resources, especially timber, influenced and altered building techniques. In the Netherlands
varying amounts of masonry were used in the construction of most
barns, but in the New World many Dutch barns were all of wood.
Pine seems to have been preferred, although oak and walnut were
also used. Such woods were more than convenient construction materials; they were a life-sustaining resource providing fire for cooking

---

16. *ERAR*, I, 169, 347, III, 424–425. For works that survey the techniques used in
constructing Dutch barns and houses, see *Boerderijen Bekijken: Historisch Boerderij-On-
derzoek in Nederland* (Amersfoort, 1985); Hermanus Van der Kloot Meijburg, *Onze
Oude Boerenhuizen: Tachtig Schetsen van Boerenhuizen in Nederland* (Rotterdam, 1912);
John Fitchen, *The New World Dutch Barn* (Syracuse, 1968); Piet van Wijk, "Form and
Function in the Netherlands' Dutch Agricultural Architecture," in Blackburn and
Kelley, eds., *Dutch Arts and Culture*, 161–169. For van Curler's dwelling on the flats,
see Lois M. Feister, "Archaeology in Rensselaerswyck, Dutch 17th-Century Domes-
tic Sites," in Bakker, ed., *New Netherland Studies*, 83.

17. *JD*, 58; *ERAR*, I, 347. For the use of hay ricks by modern Dutch farmers, see
Lambert, *Making of the Dutch Landscape*, 219.

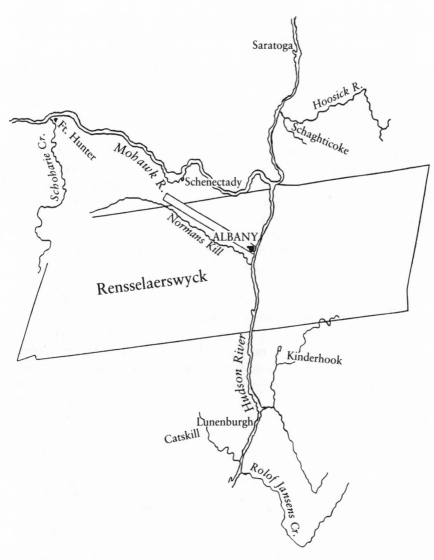

Albany, Schenectady, Rensselaerswyck, and vicinity. Drawn by Keith Prior, Colonial Albany Social History Project, New York State Museum

throughout the year and heat during the winter. Oak, hickory, ash, and elm were suitable for firewood, whereas poplar, linden, and butternut were avoided. In the Netherlands during the seventeenth century, peat served as the primary fuel, but the abundance of forests in New York allowed for an extravagance that surprised travelers such as Jasper Danckaerts: "We found a good fire, half-way up the chimney, of clear oak and hickory, which they made not the least scruple of burning profusely. We let it penetrate us thoroughly."[18]

The land and forests of the Mohawk Valley were resources to be exploited; less tractable was the river itself. The Mohawk and the streams that fed into it were a source of drinking water and water power. During the colonial period, however, the river never served as a link for travel between Schenectady and Albany. Yet it did provide an easy means of access to the interior and was not a physical barrier at Schenectady itself. The river was shallow, dotted by islands, and only a few hundred feet wide. Indeed, it was common practice for the Schenectady Dutch to take their horses and cattle across the river for pasturing on its north bank. Also, during the spring and fall, ducks and other waterfowl were hunted on the river and reeds for thatching could be gathered along its banks. By 1671 at least four individuals—Sander Leendertsen Glen, Benjamin Roberts, Claes de Graaf, and Cornelis Viele—owned land on the north side of the Mohawk opposite the village, while Daniel Jansen van Antwerpen had already acquired his property several miles upriver.[19]

During the community's earliest years, Schenectady's settlers made joint use of certain neighboring lands and resources. In 1670, when Harmen Vedder complained that Cornelis van Ness had cut reeds on his property, van Ness replied that he had "as much right to use their reed-land as they have to use his woodland." The following year, the court at Albany received a petition "by those of Schaenhechtede"

---

18. *JD*, 53. For wood used in building Dutch barns and for a variety of other construction purposes, see Fitchen, *New World Dutch Barn*, 15; *NNN*, 262; Van Laer, ed., "Van Curler and His Historic Letter," 26; Wheeler, "House of Jeremias van Rensselaer," 75–88; *ARS*, I, 102, 103. For firewood, see *ARS*, III, 508. For the use of peat for heating purposes in the Netherlands, see Lambert, *Making of the Dutch Landscape*, 210–211.

19. Even in winter the Hudson and Mohawk rivers could serve as a source of water. At Albany, holes were opened through the ice and, presumably, this also was done at Schenectady. *ARS*, I, 285. Sweer Teunissen van Velsen harnessed the water power of one of the streams leading to the Mohawk River for his grist mill. *SP*, 192–193. William Strickland estimated the width of the Mohawk as 400 yards. Strickland, *Journal*, 138. In 1670 Cornelis Cornelissen Viele petitioned the court at Albany for a piece of land on the north bank of the Mohawk River. It was granted "on condition of leaving a corner for the use of the other inhabitants in taking their horses or cattle across the river." *ARS*, I, 207. For a detailed survey of the Mohawk River done in 1792, see *DHNY*, III, 1087–1090. For an account of fishing for sturgeon at Albany in the 1700s, as well as the seasonal migration of ducks, geese, and pigeons through the region, see Anne Grant, *Memoirs of an American Lady*, 2 vols. (New York, 1901), I, 93–95.

urging that Jan Jonkers van Rotterdam and Andries Alberts (Bradt) "not enjoy [the exclusive use of] a certain parcel of land near Schaenhechtede, as it tends to the benefit of all of them." The court concurred and ruled "that for the benefit of the inhabitants no land may be taken up within three miles of the place, the same to be reserved as pasture for those of Schaenhechtede and for no other purpose."[20]

The land and water provided a rich and varied locale, but the Dutch did more than adapt to or exploit directly the natural resources that surrounded them. They altered their environment as well. This transformation was most evident in the clearing of land and cutting of timber for buildings and firewood. Also, deliberate efforts may have been made at diking and drainage. Such techniques were employed at Esopus, and at Schenectady in 1686 reference was made to "a Certain Peece of Land . . . bounded . . . to ye east [by] a low Place of ground, wh formerly hes been a Swamp." In 1687 Governor Thomas Dongan expressed the opinion that "the Dutch are great improvers of Land."[21]

The cutting of trees and the sowing of seed cleared and shaped the land for the purposes of settlement and agriculture. The erection of fences and laying out of paths established man-made boundaries and thoroughfares. All of this took time. During the first years of settlement there must have been a preoccupation with the essentials of shelter and subsistence. In 1650 Cornelis van Tienhoven reported that a community's first settlers would "dig a square pit in the ground, cellar fashion, . . . raise a roof of spars clear up, and cover the spars with bark . . . so that they can live dry and warm in these houses with their entire families for two, three or four years." No evidence exists to suggest that life at Schenectady was ever this austere. The bouwery records and Arent van Curler's letters testify that as early as 1663 and 1664 dwelling houses and barns had been raised, lands planted, and farms stocked with animals. Both at this time and later, Schenectady's lifeline was its cart road to and from Albany. Many of the necessary building materials, the pine boards and bricks employed in Dutch structures of this period, must have been produced at the sawmills and brick kilns in and near Beverwyck (Albany) and taken by wagon to the new community. On several occasions, entire dwellings were dismantled and removed to Schenectady. Many of the original proprietors owned property at Beverwyck or

20. *ARS*, I, 194, 264–265.
21. *NYCD*, III, 397; *ERAR*, II, 300. For references to the use of dikes and the drainage of land by the Dutch, see *JD*, 98; *NL*, 122.

Rensselaerswyck and probably "commuted" to their new residences at Schenectady. Arent van Curler, for example, did not sell his dwelling at Rensselaerswyck until August 1662. Presumably by this date his home at Schenectady was completed and readied for occupation.[22]

With time came an amelioration of some of the initial crudities of life at Schenectady. The community's first settlers must have had to contend with wading or bypassing the small streams that cut through their lands and fed into the Mohawk. In 1672, however, the court at Albany authorized construction of a bridge, presumably over the Binne Kill or one of the adjacent streams. Similarly, the earliest farm inventories mention buildings and gardens, animals and crops, but only at the remove of one or two decades are the first orchards listed. For example, in 1686 Ludovicus Cobes sold his property within the village which included a "Dwelling House, wth ye Orchard and Garden thereunto Belonging." Even earlier, in 1679, William Teller was raising apples on his farm.[23]

Arent van Curler, in his 1663 letter to Petrus Stuyvesant, informed the governor of the investment the Schenectady settlers had made "in building houses, barns and barracks and in horses and cattle." As important an undertaking as the erection of physical structures was the acquisition of livestock to serve as draft animals in clearing and plowing the land for planting and to provide a variety of foodstuffs essential to the Dutch diet. Years before, Kiliaen van Rensselaer correctly assessed the significance of such creatures when he expressed the hope that "after the first harvest . . . our people will no longer have lack of wheat, milk, butter or cheese." Animals could be purchased outright or acquired by way of public auctions and estate

22. *DHNY*, IV, 31. For Schenectady during the 1660s, see *ERAR*, I, 347–348, 450–451, III, 242–243, 285–287; *ARS*, III, 493–496; *SP*, 13–14. In 1663 the inhabitants of Schenectady were reported to "carry . . . Goods and Merchandises on Wagons and Horseback thither." *LONN*, 442. We can assume that not only trade goods but household furnishings, tools, and building materials were brought to Schenectady in this manner. In 1678 fire destroyed the dwellings of Sweer Teunissen van Velsen and Jacques Cornelissen van Slyck. On January 29, 1678, they both asked the court at Albany for permission to tear down houses they owned outside that community's walls "and to haul them away on their sleighs." On June 12, van Velsen's Albany house was described as "now lately taken down and carried to Schaenhechtady." *ARS*, II, 292; *ERAR*, I, 184. Van Curler sold his Rensselaerswyck property on August 17, 1662. Martin Cornelissen van Ysselsteyn sold his property in May, and Glen even earlier, in March. *ERAR*, III, 148, 157, 176–177.

23. *ERAR*, II, 315. For William Teller's orchard, see *ERAR*, III, 473. For the bridge at Schenectady, see *ARS*, I, 291–292.

Table 3. Comparison of livestock holdings on Schenectady farms

Bancker/Vedder (1663)	Brouwer (1664)	Teller (1664)	Van Ysselsteyn (1668)	Teller (1679)
6 horses	3 horses	6 horses 2 colts	4 horses	8 horses
6 cows	3 cows 2 heifers	5 cows 3 heifers 2 bull calves	5 cows	5 cows

Source: ERAR, I, 347–348, 450–451, III, 242–243, 285–287, 472–474.

sales. By this means, in 1664, Jan van Eps obtained Philip Hendricksen Brouwer's property, which included three horses, one cow, two heifers, and five sows. Although most animals were obtained locally, occasionally livestock were transported from a distance. Ludovicus Cobes, for example, procured an ox at New York City.[24]

The importance of both horses and cattle is evident from the 1651 inventory of farms at Rensselaerswyck (see Table 1). Only the smallest—that operated by Cornelis van Ness—had no cattle, and its primary reliance on horses may indicate the farm's newness and the priority given to the initial clearing and plowing of the land. Every farm had at least one horse. Arent van Curler's bouwery had as many as ten horses and eighteen cows, but the average was eight horses and ten cattle per bouwery. Father Isaac Jogues had commented years before on the prevalence of horses at Rensselaerswyck. While that animal had the advantage of being useful for both riding and labor, cattle provided food and profit. Again, it was Kiliaen van Rensselaer who most clearly expressed this relationship. In 1632 he wrote, "Our principal profit will come from the cattle, for which there is plenty of fine pasture and hay for nothing . . . while on the contrary the clearing of the land proceeds with slowness."[25]

At the time of Schenectady's founding, cattle, evidently, were still considered the more advantageous animal. Jeremias van Rensselaer complained that at Rensselaerswyck "horses have become so abun-

24. *ARS*, III, 496; *VRBM*, 199. For animals bought by Bancker and the others, see *ERAR*, I, 65, 80, 348; *ARS*, I, 124, III, 33. There also was a trade in animals at Schenectady itself. *ERAR*, III, 350.

25. *VRBM*, 199. For farms at Rensselaerswyck, see *VRBM*, 732–740. Isaac Jogues reported that the Dutch possessed horses in "great numbers." *NNN*, 262. See also Cohen, "Dutch-American Farming," 191.

dant . . . that one can not make any profit on them. Cattle are relatively still the most valuable article." The records from several Schenectady bouweries suggest that, here too, cattle were favored over
horses both in numbers and, presumably, in expected worth (Table
3). In only one instance (Teller 1679) were horses the more numerous
animal. Although at Rensselaerswyck in 1651 the average numbers of
horses and cattle were eight and ten respectively, the existing evidence suggests a slightly lower number of both per bouwery at Schenectady. Yet, in both 1664 and 1679 William Teller had eight horses,
and in 1681 Sweer Teunissen van Velsen claimed at least ten horses
divided between his property at Schenectady and at the nearby Normanskill. In attention required, productivity, and worth, such beasts
were clearly a significant part of each farmer's property. When Philip
Hendricksen Browuer's possessions were auctioned in 1664, his livestock—cattle, horses, and hogs—made up almost one-half of the
value of the estate.[26]

Although animals with distinct types of markings are mentioned in
the surviving records, neither horses nor cattle were distinguished as
true breeds during the seventeenth century. Yet livestock from particular regions were clearly preferred over others. In 1670, when
Adam Vrooman entered into an apprenticeship at Albany, it was
agreed that after six weeks of service, if he wished release from the
contract, he would "receive . . . a horse from Sprinckvielt [Spring-
field] to Albany." According to Adriaen Van der Donck, English
horses were favored as riding animals but not for farmwork. Van der
Donck also claimed that horses had been imported from Curaçao, but
that these along with Arabian horses "do not endure the cold weather
of the climate well, and sometimes die in winter." The Dutch breed
of horse was thought the most fit, but with regard to other livestock
one commentator expressed a different opinion: "The domestic cattle
are here in size and other respects about the same as in Netherland,
but the English cows and swine thrive and feed best; yea, appear to
be better suited to this county than those of Holland." Perhaps because of its usefulness for both riding and racing, the horse captured
the affection of the Dutch more than any other domestic animal. Philip Hendricksen Brouwer owned a gelding called "young Block" plus
a mare named "Col (Star)." When Jacques Cornelissen van Slyck

26. *CJVR*, 414. For the number of horses owned by Teller and van Velsen, see
ARS, III, 101; *ERAR*, III, 285–287, 472–474. In 1664 Brouwer's farmland, house, lot,
and garden sold for 1,287 guilders, his animals for 892. *ERAR*, I, 347–348.

leased part of his farm at Schenectady in 1664, the agreement included the "use of a stallion and a gelding, the one called Beyert, the other Snoeck."[27]

To the beasts' natural features, the Dutch added their own forms of identification. Hogs had their ears cut, and cattle and horses were branded. An unmarked animal was liable to be claimed by any one finding it in the woods. Both horses and cattle may have been stabled and provided with fodder during the winter months; hogs intended for slaughter were rounded up and penned in the autumn. But at other times of the year, animals roamed at will through pasture lands and woods. As a result of such freedom—or inattention—horses, cattle, and hogs were subject to indiscriminate breeding, accidents, and falling prey to wolves and other predators.[28]

Dutch farmers seem to have been particularly lax in protecting their livestock from attacks by wolves. Such incidents may have become more frequent as new settlements such as Schenectady were established during the middle half of the century. In 1671 the court at Albany received a complaint that "the destructive animals are greatly increasing and . . . do great and excessive damage to all sorts of cattle, and that the good inhabitants make no efforts or attempts to shoot or catch the same." The court issued an ordinance offering a bounty to anyone who killed a wolf and who would "exhibit some evidence thereof, in the shape of a head or a leg, or an ear."[29]

Intermittent efforts also were undertaken to improve the breeding stock of horses and cattle. Adriaen Van der Donck reported that attempts had been made at Rensselaerswyck to create a mixed breed of cattle by the mating of Dutch bulls with English cows. For horses, gelding served as a method for control and improvement of the stock. In May 1670 Governor Francis Lovelace granted Dirck Teunissen van Vechten of Rensselaerswyck the privilege of "cutting or gelding of Stone horses [stallions] in those partes." Two years later, Jeremias van Rensselaer protested to the court at Albany "that there are too

27. *ERAR*, III, 145, 280, 372–373; *AVDD*, 40; *NYCD*, I, 277. For information on seventeenth-century livestock, see Darrett B. Rutman, *Husbandmen of Plymouth: Farms and Villages in the Old Colony, 1620–1692* (Boston, 1967), 47. After a hard freeze in January 1663, Jeremias van Rensselaer wrote: "With the sleigh one could use the river everywhere without danger." *CJVR*, 307. Periodically, the court at Albany issued ordinances against horse racing, especially on the Sabbath and holidays. *ARS*, I, 148, II, 187, 402, III, 204.

28. *ARS*, II, 235, 299, 371, III, 101, 442, 478; *CJVR*, 229, 304–305; *NYCD*, XIII, 137, XIV, 285.

29. *ARS*, I, 276n–277n.

many [small] stallions at large in the spring, whereby the breed [of horses] is corrupted." Van Rensselaer requested that the local population of stallions be inspected "and that those that are not declared of sufficient size may be gelded in the spring." The court agreed that van Vechten should undertake the operation at Albany and vicinity and that he would receive a fee for his services. At Schenectady, Sweer Teunissen van Velsen and Barent Jansen van Ditmars were chosen to identify those horses which required neutering.[30]

Veterinary science was not far advanced during the seventeenth century, yet certain animal diseases were recognized and remedies prescribed. Horses in New York were reported to be "subject to a curious disease whereof many die within a few hours. The same disease attacks horned cattle that are pastured on new ground. But hay grown in salt meadows is found to be a remedy against this." While visiting Long Island, Jasper Danckaerts described an illness afflicting the local horse population, which "they call here the staggers . . . the creatures whether going or standing constantly stagger, and often fall; this increasing they fall down at last, and so . . . they die." Although it was not a perfect remedy, the ailment was controlled, according to Danckaerts, "by cutting the tip end of the tail, and letting the blood drip out; then opening a vein, giving the animal a warm drink and making a puncture in the forehead, from which a large quantity of matter runs out."[31]

If at least some attention was given to the quality of breeding stock and the standard of health of horses and cattle, little note was paid to the local hog population. There were hog pens at Schenectady, but they were used primarily in the fall when the animals were fattened before butchering, "after having picked up their food for some months in the woods, [the hogs] are crammed with corn in the fall; when fat they are killed and furnish a very hard and clean pork." During much of the year, even in winter, hogs were found in the woods. As a result, the animals were hardly domesticated and often created trouble by rooting in gardens and destroying grain.[32]

30. Ibid., 292; *BGE*, I, 347. For Van der Donck's account of attempts to create a mixed breed of cattle, see *AVDD*, 41.

31. *DHNY*, IV, 118; *JD*, 172. Adriaen Van der Donck also described several animal diseases, see *AVDD*, 40–41.

32. *DHNY*, IV, 32. In 1664, Claes Fredericksen van Petten and Isaac Cornelissen Swits leased William Teller's farm at Schenectady. The lease stipulated that they "deliver for the first time in the autumn of the year 1665 a hog fit for slaughter, and so on every year." *ERAR*, III, 286. For hogs in the woods even in winter, see *ARS*, II,

Stray animals caused continuing problems at Schenectady and else-where. Complaints of horses feeding on oats sometimes led to the animals' being clogged or hobbled to prevent their jumping over fences. Albany families employed a cattle herder to take that commu-nity's animals to pasture daily between the months of April and No-vember. At Schenectady, each owner appears to have tended his in-dividual stock; the schout assumed responsibility for impounding stray animals and received a fee for each animal restrained. In June 1670, for example, Schout Jan Gerritsen van Marcken demanded re-imbursement from Symon Volkertsen Veeder "for the care of six [stray] horses six guilders per horse." Veeder admitted that the ani-mals had broken out of their stable during the night, but maintained that he was not liable to pay the fine as the horses had "not done any damage to any one's land." Unimpressed, the court at Albany refused his plea and ordered payment.[33]

Given the damage to crops which could result from such lapses, it is surprising that Schenectady's settlers did not devote more attention to fencing in their lands. In 1668, more than a half decade after the settlement's founding, complaints were heard that "daily many ques-tions, disputes and accidents arise among the patentees of Schaen-hechtede on account of their failure to fence in their land, so that the horses and cattle go upon it and cause great damage to one another." Two years later Schout van Marcken brought suit against several in-dividuals who still had not enclosed their property. The offenders were not newcomers to the village and in fact included one of the original proprietors, a future magistrate, and the widow of Arent van Curler. Only in the fall, with the year's crops harvested and before the planting of winter wheat, was it permissible for animals to browse on the stubble left standing in the fields.[34]

As would be expected, the value of property at Schenectady in-

---

18[3]. In 1682 at Albany, one plaintiff charged that a defendant's hogs were "so wild that they jump over the fence and destroy his grain." *ARS*, III, 270.

33. *ARS*, I, 154. For stray animals and the problems they caused, see *ARS*, II, 430, III, 26. In 1669 the court at Albany allowed Jan Gerritsen van Marcken, the Schenec-tady schout, "the pound money (schutgelt)." *ARS*, I, 94. In 1670 Cornelis Viele was granted land on the north bank of the Mohawk River "on condition of leaving a corner for the use of the other inhabitants in taking their horses or cattle across the river." No mention was made of a public herder. *ARS*, I, 207.

34. *ARS*, I, 16–17. For the 1670 complaint about the fencing of land, see *ARS*, I, 138–139. In 1671 a petition was presented to the Albany court by the inhabitants of Kinderhook that two persons be chosen to "see that no one drive cattle on the land before the 25th of September." *ARS*, I, 239.

Table 4. An inventory of William Teller's farm at Schenectady, 1664 and 1679

June 1664	April 1679
house	house
barn	barn
1 rick	3 ricks
	wagon shed
2 wagons	4 wagons (1 wooden and 3 with ironwork)
2 plows	2 plows
pots and kettles	
churn and milk tub	
2 sleds	2 sleds (1 wood sled and 1 freight sled)
3 Flemish scythes	
grain winnow	
	1 harrow
6 horses and 2 colts	5 geldings and 3 mares
5 cows, 3 heifers, 2 bull calves	5 milk cows
2 sows, 3 pigs, 1 hog	hogs (unknown number)
22 sch. winter wheat	66 sch. winter wheat
4 sch. summer wheat	
3 sch. white peas	
3 sch. buckwheat	
49 sch. oats	

Source: *ERAR*, III, 285–287, 472–474.

creased as farms and lots were developed. Together with Arent van Curler, Philip Hendricksen Brouwer can be identified as one of the earliest individuals interested in a community on the Mohawk. When his estate was auctioned in 1664, the house and lands sold for 1,287 guilders. Three years later another proprietor, Martin Cornelissen van Ysselsteyn, sold his house and bouwery for 330 beaver skins. Calculated at eight guilders per beaver, his property was worth 2,640 guilders.[35]

An examination of William Teller's farm at Schenectady at two different times, June 1664 and April 1679, illustrates the improvements made to his property during these decades (Table 4). To the production of grains Teller had (by the later date) added orchard fruits such as apples while continuing to raise horses, cattle, and hogs. That Teller's male horses were all gelded may reflect the greater attention to the quality of the breeding stock first noted in

35. For Philip Hendricksen Brouwer's association with Arent van Curler, see *SP*, 10. In May 1662 Brouwer stated that he would settle at Schenectady that summer. For this and for the sale of Brouwer's and van Ysselsteyn's properties, see *ERAR*, I, 301–302, 347–348, 450–451.

1672. The inventory of farm implements and structures also suggests the improvements made to Teller's property since 1664. Two additional hay ricks and a wagon shed had been constructed. In 1664 Teller's property contained a "house, barn, rick and garden in fence." By 1679 the extent and quality of fencing had been improved, for now both the farmstead and the pasture land were "properly inclosed with a good, tight fence."[36]

In 1679 William Teller's bouwery supported eight mature horses, whereas the number of cattle was half of what it had been in 1664. This change suggests that, as draft animals needed for clearing and plowing land for grain production, horses were now a key element of the farm's profitability. When Jasper Danckaerts visited Schenectady in April 1680 he found wheat to be the community's principal commodity and compared the Mohawk Valley grains favorably with those he had seen elsewhere in the colony. Danckaerts's observations are supported by the April 1679 inventory of Teller's bouwery. Even though the summer grains had not yet been planted, there had been a threefold increase in the amount of wheat sown between 1664 and 1679. During these same years, the Board of Trade was informed that grain had now become the colony's chief resource: "Their land produces ordinarily 15 bushels on an Acre: Wheat is very good." Apparently, a return of fifteen bushels per acre was considered excellent in the seventeenth century, but greater yields may have been achieved during the next century. William Smith, Jr., in his *History of the Province of New York*, related that "the lands in the vale of Schenectady are so fertile, that . . . they till the fields every year, and they always produce full crops of wheat or pease." As late as 1795 it was reported that farmers near Schenectady commonly anticipated a harvest of twenty-five to thirty bushels of wheat per acre.[37]

---

36. *ERAR*, III, 285–287, 472–474.
37. *NYCD*, IV, 182; Smith, Jr., *History*, I, 212–213. For Schenectady farms in 1795, see Cohen, "Dutch-American Farming," 188. According to the English traveler William Strickland, by the end of the eighteenth century there may have been a decline in crop production in the Hudson-Mohawk region: "a Dutch settler told us that some years since the land generally returned 20 for one; but at this time not more than ten." Strickland, *Journal*, 134–135. For horses used in the clearing of land for grain production, see *VRBM*, 199. In 1769 Richard Smith wrote that the people of Schenectady "are supplyed altogether with Beef and Pork from New England most of the Meadows being used for Wheat, Peas and other Grain." Smith also observed that "the Indian Corn in the rich Lands is said to produce from 40 to 60 Bushels an Acre altho every Year planted in the same Earth." He gave no estimate of the quantity of wheat and peas grown per acre. Smith, *Tour of Four Rivers*, 21–22. Danckaerts wrote

The emergence of a grain economy throughout the former Dutch colony marked a significant divergence from the agricultural practices of the settlers' homeland. Lacking large tracts of arable land, the Netherlands had a rural economy that was predominantly pastoral and geared to the demands of its urban markets. Dairy products were the primary output of Dutch farms during the 1500s and 1600s. In the New World, however, by 1680 the bouweries at Schenectady, Esopus, and even near New York City were devoted to the cultivation of wheat. In 1664 William Teller's fields had been seeded with varying amounts of four different crops; wheat amounted to one-third of the eighty-one schepels sown. In April 1679, however, sixty-six schepels of winter wheat were planted. Wheat had emerged as the dominant crop at this and many other Hudson and Mohawk Valley farms. It also constituted an increasingly important element among the colony's exports. During the first decade of the eighteenth century, Governor Cornbury correctly asserted, "The Trade of this Province consists chiefly in flower and biskett."[38]

Although diverging from the economy of their homeland, the agricultural products and routines of New York's Dutch farmers were not greatly influenced by those of their Indian neighbors. Both maize and tobacco were harvested at Schenectady, but neither was a primary crop. The Dutch, as did the Indians, planted corn in hills, but New York's native peoples were apparently less ingenious than the New England tribes who taught the earliest English settlers to use fish as fertilizer. According to Adriaen Van der Donck, the New York Indians did not follow this practice. Van der Donck was emphatic, stating that "of manuring and proper tillage" the natives "know nothing."[39]

---

that the land at Schenectady "yields large crops of wheat, but not so good as that raised . . . around the city of [New] York and elsewhere, nor so productively; the latter on the other hand produce a smaller quantity, but a whiter flour. The wheat which comes from this place, the Hysopus [Esopus], and some other places is a little bluer." *JD*, 213.

38. *DHNY*, I, 711. For the Dutch rural economy, see de Vries, *Golden Age*, chap. 4; Lambert, *Making of the Dutch Landscape*, 208–209; Cohen, "Dutch-American Farming," 186. For the significance of New York's wheat economy, see Sung Bok Kim, *Landlord and Tenant in Colonial New York: Manorial Society, 1664–1775* (Chapel Hill, N.C., 1978), 157–158. Contemporaries were aware of the increased value of land and agriculture. See *CMVR*, 148.

39. *AVDD*, 96. For New York's Indians and for works that detail native horticultural practices in the Northeast, see Ceci, "Effect of European Contact and Trade," 115; Salisbury, *Manitou and Providence*, chap. 1; Bruce G. Trigger, *The Huron, Farmers of the North* (New York, 1969). In 1661 Arent van Curler joined with

What constituted "proper tillage" is uncertain. Van der Donck's account, written during the 1640s, implied that Dutch farmers fertilized their lands. Yet, in 1680 Jasper Danckaerts stated that the soils at Schenectady were worked without the use of manure. The flats were "of a black sandy soil which . . . can hardly be exhausted. They cultivate it year after year, without manure, for many years." That Danckaerts visited the village in late April, at a time when the farmers were preparing their fields for planting, lends credence to his observation. Similarly, in 1679, when William Teller leased his farm at Schenectady, he promised "to have the manure of the farm carted away clean." The year before, however, a lease for land near Albany had required the lessor "to provide a wagon and two horses for the lessee every year to draw the manure of his farmstead to said land." The evidence is not conclusive but does suggest that the latter agreement was atypical.[40]

Even when it can be established that fields were fertilized, as in the document above, it is unclear whether the manure was worked into the soil before planting or simply spread broadcast over the land. Perhaps the latter technique was used, as the lease stipulated that the manure should be drawn to the land but allowed that this might be done either "before or after seed-time." The same document required the lessor every fall "to plow said land once and to harrow the same twice and every spring the same." Such agreements provide insight into the agricultural routines of seventeenth-century Dutch farmers, but allowance also must be made for a range of individual practice. Adriaen Van der Donck noted that one farm at Rensselaerswyck had been plowed only twelve times in eleven years: "twice in the first year, and once in every succeeding year, when the stubble was ploughed in, the wheat sown and harrowed under." During the

---

Jeremias van Rensselaer and one other person at Rensselaerswyck to hire three individuals trained in the cultivation of tobacco. For the growing of corn and tobacco at Rensselaerswyck and Schenectady, see *ERAR*, III, 66–67, 313; Schenectady Court Minutes, 1684. Although native agricultural practices do not appear to have had a significant impact on European farming methods, the Dutch and English did influence their Indian neighbors. In July 1687, when the French captured and burned several Seneca villages, they found "a vast quantity of hogs." *DHNY*, I, 239. For the impact of Old World livestock in the New World setting, see Alfred W. Crosby, *The Columbian Exchange: Biological and Cultural Consequences of 1492* (Westport, Conn., 1972), chap. 3.

40. *JD*, 213; *ERAR*, III, 461, 473. For the statements of eighteenth-century observers that the Dutch did not use manure on their lands, see Grant, *Memoirs*, I, 175; Smith, Jr., *History*, I, 212. For Adriaen Van der Donck's comments, see *AVDD*, 30, 32, 96. See also Cohen, "Dutch-American Farming," 186.

1790s, William Strickland observed that Dutch farmers near Schenectady employed a rudimentary form of crop rotation. Van der Donck's information suggests that this had been so for some time.[41]

The predominance of cultivation and husbandry imposed a largely unvarying annual rhythm on the existence of the community's inhabitants. The year's routine began in the spring with the preparation of the land by plowing, seeding, and harrowing. In April 1664 Philip Hendricksen Brouwer's bouwery was described as "all being broken up land." By May the summer crops of wheat, oats, rye, buckwheat, and peas were being planted. On May 13, 1664, for example, Jacques Cornelissen van Slyck was reported to be "still daily sowing." The seeds were probably broadcast by hand over the land. Whether the crops were separated or intermixed is not known. During the 1630s, Kiliaen van Rensselaer had complained that the colonists at Rensselaerswyck were planting together both wheat and rye, "which is bad in every way, especially in reaping, as the rye is ripe sooner than the wheat." With the increased production and profitability of wheat as the century concluded, such wasteful practices may have been abandoned. July marked the month for haying and harvesting and began the busiest period of the year. By September the bulk of each year's produce had been gathered. In 1677 at Kinderhook, for example, a lessor promised to deliver up his farm "on the 10th of September . . . in stubble." It was at this time that animals were allowed to graze on the fields. Soon the fall plowing and harrowing would be under way in advance of sowing the crop of winter wheat. During these same months animals, particularly hogs, were butchered and the meat stored for consumption throughout the winter.[42]

---

41. *AVDD*, 32; *ERAR*, III, 461. Strickland, *Journal*, 135.

42. *ERAR*, I, 347, III, 281, 449; *VRBM*, 442. In 1769 Richard Smith noted that land below Albany had been "ploughed and sowed with Peas in the Broad Cast Way." On May 11, 1769, he reported: "Some of the Peas are up and some are now sowing." Smith, *Tour of Four Rivers*, 15, 19. For the harvesting of winter wheat, see *ERAR*, III, 42, 187. On May 27, 1669, a plaintiff at Albany demanded the return of a boy hired by him who had run away, "as he is much handicapped, it being in the plowing season." On August 6, 1678, Jan van Eps refused to attend the court at Albany, "on account of it being the busiest time of the harvest." *ARS*, I, 74, II, 341. Claes Cornelissen Swits was killed while plowing in September 1663. *ERAR*, III, 268. For the fall planting of wheat and for plowing and harrowing in the spring and fall, see *ERAR*, III, 159, 461. During the Esopus War of 1663, Captain Martin Kregier was responsible for providing the settlers at Esopus with armed guards. His "Journal" for the period between July and December 1663 supplies information on the day-to-day activities of the village's residents and can provide a valuable example for what must have occurred annually at other farming communities throughout the Hud-

At all times of the year, the weather, the observance of the Sabbath, as well as periods of prayer and fasting helped to break up the day-to-day routine of labor. But even the coldest months required attention to particular chores. The early months of winter were a time for threshing. In December 1675 the court at Albany ordered all people to bring to that community "their wheat, pease and maize that are thrashed, or shall be thrashed by them from week to week." Moreover, the arrival of each year's snow cover signaled the time for hauling and delivering of logs and firewood.[43]

By chance, at the community's inception, Schenectady's inhabitants were favored by several years of beneficial weather. The winter of 1658–1659 was severe, and rains in the spring damaged the winter wheat crop and delayed planting. The winter of 1659–1660 also seems to have been difficult with a heavy snowfall in January. The following year, 1661, was marked by extensive flooding in June. By contrast, the summer of 1662 and winter of 1662–1663 were evidently more pleasant. The early winter was particularly mild with no snow until January. In fact, the most remarkable event appears to have been a minor earthquake. Rains in the spring of 1663 threatened crops, but by the fall a good harvest was reported.[44]

Limits set by a variety of factors, including the length of the growing season, hours of sunshine, and annual precipitation, established boundaries for the success of each year's agricultural endeavor. Schenectady was founded during the so-called Little Ice Age that extended from approximately 1560 to 1720. The climate was cooler and perhaps somewhat drier than today. During most winters, the freezing of the Hudson River stopped all but essential communication southward and isolated the upriver communities from the rest of the colony. Even with the nominal arrival of spring, snow lingered on in

---

son-Mohawk region. *DHNY*, IV, 37–98. In the 1790s William Strickland observed Dutch farmers near Schenectady performing tasks similar to those their ancestors had done at the same time of year a century earlier. Strickland, *Journal*, 135. The alteration in the time perception of native peoples as a result of the adoption of agricultural practices has been noted in Salisbury, *Manitou and Providence*, 36. The temporal sense of the Dutch was expressed by references to religious, mercantile, and agricultural events. *FOB*, I, 132, 145, 149, 157, 199, 215, 266.

43. *ARS*, II, 54. For examples of the annual activities mentioned and the interruptions in the daily routine noted in this paragraph, see *ARS*, II, 175; *FOB*, II, 98; *ERAR*, III, 48, 406. In 1679, at his farm at Schenectady, William Teller had two sleighs, one for wood and one for freight. *ERAR*, III, 472–474.

44. For the period 1658–1663, see *CJVR*, 156, 159, 307, 321, 325, 329; *NYCD*, XIII, 134; Howell and Munsell, *History of the County of Schenectady*, 3; O'Callaghan, *History of New Netherland*, II, 404.

the woods. To demonstrate that agriculture could be successfully carried on under such circumstances, however, one need only note the
ample crops of maize raised yearly by the Iroquois in the Mohawk
Valley and western New York in the same latitude (and under similar
climatic conditions) as Schenectady.[45]

During the seventeenth century, as in the twentieth, agriculture
involved a seemingly endless series of chores and demanded the labor
to accomplish them. In 1662, when Hendrick Arentsen signed an
indenture of service to work for Jan Barentsen Wemp and Martin
Cornelissen van Slyck on their island farm at Schenectady, he bound
himself "to serve them in cultivating, plowing, sowing, mowing,
threshing, winnowing, cutting wood, and whatever else pertains
thereto." Such contracts were but one of several means by which
Schenectady farm owners recruited the labor needed to exploit and
develop their properties. The obligation involved could be short ter-
med. Arentsen, for example, seems to have been at Schenectady for
only one year. The following July, Wemp's widow and Jacques Cornelissen van Slyck (the brother of Martin, then also deceased) entered
into a similar one-year arrangement with another farmhand, Gerrit
Claessen van Nieukerck.[46]

In instances where the owner of a bouwery did not reside at
Schenectady, the farm might be leased on a long-term basis. Two of
Schenectady's original proprietors who did this with their properties
were Gerrit Bancker and William Teller, both of whom remained as
traders at Albany. Bancker in August 1663 and Teller in June 1664
leased their bouweries to younger men, individuals in their early
twenties who for a term of six years would return an annual rent in
produce and animals. As late as 1679 Teller continued this practice,
whereas Bancker by that time may have been using slaves to work his
land. In many instances, Schenectady's proprietors and inhabitants
must have worked their own farmlands, presumably with the aid of
wives and children. But even the addition of outside help did not

45. For the significance of the weather and climate, see R. Bryson, "A Perspective
on Climate Change," *Science*, 184 (May 1974), 753–760; P. M. Anderson et al., "Climatic Changes of the Last 18,000 Years: Observations and Model Simulations," *Science*, 241 (August 1988), 1043–1052. For the European climate of the sixteenth and
seventeenth centuries, see Lambert, *Making of the Dutch Landscape*, 149, 212. Jasper
Danckaerts noted the yearly freezing of the Hudson River, and in the 1700s Cadwallader Colden commented on the slow arrival of spring. *JD*, 181; *NYCD*, V, 691.
As an indication of the productivity of Iroquois agriculture, in 1687 it took the French
nine days to destroy the corn fields of four Seneca villages. *DHNY*, I, 238–239.
46. *ERAR*, III, 188. For the 1663 contract, see *ERAR*, III, 222.

release a proprietor from the necessity of expending his own labor. Having hired Gerrit Claessen van Nieukerck for the period of one year commencing with the harvest of 1663, Jacques Cornelissen van Slyck was himself recorded as "daily sowing" come the following spring.[47]

Unlike today, the seventeenth century was not yet a period of labor specialization. For instance, Pieter Danielsen van Olinda was a tailor at Beverwyck who, after marrying Jacques Cornelissen van Slyck's sister Hilletie, took up farming (and trading) at Schenectady. Hendrick Arentsen, who hired on as a farmhand for Jan Barentsen Wemp and Martin Cornelissen van Slyck in 1662, listed his principal trade as that of confectioner. Before removing to Schenectady, Sander Leendertsen Glen had acted as the master of a sloop owned by the van Rensselaer family, as a tapster, and as a trader. Perhaps because of its relationship to the Indian trade, tapping was a sought-after privilege. Both Cornelis Cornelissen Viele and Jacques Cornelissen van Slyck contested for the right to provide liquor to the natives, and others such as Douwe Aukes were complained against because they acted as unlicensed tapsters. Among the earliest Schenectady proprietors were a brewer, a baker, and a brickmaker. Later arrivals included Adam Vrooman, who had acquired skill as both a carpenter and a millwright. One might also note Ludovicus Cobes, who acted as schout first at Beverwyck and during the 1670s at Sche-

---

47. Ibid., 281. For the Brouwer and Teller leases, see *ERAR*, III, 242–243, 285–287, 472–474. In 1679 Gerrit Bancker had at least one slave at Schenectady. *ARS*, II, 429. In 1683 William Teller sued his lessee, Claes Willemsen van Coppernol, for four years back rent. *ARS*, III, 334–335. For evidence of the use of slave labor and for Schenectady inhabitants busy during the harvest, see *ARS*, II, 341, 439. For women and children working at the harvest, see *ERAR*, III, 321, 477–478. The contribution of women to the domestic and communal welfare of the communities at Schenectady and Albany remains to be explored. Women, of course, tended gardens, cooked, and looked after children. Often they also assisted their husband in whatever trade or occupation he followed. Their status reflected that of their husband, and they were subject to his authority and, at times, abuse. A few women, however, took on the public status of tavern keeper, midwife, or interpreter. Women sued and were sued, they controlled property, and much evidence suggests that their day-to-day lives were as rich and varied as that discovered for women in New England by Laurel Ulrich. *FOB*, I, 232, 257, 276, 286, 298, II, 71–72, 123, 126; *CMVR*, 9; *JD*, 52–55, 62–63, 90, 214–216, 230; Laurel Thatcher Ulrich, *Good Wives: Image and Reality in the Lives of Women in Northern New England, 1650–1750* (New York, 1983). See also Linda B. Biemer, *Women and Property in Colonial New York: The Transition from Dutch to English Law, 1643–1727* (Ann Arbor, 1983); Sherry Penney and Roberta Willenkin, "Dutch Women in Colonial Albany: Liberation and Retreat," *De Halve Maen*, 52 (Spring 1977), 9–10, 14–15, (Summer 1977), 7–8, 15; Chapter 6 below, pp. 208–209.

Table 5. Slaves at Schenectady on February 8, 1690

Slave owner	Number owned (minimum)
Sweer Teunissen van Velsen	4
Symon Schermerhorn	3
Myndert Wemp	2
Hendrick Vrooman	2
Jan van Eps	1
Douwe Aukes	1
Johannes Teller	1
Barent Jansen van Ditmars	1
Adam Vrooman	1

Source: *DHNY*, I, 304–306.

nectady. In 1655 he had petitioned the court at Beverwyck for permission to operate a day and night school.[48]

Throughout these years, village inhabitants such as Claes Fredericksen van Petten and Cornelis Cornelissen Viele were identified in contemporary records most often simply as "husbandmen dwelling at Shaenectade." Van Petten was at Schenectady by 1664 and Viele seems to have arrived in 1667; others came both earlier and later. For almost three decades they lived out their lives in a small, remote village on the frontier edge of New Netherland and New York. All of this changed within the course of a few hours on the night of February 8, 1690. How much the Schenectady settlers had achieved during the preceding thirty years is suggested by French accounts of that night's destruction. In their retreat, the French took away as many as fifty horses and calculated: "The loss on this occasion in houses, cattle and grain, amounts to more than four hundred thousand livres. There were upwards of eighty well built and well furnished houses in the town." The description is that of a village whose people had reached a measure of success and substance as an agricultural community.[49]

48. For van Olinda, Arentsen, and Glen, see *VRBM*, 821; *SP*, 183–185; *ERAR*, III, 188; *Calendar of Wills on File and Recorded in the Offices of the Clerk of the Court of Appeals, of the County Clerk at Albany, and that of the Secretary of State, 1626–1836* comp. Berthold Fernow (New York, 1896; reprint, Baltimore, 1967), 449. For the dispute between Viele and van Slyck, see *ARS*, I, 283–284, 289, 294–295, 307. For Vrooman, see *ERAR*, III, 372–373. For Cobes, see *FOB*, I, 238. The brewer, the baker, and the brickmaker were Philip Hendricksen Brouwer, Symon Volkertsen Veeder, and Pieter Jacobsen Borsboom, respectively. *FOB*, I, 201, II, 38; *SP*, 99–100.

49. *ERAR*, I, 449–450; *DHNY*, I, 301.

Unfortunately, no tax or assessment records are known to exist for Schenectady before the 1700s. One indicator of community wealth, however, is the number of residents who owned slaves at the time of the massacre (Table 5). By this index, Sweer Teunissen van Velsen emerges as the leader in the possession of human property, owning one-quarter of the slaves known to have been at Schenectady on the night of February 8, 1690. If the two slaves owned by van Velsen's stepson, Myndert Wemp, are also included, then this family possessed over one-third.[50]

Before his death in 1690 van Velsen operated a grist mill and owned land, buildings, horses, and slaves. All of this was far removed from November 1660, when Sweer Teunissen from Velsen near Arnhem in the Netherlands was engaged to come to Rensselaerswyck to serve as a hired hand on the farm operated by Jan Barentsen Wemp. Wemp had been at the colony since the 1640s, owning or working several farms and operating a sawmill and grist mill for the patroon. In 1651 he supervised "a stately farm" near the Normanskill, consisting of fourteen morgens of land and including eight horses and nine cows. Wemp exchanged this property for a larger farm on the east side of the Hudson River on what would later be known as the Poestenkill. In 1661 his home was fine enough to be leased by Jeremias van Rensselaer for use by the colony's schout. Under Wemp's tutelage, van Velsen would have acquired a solid knowledge of farm labor and mill work. Starting as a servant, he rose rapidly. After Wemp's death, van Velsen married his widow, probably in June of 1664, and with his new wife and four stepchildren removed to Schenectady. Before his death, Jan Barentsen Wemp had been one of the fourteen proprietors of the new community. Van Velsen also became an influential figure in the day-to-day life of the village. He erected a grist mill and on January 28, 1669, entered into "a contract with the commonalty . . . by which it was agreed that he should enjoy all the privileges of any Miller in this countrey, being obliged to grind every week i.e., on Tuesdays, all the corn that was to be ground." The mill was carried away by high water in 1671, but had been rebuilt by July of 1673.[51]

Van Velsen resided at Schenectady, engaged primarily in milling

50. *DHNY*, 304–306.

51. *SP*, 192. For van Velsen and Wemp, see *SP*, 192–194, 223–224; *VRBM*, 742, 831; *ERAR*, III, 283–285; *ARS*, III, 446–447, 494. For a discussion of social mobility in seventeenth-century New York, see Morton Wagman, "The Rise of Pieter Claessen Wyckoff: Social Mobility on the Colonial Frontier," *NYH*, 53 (1972), 5–24.

and farming, but he also retained title to property elsewhere. In 1667 he received a patent for land on the Poestenkill which Jan Barentsen Wemp had originally purchased from the Indians during the 1650s. To work his lands and mill, van Velsen employed slave labor. In April 1678 he paid 100 beaver skins for a twenty-four-year-old slave named Jacob. That he owned any other blacks at this time is not known, but by 1690 he possessed at least four. Equally important in the profitable working of his lands, and an additional sign of his prosperity, by 1681 he owned ten or more horses, with some at Schenectady and others at the Normanskill. By this date van Velsen was also established as a public figure. In July 1671 he was one of four persons who petitioned Governor Lovelace "in the name of the entire village of Schaenhechtede" requesting permission to trade with the Indians. Whether van Velsen enjoyed the status of a village magistrate at this time is not certain, but by the following year he clearly did so and remained one until his death in 1690. With the organization of a church at Schenectady during the 1680s, he became a deacon and later an elder.[52]

Little is known of van Velsen's physical appearance or personal characteristics. Perhaps the ability to write enabled him to advance as rapidly as he did. Having arrived during the early months of 1661, van Velsen was a relative latecomer to New Netherland. Some Schenectady proprietors and settlers such as Sander Leendertsen Glen, William Teller, and Arent van Curler had been in the colony since the 1630s. But Pieter Danielsen van Olinda was not at Beverwyck until 1663, and during that same year Douwe Aukes left the Netherlands on *De Statyn*. Neither was van Velsen the only Schenectady settler to advance his fortunes by marrying a widow. Although it would become less frequent in the eighteenth century, remarriage was an important element of Dutch family life during the 1600s. In 1676, before removing to Schenectady, Reyer Schermerhorn married the widow of Helmer Otten of Albany. Douwe Aukes's second wife was killed in February 1690, and he subsequently married again. The mother of Jan van Eps, Maritie Damen, married three times before her death in about 1682. So, too, did Cathalyna de Vos, the wife of

52. *ARS*, I, 267. For van Velsen's property holdings, as well as his slaves and horses, see *VRBM*, 756n; *SP*, 192; *ERAR*, I, 456–457, III, 446–447; *DHNY*, I, 304–306; *ARS*, III, 101. For van Velsen as a magistrate and as a deacon and elder, see *ARS*, I, 283, II, 98, 152; *NL*, 182–183; *BGE*, II, 125; *Two-Hundredth Anniversary of the First Reformed Protestant Dutch Church of Schenectady, N.Y.* (Schenectady, 1880), 241–242.

Arent Andriessen Bradt, one of Schenectady's first proprietors. Even Schenectady's founder, Arent van Curler, had married Anthonia Slachboom, the widow of Jonas Bronck.[53]

Like Sweer Teunisen van Velsen, several Schenectady settlers also passed through a period of servitude before establishing themselves at the village. Among those persons who were killed in February 1690 was Johannes Pootman, who in 1661 had been apprenticed to Philip Hendricksen Brouwer. Both Pootman and van Velsen may have been in their teens when they began their indentures. Daniel Jansen van Antwerpen, however, was a young man of twenty-six when he bound himself to serve Adriaen Appel of Beverwyck for one year beginning in September 1661. Appel's two sons went to Schenectady and, after a brief sojourn on the Delaware, van Antwerpen did likewise. Other young men attracted to the community included Claes Fredericksen van Petten and Isaac Cornelissen Swits, who in 1664 jointly leased William Teller's farm. Swits was from a New Amsterdam family, but his aunt lived at Rensselaerswyck. Van Petten may not have had any local relatives, yet both married into established Schenectady families and each would survive the 1690 attack of the French and Indians.[54]

Settlement at Schenectady in the years after 1661 offered opportunity for the acquisition of land and property and for the improvement of one's economic or social status. But removal to the new community was no guarantee of relief from present distress. In 1661 Sander Leendertsen Glen owed a debt of over nine thousand guilders. Glen may have been an extreme victim of the recession in the fur trade, for the amount was owed for the delivery of "wares and

53. Neither Jan Barentsen Wemp, van Velsen's employer, nor Wemp's wife, Maritie Myndertse, could write. *ARS*, III, 494; *ERAR*, III, 285. For Glen and Teller, see *VRBM*, 821; *SP*, 113, 152. For van Olinda, see *SP*, 183–185. For van Curler's arrival in New Netherland and his marriage to Anthonia Slachboom, see Van Laer, ed., "Van Curler and His Historic Letter," 12, 29. Van Velsen was hired in the Netherlands on November 9, 1660, and sailed for Rensselaerswyck during January 1661 on *De Hoop*. A. J. F. van Laer, ed., "Settlers of Rensselaerswyck, 1659–1664," *DSSAY*, 5 (1929–1930), 26–27. For Douwe Aukes, see "Passengers to New Netherland, 1654–1664," The Holland Society of New York, *Year Book*, 15 (1902), 27; *CHME*, LIX, 15. For Reyer Schermerhorn and Maritie Damen, see *FS*, 159, 221. For Cathalyna de Vos, see *Collections on the History of Albany, from Its Discovery to the Present Time*, ed. Joel Munsell, 4 vols. (Albany, 1865–1871), IV, 116 (hereafter cited as Munsell, ed., *Collections*).

54. For Pootman, see *ERAR*, III, 115. For van Antwerpen, see *ERAR*, III, 122; *SP*, 159. For Swits and van Petten, see *ERAR*, III, 268, 285–287; *SP*, 147, 185. For the Appel family, see *SP*, 82–83.

merchandise." In 1670 he still owed six thousand guilders and even
several years later had little money with which to pay his debts. Accidents or family constraints could also impede one's fortunes. In
1678, for example, Jan van Eps complained of "the great loss suffered
by him last winter by fire" and that his commission as lieutenant was
"not so profitable as to warrant his spending so much money for it,
he having a house full of children."[55]

Schenectady, of course, had no monopoly on attractiveness as an
agricultural settlement. Why an individual chose to reside at Schenectady as opposed to another community is often difficult to say. In
September 1662 Symon Groot recorded his intention to leave Beverwyck for Esopus, but within a year he was at Schenectady instead.
Schenectady failed to lure some potential settlers, and others left the
village after several years. Volkert Jansen Douw was an associate of
Arent van Curler at Rensselaerswyck, yet Douw never followed his
friend to the new community. Meanwhile, two of Schenectady's original proprietors, Martin Cornelissen van Ysselsteyn and Symon Volkertsen Veeder, both departed to take up lands elsewhere, van
Ysselsteyn at Claverack and Veeder on the Normanskill. Some families separated, with members to be found among several communities. Johannes Teller settled at Schenectady, but his father and
brothers stayed in Albany. Similarly, Adam Vrooman and his father
Hendrick went from Albany to Schenectady while another brother,
Jan, resided on the Normanskill. Of the three sons of Sander Leendertsen Glen, two stayed at Schenectady, but the third, Jacob, settled at Albany.[56]

New lands beyond the community also attracted settlers. In 1684
Benjamin Roberts was described as a "husbandman dwelling at Mael-
wyk above Schinnechtady." There was a movement of people to the
west of Schenectady and also interest in settlement farther north.
Cornelis Cornelissen Viele's brother Arnout resided at Albany but
also maintained a Schenectady connection. During the 1680s, Arnout
Cornelissen Viele was involved in acquiring property in two different
directions. In June 1680 he received an Indian grant for land south of
Albany, "lying on the east side of Hudson's river, over against the
Danskamer." Three years later the Mohawk's granted him "a certain

55. *ARS*, II, 341. For Glen, see *CMVR*, 15; *ERAR*, I, 369, 505.
56. For Groot, see *ERAR*, III, 191, 242–243. For Volkert Jansen Douw, see *ERAR*,
III, 66–67; *VRBM*, 826. For van Ysselsteyn, Veeder, and the Vroomans, see *SP*, 180–
181, 202–203, 212–217; *ARS*, III, 377; *ERAR*, I, 469n, II, 300, III, 427, 545.

piece of land lyeing above Schinnechtady on the Northside of the river, covering about 16 or 17 morgens." Viele's lands were located "over against the flat where Jacobus Peek lives." During these same years, Daniel Jansen van Antwerpen also lived at the flats about eight miles above Schenectady. Others moving into the Mohawk Valley included the former schout, Ludovicus Cobes, who sold his dwelling house and left Schenectady. Even Governor Thomas Dongan acquired title to land from the Iroquois in the region. During this same period, a settlement was projected north of Albany, at Saratoga, although no one from Schenectady seems to have been involved in the venture.[57]

Schenectady was not a closed or isolated community. The removal of individuals such as Arnout Cornelissen Viele or Daniel Jansen van Antwerpen from the village proper did not diminish the role they or their families were to play in Schenectady's history after 1661. In 1690 Viele's son, Arnout, Jr., was among those taken captive by the French and Indians, and during the 1690s and early 1700s, both the Viele and van Antwerpen families were active participants in the political and economic disputes that divided the community. Indeed, the history of Schenectady in the years after 1661 embodies much of the history of the New York colony during the late seventeenth and early eighteenth century.

57. *ERAR*, II, 84–85, 254; *NYCD*, XIII, 573. Viele failed to patent the land and quickly lost possession of the property. For van Antwerpen, see *SP*, 160. For Cobes, see *SP*, 103; *ERAR*, II, 315. For Governor Dongan and for the Saratoga patent, see *ERAR*, II, 195–197, 229–230.

3

A "sad and deplorable massacre"

Schenectady's founders had intended that their community would become a settlement of both traders and farmers. After 1661, however, the villagers were limited—officially—to agriculture for their subsistence and profit. Not surprisingly, an underground economy in bartered furs soon developed. This illegal traffic proved important not only for the inhabitants' livelihood but particularly for the community's relations with their fellow Dutchmen at Beverwyck (Albany) and with the colony's new English rulers.

The exclusion of Schenectady's settlers from the fur trade remained the stated policy of New York's governors and Albany's magistrates for the balance of the seventeenth century. On several occasions, however, the prohibition was breached, if only momentarily. In 1673 Governor Francis Lovelace granted Anthonia Slachboom, the widow of Arent van Curler, permission "to sell some Rumm to ye Indyans, as also some quantity of Powder & Lead." Yet the license was strictly limited. She could trade for only fourteen months, from April 1, 1673, to May 29, 1674, and the quantity of trade goods to be sold also was enumerated. Moreover, it was clear that such allowance had been granted only because of her particular circumstances, "having her House, Barnes & Corne destroyed [by fire] . . . as also the Losse of her Husband, Arent van Curler, while hee was employed in his Maties Publick Service."[1]

In 1670 Schenectady's residents as a whole were given permission to trade, but only if they did so at Albany. The Albany court members also agreed "that if any poor people living there need any necessaries for trading . . . these shall be furnished them." But at the same

1. *NYCD*, XIII, 469–470. See also Norton, *Fur Trade in New York*, chap. 4.

time the magistrates resolved to send to Schenectady "a renewal of the ordinance providing that no one of the inhabitants there shall be allowed to trade more than is required for his own needs." Except for this small concession, Albany's authorities strongly opposed any commerce in furs at the western village. Already in 1669 they had taken note of complaints that the inhabitants "openly make it their business to trade with the Indians." The court bound itself to forbid all persons from trading with the Indians and to fine those caught doing so.[2]

Thomas Norton, in his study of the fur trade in colonial New York, correctly observes that Schenectady's position within Albany County made it subject to the ordinances issued by the Albany court, an advantage Albany's magistrates exploited to enforce the prohibition of trade at the new community. This circumstance did not mean, however, that the village was completely subservient to that body, for it had its own schout and from 1672 its own subcourt. Yet the Albany authorities often ignored Schenectady's magistrates, as they did in June 1669 when they ordered the sheriff "to go to Schaenhechtede to request the inhabitants there whether they have an order from the right honorable general permitting them to trade there." If any person claimed to have such a declaration, the sheriff was to demand that it be presented. In 1678 Sheriff Richard Pretty searched the house of Jan van Eps; some trade goods were seized and van Eps was fined. Having recently been the victim of two fires, however, he was allowed to retain the merchandise long enough to dispose of it at Albany.[3]

In addition to subjecting Schenectady to its legal and administrative machinery, Albany's magistrates bolstered their local power by obtaining the support of provincial governors, both Dutch and English. In 1664 the community agreed to terms of surrender presented by Governor Richard Nicolls which confirmed that the people of Schenectady would not be allowed "to trade with the Indyans for Beaver." Subsequently, in July 1670, Nicolls's successor, Colonel Francis Lovelace, journeyed to Albany. During his stay, it was "sub-

2. *ARS*, I, 75–76, 145, 172–173.
3. Ibid., 75. For the Schenectady court and for the 1678 search of Jan van Eps' house, see ibid., 8, II, 370. For Schenectady and Albany, see Norton, *Fur Trade in New York*, 45. Counties were created in 1683. *The Colonial Laws of New York from the Year 1664 to the Revolution*, 5 vols. (Albany, 1894), I, 121–123. For the schout as a Dutch law officer, see W. Scott Van Alstyne, Jr., "The Schout: Precursor of Our District Attorney," *De Halve Maen*, 42 (April 1967), 5–6, 15, (July 1967), 7–8.

mitted for deliberation whether the inhabitants of Schaenhechtede shall enjoy freedom of trade with the Indians, or whether they shall be completely deprived thereof." Several objections were presented against Schenectady's right to trade and Lovelace concluded by prohibiting "all the inhabitants of Schaenhechtede, whatever their quality may be, to trade . . . with the Indians."[4]

Seeking to amend this restriction, Sander Leendertsen Glen, William Teller, Sweer Teunissen van Velsen, and Jan Gerritsen van Marcken (the village schout) petitioned Governor Lovelace when he was again at Albany the following year. "In the name of the entire village of Schaenhechtede," they requested that trade be allowed "as far as their own requirements are concerned." To support their appeal, they claimed "the privileges of old and the order of the honorable former general, Nicolls." Unimpressed, Lovelace rebuffed the petitioners and referred them "to the former ordinance."[5]

No evidence exists that Governor Nicolls ever sustained the villagers in their desire to trade. In making reference to "the privileges of old," however, Schenectady's magistrates may have recalled an earlier agreement by which Petrus Stuyvesant granted two of the first proprietors permission to trade at the village—a liberty that was soon revoked. In 1663 Stuyvesant had sought to coerce the proprietors into signing a bond that they would "not carry on . . . on the said Flat or thereabouts, any trade . . . with any of the savages." They refused to endorse the document and composed a letter of protest reminding Stuyvesant that "their honors have already granted a patent for land there to Jan Barents Wemp and Jacques N [Jacques Cornelissen van Slyck], without such servitude or lien as is proposed in the aforesaid draft of the bond."[6]

The recapture of New York by the Dutch in 1673–1674 compelled Albany's authorities again to seek provincial support for their community's monopoly of trade. Albany's agents appeared before Governor Anthony Colve at Manhattan to present several articles for his consideration for the "preservation of the rights of the Town of Beverwyck." Article five reiterated that "those of Schanhectede [were] not to extend their privilege any further. The land was granted them

4. *NYCD*, XIV, 559; *ARS*, I, 172–173.
5. *ARS*, I, 267.
6. Ibid., III, 492–494; *SP*, 14.

by the late General Stuyvesant solely that they should occupy themselves with agriculture." As before, Albany's trading privileges were successfully defended. Governor Colve ruled that the inhabitants of Schenectady "shall have to regulate themselves . . . by their previous instruction."[7]

To prevent the surreptitious trading of furs at Schenectady, Albany's magistrates attempted to regulate the movement of both individuals and wagons between the two communities. The sheriff was ordered to ascertain that "wagons and horses going thither . . . obtain a license before being allowed to depart, but without merchandise, to do business there, under penalty of fl. 25." Schout Jan Gerritsen van Marcken provided similar supervision over traffic exiting Schenectady for Albany. Yet in spite of such diligence, the Albany court members continued to complain that "notwithstanding of all ye means used, to Prevent the same, yet People doe dayly Profaine and trade wt strong liquors and other Indian Commodities at Shinnechtady." In 1678 Douwe Aukes was prosecuted for concealing an anker of rum and contraband goods on his wagon when he returned to Schenectady from Albany. Most likely, many other violators went undetected.[8]

At no point during these years could Albany's merchants and magistrates be assured that their community's trading privileges might not be removed to the settlement at Schenectady. In 1678 the van Rensselaer family won approval from the Stuart government for a patent for their manor which would have included both Albany and the land route to Schenectady. According to the Reverend Nicolaes van Rensselaer, "The rumor of such a remarkable change immediately alarmed the Albanians, every one being afraid of loss and damage to the beaver trade, which might be transferred to Schaneghtade." As so often before, Albany's leaders depended on the provincial authorities to preserve their advantage. A protest to Governor Edmund Andros produced the assurance that "all Indian Trade is strictly Prohibited at Schaenhechtady." Andros nullified the van Rensselaer land claims by refusing to execute the warrant from London. He further eased the Albanians' fears by telling them that "the

7. *NYCD*, II, 593–594.
8. *ARS*, I, 148–149, II, 246. For the 1678 prosecution of Douwe Aukes, see II, 377–378.

Duke [of York] intends the family of Renselaers their just Rights formerly Enjoyed . . . but without wronging any others."[9]

Not only was the court at Albany constrained to meet the chal-
lenges of outside opponents, it faced the additional burden of mon-
itoring the behavior of its own community of traders, who engaged in
"various practices to take away one another's trade." In 1684 the
court members complained of the "many evil practices and cunning
methods . . . used to meet the Indians," including the employment of
"brokers, whether Christians or Indians, to meet the Indians, under
pretext of driving to Shinnectady." That Schenectady's illicit traders
received aid from accomplices elsewhere had long been suspected by
the Albany magistrates. Merchandise found there belonging to others
was to be seized and returned to Albany.[10]

In resisting the Albany authorities, the would-be traders at Schenectady resorted to evasion, attempted bribery, threats, and violence.
In February 1680 Sheriff Richard Pretty cited Grietje, the wife of the
Schenectady proprietor Pieter Jacobsen Borsboom. Before the court
at Albany, Sheriff Pretty related that he had been "to the defendant's
house, *ex officio*, to make a search whether there were any . . . peltries
and there, under her bed, saw a beaver sticking out . . . between the
boards." When he sought to acquire the pelt, "the defendant . . .
threatened to pull his hair if he did so, so that he was forced to
leave." As he made his departure, Pretty charged, he was "offered
two beavers to settle the matter."[11]

Clearly, not only the ordinary inhabitants but the community's
proprietors and magistrates displayed little deference toward their Albany counterparts. In January 1674 Governor Anthony Colve cau-
tioned the "Magistrates of Schenechtada" that Albany's officials had
"complained . . . that you have not evinced towards them that respect
which is due them; you are, therefore, ordered, being an inferior

9. *CMVR*, 25; *ARS*, II, 363. For the van Rensselaer patent of 1678, see Norton,
Fur Trade in New York, 46; Nissenson, *Patroon's Domain*, 285–291. The charter granted
to Albany in 1686 by Governor Thomas Dongan provided that the land route to
Schenectady would remain under the city's control. *Colonial Laws of New York*, I, 200.
    10. *ARS*, III, 143–144, 461–462. As early as 1671 the Albany magistrates passed
an ordinance forbidding the inhabitants to lodge Indians at their dwellings and providing for the construction of separate huts for the use of the natives. *ARS*, I, 280,
303, 306.
    11. Ibid., II, 468–469. Pretty had another confrontation with Grietje Borsboom
and her son in the summer of 1681. The sheriff complained to the Albany court "that
the defendants committed great violence against him . . . when, on their arrival from
Schinnechtady with some beavers or peltries under their clothing, . . . grabbing him
by the throat and collar and calling him a rascal." Ibid., III, 169–170.

court to that of Willemstadt, to avoid such conduct in future." At the same time, the village schout, Harmen Vedder, received a specific reprimand. The governor expressed surprise "that said Vedder dare act in such a manner." The substance of Vedder's offense on this occasion is unclear, but on a later date he was again complained against, this time for receiving beaver skins from an Indian.[12]

A 1681 court case in which Sheriff Pretty accused a Schenectady resident (Dirck Hesselingh) of trading with an Indian at the village suggests the type of obstructionism the community's officials could employ. Pretty was forced to institute additional suits against the resident interpreters, Cornelis Cornelissen Viele and Jacques Cornelissen van Slyck. According to Pretty, both had "refused to act as interpreter in the matter of D. Hesselingh's trading at Schinnechtady, on being commanded to do so in his Majesty's name." In excusing his behavior, Viele stated that he did not refuse to do so "except conditionally." Van Slyck claimed "that he was not commanded to do so in the King's name, or, at least, . . . he did not hear it."[13]

The sheriff's convictions were in other instances more easily secured. During July 1676, Pretty brought suit against Gerrit Bancker, one of Schenectady's original proprietors who continued to reside at Albany. Sheriff Pretty demanded that the court confiscate Bancker's horses and wagon in which he had discovered "42 beavers . . . found between here and Shinnechtady, contrary to the ordinance." Had the pelts reached Albany, Bancker could have easily disguised their origin by claiming that they had been traded for at that community. The skins would then have been included with the shipments of wheat and other goods Bancker dispatched to New York City.[14]

During his 1680 visit to the community, Jasper Danckaerts described Schenectady as "twenty-four miles west of Fort Albany, toward the country of the Mohawks," the village itself a "square, set off by palisades." Years before, when Director-General Stuyvesant issued orders excluding the community's inhabitants from the fur trade, he had referred to "the dangers which unavoidably must follow

12. *NYCD*, II, 675. For Harmen Vedder, see *ARS*, III, 167.
13. *ARS*, III, 68–69.
14. Ibid., II, 129. For an example of Gerrit Bancker shipping wheat to New York City, see III, 45. Like Bancker, many Schenectady residents maintained connections with friends, relatives, and other persons which could be exploited to promote the trade in furs. Sander Leendertsen Glen, for example, retained commercial ties well beyond the local community. In 1680 two of his sons, Jacob and Sander, Jr., assumed a debt of 576 guilders in beaver skins "for merchandise received by their father" and owed to "Mons: Nicolaes d'Meyer, trader at N: York." Ibid., II, 81–82.

any trade with the Barbarians at such a distant place." Not surprisingly, Albany's magistrates and traders continued to exploit such fears in their protests against any shift of the fur trade westward, charging "that the community there, being small, might by the coming of a large troop of Indians be surprised, in which case . . . the entire country [would] be imperiled."[15]

Although the village itself was not attacked until 1690, a serious conflict between Indian rivals did occur near Schenectady only a few years after the community's settlement. In March 1669 John Pynchon reported that Indians near Springfield were "contriving to get strength to go against the Maquas." Evidently, the prime mover in this affair was a chief of the Pocumtuck tribe, Chickwallop. Little is known of either Chickwallop or his people, but he apparently sought to foster a three-way alliance against the Mohawks which would include his tribe, the Praying Indians, and the Narragansetts. The latter tribe was located in southeastern New England; the Praying Indians consisted of eleven hundred nominally Christian Indians distributed among fourteen villages under the tutelage of the Reverend John Eliot.[16]

Contemporary accounts of the invasion were provided by both Daniel Gookin of Massachusetts and the Jesuit priest Father Jean Pierron. They differ as to the number of invading Indians: Gookin stated that six to seven hundred were involved, Pierron cited a figure half as large. Both agreed, however, that the village attacked was Gandaouague (Caughnawaga), the first Mohawk village to the west of Schenectady. Whether it was taken by surprise or not is unclear. Gookin claimed that the village was besieged for "some days," whereas according to Pierron, "the enemy . . . retreated, after about

---

15. *SP*, 15; *ARS*, I, 172. *JD*, 213. During his administration, Governor Francis Lovelace urged that "a good and carefull Correspondence be maintain'd between Albany and Schanechtidee, For I look on that as a Frontier." *BGE*, I, 430. In 1691 Richard Ingoldsby described Schenectady as "the extreemest Part of all." *NYCD*, III, 792.

16. Pynchon, *Letters*, 80. Chickwallop appears to have had little success in persuading the Praying Indians to join his war party. Daniel Gookin, the Massachusetts Indian agent, later claimed that only five or six of the Praying Indians participated. Gookin also stated that by 1669 conflict between the Mohawks and the New England Indians had continued for six years with the Mohawks maintaining the upper hand to that date. His account of the Mohawks' conflict with the New England Indians is printed in Daniel Gookin, *Historical Collections of the Indians in New England*. Massachusetts Historical Society, *Collections*, 1st ser., I (1792), 162–167. For information on the New England Indians, see Bert Salwen, "Indians of Southern New England and Long Island: Early Period," in *HNAIN*, 160–176.

two hours of very obstinate fighting." In the battle's aftermath, warriors from Caughnawaga as well as Mohawks from villages farther to the west pursued the retreating Indians, now burdened and slowed by the number of their sick and wounded. The Iroquois circled ahead of the enemy to lie in wait at a site known as Kinaquariones, several leagues from the Mohawk villages and along the road that led to Schenectady. An ambush followed and after a day of resistance the New England Indians fled during the night.[17]

Existing Dutch and English documents make little comment on the attack, and the records that do so are incomplete and ambiguous. A reference to the assault in the Albany court minutes, however, suggests that the Mohawks may have approached the settlers at Schenectady for aid. On September 2, 1669, Schout Jan Gerritsen van Marcken complained "that Bastiaen Piters, negro, residing with Juffrouw Curlers, has without his knowledge dared to transport himself to the Maquas' land, in order to obtain help for the Maquas who were at Schaenhechtede." Later testimony indicated that Pieters was dispatched "to the Maquas land to warn the savages that their enemies were near there." Beyond the widow van Curler's warning, however, there is little evidence that the community at Schenectady assisted the besieged tribe. Most likely, there was general agreement with the opinion of Schout van Marcken that any involvement "might create a very grave danger, as the Christians ought to keep out of the doings of the savages."[18]

17. Gookin, *Historical Collections*, 166; *JR*, LIII, 139. For accounts of the 1669 attack, see *JR*, LIII, 137–155; Gookin, *Historical Collections*, 166–167; *SP*, 233. The leader of the New England Indians, Chickwallop, apparently survived the attack. Pynchon, *Letters*, 113. The route these Indians followed coming and going must have bypassed both Schenectady and Albany to the north. John Paine explored the region north of Albany to the Hoosick River in 1672. His account of the trails that existed there is contained in Buffington, "New England and the Western Fur Trade," 188–191. The final ambush at Kinaquariones took place at a site identified as "Within Thre dutch Myles" of the village at a steep rocky locale on the northern bank of the Mohawk River, a place that in 1672 would become the western boundary of Schenectady. In that year Kinaquariones was described as "Where The Last Battell Wass betwean The Mohoakx and The North Indiance." *NL*, 182.

18. *ARS*, I, 94, 102. On August 3, 1669, Albany's magistrates wrote the governor and council, "What relates to the war with the Indians and what occurred in consequence, your Honor can ascertain from the enclosed." The substance of this correspondence is not known, but a reference to "Mr. Wintrop," presumably John Winthrop, Jr., governor of Connecticut, indicates that the magistrates were alluding to the recent conflict between the Mohawks and New England Indians. The date of the document is confusing, however, since, according to Father Pierron, the battle at Caughnawaga did not take place until several days later. *NL*, 111. Father Pierron

Well situated for both trade and agriculture, Schenectady remained an exposed frontier community. Anglo-Dutch competition for influence with the Iroquois and control of the trade in furs were important factors leading to the creation of a village at the Mohawk Flats during the 1660s. Similarly, the breakdown of Anglo-French diplomacy and the conflict of England and France for primacy in the fur trade and for dominion over the Iroquois would contribute to Schenectady's destruction. Before Arent van Curler's death in 1667, however, an opportunity may have existed for Dutch traders led by van Curler to reorient the fur trade by exploiting the water route north to Canada.

In 1664 New Netherland passed from Dutch to English rule. At this time, both nations were rivals for the slave trade on the west coast of Africa, while in the North Sea fisheries Dutch boats frequently trespassed into English waters. Rumors of war mingled with demands for satisfaction and reparation for what were perceived as Dutch insults. The value of the Netherland's trade was known and envied in England, and the Navigation Acts of 1651 and 1660 were directed primarily at the Dutch. Additionally, the Anglo-Dutch war of 1652–1654 had already revealed the Netherland's vulnerability. In March 1664 Charles II, ignoring Dutch claims and possession (as well as earlier English grants), presented his brother James, duke of York, with control over a substantial wedge of territory between the Connecticut and Delaware rivers. James, lord high admiral of England since 1660, dispatched a fleet of four warships under Colonel Richard Nicolls, which arrived before New Amsterdam on August 26. The harbor was blocked, troops landed, and the city soon came within range of the ships' guns. On September 8 Nicolls effected a bloodless

---

stated that the attack occurred on August 18, 1669, New Style. *JR*, LIII, 137–155. For additional references to hostility between the Mohawks and the New England Indians, see *Minutes of the Executive Council of the Province of New York: Administration of Francis Lovelace, 1668–1673*, ed. Victor H. Paltsits, 2 vols. (Albany, 1910), I, 57, 60, 377–386. The Schenectady Dutch may have played a role in seeking peace between the Mohawks and New England Indians. On December 1, 1670, Governor Lovelace and his council discussed "the Peace between ye Maques & Mahicandrs" and "Ordered that a Letter of what hath past at Albany & Schanechtide with a Translation of ye Proposicons made by the Indyans there bee sent to Governor Winthrop, with a Desire of his Answer upon it." *Minutes of the Executive Council*, I, 60; *BGE*, I, 307, 308. In New England it was suspected that the attack of the Massachusetts Indians against the Mohawks was a prelude to a descent on the English settlements. *BGE*, I, 274–275; *NYCD*, XIV, 624–625; *Public Records of the Colony of Connecticut (1636–1776)*, ed. James H. Trumbull and C. J. Hoadly, 15 vols. (Hartford, Conn., 1850–1890), II, 548–551.

surrender. By October the upper Hudson and Delaware regions were also in English hands.[19]

The replacement of Dutch with English rule meant that the re-named province of New York now emerged as a pivotal colony in the imperial rivalry of England and France in North America. Although the history of French colonization in the New World extended back over a century to the voyages of Jacques Cartier, New France had not been permanently established until Champlain's founding of Quebec in 1608. The province remained short of population and retarded in its economic development. In Europe, however, French power grew at the expense of her enemies exhausted by the Thirty Years' War. Internally, after the crushing of the Fronde, the French monarchy was secure and, at the death of Cardinal Mazarin in 1661, its author-ity rested with twenty-two-year-old King Louis XIV. After 1663, New France was made a royal province and its future placed in the hands of Louis XIV's chief minister, Jean Baptiste Colbert. The col-ony was provided with a new administration, increasing numbers of settlers and troops were dispatched, and attempts were made to di-versify the economy. The fur trade, however, remained the staple economic activity in New France and, in the westward pursuit of furs, the interests of the French conflicted both with those of Iro-quois and with the English government of New York.[20]

Although there had been a brief period of peace during the 1650s, French relations with the Iroquois deteriorated thereafter. During 1666, French armies entered the Mohawk Valley on two occasions. In January the governor of New France, Daniel Rémy de Courcelle, marched southward with six hundred men to attack the Mohawks with the design "to take reuenge upon them for the seuerall murthers . . . exercised in Cannada upon the French, and the Indians of those parts." The majority of Courcelle's troops belonged to the newly ar-rived Carignan-Salières regiment and were unused to the rigors of a harsh winter march on snowshoes while carrying provisions on their backs. Lacking native guides, the army "hapned to fall short of the

19. Kammen, *Colonial New York*, 70–72; Charles M. Andrews, *The Colonial Period of American History*, 4 vols. (New Haven, 1934–1938), III, 50–63.

20. Howard H. Peckham, *The Colonial Wars, 1689–1762* (Chicago, 1964), 21; Gustave Lanctot, *A History of Canada*, 3 vols. (Cambridge, Mass., 1963–1965), II, chaps. 1–5, 7, 9; W. J. Eccles, *Canada under Louis XIV, 1663–1701* (New York, 1964), 6. For Colbert's policies toward New France, see Eccles, chap. 5. For Anglo-French conflict, see Eccles, chaps. 7–12.

castles of the Mauhaukes" and by mistake arrived on "the 9th of February within 2 myles of a small village called Schonectade."[21]

Forewarned of the army's presence, the Mohawks made a feint of retreating before the French, "but that small party drew the French into an ambuscade of neare 200 Mohaukes planted behind trees." Eleven soldiers were killed and several others wounded, after which both sides retreated. The Mohawks quickly brought word of the skirmish "to Schonecktade . . . with the heads of 4 of the ffrench to the Commissary of the Village," most likely a reference to Arent van Curler. Albany's magistrates also were informed and the following day "3 of the principle inhabitants were sent to Monsier Coursell the Governor of Cannada to inquire of his intention." Courcelle assured them that his troops would not harass the local settlements and asked only that his wounded men be looked after and that he might acquire provisions. A day later, seven of the French soldiers were taken to Schenectady, where their wounds were dressed, after which the men were removed to Albany. Next "the Dutch bores carryed to the camp such provisions as they had . . . Especially peaz and bread, of wch a good quantity was brought." Newly supplied, the army began its return march to Canada.[22]

Had it been his design, Courcelle could have occupied the village with ease. No mention is made in existing records of any defensive structure at the community before 1668. To protect the northern settlements, at this time there was at Albany only "a Captain and 60 English soldyers with 9 peece of ordinance in a small fort of foure Bastions." The French, however, intended to strike at the Mohawks. Only later was it learned that France, allied with the United Provinces, had declared war on England.[23]

In July 1666, Governor Richard Nicolls reported (incorrectly) that seven hundred French troops were marching against Albany, although he expected they would "not openly profess themselves enemies to us till they have either vanquisht the Mohawks or made peace with them." The reception the French would receive from the local Dutch communities was uncertain, but English authorities expected the worst. To the governor of Massachusetts, John Pynchon recounted that, according to Indians just returned from Albany, "the

21. *DHNY*, I, 71–72. For information on the 1666 French campaigns, see Eccles, *Canada under Louis XIV*, 41–42.

22. *DHNY*, I, 71–73.

23. Ibid., 74. For the reference to an unpalisaded blockhouse at Schenectady in 1668, see *ARS*, I, 34. The conflict between England, France, and the Netherlands is noted in Eccles, *Canada under Louis XIV*, 41–42.

Dutch . . . do speak slightly and contemptuously of the English there and say they shall be masters over the English very speedily." Similarly, in correspondence with John Winthrop, Jr., Pynchon confided the contents of his communications with the English commander at Albany. Captain John Baker was "suspicious of the Dutch" and of Arent van Curler in particular: "He writes that the French have sent word to Mr. Curlur that they will be with him e'er long with seven hundred men. . . . Curler is preparing provisions for them, and Capt. Baker is preparing powder and bullet for them." The French may have hoped to use van Curler's influence to achieve not only an alliance with the Dutch but peace with the Mohawks as well. Their contacts with van Curler continued throughout the period 1666–1667 and form a background to his fatal journey to Canada the following year.[24]

Whatever their long-range intentions, the immediate problem facing the French was to establish the credibility of their military power among the Iroquois in the wake of Courcelle's failed campaign at the year's outset. During the fall of 1666, a second army under Alexandre de Prouville, Seigneur de Tracy, entered the Mohawk's country burning villages and destroying that year's harvest of corn. Tracy's army bypassed both Albany and Schenectady, however, suggesting that Dutch expectations that the French would act as their liberators were premature. Moreover, having struck at their Iroquois trading partners, the French had severed (for the time being) the possibility of a compact with the local Dutch communities. In December, Captain Baker wrote John Pynchon that "the Dutch show greater love to us than formerly and resolve if the French propose [to come] this far to assist us." But other information suggests that the French still sought to promote an alliance with the Dutch and that Arent van Curler played a crucial role in their plans. In his December 1666 letter to Pynchon, Captain Baker also noted the return from Canada of a half-breed known variously as Canaqueese, the Dutch (Flemish) Bastard, and Smith John. Over the succeeding months, this individual performed an important role as courier between van Curler and the French.[25]

<hr>

24. *NYCD*, III, 120; Pynchon, *Letters*, 57, 59. In the Bridenbaugh edition of Pynchon's correspondence, the editor mistakenly identifies "Mr. Curler" as Jacob van Curler. For this and for the possibility of a Franco-Dutch alliance and the role of Arent van Curler, see Pynchon, 57–58, 71–72. At Springfield, John Pynchon received the same report of a French advance as did Governor Nicolls. Pynchon, 55–56.

25. For the campaign against the Mohawks led by Tracy, see Eccles, *Canada under*

That the French were in contact with the local Dutch communities at Schenectady and Albany was testified to by Baker's subsequent letters to Pynchon as well as by the correspondence that passed between Arent van Curler and Governor Tracy. In reporting Canaqueese's return from New France, Baker noted that he arrived "with letters which were five in all, all directed to the Dutch." Hoping to maintain friendly relations with the local communities, the French told Canaqueese that "the English . . . were no good people, but they had great kindness for the Dutch." In an effort at influencing opinion within the Dutch settlements, the French also sent "two or three news-books from France which say the Dutch have obtained a great victory against our [English] fleet at sea." Additionally, Baker reported the departure of "Dutch merchants come to Canada to trade there." In this manner, the French may have hoped to separate the Dutch from their dependence on the Hudson River trade route. Establishing a northern commerce might also undermine the questionable allegiance of the Dutch to their recent English conquerors. If we assume this to be the French intention, new light is thrown on Arent van Curler's journey to Canada in the summer of 1667.[26]

Throughout the winter and early spring of 1666–1667, van Curler was in contact with both the English governor at New York, Richard Nicolls, and Governor Tracy at Quebec. Canaqueese acted as the intermediary. Whatever the suspicions of the previous summer, Gov-

---

Louis XIV, 41–44. Canaqueese had been in Canada since the summer of 1666. For this and for Captain Baker's statements, see Pynchon, *Letters*, 71–72. See also Thomas Grassmann, "Flemish Bastard," *DCB*, I, 307–308. The function and status of such cultural brokers, individuals who were often half-breeds or métis, is explored in Daniel K. Richter, "Cultural Brokers and Intercultural Politics: New York–Iroquois Relations, 1664–1701," *JAH*, 75 (1988); Nancy L. Hagedorn, "'A Friend to Go between Them': The Interpreter as Cultural Broker during Anglo-Iroquois Councils, 1740–1770," *Ethnohistory*, 35 (1988).

26. Pynchon, *Letters*, 72. A 1666 letter by François Hertel of Trois Rivières to Jacob de Hinsse at Albany provides insight into those persons within the Dutch communities who were known and respected by the French. Hertel had been rescued from the Iroquois by the Dutch and wrote: "I beg you to salute in my behalf all my good friends yonder; especially Mr Montagne, Mr Corlart, M. the Minister and all the family . . . & Mr Rinzelar. I pray you to remember me to all whose names I gave you." He then continued, "Salute . . . if you please, Fellepe Jan Reut Folere Mr Abram Mr Tonnel, Jan Mr Montagne's Son, Corneli Bogardus Jan Man Andre Martin and his Brother without forgetting Mr labatit." Not all of the persons cited in this document can be identified, but it is notable that no English names are mentioned. Besides Jacob de Hinsse, other individuals who can be recognized are Johannes La Montagne, Arent van Curler, Jeremias van Rensselaer, Cornelius Bogardus, and Jean Labatie. *NYCD*, III, 132.

ernor Nicolls now professed to be "abundantly satysfied with yr care and conduct," and urged van Curler not to forget "yr promise to perfect the Cart [map] of the Lake, with the French forts, & how it borders upon the Maquais River." Both Nicolls and Tracy were evidently vying for van Curler's favor. Nicolls expressed the hope that "the publike and yr private affaires will permitt you in the Spring to visitt these Parts which you have not done since I came into the Country." Van Curler owned property at Manhattan and had journeyed there on several occasions during the 1640s and 1650s to attend to his affairs and to meet with Petrus Stuyvesant and others. His absence since the English conquest is significant.[27]

During this same period, van Curler received a series of French correspondence at least some of which he forwarded to Nicolls at New York. On February 14, 1667, van Curler wrote to the French governor, and Tracy's reply of April 30 confirms that he had been one of the recipients of the letters and news books referred to by Captain Baker. In his April correspondence Tracy remarked, "The newspapers you received and which assured us of the great Victory the Dutch gained over the English, are confirmed." Presumably, the governor's reference to the continuing Anglo-Dutch conflict was not accidental. Neither was his providing van Curler with the information that he had "granted Conditions so reasonable to the Mohawks and to all their tribes that I doubt not they will accept peace." With that the governor concluded: "If you feel inclined to come hither this summer, as you gave me to expect, you shall be . . . entertained with all my power, having great esteem for you, though I am not acquainted with your person." The wording of Tracy's letter suggests that van Curler had already expressed a desire to visit New France. He must now have requested a pass to go to Canada, and Governor Nicolls wrote to Tracy on the matter at the end of May. The date of van Curler's departure from Schenectady is not known, although it must have been in either late June or early July. Within a month word was returned of his death by drowning during an evening storm on Lake Champlain.[28]

27. *NYCD*, III, 145, 147. *The Records of New Amsterdam from 1653 to 1674*, ed. Berthold Fernow, 7 vols. (New York, 1897; reprint, Baltimore, 1976), I, 374.
28. *NYCD*, III, 151–152. For van Curler's forwarding of his French correspondence to Governor Nicolls and for Nicolls's letter to Tracy, see *NYCD*, III, 147, 156–157. Van Curler's party consisted of four other Dutchmen plus three Indians. Van Curler died fourteen days after leaving Schenectady. The Indians who returned with the news of his death started back to the village two days after he drowned and

During the same month of July, ambassadors from both the Mohawks and the Oneidas also arrived at Quebec. That spring the Iroquois' "favorable inclinations for peace" had been reported to the French. This was followed by the appearance of Canaqueese at Quebec with two accompanying Oneidas. On April 30 he was dispatched south again with Tracy's letter to van Curler as well as with a warning to the Iroquois that "if within two moons they did not obey and fulfill the proposed conditions," the French army "would go and destroy them in their own country." That twice before French armies had reached their territory was enough to convince the Mohawks and the neighboring Oneidas of the seriousness of the declaration. By the first week in July, a joint delegation had arrived at Quebec, where, submitting to French pressures, both groups requested Jesuit missionaries for their villages, the Mohawks asking for two "black gowns" and the Oneidas for one.[29]

From Tracy's letter of April 30 and through conversation with Canaqueese, Arent van Curler would have been aware both of French intentions toward the Iroquois and of the dispatch of native ambassadors to Quebec before his own departure from Schenectady. What van Curler hoped to achieve by his journey remains obscure. He might have sought an agreement to protect his village if another French army entered the Mohawk Valley. Whether he would have aided the French in negotiating a peace with the Mohawks and Oneidas cannot be said. Both van Curler and his traveling companion, Daniel Rinckhout, included a substantial amount of trade goods among the merchandise they were transporting northward at the time of their deaths. Private profit can be assumed as a certain motive; if they also hoped to promote a northern trade for the benefit of others at Schenectady and Albany, there is no clue. The *Jesuit Relation* reported that van Curler drowned "on his way to Quebec for the purpose of negotiating some important affairs." This must serve to summarize our current knowledge of the intent of van Curler's journey.[30]

---

arrived at Schenectady in ten days. As news of van Curler's death had reached Schenectady by early August, he must have left at least twenty-six days earlier, possibly during the first week in July. A. J. F. van Laer, ed., "Documents Relating to Arent van Curler's Death," *DSSAY*, 3 (1927–1928), 30–34.

29. *JR*, L, 209. For the delegation of Mohawks and Oneidas at Quebec, see *JR*, L, 211–213. The Mohawks feared a French attack at this time and, according to the French missionaries who journeyed to the Mohawk Valley, "fourteen warriors had been constantly on the watch at the entrance to this Lake [Lake George], in order to discover the army's line of march, and bear news of it with all haste to the whole Nation." *JR*, LI, 185.

30. Ibid., LI, 181. Van Curler's canoe capsized during a storm on Lake Champlain.

Shortly after van Curler's death, it was rumored that the French would attack Albany and proposed to march to Schenectady as a prelude to descending on their objective. Whether an alliance of French and Dutch against the English was still possible or if it could have been fulfilled had van Curler lived is not known, but as rumor it was an idea with a long life span. As late as 1681 the court at Albany received information from Cornelis Cornelissen Viele at Schenectady "that a Frenchman, a coureur-de-bois, came there last Monday from Sinnekes land, who divulged to a Frenchman residing, at Schinnechtady . . . that there would be war between England and Holland and France, the last two being conjoined against England." In the years after 1666–1667, however, intelligence more often spoke of a French attack rather than of a Franco-Dutch alliance. In 1673 Jeremias van Rensselaer informed his brother, "We have now and then tidings that the French from Canada intend to attack us."[31]

How serious such rumors could be taken was made evident during the summer of 1671. On orders from the court of Albany, several Frenchmen were called in and examined, including "Johan de la Rose, residing here" and "the six Frenchmen who have come here from Canada." La Rose (Jean Rosie) claimed that the French intended to divert the Albany beaver trade and in time to seize the community itself. His testimony was supported by that of several Canadian Mohawks. Others questioned included "Robertus Renatus de la Salle, a certain Frenchman who came here from the Maqua country." La Salle denied that there was any French design against Albany and charged both Rosie and the Mohawks with lying.[32]

Presented with conflicting testimony, the court decided to send one of its members "to the Maqua country . . . to make a diligent inspection of everything and . . . to send some Indians . . . to spy out all conditions and designs." It also resolved that the burghers were "to appear here next Monday, fully armed, ready to march." Evidently there was real fear over the approach of a French army and a letter on the subject was quickly forwarded to Governor Francis

Two Indians in his canoe urged him to throw his trade goods overboard, but he refused to do so. The value of van Curler's merchandise is not known, but Daniel Rinckhout, a companion who also drowned, had at least 1,100 guilders in seawan with him at the time of his death. Van Laer, ed., "Documents," 31; *ARS*, I, 28, 34, 37. The remainder of van Curler's party continued on to Canada. For their favorable reception by the French, see A. J. F. van Laer, ed., "Albany Notarial Papers, 1667–1687," *DSSAY*, 14 (1938–1939), 12.

31. *ARS*, III, 80–81; *CJVR*, 453. For the rumor that the French would descend on Schenectady before attacking Albany, see the October 5, 1667, letter of Arent van Curler's widow to the Albany magistrates. Van Laer, ed., "Documents," 33.

32. *ARS*, I, 255–257.

Lovelace. From the security of New York, Lovelace counseled against alarm, but urged the magistrates "to use those meanes that shall best conduce to our safety." Most important was that "a good and carefull Correspondence be maintain'd between Albany and Schanechtidee." In addition, the latter community was ordered to "putt themselves into some posture of Defence by keeping out Schouts, and makeing some Block house which may give some Check to the Enemy."[33]

The summer passed quietly, however, and in July, Father Jean Pierron wrote to the Albany magistrates from the largest of the Mohawk villages, Tionnontoguen. He denied all allegations that the French intended to attack or to divert the trade in furs: "It is untrue that a thousand Frenchmen are coming into this region [or] . . . that two hundred canoes were coming to beleaguer you. . . . As to the second rumor, a great many Frenchmen are in the woods . . . to trade with the Indians. You must not imagine that they will make war on you." In spite of Father Pierron's disclaimers, that same month a "Council of War" was established consisting of "the honorable Major General De la Val and the chief commissioned officers of the burgesses of Albany, colony of Rensselaerswyck and Schaenechtade."[34]

What powers this body exercised and the duration of its authority are unclear, but the council was still holding meetings as late as May 1672. A list of members included only two persons from Schenectady, but the council apparently did extend some degree of both military and civil authority over the community. On July 15, 1671, it ordered all inhabitants of Albany, Rensselaerswyck, and Schenectady "to provide themselves each with a gun." This order applied to all males over fifteen years of age and under sixty, who were also expected to supply "two pounds of powder and four pounds of lead." That the council, additionally, included certain civil powers within its jurisdiction is hinted at by a court case at Schenectady over a decade later. In March 1684 Joris Aertsen Van der Baest brought suit against Johannes Appel in an attempt to collect twelve guilders in beavers "due to him according to a judgment of the council of war at Shinnechtady." Appel protested that he was not bound to repay the debt "on account of the council of war, it being so long ago."[35]

If attacked, Schenectady would have had to depend for succor on

33. Ibid., 259–260; *BGE*, I, 430.
34. Van Laer, ed., "Albany Notarial Papers, 1667–1687," 11; *ERAR*, III, 322.
35. *ERAR*, III, 322, 324; *ARS*, III, 423. For the May 1672 list of members of the Council of War, see *ERAR*, III, 324. William Teller and Jacob Glen, one of Sander Leendertsen Glen's sons, both resided at Albany.

the military resources of its neighboring communities. During the late 1660s, the English garrison at Albany consisted of approximately sixty men. The detachment was small in numbers, supplied with only a few cannon, and surrounded by a Dutch population whose loyalty was uncertain. By this date, however, there also existed a regional defense force made up of local residents. At first a militia on foot, it was reorganized in 1667 on the initiative of Governor Nicolls, who turned one-third of their number "into horse and dragoones." Nicolls intended by this means "to prevent the incursions of the French from Canada into these parts." In 1670 Jeremias van Rensselaer was commissioned as captain of the volunteer cavalry with orders "to raise a troop of horse of 40 men." These horsemen visited Schenectady, and, although they received no pay, their social amenities included sharing "meat and drink" at Cornelis Viele's tavern.[36]

The period between 1671 and 1672 marked the first occasion at which a serious attempt was made to mobilize and coordinate the region's defenses. A second effort was undertaken in 1675 after a body of warriors led by King Philip appeared at Schaghticoke. Metacom, or Philip, as he was known to the English, had been sachem of the Wampanoag Indians since the 1660s, but not before 1675 did he commence hostilities against the local white settlements. The summer and fall were spent attacking outlying villages in Massachusetts and the other New England colonies. That December, Philip and his warriors made their way to the eastern side of the Hudson River some twenty miles above Albany. In coming this far west, he may have hoped to persuade the Mohawks to join his uprising. According to Increase Mather, Philip intended to embroil the Mohawks in the conflict by slaying several of their warriors and laying the blame for their deaths on the English. The plan went awry when one of the intended victims survived to relate what had happened. The *Jesuit Relation* reported that the Iroquois retaliated by capturing and burning several Abenakis who had been Philip's followers. Whatever the

36. *NYCD*, III, 167; *ARS*, I, 180, II, 276. For van Rensselaer's commission, see *NL*, 151. In 1670 Schenectady's inhabitants were informed "that they must make preparation to complete the block house during the winter." This structure, still incomplete after two years, remained the sole fortification at the village. Subsequently, in 1675, at a time when the Hudson and Mohawk region was threatened by warriors led by King Philip, "the Commissioners and Schout of Schaenhechtady" were ordered "without delay, to have the blockhouse in your village surrounded with palisades as a place of refuge . . . in time of need." Not until the end of the decade, however, would the village itself be palisaded. *ARS*, I, 34, 177, II, 39; *JD*, 213. The 1698 Romer map shows a community surrounded on three sides by water with a stockade covering the land approach from the east. Grassmann, *Mohawk Indians*, 527.

actual events, as late as the following July the Mohawks were still seeking opportunities to attack the New England Indians, their old enemies.[37]

The arrival of King Philip at Schaghticoke transformed the winter of 1675–1676 into a time of great uneasiness among the settlements along the Hudson and Mohawk rivers. The Dutch feared, not that Philip and his followers would attack them directly, but that their involvement in hostilities would result from conflict between the Mohawks and New England Indians. Maria van Rensselaer expressed this concern in her November 1675 correspondence: "We are daily sitting in great peril, as it is to be feared that the Maquas and the Mahicans will again become involved in war." To minimize this possibility, as early as September, the military authorities at Albany had restricted the sale of gunpowder to the eastern Indians, refusing to provide some tribes with powder while telling "the Mohegan Indians that they will try them for a while, and they shall have powder at the fall of the leaf when they hunt, and not now because they will first see and know who are at war with the English there."[38]

A council of war at Albany in late September resolved to double the community's guard but took no further action and had no instructions for the surrounding localities. At the end of October, however, all the inhabitants of Albany, Rensselaerswyck, and Schenectady were forbidden "to have any intercourse with the Indians or to question them about any matters concerning the province." Natives overheard discussing "the situation of the country" were not to be answered but were to be reported to the commander of the English garrison. On October 29, additional orders were issued for a day of

37. For the events surrounding King Philip's War, see Gary B. Nash, *Red, White, and Black: The Peoples of Early America* (Englewood Cliffs, N.J., 1974), 123–127; Jennings, *Invasion of America*, 298–326. For King Philip at Schaghticoke, see Increase Mather, *The History of King Philip's War* (Albany, 1862), 168; *JR*, LX, 133; *Public Records of Connecticut*, II, 461; *Narratives of the Indian Wars, 1675–1699*, ed. Charles H. Lincoln (New York, 1913), 87–88; Douglas E. Leach, *Flintlock and Tomahawk: New England in King Philip's War* (New York, 1958), 142; *AP*, I, 180–181, 337–345. Benjamin Church summarized the events at Schaghticoke as follows: "King Philip . . . was fled to a Place called Scattacook, . . . where the Moohags made a descent upon him and killed many of his Men, which moved him from thence." Benjamin Church, *The History of King Philip's War*, ed. Henry Martyn Dexter (Boston, 1865), 64–65.

38. *CMVR*, 15–16; Pynchon, *Letters*, 152. In 1676 Governor Andros investigated charges made by one individual at Albany, "that the north Indians have been lately here this last winter, supplyed by the . . . Inhabitants of this Place, with ammunition." The statements could not be substantiated, and the individual was fined for his "indiscreet report." *AP*, I, 345, 447, 467.

prayer to be observed on the first Wednesday of November, for the erection of a stockade at a small fort at Rensselaerswyck, and "to have the blockhouse [at Schenectady] surrounded with palisades as a place of refuge." As the village itself was not yet enclosed, shelter was offered at Albany, "if you think that the blockhouse surrounded with palisades is not sufficiently capable of defense, you may freely come to us here and you shall be welcome."[39]

Finally, in December, instructions were issued by the court at Albany to Arnout Cornelissen Viele and to Robert Sanders, a local merchant, "to go directly to Hosick, where the Northern Indians are, and address their sachems . . . investigating how many Christian prisoners they have among them." They were to seek the surrender of the captives and were to offer in exchange "duffels, clothing, or seawan, but not . . . powder, lead or provisions." The two must have departed immediately, for the next day Viele's wife represented him as plaintiff in a suit before the court. No mention was made of how large a force was at Schaghticoke, although it may have included several hundred warriors. The "northern Indians" were described as "well supplied with all sorts of munitions of war from the plunder which they have taken from the English." The Albany authorities did not underestimate the threat to their own and surrounding communities and issued an ordinance for "laying in grain and other provisions in the city of Albany . . . all the inhabitants of Albany, colony of Renselaerswyck, Schaenhechtade . . . without any exception, to bring into this place all their wheat, pease and maize that are thrashed."[40]

Schenectady's population at this time probably totaled fewer than two hundred persons. Most likely, women and children were removed to Albany while the men readied their guns, powder, and lead. The threat of hostilities continued into the new year, however, interrupting the daily routine of life by restricting the time and ability of farmers to tend to their crops and animals. As a precaution, in February 1676 the court at Albany declared, "Whereas we are informed that little or no grain can be grown this year . . . we hereby expressly forbid all the inhabitants . . . to export any grain . . . until further order."[41]

39. *ARS*, II, 37, 39.
40. Ibid., 48–49, 53–54, 56.
41. Ibid., 71. My estimate of Schenectady's population at this time is based mostly on guesswork. In 1681, however, the local Dutch church was said to have had one

One senses an expectation on the part of Schenectady's inhabitants after 1675 that their yearly efforts could be disrupted at any moment. In April 1679, when William Teller leased his Schenectady farm to Claes Willemsen van Coppernol, the agreement stipulated that "the lessee shall be holden to defray . . . all taxes . . . but in case of attack by enemies of war . . . he shall be free from all [obligation] . . . in case anything be lost in such calamities or distress." Although no fort was erected at Schenectady until 1695 and no garrison was situated at the village until after 1690, for the first time a wooden palisade was now constructed to surround the community.[42]

Ironically, this effort to strengthen Schenectady's defenses was undertaken at the onset of a brief period of calm on the northern frontier. During these years Ludovicus Cobes, Arnout Cornelissen Viele, and others sought to acquire properties to the west of Schenectady and several Albany proprietors projected a settlement to the north at Saratoga. This also may have been a period of population growth for the community. When Jasper Danckaerts visited Schenectady in 1680, he counted thirty dwelling houses. A decade later, French accounts of their 1690 attack claimed that there had been "upwards of eighty well built and well furnished houses in the town."[43]

By 1690 the settlers at Schenectady could look back over three decades of periodic threats and rumors of attack. The years 1666–1667, 1671–1672, and 1675–1676 marked the sharpest manifestations of this ever-present peril. As late as the 1680s, the fort at Albany remained the major defensive work on the upper Hudson. In 1687 it was described as "made of Pine Trees fifteen foot high & foot over with Batterys and conveniences made for men to walk about, where are nine guns, small arms for forty men four Barils of Powder with great and small shott in proportion." Although a French army was suspected of marching against Albany in 1681, for almost a decade the northern frontier remained quiet. Beginning in 1684, however, French hostilities with the Iroquois and Anglo-French rivalry for

---

hundred members. Counting spouses and mature but not yet married sons and daughters as members, this membership suggests a community of about thirty to forty households. *ER*, II, 795.

42. *ERAR*, III, 473.

43. *DHNY*, I, 301. For Danckaerts's count of houses, see *JD*, 213. Two 1690 documents (a list of persons killed and taken captive in February and a list of survivors from March) suggest that at least fifty households existed at or near Schenectady by that date. *DHNY*, I, 304–306, II, 199–202.

control of the fur trade again placed the frontier communities at risk.[44]

These years witnessed a struggle for influence among and dominance over the Iroquois by both the English and the French. During July 1667, Mohawk and Oneida ambassadors had arrived at Quebec asking for Jesuit missionaries to be sent to their villages. Returning southward with the Indians were Fathers Jacques Frémin, Jean Pierron, and Jacques Bruyas. By the early 1670s their preaching was having an impact, especially among the Mohawks. In 1672 Father Bruyas reported that the missions established "in the two villages that lie nearest to new holland" were flourishing, and he described the village closest to Schenectady as "the first and principal mission that we have among the Iroquois." That the Mohawks had received God's word "in greater abundance than the other Iroquois nations" was evidenced in several ways. The *Jesuit Relation* for 1671–1672 recorded that fifteen Christian Mohawks had settled among the Huron at Notre Dame de Foy near Quebec and that fifty more were contemplating a similar removal. At the Mohawk Valley missions, Father Bruyas claimed to have baptized thirty adults, whereas other natives had received the sacrament at the point of death.[45]

The *Jesuit Relation* for 1683 maintained that two hundred Mohawks had recently settled near Montreal. Among those persons who were most active in encouraging this resettlement was an Indian known to the French as "the great Anie" (the great Mohawk) and to the Dutch and English as "Kryn." Kryn was first mentioned in the Jesuit documents as early as 1678. In 1684 the Albany court records identified him as one of three Indians "sent by the governor of Canada to the Maquas . . . to [invite them to] move to Canada." The court ordered two of its members to go to Schenectady to investigate the matter.[46]

Not surprisingly, New York's authorities did what they could to stem this northward migration. Governor Thomas Dongan notified the Mohawks "to let none of their Indians leave their country for Canida." Subsequently, at Albany, in September 1687, several Mohawk sachems expressed their sorrow "for that misfortune that befell

44. *NYCD*, III, 391.
45. *JR*, LVII, 89–91. For the arrival of the Jesuits at the Mohawk villages, their efforts at baptizing the natives, and for the removal of numbers of Mohawks to Canada, see *JR*, L, 211–213, 323, LVI, 29, LVII, 91; Grassmann, *Mohawk Indians*, 273, 289.
46. *ARS*, III, 463. For Kryn, see *JR*, LXIII, 197, 231, 241–243, 302; Henri Béchard, "Joseph Togouiroui," *DCB*, I, 650–651.

our people in not bringing off Cryn & his company prisoners." One person who encountered Kryn at this time was Anthony Lespinard, a Frenchman resident at Albany since the 1670s. Lespinard journeyed to Montreal to inform the French of a treaty of neutrality between England and France. On returning by way of Lake Champlain, he met "Cryne the Indian General . . . at Shamble . . . [he] observed the sayd Cryne to be very true to the French . . . that the said Cryn and several Indyan Captns he saw, were in great esteem with the French Governour and officers, and that they went in very nigh Christians habitts [clothing]." In Lespinard's estimation, Kryn "would immediately joyn with the French in the warr against the Sniekes and Maques." This assessment of Kryn's loyalty proved accurate. Already that summer he had captained the Christian Iroquois who accompanied Governor Denonville's expedition against the Seneca. In February 1690 he would provide valuable assistance in the attack against Schenectady.[47]

Although the French were successful in attracting the allegiance of Mohawks such as Kryn, in other ways the 1680s were a time of travail for New France. During the summer of 1674, Louis Jolliet returned to Quebec from a voyage down the Mississippi River which brought him within a few days of reaching the Gulf of Mexico. Jolliet reported that the region contained numerous Indian tribes with an abundance of pelts they were eager to trade for European goods. A fortune in furs awaited whoever could first establish posts among the Mississippi Valley tribes. Realizing this, Governor Frontenac dispatched Robert La Salle to build a fort at Niagara in 1676. The next year La Salle crossed to France, where he received official sanction to explore the Mississippi Valley, to build forts where necessary, and to defray the costs of his enterprise by trading in the area south and west of the Great Lakes. La Salle and his associates soon monopolized the trade of the Illinois and Miami tribes and the export of furs from New France rose to ninety-five thousand pounds in 1683, an increase of over 50 percent since 1675.[48]

For the French, however, passage to the west was limited to movement along the St. Lawrence River and through the Great Lakes. Their hold on the region was secure only as long as neither the Iroquois nor the English took any preventive action. Until the 1670s the

47. *ARS*, III, 470; *NYCD*, III, 483, 487–488. For Kryn's role in Denonville's expedition against the Seneca, see *JR*, LXIII, 302.

48. Eccles, *Canada under Louis XIV*, 105–108; Lanctot, *History of Canada*, II, 98.

Iroquois were preoccupied by a conflict with the Andastes (Susquehannocks) in Pennsylvania. In 1676 this tribe was attacked by frontiersmen from Virginia and, having suffered great losses, sued for peace with the Iroquois. The years 1675–1676 also witnessed a weakening of the tribes to the east of the Iroquois as a result of King Philip's War, a process to which the Mohawks contributed with their attack at Schaghticoke. Relieved of enemies on two fronts, the Iroquois could concentrate attention on harrying New France and the French western fur trade. Almost immediately, the Jesuit missionaries reported an increasingly hostile attitude among the tribes and noted that the turn in demeanor had coincided with the defeat of "the Andastogues, their ancient and most redoubtable foes." As a result, "they talk of nothing but renewing the war against our allies, and even against the French." As the decade of the 1680s progressed, the commercial empire of the French in the west was jeopardized first by the Iroquois and then by the English. Ultimately, the French would respond to both in a similarly aggressive manner.[49]

In July 1682 Governor Frontenac received dispatches from the French court which contained his recall. His successor, Joseph-Antoine Lefebvre de la Barre, arrived in the colony during the fall of the same year. Once described as being unfit to command other men, this individual now held responsibility for counteracting the growing Iroquois menace. During the spring of 1684, reports were received at Quebec that the Iroquois had attacked Fort St. Louis in the Illinois country. La Barre reluctantly began assembling his forces. By July nearly eight hundred troops and militia were at Montreal where they were joined by four hundred allied Indians. Having reached Fort

---

49. *JR*, LIX, 251. For another report highlighting the insolent attitude and behavior of the Iroquois, see *JR*, LX, 173. For the Iroquois and the Andastes, see Eccles, *Canada under Louis XIV*, 113; Norton, *Fur Trade in New York*, 16; Anthony F. C. Wallace, *The Death and Rebirth of the Seneca* (New York, 1969), 69, 102; Francis Jennings, "Susquehannock," in *HNAIN*, 362–367. In 1682 the French estimated that there were 2,500 Iroquois warriors total and that the tribes could put "1,400 in the field." They were reported to be well supplied with firearms, powder, and lead. It also was stated "that the Senecas were preparing, with the Cayugas, to attack the French . . . being urged by the English . . . to cut off completely the trade of the Outawas." *NYCD*, IX, 196, 197. Hostilities between the French and Iroquois began in the fall of 1680 when 600 Iroquois invaded the Illinois country, threatening the Indian allies of the French and imperiling their western sources of furs. Eccles, *Canada under Louis XIV*, 114. In 1686 Anthony Lespinard of Albany informed the authorities at Montreal that the Iroquois were creating an anti-French alliance with their former enemies "the Mohegans (Loups) and other tribes towards the Andastes." *NYCD*, IX, 302.

Frontenac at the juncture of the St. Lawrence River and Lake Ontario, the governor and his troops were greeted by a declaration from
the Iroquois proclaiming that the French had "a great desire to be
stripped, roasted and eaten." La Barre's courage dwindled as rapidly
as his supplies and the number of his men fit for service. A humiliat-
ing meeting between the governor and chiefs of the Onondagas followed, at which the latter suggested that, for their safety, the French
should return to Quebec. With the conference concluded, La Barre
hurriedly did just that.[50]

Humbled by the Iroquois and having abandoned their western Indian allies, the French now entered a period of crisis in their fur
trade. Exports of skins, which had reached ninety-five thousand
pounds in 1683, tumbled to one-quarter of that figure before slowly
rising again after 1686. Having demonstrated no talent for subduing
the Iroquois, La Barre was soon recalled. His replacement, Denonville, arrived at Quebec in August 1685. The governor's most urgent
tasks were to curb the aggression of the Iroquois and to deal with all
threats to the Canadian fur trade whether from the Indians or the
English. Anglo-French rivalry now became conflict as Denonville
displayed his more aggressive stance against the English in 1686 and
against both the English and Iroquois the following year. During the
spring of 1686, an expedition of 105 men captured three English
posts on Hudson Bay and garnered fifty thousand beaver pelts. That
same year Albany merchants, encouraged by Governor Dongan, sent
a party of traders guided by renegade *coureurs de bois* to Lake Huron
to trade with the Ottawas and other Indians. There they gave more
merchandise for furs than the French traders ever had. Denonville,
however, was ready to strike here as well. In November thirty of the
traders were captured and plundered by a detachment of French and
Indians. The following May a second contingent led by Major Patrick Macgregory encountered Henri de Tonty (a former associate of
La Salle) and a band of Illinois west of Lake Erie. Tonty and his
Indian allies scattered the traders and seized their possessions. By
July many of these men, including Arnout Cornelissen Viele, were
prisoners at Montreal.[51]

50. For the Seneca proclamation to La Barre and the 1684 expedition, see Eccles,
Canada under Louis XIV, 132–134; *DHNY*, I, 95–143; *NYCD*, IX, 236–243. For a description of La Barre's character, see Lanctot, *History of Canada*, II, 85.
51. For the decline of the Canadian fur trade, see Lanctot, *History of Canada*, II, 98.
For Governor Denonville, see Eccles, *Canada under Louis XIV*, chap. 9. For the attack
against the English posts on Hudson Bay, see *Eccles*, 147–148; Nellis M. Crouse,

Having struck at the English, it was now time to vanquish the Iroquois. The Senecas were selected for chastisement because of their position adjacent to the essential western water route. By June 1687 Denonville had gathered eight hundred Troupes de la Marine, an even larger number of Canadian militia, and a body of Indians led by Kryn at Montreal. Denonville's force reached Fort Frontenac during early July. Embarking again, the army skirted the southern shore of Lake Ontario before landing well within the territory of the Senecas. After a brief skirmish, the French forces cautiously entered the nearby villages only to find them deserted. The longhouses, caches of food, and fields of corn were set ablaze. In nine days, almost four hundred thousand bushels of corn were destroyed.[52]

Throughout this period the community at Schenectady provided valuable assistance to the English cause. Except for Arnout Cornelissen Viele and Symon Schermerhorn, no one with direct ties to the village can be linked to the trading expeditions promoted by Governor Dongan. As interpreters, however, the services of the Schenectady Dutch were continually in demand. Not surprisingly, given their proximity to the Mohawk villages, members of the community were fluent in the language of the Iroquois and other tribes. In 1680, when Jasper Danckaerts sought to talk to a Mohawk who was then residing at Schenectady, the conversation took place "in the presence of five or six persons who were well versed in the Mohawk language." Cornelis Cornelissen Viele and Jacques (Aukes) Cornelissen van Slyck had acted as interpreters since the 1660s. Van Slyck, who was described in contemporary records as "formerly an Indian," was clearly trusted by the Mohawks. During a conference held in 1688, representatives of the tribe proposed to Governor Edmund Andros "that the propositions made yesterday to us, may be left in writing with Akus the Interpreter, to whom wee may have recourse for information." Of all the seventeenth-century interpreters, van Slyck may have been the best, and his services were in demand as far away as

---

Lemoyne d'Iberville: Soldier of New France (Ithaca, 1954), 14–39. For the activities of the New York traders and the response of the French, see Helen Broshar, "The First Push Westward of the Albany Traders," *MVHR*, 7 (1920–1921), 233–235; Eccles, *Canada under Louis XIV*, 148; Lanctot, *History of Canada*, II, 104; *NYCD*, III, 487, IX, 318–319; *LIR*, 110–111, 136; David A. Armour, *The Merchants of Albany, New York, 1686–1760* (New York, 1986), 7–15. For Major Patrick Macgregory, see *Calendar of Council Minutes, 1668–1783*, ed. Berthold Fernow (Albany, 1902, reprint, Harrison, N.Y., 1987), V, 175, 201, 228, VI, 9. For reference to captives held by the French, see *Calendar*, V, 202; *CMVR*, 184.

52. Eccles, *Canada under Louis XIV*, 146–154; *DHNY*, I, 191–277.

New York City, where in August 1687 he helped to examine "a Christian Maquase brought a Prisonner from Cannada."[53]

Cornelis Cornelissen Viele also was intimate with the Mohawks, who gave him the name "Keeman." His brother, Arnout Cornelissen Viele, was even better known to both the French and the Indians. In 1684 he was described in Canadian correspondence as "one Arnaud, whom Father Bruyas is well acquainted with." During that year, Arnout Viele journeyed as far as the Senecas. Dispatched to promote English trade among the Iroquois and their western neighbors, Viele acted as "the envoy of the governor of New-York, who . . . promises the Iroquois goods at a considerable reduction . . . 8 lbs. of powder for a Beaver; as much lead as a man can carry for a Beaver."[54]

The most important service rendered by the Schenectady community during these years was in gathering and relaying information and rumor concerning the activities of the French and their native allies. In 1678, for example, the Albany magistrates reported to New York that, "yesterday Mr. Windall of this towne being at Scannecstada spoake with a Mauquas that came from Cannada & he toulde him yt there was Arived from france five shipes with 2000 men and yt thay had found a Sylver mine and yt thay was bilding by it a greate fort." On occasion captive French and Indians were funneled through Schenectady to Albany; the village also served as a locale for the spying activities of both sides. Scouts, both Indian and white, were dispatched from the village. Moreover, it was not unusual for Canadian Indians to appear at Schenectady under suspicious circumstances. In 1688 the village magistrates informed Governor Andros of the arrival of "fouer Maquass formerly belonging to our Indians therefore supposed to be spies, come from Cannada." Indeed, charges were made in the aftermath of the French attack in 1690 that several of the Indians involved had visited the village in the days preceding the assault.[55]

Governor Thomas Dongan recognized the strategic significance of Schenectady and the Mohawk Valley and in 1687 advanced a plan to

---

53. *JD*, 208; *NYCD*, III, 323, 560. For van Slyck and Arnout Cornelissen Viele, see *NYCD*, 431; Trelease, *Indian Affairs*, 210–211. For the involvement of Arnout Viele and Symon Schermerhorn with the Albany trading expedition, see Broshar, "First Push Westward," 239; *LIR*, 110–111, 136. For van Slyck's abilities as an interpreter, see *LIR*, 140.

54. *NYCD*, IX, 253, 257. For Viele's Indian name, see *ARS*, III, 80n.

55. *NYCD*, III, 565; XIII, 531. For French and Indian prisoners at Schenectady, see *NYCD*, III, 480; *LIR*, 136. For the claim that several Canadian Indians visited Schenectady before the 1690 attack, see Edmund Andros, *The Andros Tracts*, ed. W. H. Whitmore, 3 vols. (Boston, 1868–1874), III, 114–115.

erect a series of fortifications "to secure the Beaver @ Peltry Trade @ the Kings right to the Country." Dongan proposed that a fort be planted "at Corlars Lake" (Lake Champlain), but his primary concern was for the western region, where he thought there should be forts "upon the great Lake, and . . . 2 or 3 little other Forts between Schonectade @ the Lake to secure our people going @ coming." With the French already stationed at Niagara and Fort Frontenac, in effect the country of the Iroquois was being encompassed by the military resources of the European rivals. Dongan, however, was also concerned with the degree of support to be expected from the local Dutch population in time of war. In his opinion, it was "a great misfortune . . . that there are so few of his Maty's natural born subjects, the greater part being Dutch, who if occasion were, I fear would not be very fit for service."[56]

Fit or not, Dongan was committed to defending the northern communities and their Dutch inhabitants, including Schenectady. After receiving "messages . . . from Albany of their apprehensions of the French," the governor determined "to carry up thither two hundred men, besides the Garrison @ go and stay there this Winter." He hoped as well "to get together five or six hundred of the five nations about Albany @ Schonectade." To protect the latter community, Dongan asked for one hundred Senecas, fifty Cayugas, sixty Onondagas, fifty Oneidas, and forty Mohawks "to be att Schannectida this winter."[57]

An attack by the French against Albany had been expected during 1686, and throughout 1687 rumors of war were prevalent in both Canada and New York. Although a neutrality agreement had been signed by England and France in Europe, in North America no treaty existed between the French and Iroquois. During the summer of 1687 the French had sought to stem the incursions of the Iroquois by launching one of their own against the Senecas, the strongest of the Five Nations and the tribe most in position to imperil the French fur trade. The chief result, however, was to promote further attacks of retaliation. In his October 1687 memoir on the state of Canada, Governor Denonville admitted, "Our enemies have parties in the woods, who from time to time, kill such as travel without precaution, and then retreat into the depths of the forest."[58]

56. *NYCD*, III, 477–478.
57. Ibid., 477, 486. Dongan stayed at Albany until March 1688. Kammen, *Colonial New York*, 117.
58. *NYCD*, IX, 353. In 1686 the authorities at Montreal were informed that Eng-

Several of these war parties departed from Schenectady, including one in September 1687 described by the Mohawk sachem Rhode as "a Compy of one hundred and thirty men that goe out . . . towards the Lake of Canida to doe all the Mischeife they can against the French." By this date the communities at Albany and Schenectady were providing the Mohawks with both provisions and shelter. Governor Dongan promised the Iroquois powder and lead as well as protection for their families. In 1689 the Mohawks also petitioned the Dutch "to assist them with Two or three pare of horses & 5 or 6 men to Ride the heaviest Stockadoes for their new Castle of Tionondage," a request to which the Albany and Schenectady magistrates readily agreed.[59]

During the winter of 1689–1690, rumors of war gave way to fact. In January 1690 Albany's magistrates notified the Iroquois "to Charge & Command them to make no Peace . . . with ye french Since his Majes Declaration of warr against them . . . by ye English nation is now come over." For the French, however, New York's authorities had long been indicted as accessories in their conflicts with the tribes. As early as 1686 Denonville charged, "I know beyond a particle of doubt, that M. Dongan hath caused all the Five Iroquois Nations to be assembled this spring at Orange . . . so as to excite them against us . . . that they must plunder our Frenchmen in the woods." The governor's solution, proposed in later correspondence, was "to go straight to Orange [Albany], storm their fort, and burn the whole concern."[60]

Two decades earlier (1666), Governor Richard Nicolls had expressed his opinion that the French would not reveal themselves as enemies "till they have either vanquisht the Mohawks or made peace with them." In January 1687, plans were proposed at Quebec for a two-pronged assault against the Iroquois with one French army marching against the Senecas and "the second, by the River Richelieu and Lake Champlain in the direction of the Mohawks." Encompassed on both sides, the tribes would be unable to come to each other's aid. Only the Senecas were attacked in 1687, but during 1688 plans were

lish forces in New York had kept guard for three months, anticipating that the French would launch an attack in retaliation for the colony's arming of the Iroquois. *NYCD*, 302. For similar fears in 1687, see *CMVR*, 184. For the 1687 treaty of neutrality, see Lanctot, *History of Canada*, II, 107–108.

59. *NYCD*, III, 483–484; *DHNY*, II, 87. For shelter and aid given to the Iroquois, see *LIR*, 122–123; *BGE*, II, 395; Grassmann, *Mohawk Indians*, 435.

60. *DHNY*, II, 142; *NYCD*, IX, 296, 309.

advanced for additional forays and, again, a double invasion was contemplated. But at this point political changes within New York and the New England colonies in reaction to the Glorious Revolution in England led to a rethinking of French designs.[61]

In January 1689 Louis-Hector, Chevalier de Callières, the governor of Montreal, attempted to explain the new state of affairs to the home authorities. Callières, however, failed to grasp the impact that the Glorious Revolution was to have in New York and New England. He incorrectly predicted, "Chevalier Andros, as well as the whole English Colony, is protestant, so that there is no reason to hope that he will remain faithful to the King of England." Callières misunderstood Andros's role but accurately assessed the political loyalties of the colonists and suggested that "as the recent Revolution in England will change the face of American affairs, it becomes necessary to adopt entirely new measures to secure Canada against the great dangers with which it is threatened." Inaction would prove disastrous: "They are about to endeavor to invest the entire of Canada and raise all the Savages against us, in order to wholly deprive us of every sort of Trade and draw it all to themselves by means of the cheap bargains they can give of goods." With the French trade ruined, the English and their Indian allies would next "fall on us, burn and sack our settlements, scattered along the River St. Lawrence." During the succeeding months, Callières emerged as the most active proponent of measures to secure Canada. He urged that the English be anticipated and that an army of seventeen hundred men be assembled with the design "to go straight to Orange, the frontier town of New-York . . . which I would undertake to carry; and to proceed thence to seize Manathe [Manhattan], the capital of that Colony."[62]

For the Dutch, it was a year of worry, rumor, and flight. Not only was there concern over an attack by the French, the allegiance of the Iroquois also was in question. At the end of July, word was received from the Mohawks above Schenectady "that four Onnongonges or Pennequid Indians . . . desired that the Maquaes and the other four nations . . . would take up the ax with them against all the Christians on this continent." The Iroquois were told that the whites "had made a compact to cut off all the Indians whatsoever." The identity of these Indians is uncertain, but they may have been Abenakis, who, as refugees, had gone to Canada after King Philip's War and who

61. *NYCD*, III, 120, IX, 321.
62. Ibid., IX, 404–405.

were now acting as agents of the French. According to the Mohawks, these Indians were encouraged by the Governor of Canada "to wage war against the English."[63]

Word of the proposed alliance reached Schenectady on July 30, and from there the information was quickly relayed to Albany. Tensions eased only after four Mohawk envoys came down to Schenectady with an explanation of what had transpired and with protestations of their tribe's continued loyalty. The situation had barely been resolved, however, before news was received that several "Skachkook Indians" had arrived at Albany proclaiming "that an army of French & Indians were Seen on this Side of ye Lake." A contingent of eighteen men was sent out "to make Discovery, which was found to be false." Two alarms within one week proved unsettling, and many persons were now reported to be "makeing Preparation to transport themselfs out of this County." In response, on August 7, the justices of the peace for Albany County ordered "that no Person . . . being fit & able to bear arms . . . shall in ye space of three monthes Presume to Depart or absent themselfs out of this County . . . without a Passe from one Justice of ye Peace."[64]

Throughout the summer and fall of 1689 the nervous inhabitants of Albany County were reported to "dayly expect to be invaded by the French." To provide warning, parties of scouts made up of soldiers from the fort at Albany plus local residents familiar with the woods and trails were kept out to the north. Few observers anticipated that such measures would prove effective. From Boston, Edward Randolph wrote the Bishop of London, "I have this day Certaine advice that the french intend to attack Albany in January next, when the Lakes & Rivers . . are all frozen. I question not but they will take it, unless Orders arrive from Engd . . . to prevent them." The killing of three persons near Schenectady by Canadian Indians was a signal of what many feared was to come.[65]

---

63. Ibid., III, 611; *DHNY*, II, 20. For the Mohawk version of this incident, see *DHNY*, II, 19–20. During the 1670s the *Jesuit Relation* took note of the arrival in Canada of "a band of a hundred and fifty abnaquis savages." *JR*, LX, 133.

64. *DHNY*, II, 82, 84. Those persons denied permission to leave Albany County without a license included only individuals "being fit & able to bear arms." Women, children, and older persons could leave and presumably did so. The following year, in May 1690, it was reported that "most of the Albany Wood men [women] are att New Yorke." *DHNY*, I, 311.

65. *DHNY*, II, 34; Randolph, *Letters and Papers*, IV, 305. For the fall 1689 killings near Schenectady, see Randolph, IV, 302, VI, 300. For the sending out of scouts, see *DHNY*, II, 99.

In fact, the major campaign of 1689 took place not on the Hudson or Mohawk rivers but along the St. Lawrence. A large body of Iroquois had departed for Canada in late June. By early August, at the very moment that the inhabitants of Albany County most feared they were to be the object of attack, the Iroquois were launching a massive raid in the vicinity of Montreal. Canadian accounts indicate that on the night of August 4, under cover of heavy rain, dozens of Iroquois crossed to the island and entered the sleeping village of Lachine. Twenty-four habitants were killed and seventy to ninety taken captive. Having been reappointed governor of New France, Frontenac reached Quebec during mid-October. At this time he learned of the deaths at Lachine. Barely one month after the governor's arrival, another party of 150 Iroquois attacked La Chesnaye near Montreal, killing twenty of its inhabitants and taking an equal number prisoner. Clearly, the situation demanded action.[66]

Returning with Frontenac was Callières, who had journeyed to France to present at court his strategy for an attack against the English. Louis XIV had hoped to restore James II to his throne and to prevent a break between England and France, but James II's forces fighting in Ireland had had little success and, in May, England declared war on France. At first rebuffed, Callières's scheme for the reduction of New York was now reconsidered. On June 7, 1689, a memoir was issued to serve as "Instructions for Count de Frontenac respecting the Expedition against New York." Callières's proposals were incorporated while leaving the governor free to adapt them as he saw fit: "Sieur de Frontenac being informed of the route he will take . . . His Majesty will not enter into further detail on that point, nor on the attack on Orange and Manathe."[67]

As originally proposed, Callières's plan called for a surreptitious approach to Albany under the guise of proceeding "to the Iroquois Country to dictate Peace to them." Having reached Albany, "invested the town and summoned it to surrender," he intended "to cut or burn the palisades, in order to make an opening, and enter the

66. One of the most graphic accounts of the village's destruction was provided by the newly returned governor. *NYCD*, IX, 435. For the departure of the Iroquois and the Lachine attack, see *NYCD*, III, 610, IX, 431; Eccles, *Canada under Louis XIV*, 164–165. For Frontenac's arrival in New France and the attack on La Chesnaye, see Lanctot, *History of Canada*, II, 114–115.

67. *NYCD*, IX, 424. For the complete document, see *NYCD*, IX, 422–426. For the outbreak of Anglo-French conflict in Europe, see Eccles, *Canada under Louis XIV*, 163–164.

place sword in hand and afterwards seize the fort, which being only about 14 feet high, can be easily escaladed . . . or by blowing in the gate with . . . small field pieces." With the inhabitants disarmed and a garrison of two hundred men left to command the town, Callières would "seize all the barks, bateaux and canoes that are at Orange, for the embarkation of my forces on the river which is navigable down to Manathe." It was an ambitious plan, probably overly so, but the Chevalier expected decisive returns: "It will render His Majesty absolute master of all the Iroquois who derive from that Colony whatever arms and ammunition they have to make war on us. . . . Having mastered the Iroquois we shall have equal control of all the other Savages who will . . . bring us all their peltries. This will cause the trade of our Colony to flourish."[68]

The targets of the French assault were Albany first and then New York City. Schenectady may have been approached, however, for Callières expected "to seize, in passing, some English Villages and Settlements where I shall find provisions and other conveniences for attacking the town of Orange." Significantly, Callières made no mention of subverting the loyalty of the Dutch to the English government. Moreover, the expedition was to be made up largely of European and Canadian troops, with only a modest number of Indian auxiliaries to serve as guides. The intent was to capture and occupy Albany and New York, not attack and retreat, and for this purpose trained troops were needed. Finally, since the communities were to be maintained, burning and plundering were to be avoided. On this latter point, the king's instructions of June 7 were explicit. The inhabitants were to be disarmed, but Frontenac was to give them "every good treatment. . . . His Majesty wishes particular care to be taken to prevent any plunder of provisions, merchandise, ammunition, property, cattle, implements and . . . household furniture." In

---

68. *NYCD*, IX, 406–407. In summarizing Callières' proposals, several significant points must be emphasized. First, the attack was expected to take place during the summer or early fall while the Hudson River was navigable. Frontenac and Callières, however, returned to Quebec in October. If carried out as intended, the campaign could not occur until the summer of 1690 at the earliest. The only winter assault launched by the French to this time had been Courcelle's which went astray and arrived near Schenectady in February of 1666. Of his journey, Courcelle later wrote: "A more difficult or longer march . . . can scarcely be met with . . . three hundred leagues on the snow . . . and endure a cold surpassing . . . that of the most rigorous European winters." *DHNY*, I, 65–66. For Callières's plan and the alterations subsequently made to it, see Eccles, *Canada under Louis XIV*, 163; David P. Hardcastle, "The Defense of Canada under Louis XIV, 1643–1701" (Ph.D. diss., Ohio State University, 1970), 197, 317–327.

the aftermath of the attacks against Lachine and La Chesnaye, Governor Frontenac had to act quickly to restore the flagging morale of the Canadian habitants. Not enough troops or supplies were available to mount an invasion, and by November winter snows already encompassed both Montreal and Quebec. The governor had to adapt his methods to the needs and resources of the moment. Although it was too late for Callières's elaborate scheme, a series of hit-and-run raids might prove effective instead.[69]

For the French, there could not have been a more propitious moment to launch an invasion. During the spring of 1689, disaffected subjects had wrested power from provincial royal appointees in both New York and the New England colonies. In response to news of the Glorious Revolution in England, Governor Edmund Andros was confined at Boston, and in New York, after some hesitation, Jacob Leisler, a New York militia captain, commandeered that colony's government. At Albany, however, the magistrates loyal to Andros refused to join Leisler in his rebellion, although there was a party within the city eager to do so. Not only was Albany divided against New York, there was little unity between Albany and Schenectady. Additionally, the latter community was split between supporters of Leisler such as Reyer Schermerhorn and backers of the anti-Leisler Convention government at Albany, who included Sander and Johannes Glen, Jan van Eps, and Sweer Teunissen van Velsen. This internal division would soon prove fatal. As early as September 1689, Sander Glen and the other Schenectady magistrates reported to Albany that at their village there was "no settlement . . . how or what way they are to Behave themselfs if ye enemy should come, since they cannot agree amongst themselves in yt particular."[70]

In November, Jacob Milborne, Leisler's lieutenant and future son-in-law, appeared before the gates of Albany with an armed body of men to demand the city's surrender. He was allowed to enter the city and to meet with the magistrates but failed in his purpose. Before

69. *NYCD*, IX, 406, 424. For the state of Canada in the fall of 1689 and Frontenac's response to the attacks of the Iroquois, see Eccles, *Canada under Louis XIV*, 164–172.

70. *DHNY*, II, 90. For the seizure of Governor Andros at Boston and Leisler's rise to power in New York, see *Narratives of the Insurrections, 1675–1690*, ed. Charles M. Andrews (New York, 1915), 170–175, 362–366. For the opponents and supporters of Leisler at Albany and Schenectady, see *DHNY*, II, 88, 349–354. The most recent study of Leisler's Rebellion is David William Voorhees, "'In behalf of the true Protestants religion': The Glorious Revolution in New York" (Ph.D. diss., New York University, 1988).

departing, however, Milborne advertised to "all the inhabitants of Schinnectady and adjoining places to repair forthwith to the aforesaid City of Albany to receive their Rights and Priviledges & Liberties." Well aware of the long-standing economic and political rivalry between the two communities, he promised that "the gentlemen of Shennechtady will be preferred to those of Albany in the approaching New Government" and that they would "have no less Privileges than those of Albany in Trading and Bolting." To consolidate the new order, on December 28, 1689, commissions were issued by Leisler for five new justices for the village.[71]

On January 12, 1690, Sander Glen notified the Albany authorities of the arrival of the commissions at Schenectady. His message was received as the Convention members debated whether Leisler was "to be Esteemed . . . Commandr in Cheefe of the Province." The documents included "a Commission to call the People together, to choose new Capt Lieft & Ensign and Toune Courte." But Glen reported that, as a body, the Schenectady officials voted "not to Obey Capt Leyslers orders, But to Protest against his Illegal Proceedings."[72]

Less than a month before the appearance of the French and Indians, the factionalism at Schenectady and between that village and Albany had again awakened. Accounts of the February 1690 attack against the village suggest how sharply divided Schenectady's inhabitants were at this time. As Robert Livingston related, "they would not watch, and where Capt. Sander [Glen] commanded, there they threatened to burn him upon ye fire, if he came upon the garde." Even families were split. Sweer Teunissen van Velsen acted with Glen, but his stepson, Myndert Wemp, was one of those who received a commission from Jacob Leisler.[73]

By early 1690 there were two focuses of power at Schenectady. Representing the weakened but still established royal authority were Captain Sander Glen, Lieutenant Jan van Eps, Ensign Johannes Sanders Glen, and Sweer Teunissen van Velsen. Opposing them was a collection of Leisler appointees who included Reyer Schermerhorn, Myndert Wemp, David Christoffelsen, Douwe Aukes, Reynier Schaats, and Johannes Pootman. Glen and his associates, however,

71. *DHNY*, II, 116, 118. For a list of justices appointed by Leisler at Schenectady, see *DHNY*, II, 350; Howell and Munsell, *History of the County of Schenectady*, 23.

72. *DHNY*, II, 148, 149.

73. Ibid., I, 310. The political differences of van Velsen and his stepson may have been rooted in family tensions. *ARS*, III, 324–326.

were responsible for the village's defenses. During the fall of 1689, the authorities at Albany had requested troops from Connecticut as a protective measure against the forces of both Leisler and the French. Governor Robert Treat agreed to send eighty men (led by Captain Jonathan Bull). On October 24, Glen and the others voted that Schenectady would "bear there Proportiones of ye Cherge of ye officers there wages and maintain them accordingly," but they did so provided the troops "be under Command and obey such orders and Instructions as they shall Receive from time to time from ye Convention of this Citty [Albany] and County." A detachment of twenty-four men led by Lieutenant Enos Talmadge took up their post at the blockhouse at Schenectady. Talmadge himself may have resided at the van Velsen household.[74]

As the new year opened, not one but three forces were advancing southward from Canada to attack New England and New York. The war parties assembled at Quebec, Trois Rivières, and Montreal. Departing Montreal in the bitter January cold, the largest party, consisting of 114 Canadians and 96 Indian auxiliaries, headed for Schenectady. The invaders were led by Nicolas d'Ailleboust de Manthet, Jacques Le Moyne de Sainte-Hélène, and Pierre Le Moyne d'Iberville. The Indian leader was Kryn. All four were veterans of the conflict of the preceding years. Since the 1670s, Kryn had recruited Mohawks for the villages of Praying Indians near Quebec and Montreal and had taken part in attacks such as Denonville's against the Senecas in 1687. The Le Moyne brothers were the sons of Charles Le Moyne of Montreal. Most recently, both brothers had participated in the 1686 assault against the English posts on Hudson Bay. Manthet, meanwhile, had taken part in one of the first counterstrokes against the Iroquois in the aftermath of Lachine. He was one of a body of twenty-eight Canadians who encountered and attacked an Iroquois war party on the Lake of Two Mountains near Montreal. Eighteen natives were killed or drowned and three prisoners were later burned. Only one of the warriors escaped.[75]

74. *DHNY*, II, 98. For Bull's troops, see *SP*, 245. Lieutenant Talmadge's body was found in the remains of the van Velsen house. *DHNY*, I, 304.

75. For the size and composition of the attacking party, see *LIR*, 158–159; Eccles, *Canada under Louis XIV*, 172. For the Le Moyne brothers and for a discussion of the Schenectady expedition, see Eccles, 160–161; Crouse, *Lemoyne d'Iberville*, 49–63; Jean Blain, "Jacques Le Moyne De Sainte-Hélène," *DCB*, I, 465–466; Bernard Pothier, "Le Moyne D'Iberville," *DCB*, II, 390–401. For Manthet, see Lanctot, *History of Canada*, II, 111; Jean Blain, "Nicolas D'Ailleboust De Manthet," *DCB*, II, 13–14.

The attackers were to inflict as much destruction against the village and its inhabitants as possible. French prisoners taken later stated that they had marched "with Positive orders to murder and DeStroy all People they mett withall at Shinnechtady Except Such as beg'd for quarters; as also to Burn ye Place and to take with them those that they could cary along."[76]

As the raiders were too few in number to act as an occupying force, Frontenac's orders had specifically stated that Schenectady rather than Albany should be attacked because it could be taken with less risk. This determined the path the party followed southward. Having traversed the frozen bodies of Lake Champlain and Lake St. Sacrament (Lake George), they struck south along a trail that led to today's Saratoga Lake (called Long Lake in 1690) and to Round Lake, north and east of Schenectady. At some point along the latter part of this route, a discussion was held whether to continue on to Schenectady as planned or to alter their goal: "When they were within some miles of Shinnechtady ye officers had a Consultation about falling upon albanie, one monsr. De Tallie who had been formerly here did Presse hard to Attaque it; Butt because there orders was Expressly for Shinnechtady ye DeSign on alby was put by." Schenectady it was to be.[77]

As the party advanced southward, thirty men were kept out as scouts about a musket shot from the main body, a number that was doubled as they neared the village. Several Christian Mohawks also may have gone ahead to visit the community two or three days before the attack. Additional information was gathered from four Mohawk women discovered in a shelter several miles from Schenectady, who were compelled to give an account of the village. At about four o'clock on the afternoon of February 8, a Saturday, the men halted to warm themselves at a fire found in the Indian women's hut. They "were harangued by the great Mohawk chief of the Iroquois from the Sault." Kryn urged them "all to perform their duty, and to lose all recollections of their fatigue, in hope of taking ample revenge for the

76. *LIR*, 158–159.
77. Ibid., 160. For the determination to attack Schenectady and not Albany, see ibid., 158–160; *DHNY*, I, 298–299; Eccles, *Canada under Louis XIV*, 172. The 1688 Franquelin map of North America indicates the trail from Lake St. Sacrament to the first Mohawk village. A 1690 map (possibly made as part of an abortive campaign against Montreal and Quebec led by Fitz-John Winthrop) denotes the trail from Lake St. Sacrament to "Long Lake," "Round Lake," and Schenectady. Grassmann, *Mohawk Indians*, 300, 523.

injuries they had received from the Iroquois at the solicitation of the English."[78]

Having left Montreal seventeen days earlier, the attackers finally reached Schenectady about eleven o'clock that night. Their intention had been to attack an hour or two after midnight, "but the excessive cold admitted of no further delay." French accounts described the village as "a sort of oblong with only two gates—one opposite the road . . . taken; the other leading to Orange." With the assistance of the Indian women, the first gate was located and found to be open. A detachment led by Iberville, however, failed to discover the Albany gate and returned to join the main force: "A profound silence was every where observed, until the two commanders, who separated, at their entrance into the town for the purpose of encircling it, had met at the other extremity." The attack was then signaled "Indian fashion." Manthet led one detachment, which besieged the blockhouse where the Connecticut troops were garrisoned. The sack of the town "began a moment before the attack on the fort. Few houses made any resistance." But at one unidentified dwelling the struggle was especially fierce: "M. de Montigny discovered some which he attempted to carry sword in hand, having tried the musket in vain. He received two thrusts of a spear. . . . But M. de Sainte Helene having come to his aid, effected an entrance, and put every one who defended the place to the sword." According to later accounts, the French method of attack was to divide into groups of six or seven before each house, "and in this manner begunn to Murther, spareing no man till they see all the houses open and master'd." Within two hours, the French controlled the village and "the remainder of the night was spent in placing sentinels, and in taking some repose." The hours before dawn must have been bitter for both survivors and attackers for "that Saturday night a Snow fell above knee deep and dreadfull cold."[79]

The Glen residence across the river from the village had not been attacked, and the following morning a small party was sent to request its surrender. Sander Glen refused and prepared to defend his prop-

78. *DHNY*, I, 299. For the precautions taken by the French as they advanced southward and for their encounter with the Mohawk women, see *DHNY*, I, 299; *LIR*, 159–160. For the claim that several French Indians visited Schenectady before the attack, see Andros, *Andros Tracts*, III, 114–115.

79. Andros, *Andros Tracts*, III, 115; *DHNY*, I, 299–300. The French accounts provide insight into the harshness of the winter march to Schenectady. Both whites and Indians "experienced inconceivable difficulties, . . . having been obliged to march up to their knees in water, and to break the ice with their feet in order to find a solid footing." *DHNY*, I, 299.

erty "with his servants and some Indians." Unattended, Iberville and
Kryn proceeded across the ice to parlay with Glen and to promise
"quarter for himself, his people, and his property, whereupon he laid
down his arms, on parole, entertaining them in his fort, and returned
with them to see the commandants of the town." The invaders were
willing to spare Glen's dwelling "in consequence of the good treatment that the French had formerly experienced at his hands," a reference to the family's past efforts in retrieving French captives from the
Iroquois. Finally, about noon on Sunday, the French and Indians
departed, taking "what Plunder they would," including "30 or 40 of
the best horses." Twenty-seven captives, both white and black,
marched away with the retreating army. Among the more grisly tro-
phies taken back to Montreal was the severed head of the village's
minister, Petrus Tesschenmaeker.[80]

Existing records offer a gruesome description of the attack on Schenectady, but the only surviving account of the death of any of the
village's inhabitants is that of Dominie Tesschenmaeker. Questioned
later about his killing, three French prisoners "confesed yt 4 or 5
french had murdered ye Minister . . . called Petrus Tessemaker, first
shooting him throu ye leggs, & then hewd him wth there Swords . . .
being asked if they had Expresse Orders to deal so Cruelly Said That
there order was to doe what was done." The bodies of many of those
killed were badly burned by the fires that destroyed their dwellings.
The burial party dispatched to Schenectady from Albany on February 10 must have needed both strong arms to dig the winter graves
and strong stomachs as well.[81]

Perspective on the killings at Schenectady can be achieved through
comparison with the loss of life which resulted from the Iroquois
attack against Lachine in 1689 and that which resulted from the raids
into New England by the other war parties dispatched from Canada
in early 1690. It may also be appropriate to include the best-known
raid of the French and Indians during the early 1700s, that at Deerfield, Massachusetts, in February 1704 (Table 6). Estimates vary, but
except at Schenectady, in each instance the number of persons killed
is substantially lower than those captured. That so many people died
at Schenectady can be attributed to two factors: the surprise of the

---

80. *DHNY*, I, 300–301; Andros, *Andros Tracts*, III, 115. For the captives and the
fate of Dominie Tesschenmaeker, see Andros, 117; *DHNY*, I, 304–306; *ER*, II, 1252;
Documents Relating to the Administration of Jacob Leisler, NYHSC, I (New York, 1868),
403.

81. *LIR*, 159. For accounts of the attack on Schenectady and its aftermath, see
DHNY, I, 285–312; Andros, *Andros Tracts*, III, 114–120.

Table 6. The 1690 attack on Schenectady compared with other French and Iroquois raids, 1689–1704, by casualties

Location	Date	Number killed	Number captured
Lachine	August 5, 1689	24	70–90
Schenectady	February 8, 1690	60	27
Salmon Falls, N.H.	March 18, 1690	34	54
Casco (Falmouth), Me.	May 27, 1690	20	100[a]
Deerfield, Mass.	February 28, 1704	38	111

Sources: Eccles, *Canada under Louis XIV*, 165; *DHNY*, I, 34–36; Peckham, *Colonial Wars*, 3, 32, 63.

[a]Nearly 100 persons who had retreated to a local fort were killed after they surrendered.

assault and the ability of the enemy to gain entrance to the stockade, which made it impossible for the soldiers and inhabitants to put up a coordinated or substantive resistance.

As if to heighten its impact, news of the killings was brought to the community at Albany in the darkness before dawn by a wounded Symon Schermerhorn. Most likely, Schermerhorn slipped out the gate to Albany which the French had been unable to discover and spurred his horse for five hours through the snow to spread the alarm. A letter was immediately sent to the community at Esopus asking for assistance, and additional riders were dispatched to warn the farmers at Kinderhook and Claverack. An express also went north toward Schaghticoke but had to turn back in the face of high water, ice, and snow. Little more was done for the moment except to fire the fort's cannon as a warning to the nearby residents at Rensselaerswyck. The city's garrison and inhabitants were immobilized, for word had been received "from Skinnechtady Informing us yt the Enemy yt had done yt Mischieffe there were about . . . 200 men but that there were 1400 in all; One army for Albany & anoyr for Sopus which hindered much ye marching of any force out of ye Citty fearing yt ye enemy might watch such an opportunity."[82]

On Monday, February 10, with the appearance of no additional enemy force, attempts were made to bury the dead at Schenectady and to provide "succor and Relieffe to ye Poor People left alive." A troop of horsemen and Mohawks sought the trail of the retreating French and Indians and a force of 140 men (Indians and Dutch) was soon in pursuit. Within a month, four prisoners, three Frenchmen

82. *DHNY*, I, 303.

and one Indian, were returned. Although only one Frenchman and one Indian were lost in the attack on Schenectady, twenty-one (seventeen French and four Indians) never reached Montreal, because they were captured, died in skirmishes with their pursuers, or succumbed to the cold.[83]

News of the French attack was quickly broadcast to other colonies, both by the authorities at Albany and by the Leisler government at New York. Before the week was out, the Albany magistrates had written to "Col. Pynchon [at Springfield] to warn the upper towns to be upon there guarde." On February 15, Mayor Pieter Schuyler also wrote to the Massachusetts government, but the task of informing more distant colonies fell to Jacob Leisler at New York. Leisler notified the governor of Maryland on March 4 "of the sad and deplorable massacre which happened at skenectady near Albany by the french & their Indians." Before long, news of the attack was current as far away as London.[84]

Clearly, the killings at Schenectady had a dramatic impact on contemporaries. The Mohawks were reported to be "much amazed to see so many People murthered and Destroyed." The devastation at the village was almost total: "they burnt all ye houses and barns Cattle &ca Except 5 @ 6." Even as late as 1694, John Pynchon still made reference to the massacre in his correspondence. What he and others learned from the events at Schenectady was expressed in his warning that the Massachusetts communities must be kept in a "warlike posture," otherwise "indiscretion may procure some smart blow (as it did to Skenectode)." That this would be so was predicted by the Mohawks: "Now you see your Blood spilt and this is the beginning of your miseries . . . make all Readinesse to master Canida . . . else you cannot live in Peace." Indeed, the attacks on Lachine and Schenectady as well as the other raids into New England were to inaugurate over two decades of conflict between England and France and their Indian allies in North America.[85]

---

83. Ibid., 304. For the pursuit of the retreating French and Indians and for an estimate of their losses, see ibid., 302, 303, 306, 309. For the three French prisoners and the captured Indian, see *LIR*, 158–162; Andros, *Andros Tracts*, III, 116.

84. Andros, *Andros Tracts*, III, 120, *DHNY*, II, 183. For Pieter Schuyler's letter, see Andros, III, 114–120. Report of the attack had reached Boston by February 24. Samuel Sewall's diary entry for that date details the events at Schenectady. Samuel Sewall, *The Diary of Samuel Sewall*, ed. M. Halsey Thomas, 2 vols. (New York, 1973), I, 251. For knowledge of the destruction of Schenectady in England, see *Narratives of the Insurrections*, 267; *DHNY*, I, 308–309.

85. *DHNY*, I, 303, 306; Pynchon, *Letters*, 238; Andros, *Andros Tracts*, III, 117.

4

White, Black, and Red at Schenectady

Between 1624 and 1664 the few hundred first inhabitants of New Netherland grew to number some eight thousand persons, white and black. The character of the migration to the colony changed over time, particularly during the 1650s, as increasing numbers of husbands, wives, and children were added to the established flow of Company employees and single young men. Existing records also report the more frequent arrival of slave ships such as the *Witte Paert* in 1655 and the *Bontekoe* the next year. Additionally, the examination of records for the patroon's settlement at Rensselaerswyck as well as genealogical materials for the province as a whole suggest that, before the English conquest, as many persons from outside the Netherlands as from the Dutch provinces settled in the colony.[1]

In the aftermath of the Schenectady massacre, representatives of the Mohawks spoke of the design of the French to "come here and kill the Dutch." Similarly, Jacob Leisler informed a correspondent of the attack of the French and Indians, "barbarously destroying the Inhabitants all being dutch." But analysis of surviving community records reveals that such statements mask the heterogeneous nature of the village's population. Over 30 percent (31.1 percent) of those persons killed or captured on the night of February 8, 1690, were not Dutch, and if one seeks to reconstruct the community's entire population, the result is much the same. At a minimum, slightly more than one-third (35.6 percent) of the individuals known to be at the village on that night cannot be classified as members of the Dutch community (Ta-

---

1. For the population history of New Netherland, see Rink, *Holland on the Hudson*, chap. 6; David Steven Cohen, "How Dutch Were the Dutch of New Netherland?" *NYH*, 62 (1981), 43–60.

Table 7. Schenectady's estimated population on February 8, 1690

	Dutch		Non-Dutch	
Killed or captured	60		27	
Survivors	25[a]			
Mohawk			20	
TOTAL	85	(64.4%)	47	(35.6%)

Dutch killed or captured			Non-Dutch killed or captured		
	Number	Percentage of total		Number	Percentage of total
Men	19	21.8	Connecticut soldiers	9	10.3
Young men	22	25.3	Slaves	16	18.4
Women	7	8.0	Indians	1	1.2
Young women	1	1.2	Other[b]	1	1.2
Children	11	12.6		27	31.1
TOTAL	60	68.9			

Source: *DHNY*, I, 304–306.
[a]Assumes all survivors were Dutch.
[b]"A french girl Prisoner among ye Mohogs."

ble 7). Not only Dutch men and women, but English, French, African, and Indian had played a role in creating the day-to-day life of the village and were caught up in its destruction.[2]

With the colony's conquest in 1664, the intrusion of English soldiers, governors, and clergy added to the mix of the province's population and opened new avenues to economic and political command. The extent of Anglicization that occurred at a frontier community such as Schenectady, however, must not be overstated. As late as 1710, Thomas Barclay, the Anglican minister at Albany, calculated that there were one hundred Dutch families at the village but only sixteen English families. A majority of those persons of English descent who came to Schenectady were, like the Connecticut soldiers

2. Andros, *Andros Tracts*, III, 118; *DHNY*, I, 308. The French claimed that "the lives of between fifty and sixty persons, old men, women and children, were spared." *DHNY*, I, 301. If twenty-seven persons were taken captive, an approximately equal number should have been left at the village. Two accounts of the French attack, each within one month of the event, stated that twenty-five survivors had remained at Schenectady. But at Albany, in March, the heads of over fifty Schenectady households were provided with aid. This discrepancy suggests that existing records undercount the number of massacre survivors or that several of the village's inhabitants may not have been at Schenectady the night it was attacked. *DHNY*, I, 307, II, 199–202; Andros, *Andros Tracts*, III, 114.

who arrived in the fall of 1689, dispatched to bolster the community's defenses. This was particularly so during the 1690s and after as a fort and a permanent garrison were established at the village. Reverend Barclay numbered the Schenectady detachment at forty men. This many or more English troops had been stationed at Albany since the 1660s but were a relatively new feature of life at the Mohawk Valley community.[3]

Before 1664 only a small number of English traders and settlers had located outside of Long Island and New Amsterdam. One of the most successful was Thomas Willett, who was active in the fur trade at Beverwyck during the 1660s. A transplanted merchant from the Plymouth Colony, Willett was fluent in Dutch and had lived in Leiden before embarking for New England in 1629. By 1640 he was at New Amsterdam, where Petrus Stuyvesant employed him in dealings with the English colonies. After 1664 he was appointed the first mayor of the renamed city of New York. At Albany, Willett continued to trade and to own property until his death in 1674. Although never as significant a figure politically or economically, during these same years Christoffel Davids, also of English descent, was at Beverwyck where he had settled by 1650. Davids was active in the fur trade and married into a Dutch family. His son, David Christoffelsen, would settle at Schenectady.[4]

During the 1650s prominent New England merchants such as John Pynchon had attempted to subvert the Dutch trade on the Hudson River. Even two decades later there were still individuals in Massachusetts who were interested in trade and settlement in the region. Acting to link the earlier and later periods was John Paine, the son of William Paine, who together with John Pynchon and William Hawthorne had sought to circumvent the Dutch merchants at Beverwyck. In 1672 the younger Paine visited Albany, where, aided by the commander of the English garrison, he provided himself with supplies and guides and spent a week examining the eastern bank of the Hudson River north of Albany as well as lands along the adjoining Hoosick River. That same year Paine acted, unsuccessfully, as an agent

3. The English conquest and its ramifications on the lives of New Netherland's inhabitants is explored in Randall Balmer, *A Perfect Babel of Confusion: Dutch Religion and English Culture in the Middle Colonies* (New York, 1989). For Barclay's information, see *ER*, III, 1866–1867. As early as 1666 there was an English garrison of sixty men at Albany. *DHNY*, I, 74.

4. For Willett, see Elizur Yale Smith, "Captain Thomas Willett, First Mayor of New York," *NYH*, 21 (1940), 404–417; *ERAR*, I, 487, 495, III, 32–34, 417–418. For the Davids family at Albany and Schenectady, see *SP*, 102–103; *FS*, 36.

for the Massachusetts government, which sought "free Egress, and Regress upon Hudsons River for Transportacion of People and Goods."[5]

Between 1669 and 1670 a direct trade with New England had already been established by the patroon Jeremias van Rensselaer. The exchange involved the shipment of wheat to Boston and the westward transport of cattle and horses. Van Rensselaer found the enterprise rewarding but difficult to sustain. After the commander of the fort at Albany complained that the New Englanders were trading "wth Horses and Cattle for Beaver," Governor Lovelace (in 1670) prohibited any further "Importacõn of Cattle, Horses, or Goods from any other Government to that Place over Land, or the Exportacõn of Beaver or Peltry from thence that way." This attempt to protect the colony's revenues was coupled with an order against the exportation of grain except in the form of "fflowre, Bread, or Bisquett." By August 1671 van Rensselaer lamented, "Times are bad here. . . . last spring an order was issued prohibiting the transportation of grain to Boston, and it is said that it will remain in force." A temporary phenomenon, there is no evidence that this abortive Anglo-Dutch economic contact had any impact on the inhabitants of Schenectady.[6]

During the seventeenth century, English travelers only rarely visited the community at Schenectady. In the summer of 1677, Wentworth Greenhalgh journeyed westward from Albany to the Iroquois country, but left no record of his impression of the village. One individual who did was the Reverend John Miller, chaplain to two companies of grenadiers at New York. Miller was in the province from 1692 to 1695 and had occasion to be at both Albany and Schenectady. On returning to England, Miller drew a plan of the new fort at Schenectady from memory and his own observations related specifically to that structure: "Dependent on this City [Albany] and about twenty miles northward from it, is the Fort of Scanectade, quad-

---

5. *BGE*, I, 498. For Paine's 1672 journey to Albany, see Buffington, "New England and the Western Fur Trade," 188–191. Paine was again at Albany in 1674. See Pynchon, *Account Books*, 451–452.

6. *Minutes of the Executive Council*, I, 56–57; *CJVR*, 441–442. For further information on the New England trade, see *CJVR*, 416, 430; Pynchon, *Account Books*, 207, 394. During the early 1670s, John Pynchon maintained Timothy Cooper as his trading partner at Albany. In 1671 Adam Vrooman was employed by Pynchon in the construction of a (grist?) mill. Pynchon, 66–69, 134–138, 393–394. By the eighteenth century, many of the cattle and hogs consumed at Schenectady were supplied from New England. Smith, *Tour of Four Rivers*, 22.

rangular with a treble stockado with a new block house at every angle and in each block house two great guns."[7]

The conquest of New Netherland in 1664 and the placement of English troops at Albany (Beverwyck) and Kingston (Esopus) resulted in difficulties between the townspeople and the soldiers. Within two years, it was reported that the Dutch at Albany spoke "contemptuously of the English," claiming that they would be "masters over the English very speedily." In fact, in 1673 a Dutch squadron did recapture the colony, but the satisfaction of the local population at this event gave way to disappointment the following year as English control was reestablished.[8]

A residue of suspicion and distrust existed between the English and Dutch for many years. New York officials at all levels expressed reservations about the loyalty of their conquered subjects. In 1666 Captain John Baker commanding at Albany suspected Arent van Curler's dealings with the French. Twenty years later, Governor Thomas Dongan also voiced his concern that at New York "there are so few of his Maty's natural born subjects, the greater part being Dutch, who . . . I fear would not be very fitt for service." At Schenectady, moreover, an element of ethnic tension between the Scottish-born Sander Leendertsen Glen and the majority of Dutch settlers may have accounted for Glen's establishment of a plantation across the Mohawk River from Schenectady on land he named "Nova Scotia." Glen was initially the only settler to separate himself from the village in this manner, but he was soon joined on the north bank of the river by Benjamin Roberts, who also may have been of Scottish or English origin.[9]

7. *SP*, 310n. For Greenhalgh, see *DHNY*, I, 11–12; *ARS*, II, 212; *NYCD*, III, 250–252. For Miller, see *NYCD*, IV, 182n. Miller's sketch should be compared with the map of Schenectady prepared by Colonel Wolfgang William Romer in 1698. Grassmann, *Mohawk Indians*, 527.

8. Pynchon, *Letters*, 59. For Anglo-Dutch tension at Albany and elsewhere, see *CJVR*, 460–461; *NYCD*, III, 94; *Kingston Papers*, ed. Peter R. Christoph et al., trans. Dingman Versteeg, 2 vols. (Baltimore, 1976), I, 208; Donna Merwick, "Becoming English: Anglo-Dutch Conflict in the 1670s in Albany, New York," *NYH*, 62 (1981), 389–414. For the capture of the colony by the Dutch and the subsequent reestablishment of English control, see *AP*, 12–15, 61–84.

9. *NYCD*, III, 478. For Sander Leendertsen Glen and Benjamin Roberts, see *SP*, 115, 139–140. The Glen family property was known as Scotia throughout the seventeenth century. *DHNY*, I, 303. The August 1668 instructions given to Captain Baker at Albany by Governors Nicolls and Lovelace read: "Lett not your eares bee abused with private Storyes of the Dutch, being disaffected to the English, for generally we cannot expect they love us." *BGE*, I, 162.

The extended Anglo-Dutch ill-feeling that can be documented for a community such as Albany may have had less chance for expression at the more isolated village on the Mohawk. No English troops were stationed there and few English settlers arrived prior to the 1690s. Nevertheless, the available evidence suggests that Schenectady's population harbored the same anti-English suspicions and animosities as did their Albany neighbors. In 1677 the Connecticut River towns of Hatfield and Deerfield were attacked by a party of Indian raiders from Canada. The wives and children of Benjamin Waite and Stephen Jenning were among those persons taken captive. Both men received permission from the Massachusetts government to travel to Albany to arrange for Indian guides to accompany them in their search for family members. For whatever reason, having reached Albany, they continued on to Schenectady. Here they were accused of claiming that the village "did belong to Boston." Arrested and transported to New York City, they were examined before Governor Andros, who questioned Waite first. "Being demanded of the discourse between them and some of Schanectade," Waite denied that he had claimed the region for New England, "pretending it some mistake, they not understanding one anothers Language." Jenning concurred; he too claimed that "they not understanding one another well Might Mistake." With the interviews completed, both men were allowed to depart. Nothing indicates that the designs of either man included anything more than the retrieval of lost relatives. Yet, whatever the source of their difficulty, whether inopportune boastfulness or the poor command of English or Dutch by both sides, the incident signaled the unextinguished distrust of the Schenectady Dutch for their English neighbors.[10]

Even more striking evidence for the continuation of Anglo-Dutch animosity at Schenectady derives from the 1690s, at the time of King William's War. The construction of a fort in 1695 resulted in the establishment of a permanent English garrison at the village. One might expect that the community would welcome whatever protection could be provided, little matter whether the troops were Dutch or English. Yet only a few months later, on the night of January 10, 1696, the company deserted: "the whole guard, except one . . . to the

10. *Papers concerning the Attack on Hatfield and Deerfield by a Party of Indians from Canada September* 19, 1677, ed. Franklin Benjamin Hough (New York, 1859), 59–60. See also Pynchon, *Letters,* 172–174; C. Alice Baker, *True Stories of New England Captives* (Greenfield, Mass., 1897), 109–125.

number of sixteen broak through the north west Blockhouse next the water side." Seeking to escape across the frozen Mohawk River, their flight was discovered by the fort's commander,who pursued the deserters with a contingent of soldiers and Schenectady inhabitants. An exchange of musket fire killed five and left two men wounded. Eventually, ten of the soldiers were captured and court martialed. In excusing their actions, the men predictably complained of the harsh discipline that was their lot at the frontier post. But several gave as the single most important reason for their desertion "that the inhabitants were very unkind . . . in calling them English doggs."[11]

In 1664 Beverwyck's submission to English authority had been effected by Colonel George Cartwright; over the years a succession of military figures established a continuing English presence at the community. The importance of maintaining communications between Albany and Schenectady was recognized, and the latter settlement urged to keep out scouts whenever a French army was rumored to be approaching. Before the 1680s, however, Schenectady played only a minor role in the routine military calculations of the English authorities. The August 1668 instructions to Captain John Baker for "the well regulating of the Militia and other Affaires at Albany" did not mention the nearby village. Only during the 1680s did Schenectady begin to receive greater attention, a recognition of its strategic position on the trade route to the western sources of furs whose exploitation Governor Thomas Dongan was then seeking to promote.[12]

With the threat of war from the mid-1680s on, Schenectady figured even more prominently in the designs of the English provincial government. In 1687 the village was ordered fortified, and Governor Dongan proposed a series of frontier garrisons in the Mohawk Valley stretching from Schenectady to Lake Ontario. Dongan's recall and the upheaval associated with Leisler's Rebellion prevented any action being taken. But the commencement of hostilities in 1690 again produced concern for the stationing of troops at the village. The blockhouse was rebuilt and a fort constructed. At the suggestion of Richard Coote, earl of Bellomont, Schenectady would have figured even more prominently in English military planning. In 1699 Governor Bellomont endorsed Dongan's previous proposals and more. Reasoning that "a desert Country . . . is frightfull to people unless there be

11. *NYCD*, IV, 161, 163–164.
12. For the 1664 surrender of Albany, Captain Baker's instructions, and Schenectady's role in English military planning, see *BGE*, I, 44, 161–163, II, 391, 394.

Forts to protect 'em," he recommended a frontier force of one thousand troops with the majority to be stationed at Schenectady and
Albany. Even a decade later, however, as the Reverend Barclay's figures reveal, the actual English presence at Schenectady continued to
fall far short of such grandiose schemes.[13]

For Schenectady's inhabitants, of course, the single most important
factor of English rule was the continued prohibition on trade at their
village. That this would be so had been made clear as early as October 1664 at a conference between Governor Richard Nicolls and
three deputies from Albany. The result was a series of seventeen
articles agreed to concerning the rights and duties of the Albany government and providing for the accommodation of the town's new
English garrison. Article eleven ensured Albany's monopoly of trade:
"That the former Order forbidding the Inhabitants of Schonecstade
to trade with the Indyans for Beaver, and the penaltyes therein be
strictly observed." Orders prohibiting trade at Schenectady were re-
issued in 1669, 1670, and later.[14]

At the surrender of New Netherland in 1664 the colony's English
conquerors acted to preserve the existing political situation. It was
agreed that "all inferior civill Officers and Magistrates shall continue
as now they are," but instructions also were issued that at "the Customary time of New Eleccon . . . new ones [are] to be Chosen, by
themselves, provided that such new Chosen Magistrates shall take the
Oath of Allegiance to his Majesty of England, before they enter upon
their Office." The involvement of the Schenectady Dutch with English legal and political institutions nevertheless remained slight. Juries
were instituted to try criminal cases, and in 1672 the village was provided with its own court, although it was still an inferior body to the
court at Albany. Such changes were more of form than substance.
Lacking a settled English population, local political and military offices continued in the hands of Dutchmen such as Sweer Teunissen
van Velsen and Jan van Eps, or of those long domiciled among the
Dutch such as the Glens (see Table 14).[15]

13. *NYCD*, IV, 505. For Governor Dongan's plan to fortify the Mohawk Valley,
see *NYCD*, III, 477.
14. *BGE*, I, 50. For the prohibition of trade at Schenectady, see *BGE*, I, 261, 328,
459; *ARS*, II, 363; Norton, *Fur Trade in New York*, 45.
15. *BGE*, I, 37. For the colony's surrender in 1664, see *BGE*, I, 35–38, 49–50. For
the court at Schenectady, see *BGE*, II, 125, 139–140; *ARS*, II, 362; *Minutes of the
Executive Council*, I, 146. As late as 1676 the "customary practice" at Schenectady was
to provide the governor with a list of "suitable persons for the administration of the

Except in performing services as interpreters at Indian conferences or as ambassadors to the Iroquois, Schenectady's settlers had little occasion to act for or to have contact with the colony's English hierarchy. Those who did constituted but a handful of the village's population. During the seventeenth century they included not only persons of mixed Dutch and native descent such as Jacques Cornelissen van Slyck and his sister Hilletie, but also Cornelis Cornelissen Viele and his brother Arnout. By the early 1700s, Jan Baptist van Eps and Lourens Claesen Van der Volgen were similarly employed. In 1667 Governor Richard Nicolls spent two days at the village, and in 1687, at a time when a French attack was anticipated, Governor Thomas Dongan wintered at Albany and was briefly at Schenectady as well. Here he received proposals from the Five Nations presented to him by Jacques Cornelissen van Slyck and Daniel Jansen van Antwerpen. In the usual course, though, visits by the governor and his entourage were decidedly rare.[16]

The English conquest of 1664 and its aftermath had little impact on the day-to-day existence of the Schenectady inhabitants. Prohibitions against trade and restrictions on the export of grain affected the villagers' livelihood, but until the end of the seventeenth century there was little or no English presence at Schenectady, political, military, or otherwise. Occasionally, however, village affairs received the attention of the provincial authorities. During the 1670s, Cornelis Cornelissen Viele and Jacques Cornelissen van Slyck both contested for the privilege of tapping at Schenectady. Enough dissension was created for the case to become the concern of the governor and council. Similarly, in 1678 the governor's council was compelled to issue an order regarding "a dispute between Johannes Provost sheriff of Albany, and Ludovicus Cobet schout of Schenectady, about their

---

magistrates' office." The number of candidates would be greater (often double) the number of available positions. As had been typical in New Netherland before 1664, the governor would then select from among those persons whose names had been supplied to him. See *AP*, I, 425–426.

16. For the activities of the van Slycks and Vieles, as well as for Van der Volgen and van Eps, see *Calendar of Council Minutes*, III, 113, V, 165, VII, 91, 98, VIII, 61, 100, 101, 115, 128, IX, 164, 193, 267. For Governor Dongan's stay at Albany and his visit to Schenectady, see *Calendar*, V, 212, 220; *NYCD*, III, 477; *LIR*, 140–143. Governor Richard Nicolls was at Schenectady in October 1667. See *NYCD*, III, 162–163. During the 1690s, Governors Henry Sloughter and Benjamin Fletcher visited Schenectady, as did Governor Cornbury and Governor Robert Hunter in the first decades of the eighteenth century. *NYCD*, III, 779, 792, IV, 14, 21, 41, 222, 430, 993, V, 175.

jurisdiction." That same year, the council allowed for land opposite Schenectady to be set aside for the support of a minister. Privileges also were extended to individual community members. In 1673, because of losses she had suffered from fire, Arent van Curler's widow was granted the right to trade at the village, and in 1684 Johannes Sanders Glen successfully petitioned "that no one but himself be allowed to plow the Mohawks sachems' land."[17]

The daily lives of the majority of villagers were circumscribed more by the events of their own and nearby communities than by the actions of distant English officials. Except for those of the Glen, van Slyck, and Viele families, the names of most of the community's inhabitants were unknown beyond the boundary of the village and their circle of family, friends, and acquaintances. One individual who did succeed in transcending the confines of the Mohawk Valley community was Reyer Schermerhorn, the son of Jacob Jansen Schermerhorn of Albany. Schermerhorn moved to Schenectady after his 1676 marriage to Arriantje Bradt, the widow of Helmer Otten. He acquired a portion of Otten's property at the village, where he resided until his death in 1719. Between 1683 and 1685 he was Schenectady's representative to New York's first assembly as well as a member of several assemblies during the 1690s. Additionally, Schermerhorn was active providing supplies to the English troops at Schenectady and after 1699 was associated with Governor Bellomont in a project to produce naval stores from timber lands along the Mohawk River.[18]

At the outset of the eighteenth century, the English presence at Schenectady, although far from dominant, was the greatest it had yet been. Not only were there a garrison in residence and an additional dozen or more English families, the thread of English imperial and ecclesiastical influence now extended even more prominently into the Mohawk Valley. By 1712 a company of twenty men was situated at Fort Hunter near the Schoharie River. Also during these years, the Reverend Thomas Barclay made his greatest effort to Anglicize the

17. *Calendar of Council Minutes*, III, 182, V, 38. For affairs at Schenectady being brought to the attention of the governor and council, see *Calendar*, III, 91, 125, 182. Prohibitions on the export of grain were issued in 1671, 1672, 1673, 1675, and 1676. *Calendar*, III, 24, 51, 87, 104, 145.

18. For Reyer Schermerhorn, see *SP*, 135, 142–145. For his years in the assembly, see *ER*, II, 863; Patricia U. Bonomi, *A Factious People: Politics and Society in Colonial New York* (New York, 1971), 296–298; *Calendar of Council Minutes*, V, 1. For his wartime activities and involvement with Governor Bellomont, see *Calendar*, VIII, 71, 140; *NYCD*, IV, 785, 833.

village's religious and educational institutions. In the fall of 1710, at Albany, Barclay wrote of his accomplishments to the secretary of the Society for the Propagation of the Gospel in Foreign Parts:

> Att Schenectady I preach once a month, where there is a garrison of forty soldiers, besides about sixteen English and about one hundred Dutch families; they are all of them my constant hearers. I have this summer got an English school erected amongst them, and in a short time, I hope, their children will be fit for catechising. . . . In this village there has been no Dutch ministers these five years. . . . I have taken pains to show them the agreement of the articles of our church with theirs. I hope in some time to bring them not only to be constant hearers, but communicants.

Barclay's expectations were premature. Although he succeeded in establishing an Anglican congregation and church at Albany, the attentiveness of the Schenectady Dutch was due primarily to their village's being without a minister, a lack that was remedied in 1714 with the arrival of Dominie Thomas Brouwer.[19]

No Anglican church was founded at Schenectady until the mid-eighteenth century. During most of the period covered here, English settlers played only a secondary role in the community's civil and religious life. In large part the Dutch community was able to absorb these new arrivals. A 1697 census of households at Schenectady includes seven individuals of English descent. Five of these men are known to have married Dutch women, all widows, and a sixth married Lea, a Mohawk woman (and the widow of Claes Willemsen van Coppernol). Similarly, a 1719 assessment roll for the village includes the names of almost 130 heads of households but lists only a dozen individuals whose surnames betray their English origins. Nine of these men had not been at the village in 1697. Of these recent arrivals, at least three had married into Dutch families and their children were baptized at the Dutch Reformed church.[20]

19. *ER*, III, 1866–1867. For the establishment of Fort Hunter, see John W. Lydekker, *The Faithful Mohawks* (New York, 1938), 26–34; *NYCD*, V, 279–281. For Reverend Barclay at Albany, see George R. Howell and Jonathan Tenney, *History of the County of Albany, N.Y., from 1609 to 1886* (New York, 1886), 759; Balmer, *Perfect Babel*, 102. For Dominie Brouwer at Schenectady, see John J. Birch, *The Pioneering Church of the Mohawk Valley* (Schenectady, 1955), 45. For the erection of an Anglican church at Schenectady, see *ER*, V, 3736, VI, 3813.

20. For the 1697 census of Schenectady households, see *The Annals of Albany*, ed. Joel Munsell, 10 vols. (Albany, 1850–1859), IX, 88–89 (hereafter cited as *Annals*).

During the eighteenth century, the greater ethnic diversity of Schenectady's population was reflected in names recorded on tax lists, church documents, and other community records. But even during the seventeenth century the migration to New Netherland had included individuals from a variety of European locales. In fact, the first settlers at Fort Orange in the 1620s had been French-speaking Walloons from the southern Netherlands. Also, one of the early colonists at Rensselaerswyck was Jean Labatie, a Frenchman. Labatie was at Rensselaerswyck after 1637, where he traded with the Mohawks. His status with the tribe was such that in 1650, together with Arent van Curler, he was among several persons chosen to attend a conference at the Mohawk villages. Like the Scotsman Sander Leendertsen Glen and the Englishman Christoffel Davids, Labatie established himself within the Dutch community. Through his wife he was the uncle of Isaac Cornelissen Swits, who leased William Teller's farm at Schenectady in 1664. By 1669 Labatie himself was purchasing property at the village, although he never resided there.[21]

During this period, other Frenchmen filtered southward from Canada, including Anthony Lespinard and Jean Rosie, both of whom had established themselves at Albany by 1670. There is little evidence, however, that any Frenchmen permanently transplanted themselves to Schenectady, although by 1704 Philip Bosie was residing at the village. He may have been the son of Peter Bosie of Albany, who in

---

Information on the marriage patterns and family histories of the Englishmen who settled at Schenectady is contained in *FS*; *SP*, 82–230; Records of the First Reformed Church at Schenectady, N.Y., 1683–1852, 3 vols. New York State Library, Albany, I. For English settlers at Schenectady in the years after 1690, see Table 20; Schenectady Tax List, 1719, Schenectady County Historical Society, Schenectady. The continued adherence of Dutch New Yorkers to the Dutch Reformed church and the incorporation of English or French men married to Dutch women by that institution were phenomena that also occurred at New York City (at least before 1720). Joyce D. Goodfriend, "The Social Dimensions of Congregational Life in Colonial New York City," *WMQ*, 3d ser., 46 (1989), 252–278.

21. For Labatie, see *SP*, 125–127; *VRBM*, 813–814; *ERAR*, I, 459–460, 474, III, 267–268; *FOB*, I, 56; *LIR*, 144–146. Two articles that explore the ethnic diversity of New Netherland's population are Rink, "People of New Netherland," and Cohen, "How Dutch Were the Dutch of New Netherland?". Schenectady's early settlers included the Lutheran Bradt family from Norway and the Truax family of Walloon origins. Arent van Curler's wife, Anthonia Slachboom, may have been Danish. The ethnic makeup of the community during the eighteenth century may be gathered from local tax records. See, for example, the tax lists of 1705, 1708, 1719, 1738, 1751, and 1779. Livingston-Redmond Papers (microfilm), roll 10, New York State Library, Albany; Schenectady Tax List, 1738, New-York Historical Society, New York; Garret Y. Lansing Papers (microfilm), New York State Library, Albany; Schenectady Tax Lists, 1719 and 1751, Schenectady County Historical Society.

seventeenth-century documents was referred to as Peter the French-man. The English presence at Schenectady can be given some quan-titative expression in terms of the size of the garrison or counts of families such as that transmitted by Reverend Barclay. Unfortu-nately, the French presence must often be derived from more ob-scure references such as that found in the records of the Dutch Re-formed church in 1687 for an outlay of eight guilders for "a shirt for a captive Frenchman."[22]

Of the French traders and missionaries who visited Schenectady, best known today is Robert La Salle, who passed through the village in 1671 on his way to testify before the court at Albany. Other visi-tors included the Jesuit fathers Jean Pierron and Jacques Bruyas, who ministered to the Mohawks in the villages west of Schenectady. Both journeyed to Albany for supplies or to appear before the court, and the Dutch at Schenectady were responsible for providing horses for their return to the Mohawk country. In 1667 Governor Richard Nicolls suggested that he and Father Pierron might profit from a meeting at the village, but no conference took place. Over the years, however, a number of Frenchmen were aided by the Dutch in escap-ing from their Iroquois captors, and for this reason Arent van Curler and in later years the Glen family were known and respected in New France. In fact, in 1643, when he first saw the flats along the Mo-hawk River, van Curler had been on his way to treat with the Mo-hawks for the release of Father Isaac Jogues.[23]

More typical of the Frenchmen who arrived at Schenectady during these years was Matthys Boffie (Bovie), who in 1685 was charac-terized as "a vagrant fellow of no settled habitation." Indeed, the ma-jor French presence at both Schenectady and Albany was made up of such persons, who were attracted by the clandestine trading of furs. At least one Schenectady inhabitant, Cornelis Cornelissen Viele, is known to have employed a Frenchman named Jacques. This individ-ual may have been useful to Viele in running his tavern and in pro-moting contacts with the Indians and other coureurs de bois. Viele

22. For Lespinard, Rosie, and Bosie, see *ARS*, I, 32n, 42, 114, III, 87; *NYCD*, IV, 715; *FS*, 17. For the March 1687 reference to a French captive at Schenectady, see *Two-Hundredth Anniversary of the Dutch Church of Schenectady*, 183.

23. For La Salle and for Fathers Pierron and Bruyas, see *NYCD*, IV, 715, IX, 122–125, 127, XIII, 523–524; *JR*, LI, 219; Van Laer, ed., "Albany Notarial Papers, 1667–1687," 12; *ARS*, I, 14–15, 186, 256. For Governor Nicolls and Father Pierron, see *ER*, I, 590. For Arent van Curler, see Van Laer, ed., "Van Curler and His Historic Letter," 27–28; Van Laer, ed., "Documents," 31; *JR*, XXIV, 283, 297. François Her-tel was one of those rescued from the Iroquois in the 1660s. *NYCD*, III, 132.

had settled at Schenectady in 1667 and three years later his brother Pieter, together with another man, Elias van Gyseling, purchased a farm at the new community. Whether either Viele was fluent in French is not known, but it is likely since their mother, Marie du Trieux, was of Walloon descent. Certainly, van Gyseling spoke the language and may have been of assistance to the two brothers. The extent of Cornelis Viele's contacts with coureurs de bois is impossible to judge, but in 1683 he brought suit against Matthys Boffie and two other Frenchmen identified as Tardivett and Duplicee for payment of beaver skins owed him by the trio.[24]

The surviving evidence suggests a more intimate relationship between the French and the Dutch than between the Dutch and the English. Even so, Frenchmen who were at Schenectady occupied a marginal position within the community. Individuals and on occasion entire families journeyed southward from Canada and several Frenchmen were resident not only at Albany but at Schaghticoke and at Saratoga as well. Yet none is known to have resided at Schenectady on any long-term basis, and those who visited the village were accused of sedition, theft, Sabbath breaking, of fornication with slaves and seeking to entice them to escape to Canada.[25]

Frenchmen who aligned themselves with the Dutch and English were treated as renegades by the authorities in New France, and amid the growing tensions of the 1680s, they also found themselves distrusted within New York. Occasionally, an individual such as Anthony Lespinard sought to maintain a link between both worlds. An inhabitant of Albany since the 1670s, where he made a living as a baker, Lespinard continued to place his children with the Jesuits at Montreal for their instruction. Burgeoning imperial rivalry, however, constricted the fluidity of loyalty and opportunity characteristic of earlier years. In 1687 Lespinard was employed by the Albany magistrates to deliver notification of a treaty of neutrality between England and France to the French governor; by 1689, with renewed expectations of conflict and fear of Roman Catholicism among the Dutch

24. *ARS*, III, 527. For Viele, see *ARS*, III, 80–82; Kathlyne Knickerbacker Viele, *Viele Records*, 1613–1913 (New York, 1913), 13–18. For the seventeenth-century trade with Canada, see Norton, *Fur Trade in New York*, 121–126. For Viele's suit against Boffie, see *ARS*, III, 382, 393. For the Vieles and van Gyseling, see *SP*, 181–182, 207–211. The case continued into 1684. Schenectady Court Minutes, 1684.

25. For the French at Schaghticoke and Saratoga, see *ERAR*, II, 344; *ARS*, II, 48–49, 171. For French families at Albany and Schenectady and for complaints against the French, see *ARS*, III, 306, 310, 398.

Table 8. Number of slaves killed or captured at Schenectady, February 8, 1690, by owner

Owner	Number of slaves killed	Number of slaves captured
Jan van Eps[a]	1	
Douwe Aukes	1 (Francyn)	
Sweer Teunissen van Velsen[a]	4	
Hendrick Vrooman[a]	2	
Symon Schermerhorn	3	
Johannes Teller[b]		1
Myndert Wemp[a]		2
Barent Jansen van Ditmars[a]		1
Adam Vrooman		1
TOTAL	11	5

Source: *DHNY*, I, 304–306.
[a]Owner killed.
[b]Owner captured.

populace, he was subjected to detention and interrogation by these same officials.[26]

Presumably, most persons of European descent who came to Schenectady did so out of their own motivation. Such was not the case with the village's black population, whose arrival resulted either from their purchase by a Schenectady resident or from the relocation of a slave-owning household from Albany or Rensselaerswyck to the new community. Unfortunately, it is not possible to state accurately the number of black men, women, and children who lived at the village before 1714 (see Table 12). Moreover, not only is the slave population hard to identify statistically, the lives of these men and women are difficult to detail at a more personal level as well. Of those blacks who were at Schenectady on the night of February 8, 1690, the name of only one can be recalled today: among the eleven dead slaves was a woman, Francyn, owned by Douwe Aukes. Like small children, slaves were included among the count of killed or captured but were not named. Yet clearly they represented a significant segment of the

26. For Lespinard, see *ARS*, I, 171; *ERAR*, III, 593–594; *NYCD*, IX, 302; *DHNY*, II, 82, 83. In 1687 Lespinard and Jean Rosie journeyed from Albany to Canada. At Quebec they were jailed briefly by the French authorities. *DHNY*, I, 254–255. Fear of a French attack and of Roman Catholicism were important components of the support that Jacob Leisler received after 1689. Balmer, *Perfect Babel*, 31–32.

Schenectady population, amounting to over 18 percent of those persons killed or captured (Table 7).[27]

In three instances, masters and slaves met the same fate, dying at the hands of the French and Indians. Additionally, one individual, Johannes Teller, joined his slave as a captive journeying north to Canada. Existing evidence suggests that the sixteen slaves enumerated as killed or captured constituted the major part of those owned at the village not counting slaves at the Glen residence. Some slaves—those unable to travel—may have remained among the survivors. Moreover, because of heavy snows the French had determined to take only male prisoners, so female slaves may have been allowed to stay at the village. Assuming, however, that the French considered slaves an important part of their booty, it is likely that the five individuals taken captive represent the majority if not the totality of the slaves who remained alive.[28]

Black men, women, and children are known to have resided at the village in the years before the massacre, yet, one is left with the impression that on this night the population was predominantly male. Perhaps Francyn was an individual of some special stature within the community, but it is suggestive that her death is the only one recorded without the the asexual designation "Negro" or "Negroes." It seems likely that if other black women were killed, they also would have been identified by sex if not by name. Also, it may be coincidental, but all of the five slaves who are known to have survived the massacre and been taken captive were men or boys.[29]

As an institution, slavery was established in New Netherland long before the Schenectady settlement, the first slaves having been brought to Manhattan in 1626. At first, many of the colony's unfree

27. For the number of slaves at Schenectady the night of February 8, 1690, see *DHNY*, I, 304–306. For works that discuss slavery in New Netherland and New York during the seventeenth and eighteenth centuries, see Joyce D. Goodfriend, "Burghers and Blacks: The Evolution of a Slave Society at New Amsterdam," *NYH*, 59 (1978), 125–144; Morton Wagman, "Corporate Slavery in New Netherland," *Journal of Negro History*, 65 (1980), 34–42; Edgar J. McManus, *A History of Negro Slavery in New York* (Syracuse, 1966), 1–39; Joyce D. Goodfriend, "'Too Great a Mixture of Nations': The Development of New York City Society in the Seventeenth Century" (Ph.D. diss., University of California, Los Angeles, 1975); Kruger, "Born to Run."

28. For slaves and masters at Schenectady on February 8, 1690, see *DHNY*, I, 304–306. For the French decision to take only male captives, see Andros, *Andros Tracts*, III, 117.

29. In 1685, reference was made to the "Negroes and Negresses of Shinnechtady," indicating that a population of both male and female slaves resided at the village. *ARS*, III, 526.

blacks remained the property of the Dutch West India Company. A majority of the Company's slaves were located at New Amsterdam, but a few could also be found throughout the colony at Fort Orange and on both the Connecticut and Delaware rivers. Blacks were employed in construction work, as farm laborers, and even occasionally in military service against the Indians. Eventually the Company found it more profitable to lease its slaves to private individuals, Company officials, and to local governments. Not until the 1650s, however, did the private ownership of slaves become prevalent.[30]

Many slaves were acquired by the Dutch through the capture of Spanish and Portuguese prizes; others arrived in New Netherland after a period of labor in Brazil or Curaçao. With the loss of Brazil in 1654, the position of New Netherland in the Dutch slave trade was recalculated and the colony became an increasingly important market, both for the Company and for private traders. Between 1660 and 1664 at least four hundred slaves were delivered at New Amsterdam, mostly on the Company's account. Not surprisingly, a majority of slave owners were persons of some status, merchants and Company officials, but slaves also were held by tavern keepers, mariners, butchers, and other trades people. By 1664 slavery was a form of labor exploitation long familiar to the Dutch community. With the colony's conquest in that year and the adoption of the first English legal code in 1665, the so-called Duke's Laws, service for life was unhesitatingly incorporated into New York's legal system. Slavery prospered, and by the eighteenth century New York had a higher proportion of slaves than any other colony north of Delaware.[31]

Substantial evidence exists that by 1690 black slaves had been an important factor in Schenectady's demography, economy, and culture for many years. Included in Table 8 is a list of those persons who owned slaves in 1690, in Table 9 the evidence for slave owner-

30. Wagman, "Corporate Slavery," 35–37; A. Judd Northrup, *Slavery in New York, A Historical Sketch*, State Library Bulletin, History No. 4 (Albany, 1900), 246; Goodfriend, "Burghers and Blacks," 127, 131, 132. See also "Blacks in New Netherland and Colonial New York," proceedings of the sixth annual Rensselaerswyck Seminar, in *Journal of the Afro-American Historical and Genealogical Society*, 5 (1984). For the Dutch involvement in the African slave trade, see Kruger, "Born to Run," 34–35.

31. Goodfriend, "Burghers and Blacks," 128, 133–134, 138, 142, 144; Winthrop D. Jordan, *White over Black: American Attitudes toward the Negro, 1550–1812* (Baltimore, 1968), 84. Between 1620 and 1623 the Dutch imported over 15,000 slaves to work on sugar plantations in Brazil. Also, between 1623 and 1630 the Dutch captured more than 2,000 slaves from the Spanish. Northrup, *Slavery in New York*, 248. For the Dutch and English systems of slavery, see Kruger, "Born to Run," 19, 56, 70.

Table 9. Evidence of slave ownership at Schenectady before 1690

Owner	Date	Evidence
Anthonia Slachboom	1669	Bastiaen Pieters, "negro, residing with Juffrouw Curlers"[a]
	1676	slave Dina given her freedom in Juffrouw van Curler's will; slave Anna (who had a child) appraised in settlement of estate
William Teller	1676	owned a female slave
Sander Leendertsen Glen	1677	owned three slaves
Sweer Teunissen van Velsen	1678	bought a slave named Jacob
Claes Fredericksen van Petten	1682	bought a slave named Jan
Gerrit Bancker	1679	owned the slave Claes, who was found guilty of theft
	1683	complained that Douwe Aukes tapped "to his Negroes or slaves"
Reynier Schaats	1684	demanded that Douwe Aukes pay for use of his slave
Dominie Petrus Tesschenmaeker	1686	complained to Governor Denonville that two of his slaves had fled to New France

Sources: *NYCD*, III, 458; *ERAR*, II, 83, III, 447, 537; *ARS*, I, 94, 102, II, 137, 231–232, 429–444, III, 383; Schenectady Court Minutes, 1684; *AP*, I, 483–484.
[a]May have been a freed slave.

ship at Schenectady in the years before the French attack. At least fifteen individuals can be identified as possessing slaves at Schenectady during the years after 1661, a figure that represents nearly one-sixth of the heads of families known to have resided at the village prior to 1690. Moreover, in the years between 1667 and 1676 Anthonia Slachboom, the widow of Arent van Curler, also directed a household that included several slaves. Some individuals had been slave owners for many years. In 1677 Sander Leendertsen Glen had at least three slaves, but he was first identified as a slaveholder as early as 1652 when he owned a female slave. In 1678 Sweer Teunissen van Velsen purchased a twenty-four-year-old slave named Jacob. Twelve years later, van Velsen owned at least four slaves, who perished as he did.[32]

Slaves were bought like any other property, under the same terms and conditions as houses or horses. In 1678 Governor Edmund An-

32. For Schenectady's settlers before 1690, see *SP*, 82–230. For van Velsen and Glen as owners of slaves, see *ERAR*, II, 82–83, III, 446–447; *DHNY*, I, 304; *FOB*, I, 16. For Anthonia Slachboom, see *AP*, I, 483–484. The private ownership of slaves was not common in New Netherland until the 1650s. Goodfriend, "Burghers and Blacks," 134.

dros complained that throughout the colony there were "but few Servts, much wanted & but very few slaves." Possibly the demand for slaves accounted for their doubling in price during the two decades after Schenectady's settlement. In 1659 Jan Baptist van Rensselaer reported that slaves who had spent several years in the West Indies "and who for a year or two had always lived here with Dutch people have been sold . . . for 300 or 350 guilders." In 1678, however, when Sweer Teunissen van Velsen purchased a slave named Jacob, "aged about twenty-four years . . . hearty and sound," he paid one hundred "whole, salable beaver skins" worth eight guilders each. In 1684 the Frenchman Matthys Boffie offered sixty beavers for a female slave owned by one of Sander Leendertsen Glen's sons.[33]

For those who hesitated to purchase a slave outright, it also was possible to acquire one by lease. Arnout Cornelissen Viele did so in 1682 when he hired a young slave named Sara for three years. Viele's agreement with her owner, Johannes Clute of Albany, is an important document as it illustrates the type and number of duties expected of a female slave:

> Said Capt. Johannes Clute promises to fit out said negress with proper clothing, woolen as well as linen, stockings and shoes, and that said negress (now about nine and a half years old) shall serve out said term with said Aernout Cornelisz and his wife with all diligence and faithfulness . . . but if said Capt. Jan Clute has use for said negress one month every year in harvest time she shall serve him. . . . And Aernout Cornelisz promises to fit out said negress again at the end of the . . . term as well with woolen as linen, shoes and stockings . . . and Aernout Cornelisz . . . promises to exercise her in godly prayers and to bring her up in the fear of the Lord, likewise to teach her to sew, knit and spin according to her capacity.

If the agreement seems overly solicitous of Sara's welfare, one might contrast it with a mortgage and bond entered into by Clute two years

---

33. *DHNY*, I, 91; *CJVR*, 167; *ERAR*, III, 446–447. For Boffie, see *ARS*, III, 480–481. For examples of the sale of slaves at Albany, see *ERAR*, III, 446–447, 492, 493, 522–523, 537. In 1664 Jeremias van Rensselaer bought a male and a female slave for 400 and 350 guilders in beaver skins. *CJVR*, 365. Most slaves in New York probably came from the West Indies rather than directly from Africa. For this and for the increasing price of slaves from 1687 to 1720, see Goodfriend, "Burghers and Blacks," 143; McManus, *Negro Slavery in New York*, 28, 43. Additional information on the origins of slaves in New York is contained in Kruger, "Born to Run," 35, 40, 78.

later. For payment of a debt, Clute bound his house "and also specially my negroes, horses, cattle and other property."[34]

That slaves were considered as much a part of an estate as any
other property, and were subject to the same vagaries of disposal,
was made clear at the death of Anthonia Slachboom in 1676. William
Beekman of New York acted as administrator in the settlement of the
estate's debts. In 1677 he asked the court at Albany to rule on the
disposition of two female slaves. Beekman first requested that the
court "appoint two impartial men to appraise the negress Anna (without her child), as by mortgage dated December 1, 1676, she is bound
to Capt. Delavall." The court did so, and Beekman next petitioned
that it "render a decision regarding a negress called Dina, whom the
widow Corlaer in her will set free, namely, what is to be done in the
matter." The judgment of the court made clear that the interests of
the creditors and payment of the estate's debts came before the freedom of a slave.[35]

Slaves, both male and female, were used like any other bound labor, as messengers, cowherders, and as agricultural workers, particularly at harvest time. They provided a long-term work force to supplement the labors of family members, hired hands, and servants. In
fact, they may have acted in lieu of white servants. It is noteworthy
that, except for one young girl, all of those persons killed or captured
at Schenectady on February 8, 1690, can be identified as members of
an established village family, as soldiers, or as slaves—no servants are
mentioned in the existing records. Moreover, reconstruction of the
van Velsen household on that evening suggests that slaves lived in
close proximity to their masters (at least during the winter months).
Perishing together were Sweer Teunissen van Velsen, his wife, four
slaves, and "Antje Janz doughter of Jan Spoor." Antje Spoor was the
daughter of Jan Spoor of Albany. She was not related to the van
Velsens and may have been at Schenectady to care for Sweer Teunissen and his elderly wife.[36]

34. *ERAR*, II, 249, III, 545–546. See also Kruger, "Born to Run," 100.
35. *ARS*, II, 232. The breakup of slave families is noted in Kruger, "Born to Run,"
23.
36. *DHNY*, I, 304. In 1664 van Velsen had married the widow of his employer, Jan
Barentsen Wemp. *SP*, 192; *ERAR*, III, 285. In 1699 Governor Bellomont noted the
scarcity of white servants in New York and the use of slaves in their stead. McManus,
Negro Slavery in New York, 41–42. For the employment of slaves as messengers, as
cowherders, and in the harvest, see *CJVR*, 220; *FOB*, II, 217; *ERAR*, III, 545–546;
ARS, I, 102, II, 115, 439, III, 29; Kruger, "Born to Run," 41, 93, 97–101. The extent
to which slaves were hired out by their owners or self-employed is not known. In

Provided with similar clothing, dubbed with Dutch names, living in close proximity to their masters, superficially Schenectady's population of slaves may have seemed little more than black-skinned Dutch men or women. Yet one must question how assimilated they were into Dutch life and culture. Not only would racial prejudice and the difficulties of the Dutch language have proven stumbling blocks, it is possible that where blacks sought assimilation, for example, in the area of religion, they did so on their own terms and out of motives their masters could not condone. During the 1640s, it had been reported that the slaves of New Netherland contrasted favorably with the local Indian population in acquiring the tenets of the Dutch religion: "The Americans (Indians) come not yet to the right knowledge of God; but the negroes, living among the colonists, come nearer therto, and give better hope." However, a motive for such receptiveness was supplied by the minister at Brooklyn: "The negroes occasionally request, that we should baptize their children, but we have refused to do so . . . because of the worldly and perverse aims on the part of said negroes. They wanted nothing else than to deliver their children from bodily slavery, without striving for piety and christian virtues."[37]

That at least some owners were concerned for the religious upbringing of their slaves is clear from the agreement between Johannes Clute and Arnout Cornelissen Viele, but this may have been an extraordinary example. Both in the Netherlands and in the Dutch colonies, representatives of the Dutch Reformed church condoned the institution of slavery. Moreover, at Schenectady, formal indicators of religious practice, including church membership lists and marriage and baptism records, reveal an almost total lack of black participation. In over six decades, beginning in the 1690s, no slaves were married at the Dutch church, none became members of the congregation, and in only three instances were slave children baptized at the church (Table 12).[38]

1676, however, Anthonia Slachboom was ordered by the court at Albany to settle with several creditors. One debt in beavers and seawan was to be paid in full, "discounting three beavers earned by her Negress." *AP*, I, 484. Blacks suffered similar work-related injuries as whites, see *ARS*, II, 318. For the Spoor family of Albany, see Munsell, ed., *Collections*, IV, 167.

37. *ER*, I, 142, 548. For the prejudices of the Dutch, see McManus, *Negro Slavery in New York*, 18–19; *CJVR*, 255; *ARS*, II, 115. The latter citation also suggests that some slaves found, or pretended to find, the Dutch language difficult to master.

38. For Dutch ministers and slavery, see Goodfriend, "Burghers and Blacks," 131–

The extent to which blacks at Schenectady were intimate with the cultural and spiritual world of their masters is not known. Existing records suggest that, like the coureurs de bois who frequented the village, the black population occupied a position within but not fully a part of the community. Indeed, on several occasions reference was made to the sexual intimacy of French men and black women. In 1676 a slave belonging to William Teller accused Anthony Lespinard of fathering her child, a charge that was withdrawn on further questioning. One Frenchman who admitted to having an extended relationship with a slave woman was Matthys Boffie (Bovie), who was in the vicinity of Schenectady during the early 1680s. In 1684 Jacob Glen, Sander Leendertsen Glen's eldest son, informed the court at Albany that Boffie had threatened to poison his slave, Pey. Boffie admitted that he had slept with the woman for two years, had had "2 children by her and that he would like to buy her." He offered fifty or sixty beaver skins for the woman, threatening that, if Glen refused to sell her, he would "get a root out of the woods and break it in two and give the Negress one half and eat the other half myself and thus die before your door." Both Pey and another slave woman accused Boffie of encouraging Pey to escape to Canada with him. To their testimony was added that "of various Negroes and Negresses of Shinnechtady . . . in which they unanimously charge him with having employed every means to entice her to run away to Canada, saying that he would show her the way and make her free."[39]

Before the court, Pey and the other slaves claimed to have spurned Boffie's entreaties. Yet it may be that such testimony reflected only a desire to please their listening masters. Two years later, in 1686, Governor Denonville wrote to Governor Dongan: "One of your officers, the clergyman of Kannestaly (Schenectady), demands of me two

---

132. For the 1682 agreement between Clute and Viele, see *ERAR*, III, 545–546. In the 1680s Governor Thomas Dongan noted that slave owners in New York did little to further the conversion of their slaves. During both the Dutch and the English periods, the notion was prevalent that the conversion or baptism of a slave would effect the slave's emancipation. The legal marriage of slaves also was suspected of having the same result. Northrup, *Slavery in New York*, 250–251, 257, 280. Still, blacks were married and their children baptized at the Dutch Reformed church at New Amsterdam. Kruger, "Born to Run," 43–47.

39. *ARS*, III, 480, 526. For the accusation against Anthony Lespinard by William Teller's slave, see *ARS*, II, 137. Occasionally, reference was made to mulatto children. There seems to have been some sentiment against the sale of such children by their Dutch fathers. *ARS*, I, 254. For Boffie, see Munsell, ed., *Collections*, IV, 101. He later married a Barrois girl, the daughter of a French family resettled at Albany.

negro slaves who . . . he believes have come hither. I had them looked for every where. I assure you . . . should they turn up in the colony, that I will in good faith have them bound and manacled to be sent to you." Dominie Petrus Tesschenmaeker's slaves may have escaped to Canada, but not all of the blacks taken captive in 1690 looked on their journey northward as a march to freedom. Two Dutchmen who joined the Mohawks in trailing the retreating French and Indians reported that their party "would have overtaken them had they not been Spyed by some of ye Enemy Indians." These Indians had gone out "to looke for 2 negroe boys yt were Runn away from them." Presumably the boys were motivated by a desire to rejoin family and friends and to accept bondage among the Dutch as opposed to an unknown fate at the hands of the French and Indians.[40]

Short of flight, there were a variety of ways by which a slave could prove troublesome to his or her Dutch owner. In 1683 Gerrit Bancker entered a complaint against Douwe Aukes, "that the defendant taps to his Negroes or slaves and trades and bargains with them without their master's consent." Specifically, Bancker charged Aukes with buying "silver buttons from his Negro . . . thus trading with his slaves in such a way that he can not get a sight of his Negro, who hides himself, to the great detriment of the plaintiff." Bancker's protest was well founded, and Aukes promised not to have "any intercourse with Gert. Banker's Negro and never allow him to come into his house, nor sell him any drink."[41]

Although racial slavery was established in New Netherland as early as 1626, historians have debated the nature of that system. Slavery in New Netherland has been pictured as a haphazard and inconsistent institution, allowing blacks a degree of freedom which became increasingly constricted only after the advent of English rule. Gerrit Bancker's confession that he could not locate his slave, as well as the testimony of Pey that she had maintained a relationship with the Frenchman Matthys Boffie for over two years, suggests a surprising degree of autonomy in the behavior of at least some slaves at Schenectady. That there were boundaries beyond which one could not go, however, was made clear by the 1679 trial of Gerrit Bancker's slave Claes, and Jacob, the recently acquired slave of Sweer Teunissen van Velsen. Both were accused of theft. Claes was quickly arrested, but Jacob stole a horse, with which he was able to reach

40. *NYCD*, III, 458; *DHNY*, II, 163.
41. *ARS*, III, 383–384, 402.

Albany. There, with the help of a Mohawk Indian, he crossed the Hudson River. Traveling south, he obtained a canoe at Esopus and with that reached New York City before being apprehended.[42]

The case is important for what it reveals of the behavior and motivation of the slaves, their Dutch masters, and other persons who became involved, both black and white. Although Jacob was judged the primary culprit, he had been aided by Gerrit Bancker's slave Claes, as well as by Black Barent, who belonged to Dominie Gideon Schaats of Albany. The degree of contact which existed between the slave populations of Albany and Schenectady is difficult to assess, but Jacob had been purchased by Sweer Teunissen van Velsen at Albany, which also was Gerrit Bancker's residence. Meanwhile, Dominie Schaats's slave, Black Barent, most likely accompanied the minister to Schenectady on those occasions when he went there to preach. It was Black Barent who later testified that he came into possession of a silver thimble and a silver needle "from Jacob, the negro of Sweer Teunise, who ordered him to take them to Maritje Daeme, to have a pair of silver breeches buttons made for the said Jacob."[43]

Ultimately, both Claes and Black Barent were found guilty of theft and were condemned to receive twenty and thirty lashes respectively. Barent, "it being his third offence," also was to be "branded on his right cheek as an example to other rogues." The sentences were carried out as ordered by the Albany court, except that on petition of Dominie Schaats his slave was branded on the back rather than on the face. The following month van Velsen's slave Jacob was returned from New York to receive his punishment, thirty-eight lashes on the bare back, and van Velsen was obliged to pay the court for its costs in the case.[44]

Peter Wood and Gerald Mullin have examined the life experiences of blacks in colonial South Carolina and Virginia. The detail their studies provide of diet, clothing, work habits, and family relations is unfortunately lacking for the Schenectady slave community. More-

42. Under the Dutch system of slavery it was possible for some slaves to achieve their freedom. Most of the first slaves transported to New Netherland during the 1620s did so. Kruger, "Born to Run." For the slave Jacob's flight to New York and the resulting court case, see *ARS*, II, 429–444. Jacob could speak Dutch, English, and the Mohawk and Mahican languages. *AP*, III, 140–141.

43. *ARS*, II, 431. For van Velsen's purchase of Jacob at Albany, and for Dominie Schaats, see *ERAR*, III, 446–447; *ARS*, II, 36–37, 383.

44. *ARS*, II, 437. For the sentence imposed on the slave Jacob, see *ARS*, II, 443–444. For Bancker and Maritie Damen, see *FS*, 4–5, 221.

over, there are apparent differences between the southern slave societies and that of New York. During the colonial period, blacks accounted for 40 percent of the population of Virginia and 60 percent of South Carolina's inhabitants, but were only 14 percent of the population of New York even in the mid-1700s. New York also was a geographically extensive colony lacking the seaboard concentration of white and black population characteristic of Carolina and Virginia. Fewer in number and less concentrated in settlement, slaves in New York may have experienced more difficulty in maintaining cultural remnants of their African homeland. Nevertheless, the 1679 incident, with its testimony of petty thievery and the passage of stolen goods from Schenectady to Albany, reveals something of the half-hidden world of the New York slaves' existence and of their relations with their Dutch masters. It also suggests a desire to transform normally unobtainable objects from the world of their masters into symbols of status (silver buttons) within the slave community.[45]

The behavior of several members of the Dutch community involved in the theft case was also less than prudent. Most compromised was Maritie Damen, whose statements before the court were littered with denials and alterations of testimony. Eventually, she was forced to admit to having received a silver coin from Jacob "to have a pair of silver breeches buttons made of it." Jacob had heard that she was going to Albany, where there were silversmiths, and so made the request. Damen, who was Gerrit Bancker's mother-in-law, did not question Jacob as to the source of the coin and took it together with other pieces of silver given her by Black Barent, placing them in a small bag under her bed. Possibly Damen might have acted differently had she known that Bancker's slave Claes also was involved in the thefts, but she displayed no hesitation at receiving such suspicious articles from someone else's slave. The court found her actions so upsetting as to fine her one hundred guilders in seawan. But even the woman whose property was stolen was more interested in

---

45. Jordan, *White over Black*, 103; Gerald W. Mullin, *Flight and Rebellion: Slave Resistance in Eighteenth-Century Virginia* (New York, 1972); Peter H. Wood, *Black Majority: Negroes in Colonial South Carolina from 1670 through the Stono Rebellion* (New York, 1975). The records of the Albany Dutch Reformed church, during the period I cover in this book, contain only one reference to the burial of a black (in 1671). Hannay, comp., "Burial Records," 8. Two recent studies of slavery in colonial New York are Thomas J. Davis, *A Rumor of Revolt: The "Great Negro Plot" in Colonial New York* (New York, 1985) and Kruger, "Born to Run." Vivienne Kruger's work contains statistics on the number and distribution of slaves in New York and compares New York with other colonies. "Born to Run," 11–12, 17.

regaining her lost silver than in making an example of the slaves involved. Before the court she acknowledged that, suspecting the identity of the culprits, she had asked "the negroes to come to her house to hear what Claes would say and that she gave Barent, the negro, and Philip the Moor, each a piece of pancake." Finally, the greatest concern of Sweer Teunissen van Velsen was that his slave Jacob had absconded during the harvest season when his labor was most needed. Van Velsen requested that the court deal quickly with "his run-away negro . . . in case he be found guilty, to punish him as speedily as possible in order that he may have him home, as he needs him very much."[46]

The crimes of slaves at Schenectady included theft, running away, unsupervised drinking and trading, and fornication, but there was nothing so serious as at Albany, where in 1682 a slave cut the throats of two of his master's children and critically wounded a third person before fleeing up the Mohawk River. There he may have committed suicide, for his body was found several days later, and the sheriff was ordered "to commandeer some Negroes along the road and to bring the dead body of the murderer here [Albany] . . . in order that it may be hung as an example to others." This slave may have hoped to find refuge among the Iroquois. Whether it would have been accorded him is not known. In 1679 the slave Jacob had been aided in crossing the Hudson River by a Mohawk whom he met near Albany, but during that same decade, on one occasion, the tribe returned a slave who had escaped to their villages.[47]

Possibly some few blacks at Schenectady found freedom short of flight or death. Bastiaen Pieters, who lived with the widow van Curler, may have been a freed black. Pieters was complained against in 1669 for going to the Mohawks to warn them of the attack of the New England Indians. The court records described him as a "negro residing with Juffrouw Curlers." Pieters himself testified "that he went to the Maquas land by order of Juffrouw Curlers (whose servant he is)." The use of "residing with" rather than the possessive "belonging to" and particularly of the appellation "servant" and not "slave" suggests that Pieters had achieved some degree of liberation in his status.[48]

46. *ARS*, II, 433, 434, 439.

47. Ibid., III, 278. For the 1670 return of a slave to the Dutch by the Mohawks, see ibid., 291. The best recent study of white reaction to slave violence in New York is Davis, *Rumor of Revolt*.

48. *ARS*, I, 94, 102. The freeing of blacks by the Dutch is noted in Kruger, "Born to Run," 42, 52.

Before her death in 1676, Anthonia Slachboom had intended to free her slave Dina. Other Schenectady residents also made arrangements for the independence of their slaves. In 1691 Cathalyna de Vos entered into a marriage contract with Claes Jansen van Bockhoven of Albany. Mentioned in the document were five slaves, "the two negros named Sam and Jack, a negress named Isaabelle and also two children of said negress, the one named Sussanna and the other Rachel." It was agreed that "after the death of us both [they] shall have and enjoy their full freedom without any one's having power to burden them further with any servile labor . . . and if the aforesaid negress shall come to have any more children they shall likewise at the same time have their freedom." Indeed, in one instance a former slave may have acquired property near Schenectady. This individual, Philip the Moor, had, together with Claes and Black Barent, attended the interrogatory dinner at the time of the theft of silver in 1679. This is likely to be the same Philip Philipsen de Moor who in the 1680s and 1690s owned a farm of twenty morgens lying above Schenectady known as De Willigen [the Willows].[49]

The number of slaves who escaped death or capture or who belonged to Dutch families not at Schenectady on the night of February 8, 1690, must have been small. That several years later many of the inhabitants who survived the French attack owned few or no slaves suggests strongly that the sixteen blacks who can be enumerated in 1690 were, excluding those who belonged to the Glen family, the total complement of slaves then at the village. The arrival of slave owners such as Claes Jansen van Bockhoven, who removed to Schenectady from Albany after marrying Cathalyna de Vos, helped to restore the number of unfree blacks at the village. But in 1697 only fourteen slaves were present at Schenectady, including those owned by the Glen family. Two former slaveholders, Symon Schemerhorn and Johannes Teller, were either dead or not residing at the village. Of those who remained, Douwe Aukes now had no slaves, while Adam Vrooman owned a single slave, as he also seems to have done in 1690. The number of slaves owned by the Vrooman family had in fact declined since 1690, when between them Adam and his father, Hendrick, had possessed at least three. A similar decline in slave

49. *ERAR*, II, 404. For de Moor, see *ARS*, II, 432–433; *ERAR*, II, 355–356, 393–394, IV, 123; *SP*, 70, 137; *FS*, 141. Land ownership by blacks is discussed in Kruger, "Born to Run," 53, 55.

Table 10. Slave ownership at Schenectady, 1690 compared with 1697

February 8, 1690		June 16, 1697	
Slaveholder	Number owned	Slaveholder	Number owned
Johannes Glen	?	Johannes Glen	2
Sander Glen^c	?	Abraham Groot (married widow of Sander Glen)	3
Douwe Aukes	1	Douwe Aukes	0
Sweer Teunissen van Velsen^a	4		
Myndert Wemp^a	2	Barent Wemp (brother of Myndert)	1
Hendrick Vrooman^a	2		
Adam Vrooman	1	Adam Vrooman	1
Jan van Eps^a	1	Jan Baptist van Eps (son of Jan van Eps)	0
Symon Schermerhorn^c	3		
Johannes Teller^bd	1		
Barent Jansen van Ditmars^a (second husband of Cathalyna de Vos)	1	Claes Jansen van Bockhoven (third husband of Cathalyna de Vos)	5
		Harmanus Vedder (married widow of Andries Bradt)	1
		the widow Makelyk^e	1

Sources: *DHNY*, I, 304–306; *FS*; *Annals*, IX, 81–89.
^aKilled February 8, 1690.
^bTaken captive by the French and Indians.
^cDead by 1697.
^dResiding at Albany in 1697.
^eWidow of Pieter Adriaensen van Woggelum.

ownership affected the van Velsen, Wemp, and van Eps families. In 1690 Sweer Teunissen van Velsen and his stepson Myndert Wemp owned at least six slaves. In 1697 Barent Wemp, Myndert's surviving brother, had only one. Jan Baptist van Eps owned no slaves, whereas his father had possessed at least one at the time of the massacre.[50]

In 1690, including Johannes and Sander Glen, eleven Schenectady residents, members of eight separate families, possessed a minimum

50. For slave ownership at Schenectady in 1690 and 1697, see *Annals*, IX, 88–89, *DHNY*, I, 304–306. The ownership of small numbers of blacks was characteristic of slavery in New Netherland and New York. Kruger, "Born to Run," 20.

of sixteen slaves (Table 10). In 1697 seven individuals owned four-teen. Only two persons who possessed slaves at Schenectady in 1690 continued to do so seven years later. These individuals (Johannes Glen and Adam Vrooman) were joined by Barent Wemp, who had succeeded his slain brother and stepfather as an owner of human property. Additionally, several persons who had not owned slaves in 1690 now did so. They included Abraham Groot and Harmanus Vedder, who came from established Schenectady families, but who were unmarried and too young to be slave owners in 1690. Claes Jansen van Bockhoven and the widow of Pieter Adriaensen van Woggelum (one of Schenectady's original proprietors) also now resided at the village. Van Bockhoven's five slaves and Juffrouw van Woggelum's one slave accounted for almost half of the blacks then at Schenectady. There was thus both a lack of continuity in individual slave ownership and a reduction in the number of slaves altogether between 1690 and 1697.[51]

The reduced number of slaves and slaveholders at Schenectady re-flected the fortunes of Albany County's inhabitants as a whole in the years after 1690. In 1689 the county's white population numbered 2,016 persons. By 1698 more than one-quarter of the county's resi-dents, had departed, died, or been taken prisoner by the French and Indians, leaving but 1,476 persons both white and black (see Appen-dix at end of chapter). During the next decade and a half, the free and unfree populations of Albany County again rose until 1714, when 3,329 persons were listed in that year's census. By this date, blacks were again an important part of the county's population, amounting to 13.7 percent of the total. Equally significant, however, was the fact that the population of slaves was not evenly distributed among the county's several communities. While unfree blacks consti-tuted 13.7 percent of the total county inhabitants, they made up 7.4 percent of those persons living at Schenectady and a slightly larger 9.9 percent of the Albany population. But at Rensselaerswyck a sharply higher proportion—29.7 percent of the manor's population—was recorded.[52]

51. For Barent Wemp, see *FS*, 289. For van Bockhoven, see *ERAR*, II, 404; *ARS*, III, 303.

52. For Albany County's population of slaves between 1689 and 1714, see *DHNY*, I, 689–690, III, 905; *Annals*, IX, 88–89. For the increase in New York's slave popula-tion after 1698, see McManus, *Negro Slavery in New York*, 24–26, 42. The statistics for slaveholding in Albany County correspond to those elsewhere in the colony. Kruger, "Born to Run," 11–12.

Table 11. White and slave populations of Albany, Schenectady, and Rensselaerswyck in 1714, by sex and age group

| | Whites | | | | | | Slaves | | | | |
| | Males | | | Females | | | Males | | Females | | |
	Over 60	16–60	Under 16	Over 60	16–60	Under 16	Over 16	Under 16	Over 16	Under 16	TOTAL
Albany											
1st ward	3	102	117	4	122	104	9	14	22	13	510
2nd ward	4	75	54	7	81	61	3	5	12	4	306
3rd ward	10	62	68	6	82	61	6	10	6	9	320
TOTAL	17	239	239	17	285	226	18	29	40	26	1,136
Schenectady	12	110	154	13	107	151	7	10	19	8	591
Rensselaerswyck	11	112	123	5	93	83	73	41	36	31	608
Albany County	54	688	753	49	676	651	155	98	122	83	3,329

Source: DHNY, III, 905.

Examination of the age and sex profiles of the three slave populations presents the most striking differences among them and suggests
a significant contrast in the internal economies of Schenectady and
Albany as compared with Rensselaerswyck (Table 11). Rensselaerswyck's labor requirements demanded a mature force of male workers
capable of sustained effort particularly at the time of harvest. Schenectady, too, was primarily an agricultural community, but, the resources of the van Rensselaer family appear to have been such that
they could supplement the labor supplied by their tenants with the
addition of black slaves. Among the manor's white population there
was a greater number of males sixteen or older than females, and
within the black community the difference was even more dramatic.
There were twice as many mature male slaves as female (73 to 36),
and women and children under the age of sixteen constituted less
than two-thirds of the total slave population. Just the reverse was the
case at Schenectady and Albany. At Albany there were twice as
many mature female slaves as male; at Schenectady the ratio approached three to one. At both communities women and children
under the age of sixteen constituted the same proportion of the total
slave population—a commanding 84 percent. There being such a
large number of women and children and so few mature males, at
Schenectady and Albany individual slaves may have been employed
as much for domestic chores and as servants as for farmwork and as
craftsmen. Finally, it is possible that the disproportionate number of
women and children at Schenectady reflected a population of unfree
blacks which was being replenished by means of natural increase
rather than through the purchase of additional slaves.[53]

Throughout this period there seems to have been a complete disregard for the proprieties of marriage for slave couples on the part of
their Dutch owners. The 1691 marriage contract between Claes Jan-

53. For the 1714 population of Albany, Schenectady, and Rensselaerswyck, see
DHNY, III, 905. An unbalanced sex ratio among adult slaves was common in New
York, as was a high percentage of dependent individuals (children and the elderly)
among the slave population as a whole. Kruger, "Born to Run," 22, 101–102. For
slave populations elsewhere in early America, see Russell R. Menard, "The Maryland
Slave Population, 1658 to 1730: A Demographic Profile of Blacks in Four Counties,"
WMQ, 3d ser., 32 (1975), 29–54; Allan Kulikoff, "A 'Prolifick' People: Black Popula-
tion Growth in the Chesapeake Colonies, 1700–1790," *Southern Studies*, 16 (1977),
391–428; Allan Kulikoff, "The Origins of Afro-American Society in Tidewater
Maryland and Virginia, 1700 to 1790," *WMQ*, 3d ser., 35 (1978), 226–259; Jean
Butenhoff Lee, "The Problem of Slave Community in the Eighteenth-Century Chesa-
peake," *WMQ*, 3d ser., 43 (1986), 333–361.

Table 12. Schenectady church records documenting ceremonies for Indians and slaves, 1694–1760

	Indians[a]			Slaves	
Year	Baptisms	Marriages	Year	Baptisms	Marriages
1698	3		1708	1	
1700	30		1758	1	
1701	47	13	1760	1	
1702	13	2			
1703	10				
1704	9	3			
1705	4				
1707	3				
1711	10				
1712	23	1			
1732	1				
1733	1				
1737	1				
1746	3				
1747	5				
1748	1				
1749	3				
1750	1				
1751	1				
1753	1				
1756	4				
1758	1				
1759	4				
1760	1				

Source: Records of the First Reformed Church at Schenectady.
[a]The same individual may be listed under more than one category.

sen van Bockhoven and Cathalyna de Vos mentioned five individuals: "the two negros named Sam and Jack, a negress named Isaabelle and also two children of said negress . . . Sussanna and . . . Rachel." These may have been the same five slaves owned by van Bockhoven in 1697. In any case, there was no acknowledgement of a familial bond between either Sam or Jack and Isaabelle and her two daughters. The girls were listed simply as the "two children of said negress." Similarly, in 1677, when William Beekman acted as administrator for the estate of Anthonia Slachboom, he asked the court at Albany to appoint "two impartial men to appraise the negress Anna (without her child)." There was no suggestion that Anna was then living with the child's father. The records of the Dutch Reformed church at Schenectady present no instance of a marriage between slaves at the village during any of the years of this study. In fact, the only evidence of a slave couple who may have gained recognition as living together as husband and wife comes from the October 1708 baptism of Volkje, the daughter of Susanna and Symon, a slave owned by the Glen family (Table 12).[54]

Even had their Dutch owners exhibited a greater concern for legitimizing the family relations of Schenectady's adult slaves, the imbalance in the ratio of men to women at the village and throughout Albany County evident in the 1714 census figures would have severely limited the opportunities of blacks to join together as husbands and wives. Moreover, the short-term evidence suggests no dramatic alteration in the ratio of male and female slaves. By 1723 Albany County's population was 6,501—almost double what it had been a decade earlier. The white population had expanded 98 percent, from 2,871 to 5,693 persons. The slave population climbed, but more slowly, from a figure of 458 in 1714 to 808 in 1723, an increase of 76 percent. (As a percentage of the county's total inhabitants the slave population was actually reduced from 13.7 to 12.4 percent.) Even with the overall increase in numbers, there was no correction in the imbalance between unfree men and women. One can surmise that in 1723 as in 1714 Schenectady's slave community accounted for less than 10 percent of the village's total population and that a majority of the slaves were women and children.[55]

By 1723 the slave population of Albany County may have included more than just black men and women. For the first time the census of that year classified the unfree as "Negroes and other Slaves." It is not certain, but the additional slaves may have been male Indians shipped northward from the Carolinas. In 1708 the unfree population of South Carolina amounted to 2,900 African and 1,400 Indian slaves. The Indians had been garnered by means of alliances between the Carolinians and coastal tribes who were armed by the whites and rewarded for raiding weaker interior groups. Because of the problem

---

54. *ERAR*, II, 404; *ARS*, II, 232. Examples of slave mothers and children living with unrelated black men could be found elsewhere in the colony. For this and for further discussion of slave marriages and families, see, Kruger, "Born to Run," chaps. 4 and 7. For the 1708 baptism, see Records of the First Reformed Church at Schenectady, I, 172.

55. For the censuses of 1714 and 1723, see *DHNY*, I, 693, III, 905. For Indians held as slaves in New York, see Kruger, "Born to Run," 71–72, 332.

of preventing captured Indians from escaping or rebelling, by the second decade of the eighteenth century hundreds of male Indian slaves were being shipped out of South Carolina to the West Indies and to New York and the New England colonies. This exportation would account for the reclassification of the slave population of Albany County, and it may also explain what appears to be an increase of adult male slaves in the county as a whole. In 1714, for Albany County in its entirety, there was a rough correspondence of mature male and female slaves. Women amounted to 44 percent and men 56 percent of the slaves over the age of sixteen. The 1723 categories were not age specific; adult slaves were listed simply as "Men" and "Women." Within these groupings there were 307 males and 200 females. Without age specification, by this classification female slaves accounted for only 39 percent of the adult population, while males were 61 percent of the total.[56]

The possibility that by the 1720s Indians were being held as slaves within Albany County marks a dramatic contrast with the situation of the seventeenth century. In 1683 Jonathan Bull of Connecticut arrived at Albany with two Indian servants. Both quickly ran away and Bull's attempts to retrieve them from the Indians at Schaghticoke by whom they were harbored were unsuccessful. The court at Albany could do no more than recommend that the two Indians be returned. Finally, Bull accepted an arrangement by which "the Indians living at Skachkook . . . would give him 30 beavers for the two Indians." In recording the incident, the court minutes simply stated that Bull "was not allowed to take them away by force, because all Indians here are free."[57]

---

56. *DHNY*, I, 693, III, 905. For New York's slave trade after 1700, see James G. Lyndon, "New York and the Slave Trade, 1700 to 1714," *WMQ*, 3d ser., 35 (1978), 375–394. For the Indian slave trade in the Carolinas, see Nash, *Red, White, and Black*, 113–114. For the enslavement of Indians in New Netherland and New York, see Almon W. Lauber, *Indian Slavery in Colonial Times within the Present Limits of the United States* (Williamstown, Mass., 1970), 112–115, 193. In 1702 a duty of fifteen shillings was placed on every black or Indian slave imported into the colony. This was the first act to mention Indian slaves. *Colonial Laws of New York*, I, 484. In 1708 Governor Cornbury informed the Lords of Trade of the execution of an Indian slave and three black slaves who had murdered their owner and his family. *NYCD*, V, 39. At Albany in 1693 the Iroquois referred to slaves they owned, but it is not clear if these were blacks or other Indians. Northrup, *Slavery in New York*, 259. For Indian slavery elsewhere in early America, see James Leitch Wright, *The Only Land They Knew: The Tragic Story of the American Indians in the Old South* (New York, 1981).

57. *ARS*, III, 367.

The recognition of native autonomy tendered by the Albany court illustrates what, according to Gary Nash, "can be regarded as a kind of litmus test of the balance of power between the two cultures." In New Netherland and New York, during the seventeenth century, Indian-white relations in the Hudson-Mohawk region took place within a framework of peace and regard for tribal sovereignty. It was a relationship that, as detailed by Allen Trelease, both sides valued: "The two races regarded each other less often as corn thieves, trespassers, or Indian givers than as sources of economic prosperity; what they thought of each other personally was beside the point."[58]

Throughout these years Albany remained the locale for the formal handling of Indian affairs—economic and diplomatic. Except for Reyer Schermerhorn, no one from Schenectady served as a member of the Albany-based Commissioners of Indian Affairs and only rarely was the community the site of a full-fledged Indian conference such as the one that occurred in July 1702 between the Mohawks and Governor Cornbury. Yet during both the seventeenth and the early eighteenth centuries, a number of Schenectady's inhabitants emerged as essential intermediaries in the machinery of Indian affairs as interpreters and provincial emissaries. One of the most active in the first half of the eighteenth century was Lourens Claesen Van der Volgen. Captured by the French in 1690, he returned from Canada nine years later having acquired fluency in the Iroquois language. Until his death in about 1740, Van der Volgen was employed as a provincial interpreter among the Five Nations. Details of his activities can be gained from the minutes of conferences such as that held between Governor Robert Hunter and the Iroquois at Schenectady in 1710. It was recorded that "the Interpreter Lawrence Clace being come from ye Sinnekes Country & ye rest of ye 5 Nations westward, doth relate to his Excelly Robt Hunter . . . what has occurred to him among sd Indians in ye 3 months that he has been from Albany." Undertaken during a time of war, Van der Volgen's mission had strategic significance, but it also included an important commercial component. Ever since the 1680s, attempts had been made to tap the peltry supplies of the tribes to the west of the Iroquois. Van der Volgen had been "sent

58. Nash, *Red, White, and Black,* 97, 106; Trelease, *Indian Affairs,* 115. To a large degree, Indian-white relations in the Hudson-Mohawk region during the seventeenth century corresponded to the situation in New France, where, according to William Eccles, the French colony "had divided sovereignty, French and Indian." Quoted in Nash, *Red, White, and Black,* 107.

to ye five Nations to watch ye motions of ye French & to perswade those Indians to give free passage to ye farr Indians through their Country to Come here to Albany to trade."[59]

Van der Volgen's labors were complemented by those of another former captive, Jan Baptist van Eps. In 1701 both were granted land above Schenectady by the Mohawks. Most often dispatched individually to the Iroquois, at times they worked together, as in 1713 when Hendrick Hansen of Albany "assisted by Capt. John Bleker and Lowrens Clasen" journeyed to Onondaga. At Schenectady they encountered van Eps, who accompanied them when they departed the village the following morning ("he had also with him his wife and some [namely, two] Cayuga lads"). Such travelers often went by horse; Arent van Curler had done so in 1643 when he sought the release of Father Isaac Jogues from the Mohawks and so had Arnout Cornelissen Viele in 1684 when he journeyed as far as the Senecas. Indeed, the French envied the ease with which the Dutch and English could penetrate the Iroquois country in this manner.[60]

By the end of the seventeenth century it was common for such envoys to remain among the tribes for some time. In February 1699, for example, Jan Baptist van Eps received instructions from Governor Bellomont to wait "at Onnondage to watch the motion of the said Indians that they send no body to Canada, nor receive any messengers from thence." Similarly, Lourens Claesen Van der Volgen had

59. *NYCD*, V, 217–218. For Cornbury's 1702 conference, see *NYCD*, IV, 994. For Van der Volgen, see *SP*, 174–175. For the Commissioners of Indian Affairs, see Norton, *Fur Trade in New York*, 73–82; Edgar A. Werner, *Civil List and Constitutional History of the Colony and State of New York* (Albany, 1888), 181.

60. *NYCD*, V, 372. In 1682, according to Jacob Glen, Arnout Viele estimated that a journey to the "Seneca country" would take twenty days. *CMVR*, 72. Cadwallader Colden noted that it was equally possible to contemplate a water passage through the heart of the Five Nations by way of the Mohawk River "to the Carrying-place . . . which runs into the Oneida Lake. . . . From thence they go with the Current down the Onondaga River to the Cataracui Lake [Lake Ontario]. The Distance between Albany and the Cataracui Lake (this Way) is nearly the same . . . with that between Monreal and the Cataracui Lake, and the Passage much easier." Cadwallader Colden, *The History of the Five Indian Nations*, 2 vols. (New York, 1902), II, 44–45. The party led by van Eps left Schenectady on September 12, 1713. His wife, Helena Glen, may have just given birth to the couple's sixth child (Jan Baptist van Eps), who was baptized at Schenectady on September 27. *FS*, 221–222. For the 1701 grant to van Eps and Van der Volgen, see *Calendar of Council Minutes*, VIII, 265. For travel by horse, see Van Laer, ed., "Van Curler and His Historic Letter," 27; *JR*, XXIV, 283, *LIR*, 81; *NYCD*, IX, 257. In 1685 a Canadian correspondent noted, "It is quite easy to go from Manatte and Orange to Lake Ontario on horseback, the distance being only one hundred leagues through a beautiful country." *NYCD*, IX, 282.

spent three months with the Iroquois before meeting with Governor Hunter. Van der Volgen and van Eps were most active in these ventures, but they were not alone. As an agent for Governor Bellomont, Reyer Schermerhorn visited the Mohawks to gain permission for the felling of timber for the production of naval stores. Most adventuresome of all was Arnout Cornelissen Viele. Between 1692 and 1694, Viele was on the Ohio and Wabash rivers trading with the Shawnees and Miamis.[61]

Ease of access meant not only that Schenectady's inhabitants visited the Iroquois villages but that even more frequently Indians journeyed to the Dutch community. Schenectady lay across the long-established trail between the Hudson and Mohawk rivers, a route traveled by the Iroquois on their way to trade at Albany. In August 1665, for example, four hundred Mohawks and Oneidas were at Albany and a contingent of Onondagas was expected shortly. Often these same Indians lingered at Schenectady, although their presence was not always welcome. In 1687 it was reported that "70 Maquase" were "ly[ing] still at Shennectady and doing nothing." Most distracting was the prevalence of drink among such warriors. Mayor Pieter Schuyler of Albany complained to Governor Dongan, "We find that the selling of strong Liquor to the Indians is a great hinderance to all designs they take in hand, [they s]tay a drinking continually at Shinectady."[62]

During the years of war after 1690, even greater numbers of Indians were, on occasion, at the village. In August 1692 almost 350 Iroquois were encamped there in preparation for departure against the French. The presence of several dozen, much less several hundred, Iroquois must have had a dramatic impact on daily life at Schenectady, for as late as 1697 only 238 persons, white and black, were living at the village, and it is doubtful if the pre-massacre population had been much larger (certainly, far fewer persons were in residence during the first decade of settlement). During the summer trading months, the village must have hosted large numbers of Indians passing to and from Albany. In fact, there was some native presence year round; we know that on the night of February 8, 1690, at least twenty

61. *NYCD*, IV, 497. For Van der Volgen, see *NYCD*, V, 217–218. For Reyer Schermerhorn, see *ER*, II, 1303; *Calendar of Council Minutes*, VIII, 282. For Viele's journey to the Ohio, see Broshar, "First Push Westward," 239–240.

62. *NYCD*, III, 479, 481. For the 1665 count of Indians, see *CJVR*, 381. In 1688 Edward Randolph reported that two hundred Indians were at Albany and others were at Schenectady. Randolph, *Letters and Papers*, VI, 262.

Mohawks were at the village. Indeed, the appearance of Indians at Dutch dwellings must have been routine. In 1683, at Albany, a Mohawk warrior was accused of attempting to kill a Dutch boy. Court testimony revealed that they had both been sleeping in the same house. Among those questioned in the case were several Indian women then in residence at William Teller's Albany home. Such intimacy worried at least one commentator, who argued that the opening of the fur trade to private individuals had "produced . . . too much familiarity with the Indians. . . . For, not satisfied with merely taking [the Indians] into their houses in the customary manner, they attracted them by extraordinary attention, such as admitting them to Table, laying napkins before them, presenting Wine to them."[63]

The Iroquois presence provided both additional defense for the exposed Schenectady community and support for the clandestine trade in furs. Throughout the seventeenth century, the exchange of beaver and other skins remained the staple element of Dutch-Indian relations. During the eighteenth century, however, some of Schenectady's settlers ventured into Iroquois territory for purposes other than trade. As an associate of Governor Bellomont, Reyer Schermerhorn sought agreement by the Iroquois for the use of Mohawk Valley timber in the production of naval stores. Several members of the Schenectady community also were engaged to promote the English imperial presence among the Five Nations. In 1711 five Schenectady carpenters signed an indenture with Governor Robert Hunter by which they agreed to "Build two forts in the Indians Country," repairing first "into the Moehoques Country and there Build a ffort . . . att Each Corner a Block house . . . And also a Chaple." Similar structures were to be erected among the Onondagas, but only the first were completed, to become known as Fort Hunter and Queen Anne's chapel. Finally, the Schenectady Dutch provided services needed by the Iroquois at their villages. On one occasion the Senecas

---

63. *NYCD*, I, 182. For Indians at Schenectady the night of the French attack as well as in 1692, see *LIR*, 162; *DHNY*, I, 301. For Schenectady's 1697 population, see *Annals*, IX, 88–89. In 1658 information was provided to the Beverwyck court regarding the actions of one individual who, at his dwelling, gave drinks to "two savages who were lodging there and sat by the fire." *FOB*, II, 100. At Albany during the 1670s, there were attempts to establish a greater segregation of whites and Indians. Ordinances were passed against giving lodging to any natives "except some old sachems." The evidence from the 1683 trial of the Mohawk for attempted murder suggests that such regulations were poorly enforced. *ARS*, I, 303, III, 331–332. The map of the fort at Schenectady drawn during the 1690s by the Reverend John Miller depicts huts erected for the accommodation of visiting Indians. *SP*, 311.

asked for two men from Schenectady, "a Smith and an Armourer," to come and live among them.[64]

In assessing the native peoples who surrounded them, the Dutch most frequently resorted to comparing Indian institutions with their own, with invariably negative results. One commentator found, for example, that "traces, and nothing more, of the institution of marriage can be perceived among them. The man and woman unite together without any special ceremony." The physical appearance of the natives alone must have given pause to some Dutch; one Indian accused of a crime at Albany was described as having "the mark of a dog on the right cheek, two stripes on the chin and long hair." Not looks, however, but behavior was most condemned. During the 1620s, Dominie Jonas Michaëlius characterized the Indians at Manhattan "as thievish and treacherous as they are tall; and in cruelty they are altogether inhuman, more than barbarous, far exceeding the Africans." Even a sympathetic minister such as Johannes Megapolënsis anticipated only "the conversion of the heathens or Indians here." This would be achieved when "by the numbers and power of our people, they are reduced to some sort of civilization."[65]

Evidence from Schenectady suggests that the Dutch not only abused the Indians with whom they traded but also directed hostility against those persons of mixed blood domiciled among them. Cornelis Anthonisz van Slyck was a carpenter and mason who settled at Rensselaerswyck as early as 1634. In 1646 he received a patent for land at Catskill from Governor William Kieft, a reward for services

64. *NYCD*, V, 279–280, 867. The five Schenectady carpenters were Gerrit Symonsen Veeder, Barent and Hendrick Vrooman, John Wemp, and Arent van Petten. The two men requested by the Seneca were Joseph van Sice and Hendrick Wemp. In 1722 Wemp's brother, Myndert, also was working among the Seneca as a smith. *NYCD*, V, 718, 719; *FS*, 290.

65. *NYCD*, I, 282; *ARS*, III, 333; *ER*, I, 56–57; *NNN*, 309. The Dutch compared the Indians of New Netherland to "Brazilians" and "Gipsies." One account stated, "Thus these savages resemble the Italians, being very revengeful." *NYCD.*, I, 281; *NNN*, 213. See also Charles T. Gehring and Robert S. Grumet, "Observations of the Indians from Jasper Danckaerts's Journal, 1679–1680," *WMQ*, 3d ser., 44 (1987), 104–120. A broader perspective on Indian society and culture as perceived by Europeans in North America is provided by the following works: Karen Ordhal Kupperman, *Settling with The Indians: The Meeting of English and Indian Cultures in America, 1580–1640* (Totawa, N.J., 1980); James Axtell, *The Invasion Within: The Contest of Cultures in Colonial North America* (New York, 1985); Robert F. Berkhofer, Jr., *The White Man's Indian: Images of the American Indian from Columbus to the Present* (New York, 1978). For the Native American perception of Europeans, see Cornelis J. Jaenen, "Amerindian Views of French Culture in the Seventeenth Century," *CHR*, 55 (1974), 261–291.

rendered in concluding a peace between the Dutch and Indians. Four years later, together with Arent van Curler, he was chosen to act as an ambassador to the Mohawks. By this date van Slyck already had begun a liaison with a Mohawk woman which was to produce at least three children. The oldest, Martin Cornelissen, witnessed the July 1661 deed between Arent van Curler and the Mohawks. Together with Jan Barentsen Wemp, Martin acquired land at Schenectady, property that passed to his younger brother, Jacques Cornelissen, on Martin's death. Jacques married a Dutch woman, Gerritje Ryckman, and they were joined at Schenectady by his sister Hilletie, who married another proprietor, Pieter Danielsen van Olinda.[66]

Children of a Dutch father and a Mohawk mother, brother and sister occupied a strategic position among the Dutch, English, and Iroquois, and both became trusted interpreters for the province. That they were also uncomfortably perched between two worlds was revealed by an extraordinary conversation that Jasper Danckaerts had with Hilletie van Olinda. While at Schenectady in 1680, Danckaerts was introduced to "a certain Indian woman, or half-breed, that is, from a European and Indian woman." She had been brought up among the Mohawks with whom her mother remained, but Danckaerts determined "that she was a Christian, that is, had left the Indians, and had been taught by the Christians and baptized; that she had made profession of the reformed religion, and was not of the unjust."[67]

Although Cornelius van Slyck's marriage to their Mohawk mother was never formalized by a minister of the Dutch Reformed church, both Jacques and Hilletie were able to reside among and marry within the Dutch community. In this, Dutch experience in New Netherland paralleled that of their fellow countrymen in the East Indies, where the Dutch settlers seldom wed the Asian women who bore them children but did not hesitate to marry the Eurasian offspring of such liaisons. At Schenectady, however, as Hilletie explained to Jasper Danckaerts, she found herself an object of scorn among both the native and the white communities. As a young woman, she would visit the Dutch villages with her mother to trade, but at her decision to leave the Mohawks to go live among the Dutch, "her mother . . . began to hate her. . . . Her brothers and sisters

---

66. *VRBM*, 809; *SP*, 11–12; *ER*, III, 188, 222–223; *FS*, 229.
67. *JD*, 201–202. See also Richter, "Cultural Brokers and Intercultural Politics," 40–67; Hagedorn, "'A Friend to Go between Them.'"

despised and cursed her, threw stones at her, and did her all the wrong they could." By the Dutch she was taught "to read and write and do various handiwork." She mastered the New Testament and "she made her profession, and was baptized." To Danckaerts, however, she expressed her disappointment: "How many times . . . have I grieved over these Christians, not daring to speak out my heart to any one, for when I would sometimes rebuke them a little for their evil lives, drunkenness, and foul and godless language, they would immediately say: 'Well, how is this, there is a sow converted. Run, boys, to the brewer's, and bring some swill for a converted sow,' words which went through my heart, made me sorrowful and closed my mouth."[68]

During Kieft's War in the 1640s, Indians attacked near New Amsterdam denounced the Dutch for killing their own children. The degree to which sexual relations occurred between Dutch men and Iroquois women, however, is not known. Kiliaen van Rensselaer had warned his settlers not "to mix with the heathen . . . women, for such things are a great abomination to the Lord God and kill the souls of . . . Christians." In 1652 the ban was renewed during the patroonship of Jeremias van Rensselaer, but such prohibitions failed to prevent Cornelis van Slyck from maintaining an extended liaison with a Mohawk woman. They also had little impact on the behavior of Schenectady's founder, Arent van Curler, who, although married to Anthonia Slachboom, had fathered a daughter who continued to live among the Mohawks.[69]

Van Curler's daughter was not the only individual of mixed European-Indian descent who resided among the Mohawks. Hilletie van Slyck stayed with her mother for some years before marrying Pieter Danielsen van Olinda and settling at Schenectady. Best known of the half-breeds who lived out their lives among the Mohawks was Canaqueese, who as early as 1653 was mentioned in Dutch records as "a savage who is much beloved by the Maquas." The *Jesuit Relation* a year later was more explicit, stating that he was the "son of an Iroquois mother and a Dutch Father." Canaqueese was entrusted with missions of importance by both the Mohawks and the Dutch. In July 1654 he arrived at Quebec to voice the opposition of the Mohawks to

68. *JD*, 203–204. Hilletie van Olinda was stated to have been the convert of Dominie Godfridus Dellius of Albany. *NYCD*, IV, 364. For the Dutch in Asia, see Boxer, *Dutch Seaborne Empire*, 223–229.

69. *VRBM*, 442. For the 1652 ban, see *ER*, I, 310. For van Curler's daughter, see *ARS*, II, 86. For the Indians attacked by the Dutch in the 1640s, see *NNN*, 231.

an economic and diplomatic alliance recently negotiated between the French and the other Iroquois. Canaqueese also was employed by the Beverwyck court to deliver messages to the governor of New France. For much of 1666 he was in Canada, where the French were reported to have "used him kindly and clad him well." Finally, during 1666–1667, it was Canaqueese who acted as the envoy of the French governor, Tracy, in his negotiations with the Mohawks and Oneidas and as a courier bearing the correspondence that preceded Arent van Curler's summer journey to Canada.[70]

The effect of such intimacy with the Indians on the character and behavior of the Dutch at Albany and Schenectady was gauged by Jasper Danckaerts during his visit in 1680. In April, journeying by boat from New York City to Albany, Danckaerts noted of his fellow passengers that "As these people live in the interior of the country . . . they are more wild and untamed, reckless, unrestrained, haughty, and more addicted to . . . cursing and swearing." A half century earlier Dominie Jonas Michaëlius had written of the Indians: "As to the natives of this country, I find them entirely savage and wild, strangers to all decency, . . . uncivil and . . . proficient in all wickedness and godlessness." There is a striking correspondence between Michaëlius's description of "the natives of this country" and that offered by Danckaerts of those Dutch who lived "in the interior of the country." Newly arrived from the Netherlands, Danckaerts clearly perceived a distinction between himself and those persons who had long resided within the upper reaches of the colony. It was a perception shared by a number of River Indians whom Danckaerts and his traveling companion, Pieter Sluyter, encountered on a visit to the falls at Cohoes. En route, "there were some families of Indians living. Seeing us, they said to each other, 'Look these are certainly real Dutchmen, actual Hollanders.'" Asked how they could be certain, the Indians replied, "We see it . . . in their faces and in their dress." As the Indians at Cohoes discerned, after seventy years of trade and settlement, there had indeed come to be a difference between the transplanted Netherlanders they knew and "real Dutchmen, actual Hollanders." Danckaerts himself may have supplied a key to the distinction with his observation that it was the people of

---

70. *FOB*, I, 91; *JR*, XLI, 85; Pynchon, *Letters*, 72. For Canaqueese, see Pynchon, 71; Grassmann, *Mohawk Indians*, 154; Grassman "Flemish Bastard," 307–308. *JR*, L, 209. For his role as a courier to and for van Curler, see *NYCD*, III, 147, 151, 152.

the interior who lived "somewhat nearer the Indians." Of all the seventeenth-century Dutch communities, the nearest was Schenectady.[71]

Until the eighteenth century, Indian affairs at Schenectady were in the hands of laymen—traders, interpreters, and half-breeds such as the van Slycks. Only after the arrival of Dominie Bernardus Freeman in 1700 was there any sustained effort to bring a Christian influence to bear on the surrounding natives. New Netherland had been founded as a colony of traders and settlers with little religious vision or motivation. Seventeenth-century Dutch attempts to convert the native population were meager both in effort and effect. Most active of the early ministers was Dominie Johannes Megapolensis, who for several years in the 1640s served at Rensselaerswyck. During his term at the colony he sought to preach to the Mohawks, but the necessity of learning their language hindered his efforts. Even more discouraging was the attitude of the Indians themselves, "When we pray they laugh at us. Some of them despise it . . . and some . . . stand astonished." Megapolensis departed for New Amsterdam in 1649, leaving no record of having converted even one Indian. His successor, Gideon Schaats, arrived at Rensselaerswyck three years later with instructions to "bring up both the Heathens and their children in the Christian Religion." There is little evidence that he ever did so.[72]

No minister was established at Schenectady until the arrival of Petrus Tesschenmaeker in the 1680s. Like Schaats, who had now removed to Albany, Tesschenmaeker initially gave little concern to the spiritual welfare of the natives. During these same years, however, Jesuits such as Father Jacques Bruyas succeeded in baptizing nu-

---

71. *ER*, I, 56; *JD*, 196, 200. For a general discussion of the impact of Indian culture on Europeans, see Axtell, *European and Indian*, chap. 10. Gary Nash has commented on the process of "transculturation between Indians and Europeans." He notes that in most instances authors discuss the "Europeanization of Indians" rather than the "Indianization of whites." According to Nash, the latter phenomena occurred only when white colonists were captured or ran away to Indian settlements. Nash, *Red, White, and Black*, 283–285. Schenectady and Albany, however, were communities where whites and Indians lived together, traded with each other, slept in the same rooms, and ate at the same table. It is difficult to imagine that the cultural, personal, and biological impacts of these relationships ran only in one direction. For this reason, the comments of the Indians at Cohoes as well as those of the Dutch traveler Jasper Danckaerts strike me as enlightening and useful.

72. *NNN*, 177–178; O'Callaghan, *History of New Netherland*, II, 567. See Megapolensis's "Short Account of the Mohawk Indians" in *NNN*, 168–180. For Megapolensis and Schaats, see Trelease, *Indian Affairs*, 169–170; *ER*, I, 326–327.

merous Mohawks, particularly in the village nearest to Schenectady. Whether Dutch efforts in this direction would have produced similar results cannot be said. The impression left by Jasper Danckaerts was that the community at Schenectady offered little ground for missionary work. A half-breed such a Hilletie van Olinda who did convert met scorn and slights. Even less concern was expressed for the conversion of those Indians who visited the village or who resided only a few miles to the west. Hilletie, for example, had a "nephew, a full-blooded Mohawk, named Wouter. The Lord has also touched him, through her instrumentality." Like Hilletie, Wouter too was taunted and ostracized: "He has betaken himself entirely to the Christians and dresses like them. He has suffered much from the other Indians and his friends." At Schenectady, Wouter lived with his uncle, Jacques Cornelissen van Slyck. According to Danckaerts, van Slyck valued his nephew's services as a trapper so highly that he not only failed to encourage Wouter's conversion but actively hindered him in this design: "His uncle, with whom he lived, was covetous, and kept him only because he was profitable to him in hunting beaver. He therefore would hardly speak a word of Dutch to him, in order that he might not be able to leave him too soon, and go among the Christians and under Christianity."[73]

Until the end of the 1600s, the most impressive efforts at conversion remained those of the French Jesuits, and the Mohawks were still their most receptive audience. During the last decade of the seventeenth century, however, Dutch ministers such as Dominie Godfridus Dellius of Albany also exhibited a growing missionary concern. By 1698 Dellius and another minister, Johannes Petrus Nucella, were baptizing Indians at Schenectady. Even greater progress was made after the arrival of Dominie Bernardus Freeman. Yet the foundation for Freeman's efforts appears to have been laid almost a decade earlier. Just before his death in 1690 Dominie Tesschenmaeker had begun ministering to the natives. Accounts of his activities, however,

---

73. For Dominie Tesschenmaeker, see Balmer, *Perfect Babel*, 22–24. For Danckaerts's description of Schenectady, see, *JD*, 205–206. For Father Bruyas's activities among the Mohawks, see *JR*, LVII, 89–93. For an evaluation of the work of the Jesuits among the eastern tribes, see Axtell, *European and Indian*, 69–72. For the missionary efforts of the Dutch compared with the French, see Frederick J. Zwierlein, *Religion in New Netherland: A History of the Development of the Religious Conditions in the Province of New Netherland, 1623–1664* (Rochester, 1910), 266–316. As late as 1660, there were only six Dutch ministers in New Netherland and only one (Dominie Schaats) at Beverwyck. *DHNY*, III, 109–110.

included the admission that he was "the first who ha[d] taken upon himself at his own expense, and of his own motion and out of pure love, the troublesome labor of converting the heathen."[74]

During 1691, reports forwarded to King William III explained that, with the outbreak of war, the Jesuit missionaries had left the Mohawk villages and that since their departure "the Dutch Minister at Albany hath been very successfull in converting many of them to the true religion." The minister referred to was Dominie Godfridus Dellius. That same year "the praying Indians of the . . . Maquass" informed Governor Henry Sloughter that they were "extreamly obliged" for the restoration of the dominie to them. Dellius himself notified the Classis of Amsterdam of his efforts. He had translated "several prayers, the Ten Commandments, the Creed, and eight or ten Psalms . . . into the language of the Indians."[75]

Dominie Bernardus Freeman, who was installed at Schenectady in 1700, also was expected to preach to the Iroquois. More fluent in the Mohawk language than Dominie Dellius, Freeman was an instant success. By 1701 the Mohawks claimed to "have now two Castles that are begun to pray or turn Christians." Yet, the most definitive index of Dominie Freeman's progress among the tribe was the record of baptisms and marriages at the Dutch church at Schenectady (see Table 12). These same figures, however, also demonstrate clearly the coincidence of Indian baptisms and marriages with Freeman's pastorate. As early as 1702 Freeman was petitioning the governor for permission to move elsewhere. With his departure in mid-1705, the number of baptisms declined dramatically and, except for one instance, no further Indian marriages were recorded at the Dutch Reformed church. Only briefly, in 1711 and 1712, did the level of baptisms approach the numbers current during Dominie Freeman's tenure. In 1710 the Anglican minister, Thomas Barclay, presented a

74. *ER*, II, 1003. Regarding Tesschenmaeker's efforts among the natives, after 1690 it was reported that "his taking off grieves also the very heathen; for during the past year his Reverence made it his duty to instruct them and . . . he had already incorporated quite a number, after public confession and baptism, in the church, much to the astonishment of everybody." *ER*, II, 1003. For Dellius and Nucella at Schenectady, see Records of the First Reformed Church at Schenectady, I.

75. *ER*, II, 1103; *NYCD*, III, 771, 799. In 1694 Pieter Schuyler recorded: "We went from Schinnechtadij, and arrived yt day to ye Praying Maquase Castle called Tionondoroge." *NYCD*, IV, 81. Not all of the Mohawks were happy with these developments. Grassmann, *Mohawk Indians*, 294. To compensate for his language difficulties, Dominie Dellius used Hilletie van Olinda as his assistant. *NYCD*, IV, 566.

disheartening picture of the condition of the Praying Indians: "The Indians have no ministers; there are about thirty communicants, and of the Dutch church, but so ignorant and scandalous, that they can scarce be reputed Christians." But the influence of Dominie Freeman lingered on: "The sachems of the five nations . . . desired . . . that Mr. Freeman, present minister of the Dutch congregation of Flatbush, near New York, be one of those two missionaries which the queen promised to send them."[76]

Although Dominie Freeman did not return, within a year both a fort and an Anglican chapel were constructed among the Mohawks. This initial movement of an English imperial and ecclesiastical presence into the Mohawk Valley was followed, during the 1720s, by the establishment of Oswego on Lake Ontario as a center for the fur trade. By this date the Iroquois had already begun to lose their aboriginal sovereignty and strength. As early as the 1630s, smallpox had reduced the Mohawks' population and the trade wars of the 1640s and after took a particularly heavy toll on the male members of Iroquois society. In 1666 and again in 1693, the Mohawks were besieged by invading French armies. During the 1660s the tribe may have had as many as 500 warriors. By 1698, however, at the end of King William's War, this figure had been reduced to 110. Although the Mohawks compensated for their declining military fortunes by the use of their diplomatic talents, it proved increasingly difficult for the tribe to maintain either its territorial or its cultural hegemony. The nearness of colonial settlements, the impact of disease, the desire for European-made luxuries that had now become necessities, and the alliances by which the Mohawks were alternately forced to embrace or play off colonial governments all took their toll. Reduced in numbers and military power, they could no longer withstand the movement of settlers into their lands. In 1724 the Mohawks were reported to live, "but forty Miles directly west from Albany, and within the English Settlements, some of the English Farms upon the same River being thirty Miles further West."[77]

---

76. *DHNY*, III, 898–899; *NYCD*, IV, 906. For Dominie Freeman's fluency in the Indian language and for his arrival at and eventual departure from Schenectady, see *NYCD*, V, 227; *ER*, III, 1471–1472, 1476, 1532–1543, 1596, 1607, 1623–1635; Birch, *Pioneering Church*, 35–39.

77. Colden, *History*, II, 15–16. For the reduced status of the Iroquois and other Indians, see Axtell, *European and Indian*, 83; Elisabeth Tooker, "The League of the Iroquois: Its History, Politics, and Ritual," in *HNAIN*, 421. By the 1630s smallpox already was reducing the Mohawk population. *HMVDB*, 4. For the Mohawks in the

The activities of the French Jesuits and Dutch dominies presaged the physical and cultural penetration of Iroquois society evident by the eighteenth century. According to James Axtell, "all the European missionary societies, Protestant and Catholic, began and with few exceptions ended their American efforts with the belief that it was necessary to 'civilize Savages before they can be converted to Christianity.'" Names, clothing, marriage ceremonies, hairstyles, even burial practices were altered to the white man's pattern as a prelude to acceptance of the white man's religion. This was the "dilemma of civilization" which confronted Hilletie van Olinda, Wouter, and the other Mohawk converts during the 1600s and early 1700s. Their attempted assimilation into white culture often proved unsatisfactory. At the end of the eighteenth century, in response to the continued deterioration of their native culture, other Iroquois would embrace a different response—not assimilation but the preservation and revitalization of Indian ways. Both the half-breed Jacques Cornelissen van Slyck and his sister Hilletie, however, were to live out their lives among the Mohawk Valley Dutch. As for Wouter, he departed Schenectady in 1680, intending to rendezvous with Jasper Danckaerts at Boston and to journey to the Netherlands. His fate is not known.[78]

Situated on the northern frontier of New Netherland and New York, between 1661 and 1710 the community at Schenectady was simultaneously both a point of beginning and an end. Within New York, it marked the terminus for settlement, trade, and agriculture. To the west were the villages of the Iroquois, to the north the settlements of New France. Yet such racial, political, and cultural boundaries as existed were permeable, and Schenectady quickly emerged as

---

later seventeenth century, see Daniel K. Richter, "War and Culture: The Iroquois Experience," *WMQ*, 3d ser., 40 (1983), 537–538, 542–543, 545–547, 551. As early as 1686 the charter granted to Albany by Governor Thomas Dongan gave the city control of land near the future site of Fort Hunter. *Colonial Laws of New York*, I, 199.

78. Axtell, *European and Indian*, 44; Wallace, *Death and Rebirth of the Seneca*, 202–208. Some of the most graphic descriptions of the Iroquois in the eighteenth century are contained in the *Moravian Journals Relating to Central New York, 1745–66*, ed. William M. Beauchamp (Syracuse, 1916). For the alteration that occurred in Indian culture as a result of contact with Europeans, see Axtell, *European and Indian*, chap. 3, and James Axtell, "The Ethnohistory of Early America: A Review Essay," *WMQ*, 3d ser., 35 (1978), 120–144. Also excellent is Wallace, *Death and Rebirth of the Seneca*. For the Iroquois adaptation to their declining military fortunes, see Richard Aquila, *The Iroquois Restoration: Iroquois Diplomacy on the Colonial Frontier, 1701–1754* (Detroit, 1983); Richard L. Haan, "The Covenant Chain: Iroquois Diplomacy on the Niagara Frontier, 1697–1730" (Ph.D. diss., University of California, Santa Barbara, 1976); Richter, "Cultural Brokers," 40–67.

a locale for economic exchange and cross-cultural contact. The village's inhabitants, white and black, arrived seeking opportunity, to provide defense, or (in the case of blacks) to be exploited. The resulting mixture of peoples produced a community whose inhabitants clearly reflected the heterogeneous population that made New York unique among England's North American colonies.

Appendix. The Population of Albany County, 1689–1698

The following population count exists for Albany County in 1689:[79]

Whites			Slaves	Total
Men	Women	Children		
662	340	1,014	—	2,016

There exist, however, two counts of Albany County's population in 1697 and 1698:

	Whites			Slaves	Total
	Men	Women	Children		
1697	382	272	805	—	1,459
1698	380	270	803	23	1,476

These figures may be in error. In 1697 there were 14 slaves at Schenectady. It would be surprising if only 9 more slaves were to be found in all of Albany County a year later. The figures for the decline in the county's population between 1689 ad 1697 are also questionable. There are 557 fewer persons indicated in the census for Albany County in 1697 than in 1689:

	Men	Women	Children
Departed	142	68	209
Taken prisoner	16		
Killed	84		
Died	38		
TOTAL	280	68	209

Two problems exist with these figures. There is no count of the slaves who may have left the county with their owners or of those slaves who remained but who died, were killed, or were taken prisoner between 1689 and 1697. Second, even for the white population, the enumeration is incomplete and does not reflect the number of women or children killed at Schenectady in 1690.

79. *DHNY,* I, 689–690; *Annals,* IX, 88–89.

5

A Divided Community

The attack against Schenectady in 1690 occurred at a moment of provincial political division, confirming rumors of a French invasion and heightening the fear of Roman Catholicism among the Dutch colonists. The community's destruction was quickly seized on by both the supporters and the foes of Jacob Leisler to demonstrate the malicious folly of their opponents. Robert Livingston, the Albany city clerk, provided Sir Edmund Andros with an account of the massacre which laid full blame for the tragedy squarely on the Leislerians: "The people of that Towne . . . would not obey any of ye Magistrates neither would they entertain ye souldiers sent thither by yt Convention of all; nothing but men sent from Leysler would do theire turn. Thus had Leysler perperted yt poor people by his seditious letters now founde all bloody upon Skinnechtady streets, with the notions of a free trade, boalting &c. and thus they are destroyed." In his correspondence, Jacob Leisler cast similar responsibility back on his enemies: "It is such newes as we feared long since, Alase what could there be expected of a certane number of rebellious people that remained ruling under that arbitrary Commissione of sir Edmund at Albany." Moreover, word of the killings provided Leisler with an opportunity to move against opponents at New York City and throughout the colony. Realizing his vulnerability, Livingston quit Albany for Connecticut in March 1690, ostensibly to search for aid from the New England governments against further attacks by the French and their Indians.[1]

---

1. *DHNY*, I, 309–310, II, 184. The attack at Schenectady confirmed the Leislerians' fear of a French invasion and of Roman Catholicism. Balmer, *Perfect Babel*, 31–32. After the Schenectady massacre, Jacob Leisler wrote: "Att the first

Undeterred by Livingston's departure, Leisler's agents at Albany gathered evidence of his misdeeds, including "the Minutes and other Books & papers &c. belonging to this City and the County of Albany." Since they could find registers dating only to December 1685, they also forwarded "six sworn affidavits against the aforesaid Livingston in behalf of his majesty [James II]." Among those who provided testimony were Reyer Schermerhorn and his brother, Symon, as well as their brother-in-law, Myndert Harmensen Van den Bogaert. Additionally, Reyer Schermerhorn was chosen one of "2 proper persons to consult & conclude at New York concerning his Majesty's interest in this conjuncture." In combination with Myndert Wemp, David Christoffelsen, Johannes Pootman, Reynier Schaats, and Douwe Aukes, Schermerhorn had contested for authority at the village with the established magistrates in the weeks just before the Schenectady massacre. Reyer Schermerhorn, however, was, and would remain, a central figure in the events of Leisler's Rebellion and its divisive aftermath at Schenectady.[2]

Historians of early New York long presumed that the uprising initiated by the New York City militia and controlled by Jacob Leisler was an event that focused most significantly on New York and the adjacent areas of Long Island and Westchester County. More recently, Leisler's Rebellion has been portrayed as the result of Anglo-Dutch ethnic hostility and economic competition that developed during the decades before 1689. In addition, the revolt is recognized as having initiated a period of extended political factionalism, although most analysts conclude that provincial dissension dissipated shortly after the arrival of Governor Robert Hunter in 1710.[3]

---

hearing of the sd newes I immediately made an alarum and . . . imprisoned about 40 commissioned officers by sir Edmund." *DHNY*, II, 185. For Robert Livingston, see *DHNY*, II, 174–177; *Narratives of the Insurrections*, 338; Kim, *Landlord and Tenant*, 50–51; Lawrence H. Leder, *Robert Livingston, 1654–1728, and the Politics of Colonial New York* (Chapel Hill, N.C., 1961), chap. 4. Livingston was among those persons at Albany who were most active in obstructing the armed force headed by Jacob Milborne and dispatched by Leisler in the fall of 1689.

2. *DHNY*, II, 205. Seven persons testified against Livingston. *DHNY*, II, 206–210. For Van den Bogaert, see *FS*, 159, 214. Leisler's agents at Albany included Johannes de Bruyn, Johannes Prevoost, and Jacob Milborne. *DHNY*, II, 191. For the Schenectady magistrates and those commissioned by Leisler, see *DHNY*, II, 98, 149, 350.

3. For Leisler's Rebellion, see Kim, *Landlord and Tenant*, chap. 2; Lawrence H. Leder, "The Politics of Upheaval in New York, 1689–1709," *NYHSQ*, 44 (1960), 413–427; Thomas J. Archdeacon, "The Age of Leisler—New York City, 1689–1710: A Social and Demographic Interpretation," in *Aspects of Early New York Society and Poli-*

An examination of the events at Schenectady, however, compels a reassessment of these conclusions. In total, the evidence suggests that Leisler's Rebellion was not solely a New York City–based phenomenon and that, at least for the frontier, farming community at Schenectady, the consequences were divisive and enduring. The events surrounding Leisler's Rebellion crystallized dissension within the community and established a lasting pattern for dispute. The issue of land ownership and acquisition was fundamental. The conflict was played out, though, not between a constellation of English and Dutch antagonists but rather between groups of "ins" and "outs," first settlers and later arrivals seeking access to the one resource that mattered—land.[4]

For the period 1689–1691 the political allegiance of only twenty-one persons can be determined, but, this number represents members of almost half of the households known to have been established at Schenectady in 1690. Those persons who aligned themselves with the anti-Leislerian party included surviving village proprietors such as William Teller, Gerrit Bancker, Jacques Cornelissen van Slyck, and Pieter Danielsen van Olinda, as well as the sons of proprietors such as the Glen brothers, Sander and Johannes Sanders Glen. Alternately, the Leislerians impress one as a group of men somewhat younger than their opponents—individuals who had arrived at Schenectady after its initial decade of settlement or under circumstances less favorable than their rivals (Table 13). Douwe Aukes, David Christoffelsen, Reynier Schaats, and Reyer Schermerhorn must all be counted among those persons who settled at the village after 1670. Of the others, Claes Fredericksen van Petten, Isaac Cor-

tics, ed. Jacob Judd and Irwin H. Polishook (Tarrytown, 1974), 63–82; Thomas J. Archdeacon, *New York City, 1664–1710: Conquest and Change* (Ithaca, 1976); Bonomi, *Factious People*, 75–81; Jerome R. Reich, *Leisler's Rebellion: A Study of Democracy in New York, 1664–1720* (Chicago, 1953); David S. Lovejoy, *The Glorious Revolution in America* (New York, 1972); Voorhees, "'In behalf of the true Protestants religion.'" Coinciding with the three-hundredth anniversary of Leisler's Rebellion, several articles on the subject characterize the personalities and events surrounding the rebellion and its aftermath: Randall Balmer, "Traitors and Papists: The Religious Dimensions of Leisler's Rebellion," *NYH*, 70 (1989), 341–372; Donna Merwick, "Being Dutch: An Interpretation of Why Jacob Leisler Died," *NYH*, 70 (1989), 373–404; Thomas E. Burke, Jr., "Leisler's Rebellion at Schenectady, New York, 1689–1710," *NYH*, 70 (1989), 405–430; Adrian Howe, "The Bayard Treason Trial: Dramatizing Anglo-Dutch Politics in Early Eighteenth-Century New York City," *WMQ*, 3d ser., 47 (1990), 57–89.

4. In his study of religion and the Dutch church in early New York, Randall Balmer notes the divisions which existed within the Dutch community during the Leisler years. Balmer, *Perfect Babel*, 33–34.

Table 13. Opponents and supporters of Jacob Leisler at Schenectady

Opponents

Name	Age in 1689	Evidence of political allegiance
Gerrit Bancker[a]	?	Supporter of Albany Convention
William Teller[a]	69	"
Johannes Appel	?	Held office under Albany Convention
Johannes Sanders Glen	41	Schenectady magistrate and backer of Albany Convention
Sander Glen, Jr.	42	"
Jan van Eps	?	"
Sweer Teunissen van Velsen	?	"
Jacques Cornelissen van Slyck	49	Aided Albany Convention with Indian affairs
Adam Vrooman	40	Rejected letter from Jacob Milborne
Pieter Danielsen van Olinda	?	Wife Hilletie later rewarded by Governor Fletcher

Supporters

Name	Age in 1689	Evidence of political allegiance
Symon Schermerhorn	31	Testified against Robert Livingston
Reyer Schermerhorn	37	Received commission from Leisler
Myndert Wemp	40	"
Douwe Aukes	50	"
David Christoffelsen	39[b]	"
Johannes Pootman	44	"
Claes Fredericksen van Petten	48	"
Barent Wemp	33	"
Isaac Cornelissen Swits	45	"
Arnout Viele	50	"
Reynier Schaats	?	"

Sources: For ages, see *NYCD*, IV, 352; *DHNY*, II, 206–208; *ERAR*, III, 115, 284, 268, 372; *SP*, 85, 102, 185; Viele, *Viele Records*, 19. For political allegiance, see *DHNY*, II, 94, 99, 111, 112, 137–139, 143–144, 149, 207, 314, 350, 353.

[a]Bancker and Teller resided at Albany but are included here as Schenectady proprietors.

[b]Christoffelsen's father arrived at Beverwyck in 1650 and subsequently married. His mother died in 1657. Christoffelsen would have been at most 39 years old in 1689.

nelissen Swits, and Johannes Pootman were residents of the village during the 1660s. Van Petten and Swits, however, arrived as the tenant farmers of William Teller, whereas Johannes Pootman reached the village as the indentured servant of another proprietor, Philip Hendricksen Brouwer.[5]

Recent studies of Leisler's Rebellion focus prominently on New York City and emphasize the class and ethnic elements that separated Leisler and his followers from their opponents. With no settled English population at Schenectady, the ethnic dissension that may have characterized New York City's politics at this time was not so prominent. Two of the most active anti-Leislerian leaders in 1690, however, were Sander and Johannes Sanders Glen. Sons of a Scottish father who had married a Dutch woman, they also married local Dutch women. The union of English or Scottish settlers with Dutch women provides an element of ethnic complexity neglected by most analysts of the events surrounding Leisler's Rebellion at New York City or elsewhere in the province. Nonetheless, the overwhelming fact of the divisions associated with the rebellion at Schenectady is that they occurred within the Dutch community and not between mutually hostile ethnic groupings.[6]

It has been asserted that in New York City the Leisler government drew support from "persons of humble background" and "created a precedent for popular politics." At Schenectady, the adherence of Claes Fredericksen van Petten, Isaac Cornelissen Swits, and Johannes Pootman indeed suggests that the Leislerian party proved attractive to men of lesser means. Yet the Leislerians were not devoid of individuals of substance. Douwe Aukes, Myndert Wemp, and Symon Schermerhorn, as well as (probably) Reyer Schermerhorn, all were owners of slaves. In addition, Symon and Reyer were sons of Jacob Jansen Schermerhorn, who in 1660 had been counted as one of the principal traders at Beverwyck and who at his death in 1688 left an estate valued at over fifty thousand guilders. Because we lack assessment records for this period, it is difficult to judge if differences in

5. The dates of arrival of Schenectady's settlers are noted in *SP*, 82–230. For van Petten, Swits, and Pootman, see *ERAR*, III, 115, 285–287.

6. Gary B. Nash, *The Urban Crucible: Social Change, Political Consciousness, and the Origins of the American Revolution* (Cambridge, Mass., 1979), 46, 47. Sander Glen married Antje Wemp and Johannes Sanders Glen married, first, Annatie Peek and, second, Diwer Wendel, the widow of Myndert Wemp. *FS*, 76, 289. Among Leisler's supporters was David Christoffelsen, who was of English descent. *FS*, 36. For the marriage of Englishmen with local Dutch women at Schenectady, see Table 20. For New York City, see Nash, *Urban Crucible*, 45; Archdeacon, "Age of Leisler," 70.

economic status may have separated the two factions. Yet support for this surmise may be gained from a brief recounting of the experiences of the Leislerian Johannes Pootman and those of the Leisler opponent Adam Vrooman in the years before 1690.[7]

On September 14, 1661, Pootman, "a young man, at present about sixteen years of age" was engaged to Philip Hendricksen Brouwer "to serve him, Phillip Hendricxsz, faithfully in all his business and affairs . . . for the term of three successive years." Brouwer, a brewer at Beverwyck, was already associated with Arent van Curler as one of the first Schenectady proprietors. The extent to which Pootman was to be instructed by Brouwer in his trade is not clear, and it may be significant that this was not specified in the contract. Moreover, with Brouwer's death in 1664, the major share of his estate, including his brewing equipment, passed to Jan van Eps, a future Leisler opponent. There is no evidence that Pootman ever established himself as a brewer at Schenectady.[8]

Unlike Pootman, Vrooman was fortunate to have the support of other family members, including a father concerned that his son acquire skill in a trade. On May 23, 1670, at Albany, twenty-one-year-old Adam Vrooman, "with the consent of his father, Heyndrick Meesz Vrooman," bound himself for two years to Cornelis Willemsen Van der Burgh to learn "carpentering and millwrighting." Vrooman and his father did not settle at Schenectady until 1677, but by 1683 he had constructed the community's second grist mill and in 1688 owned land both at the village and above Schenectady along the Mohawk River. By 1690, between them, father and son possessed at least three slaves. When approached in the fall of 1689 by Jacob Milborne "to advise and require all the Inhabitants of Schinnectady . . . to repair forthwith to the aforesaid City of Albany to receive their

7. Archdeacon, "Age of Leisler," 46, 47. For Jacob Jansen Schermerhorn, see *FS*, 158–159; *FOB*, II, 255. For the slaves captured or killed at Schenectady in 1690 who belonged to Symon Schermerhorn, Douwe Aukes, and Myndert Wemp, see *DHNY*, I, 304–306. Reyer Schermerhorn's will, written in 1717, mentions two slaves. Richard Schermerhorn, *Schermerhorn Genealogy and Family Chronicles* (New York, 1914), 64–66; *Abstracts of Wills on File in the Surrogate's Office, City of New York, 1665–1800*, *NYHSC*, XXV–XLI (1893–1909), XXVI, 335–336. In 1682 Claes Fredericksen van Petten bought a slave named Jan, but it is not known if he still owned this slave in 1690. *ERAR*, III, 537.

8. *ERAR*, III, 115. The sale of Brouwer's estate took place in April 1664. *ERAR*, I, 346–348. For Johannes Pootman, see *SP*, 137–138. Pootman appears to have had no local family members. In 1661 he was bound out for three years of service to Philip Hendricksen Brouwer by a Beverwyck trader departing for the Netherlands, Jan Hendricksen van Bael. *ERAR*, III, 115; Munsell, ed., *Collections*, IV, 176.

Table 14. Schenectady officeholders, 1669–1690

Officeholder	1669[a]	1670	1671	1672	1673	1674	1675	1676	1677	1678	1679	1680	1681	1682	1683	1684	1685	1686	1687	1688	1689	1690
Jan Gerritsen van Marcken	P[b]	P																				
Sander Leendertsen Glen	P		P	P	P		P															
Pieter Danielsen van Olinda		P	P	P																		
Jan van Eps		P	P	P	P		P	P		PM		P	P	P		PM	M				PM	
Sweer Teunissen van Velsen		P	P	P	P										C					C	P	
Teunis G. Swart				P																		
Harmen Vedder					P	P	P	P														
Barent Jansen van Ditmars					P								P			P						
Ludovicus Cobes							P	P	P	P		P	P			P						
Daniel Jansen van Antwerpen							P	P	P	P		P	P			P						
Sander Glen, Jr.											P	P	P		P	PM	PM			P	PM	PM
Reyer Schermerhorn												P	P			M	M	P		P	*p*	*p*
Johannes Glen																M	M	C	C	PC	PM	PM
Myndert Wemp																			C		*p*	
David Christoffelsen																					*p*	
Reynier Schaats												C								C	*p*	
Douwe Aukes																				C	*M*	*P*
Claes Fredericksen van Petten																					*M*	*P*
Barent Wemp																				C	C	
Isaac Cornelissen Swits																				C	C	*M*
Johannes Pootman																					*p*	

Sources: NYCD; DHNY; ERAR; SP; CHME; ARS; LIR; ER; NL; BGE; AP; Calendar of Council Minutes; Records of the First Reformed Church at Schenectady; Schenectady Court Minutes, 1684.

[a] There is no information on officeholders at Schenectady before 1669. Individuals such as Adam Vrooman who held a church office but no political or military position have not been included in the list.

[b] P = political; M = military; C = church; *P* = political by commission from Jacob Leisler; *M* = military by commission from Leisler.

Rights and Priviledges," Vrooman declined to cooperate and notified the anti-Leisler Convention government at Albany instead.[9]

Before 1689, neither Pootman nor Vrooman had been politically active, although both had held positions within the Schenectady Dutch Reformed church. The anti-Leislerians included several individuals who had held both civil and military office either at Schenectady or Albany, but Pootman's lack of political position was characteristic of Leislers's supporters as a whole. Myndert Wemp served one term as a village magistrate, but only Reyer Schermerhorn, who acted both as a magistrate and as Schenectady's assemblyman from 1683 to 1685, had had any extended political experience. For the majority of those persons who can be identified as Leislerians, their commissions from Jacob Leisler marked their first advancement as officeholders (Table 14). The bitterness engendered by this political upheaval is suggested by Robert Livingston's already quoted remark that at Schenectady before the massacre Leisler's supporters had threatened "to burn [Captain Sander Glen] . . . if he came upon the garde." Schenectady was a small community in both size and population, and individual hostilities must have been exacerbated by the inability of antagonists to avoid each other during their daily round of activities. Both the Leislerian Myndert Wemp and the anti-Leislerian Glen family, for example, were owners of house lots on the west side of the village. On the nearby cultivated flatland, Reyer Schermerhorn's bouwery Number Four was, in its division farthest from the village, adjoined by farms owned by the Glens and by Gerrit Bancker.[10]

Existing antagonisms may also have been heightened by the fracturing of family loyalties. This situation was particularly apparent in the Bradt family. Two of the sons of Cathalyna de Vos (by her first husband, Arent Andriesen Bradt) were married to daughters of

9. *ERAR*, III, 372–373; *DHNY*, II, 116. For Adam Vrooman, see *DHNY*, I, 304–306, II, 116–117; *FS*, 276–277; *SP*, 212–216.

10. *DHNY*, I, 310. In November 1689 Adam Vrooman rejected Jacob Milborne's request that he assist Leisler's supporters at Schenectady with the explanation, "I am a person of no power nor authority." *DHNY*, II, 117. Some members of the anti-Leislerian party, for example, William Teller, had held office at Albany. *BGE*, II, 316; *ARS*, II, 241, III, 458. In 1676 Johannes Pootman was one of six persons selected as "suitable . . . for the administration of the magistrates' office" whose names were submitted to Governor Andros for his preference. There is no evidence that Pootman was chosen. *AP*, I, 425–426. For the property holdings of the Glen family, Myndert Wemp, and Reyer Schermerhorn, see *SP*, 64, 115, 224–225. Evert Bancker, Gerrit Bancker's son, was an active supporter of the anti-Leislerian Albany Convention in 1689 and 1690. *DHNY*, II, 88–146.

Jacques Cornelissen van Slyck and a third married into the van Eps family. Although the Bradt brothers were associated with families connected to the anti-Leislerian party, their sisters were the wives of Reyer Schermerhorn, Claes Fredericksen van Petten, and Johannes Pootman, all individuals who held commissions issued by Jacob Leisler. Equally divided were the family and political relations of the Wemp brothers, Myndert and Barent. Both held office under Jacob Leisler, but their sister Antje had married Sander Glen, Jr., and their stepfather was Sweer Teunissen van Velsen. Sons of a proprietor (Jan Barentsen Wemp), stepsons of one magistrate and related by marriage to another, the appearance of the Wemp brothers in the Leislerian camp is puzzling. The explanation may lie in a prior (1683) dispute between the brothers and their stepfather, van Velsen, concerning the distribution of the inheritance of a deceased sister to the remaining Wemp offspring. In pressing their claim, the brothers were aided by Arnout Cornelissen Viele, also a future Leisler adherent and, since the death of Jan Barentsen Wemp, the children's guardian.[11]

The political divisions that emerged at Schenectady appear to have paralleled those provincewide. Neither at Schenectady nor within the colony were the Leislerian leaders inconsequential men. All were property holders and some, such as the Schermerhorns, were possessed of real wealth. Yet on various levels the Leislerians must be counted among the provincial "outs." Although one of the wealthiest traders at New York City, Leisler himself "was never accepted by the social elite or accorded any government office, except for a captaincy of the city militia." Similarly, at Schenectady, those Leislerians who can be identified were predominantly individuals who had exercised little social or political authority before 1689. As the allegiance of only about half of the village's households can be determined, however, it must be admitted that the contours of Schenectady's politics at this time remain inexact.[12]

11. For the family relations of the Bradts, Pootman, van Petten, and Schermerhorn, see FS. Another Leisler appointee, David Christoffelsen, was a cousin to the Bradts. His mother and Cathalyna de Vos were sisters, both being the daughters of Andries de Vos of Rensselaerswyck. SP, 93, 102; VRBM, 825. For the Wemp family, see FS, 289; DHNY, II, 350, 353; ERAR, III, 283–285; ARS, III, 324–326, 344.

12. Kim, Landlord and Tenant, 52. For an analysis of the supporters and opponents of Jacob Leisler, see Kim, 51–54. Leisler was not only an officer of the militia; in 1685 he became a justice of the peace for New York City. Calendar of Council Minutes, V, 128.

Both at Schenectady and throughout the province, the immediate tenure of the Leislerians was short-lived. Jacob Leisler and his son-in-law, Jacob Milborne, were executed for treason in May 1691. During the subsequent administrations of Governors Henry Sloughter, Richard Ingoldsby, and Benjamin Fletcher (1691–1698), the province's anti-Leislerian faction remained firmly in control. After a period of political paralysis, however, leading Leislerians, including Jacob Leisler, Jr., and Abraham Gouverneur, sought recognition from the English government for what they claimed was the colony's corrupt and miserable condition. Their petitions were ultimately successful, resulting in the removal of Fletcher and his replacement by Richard Coote, earl of Bellomont, who arrived at New York in April 1698. Although Bellomont displayed no initial favoritism, within a short time the governor had "clearly become as zealous a Leislerian partisan as the Leislerians themselves." Anti-Leislerian political figures were purged, and Bellomont also acted to revoke the "extravagant" land titles issued by his predecessor. Among those grants he considered the most notorious was one that had been awarded to several prominent Albany officials including Dominie Godfridus Dellius, Pieter Schuyler, and Dirck Wessels Ten Broeck. The patent encompassed some two hundred square miles of Mohawk Valley land above Schenectady.[13]

Needing firsthand intelligence about the region, in May 1698 the governor dispatched Colonel Wolfgang William Romer to examine the fortifications at Albany and Schenectady. Romer's mission, however, was not restricted to the investigation of local defenses. In all, he covered some forty miles of territory before rendering judgment on the cupidity of the previous administration's adherents: "It is a

---

13. Kim, *Landlord and Tenant*, 72. For the arrest, trial, and execution of Leisler and Milborne, see *DHNY*, II, 362–382. For the petitions of Leisler's son and others, and for Governor Fletcher's replacement by the earl of Bellomont, see *NYCD*, IV, 212–220, 261; John C. Rainbolt, "A 'great and usefull designe': Bellomont's Proposal for New York, 1698–1701," *NYHSQ*, 53 (1969), 334–336. Bellomont may have arrived with a list of Leislerians to be favored by his administration. Robert C. Ritchie, *Captain Kidd and the War against the Pirates* (Cambridge, Mass., 1986), 49. For the purging of anti-Leislerian political figures, see Kim, *Landlord and Tenant*, 72–74. Those involved in the Dellius grant included not only Dellius, Schuyler, and Ten Broeck, but also Evert Bancker and William Pinhorne. They had been rewarded by Governor Fletcher for their political loyalty, aid in prosecuting the war effort, and influence with the Iroquois. Kim, 62–71, 76; *NYCD*, IV, 170. Governor Bellomont expressed his desire to vacate the Fletcher land grants in his correspondence with various home officials. Of the Dellius grant, he wrote: "The Mahawcks land, 50 miles in length, I hear the Grantees value at 25,000 [pounds]." *NYCD*, IV, 327.

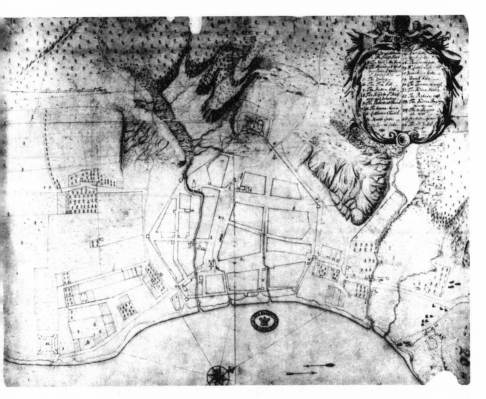

The 1698 Romer map of Albany. From *DSSAY*, 2 (1926–1927)

pity, and even a shame, to behold a frontier neglected as we now perceive this is; and had the public interest been heretofore preferred to individual and private profit, which has been scattered among a handful of people with diabolical profusion, the enemy had never committed pernicious forays on the honest inhabitants generally."[14]

Romer's visit to Schenectady in conjunction with Governor Bellomont's determination to vacate the Dellius grant proved instrumental in restoring the influence of Leislerians such as Reyer Schermerhorn and Arnout Cornelissen Viele. In a report to the governor dated June 13, 1698, Romer recommended Viele's talents as an interpreter: "I take the liberty to propose to you a good and faithful interpreter, name Arnout Cornelissen Vile, living in The Bay, on Long Island." In 1690 Viele had been commissioned by Jacob Leisler's government

14. *NYCD*, IV, 328.

"to be agent for this their Majties Province . . . to go to Onnondago
& there reside . . . amongst the sd Indians." Superseded as an interpreter by Hilletie van Olinda the following year, he next undertook
an expedition through Pennsylvania as far as the Ohio River in search
of furs. After Viele returned in 1694, his services as an interpreter
and emissary to the Iroquois were too valuable to be entirely ignored,
but he remained out of favor and soon retired to Long Island.
Romer's correspondence was not, however, the first notice Governor
Bellomont had had of Viele. Already on May 31, at New York, the
governor had employed him to examine two Mohawks, Henry and
Joseph, regarding the lands acquired by Dellius and the others.[15]

Reyer Schermerhorn's diminished authority had been apparent as
early as June 1691 when Governor Henry Sloughter met in conference with the Iroquois at Albany. Captain Sander Glen of Schenectady was present, but Schermerhorn, noticeably, was not. Glen, who
served as justice of the peace at Schenectady until his death in 1695,
instituted proceedings against Schermerhorn which, on April 9,
1696, resulted in an order for his arrest "for obstructing repairs to the
fortifications." Although harassed by his opponents, Schermerhorn
was not entirely superseded as a political figure and in 1693 and 1694
was elected an assemblyman from Albany County. In each instance,
though, his fellow representative was a Fletcher adherent, Dirck
Wessels Ten Broeck of Albany. Writs for new elections were issued
soon after Governor Bellomont's arrival in 1698, and Schermerhorn
was again chosen to represent Albany County but was now paired
with another Leislerian, Jan Jansen Bleecker. For former Leislerians
such as Reyer Schermerhorn, it was a propitious moment. Governor
Bellomont's correspondence makes clear that throughout the spring
and summer of 1698 he was marking out political friend from foe and
his sentiments were decidedly in favor of the Leislerian party. According to Bellomont, they possessed the character of a "sober and
virtuous people" whom he estimated comprised two-thirds of the provinces population, "and better affected to His Majesty's government

---

15. Ibid., 329; *DHNY*, II, 314. Colonel Romer was chief engineer at New York.
NYCD, IV, 305. For Viele's dismissal, his replacement by Hilletie van Olinda, and
subsequent reemployment by Governor Bellomont, see *NYCD*, IV, 198, 345–346;
Calendar of Council Minutes, VI, 135; Trelease, *Indian Affairs*, 212. For his 1692–1694
trading expedition, see *NYCD*, IV, 96; Charles A. Hanna, *The Wilderness Trail or the
Ventures and Adventures of the Pennsylvania Traders on the Allegheny Path*, 2 vols. (New
York, 1911), I, 136–143; Broshar, "First Push Westward," 239. After 1694, Viele was
occasionally used to treat with the Iroquois but soon retired to Long Island. *NYCD*,
IV, 123; Viele, *Viele Records*, 32.

then the other party, I averr it for a truth." To the Lords of Trade, Bellomont wrote that he could see no reason why "the English and Dutch that are called Leislers party should be any longer excluded from a share in the government."[16]

As assemblymen, Schermerhorn and Bleecker aligned themselves with the governor in Bellomont's drive against the Dellius grant. Fearing that Albany's influence over the fur trade would be diminished, the city's common council had already sought, but failed, to persuade Dominie Dellius and the other grantees to relinquish their patent to it. A February 1698 petition to Governor Fletcher was equally unsuccessful. Subsequently, on June 6, 1698, Schermerhorn and Bleecker expressed the city's concerns to Governor Bellomont stating "that they [were] informed of a Certeine grant that was made by Coll: Fletcher . . . of the Maquase Land which grant . . . will Constraine and force the Indians of the Maquase Nation to desert this Province and fly to the French."[17]

A short time later both men provided even stronger evidence of their political loyalty when they supported Bellomont in his conflict with the recently elected provincial assembly. Indeed, they went so far as to announce their intention to withdraw from the assembly. The governor distrusted the majority members of the assembly and as early as May 17 had proposed increasing their number from nineteen to thirty, in an effort to dilute his opponents' influence. At Bellomont's urging, both Schermerhorn and Bleecker retained their

16. *Calendar of Council Minutes*, VII, 183; *NYCD*, IV, 379–380. For Governor Sloughter's visit to Albany, see *NYCD*, III, 773. The date of Sander Glen's death is not known, but his wife remarried on April 15, 1696. As early as March of that year his brother Johannes had replaced him as a justice of the peace at Schenectady. *NYCD*, IV, 161; *FS*, 76, 81. After his arrest, Reyer Schermerhorn appeared before the governor and council and was ordered to reappear at the next session of the supreme court. He did so in New York on October 10, 1696. *Minutes of the Supreme Court of Judicature, 1693 to 1701, NYHSC*, XLV (1912), 105; *Calendar of Council Minutes*, VII, 188. As early as 1690 Schermerhorn was identified as the representative for the town of Schenectady. *DHNY*, II, 283. For the 1698 election and Schermerhorn's career as an assemblyman, see *Calendar of Council Minutes.*, VIII, 34; Bonomi, *Factious People*, 296–299.

17. *NYCD*, IV, 330–331. The concern of the Albany traders for control of the fur trade was expressed by Robert Livingston, *NYCD*, IV, 874. The city's attempt to gain control of the Dellius grant is noted in Kim, *Landlord and Tenant*, 75–76. In presenting their memorial to the governor, Schermerhorn and Bleecker were presumably aware of the interrogation of two Mohawks, Henry and Joseph, at New York on May 31. With Arnout Cornelissen Viele acting as interpreter and Governor Bellomont present, they denied that the land had been sold by their tribe to Dellius or to anyone else. *NYCD*, IV, 345.

seats. On June 14, however, the governor dissolved the body of which he had complained so bitterly. Elections for its successor were held early the following year. Schermerhorn and Bleecker were again returned as representatives for the city and county of Albany, as was a third individual, Hendrick Hansen, also a former Leislerian.[18]

Beginning in 1699, Reyer Schermerhorn proved himself doubly useful to Governor Bellomont, both in vacating the Dellius grant and in advancing a project conceived by the governor for the extraction of naval stores from timber lands located above Schenectady. In fact, there was a direct link in Bellomont's plans between the two objectives, as he admitted to the Lords of Trade: "These pines I fancy will be found to grow on Mr Dellius's grant." In an initial letter of April 17, 1699, the governor presented "a first essay or a rude sketch" on which he expanded in later correspondence. He also acknowledged a debt to Schermerhorn in the project's origins: "My thoughts have been so at worke about Naval Stores and Masts for the Kings ship's, That understanding last spring from two honest Dutch men that had found out a parcell of vast pines . . . which they said were big enough for masts for the biggest ship in the world; I resolved to take an account of them, and for that end sent Mr Schermerhoorn, one of the Dutchmen that discovered them to me, and with him John Latham an able shipwright, who learn't his Trade in one of the King's yards in England to view them." Schermerhorn received instructions from Bellomont to report "what trees he found fit for Masts, what Pitch Pines for making Pitch, Tar and Rozin, and all other timber fit for building Ships of War."[19]

---

18. Bellomont provided the Lords of Trade with an account of the affair: "I found the Sheriffs of the Counties here, appointed by Coll: Fletcher, to be of the scum of the people . . . who . . . made corrupt and false returns of Members, in so much, that of nineteen persons that make up the members of this Assembly eleven of their elections were disputed, but they being a Major vote of the house have established themselves, and have proceeded with the greatest confusion . . . which hath occasioned six of the nineteen to make remonstrance to the house . . . but the major part rejected it, on which the six withdrew, and did petition myself and Councill and made a protestation against the proceedings of the house." *NYCD*, IV, 322. For the withdrawal of Schermerhorn and Bleecker from the assembly, see Bonomi, *Factious People*, 298–299; *Journal of the Votes and Proceedings of the General Assembly of the Colony of New York, 1691–1765*, 2 vols. (New York, 1764–1766), I, 90. Governor Bellomont's proposal to increase the number of assemblymen is noted in Kim, *Landlord and Tenant*, 72.

19. *NYCD*, IV, 588–589, 785. For the annulment of Dellius's grant, see *NYCD*, IV, 510. The assembly concluded its session on May 16, 1699. On May 19, at New York, Governor Bellomont provided Reyer Schermerhorn and Hendrick Hansen of Albany with instructions to visit the Mohawks "to give them an account of the justice

Bellomont was at Albany during July 1698 to meet with the Five Nations. His correspondence at that time offers ample evidence of his determination to nullify the Dellius grant, but no indication that he had yet settled on a project for extracting naval stores from these lands. The governor had, however, arrived in the province with instructions that clearly emphasized the interest of imperial officials in the development of a naval stores industry in the colony. That Dominie Dellius had already begun to exploit the timber resources of his grant to this end may also have provided impetus for a similar project on the governor's part. At a later date, Bellomont integrated his observations made at Albany into his maturing plans. Even the falls at Cohoes were not expected to be a fatal impediment: "I am satisfied the Trees might be floated down the great fall (which I have been at) and then they will be the cheapest in the world, for they may be floated all down Hudson's River to the Ships side that take 'em in to carry them to England. . . . to be sure the seasons of the year must be watch'd when there are floods in the River, and then I am confident those trees may be safely floated."[20]

The proposals and surveys made in 1699 became reality the following year with the first felling of trees. Although the governor had been assured that "there are pines enough in those woods on the Mohack's river to furnish the navy these thousand years to come," the initial contract was for a modest number of masts, twenty-four, the largest of which were to be thirty-seven and forty inches in diameter. The work began in the spring and continued through the ensuing winter. On January 2, 1701, Bellomont reported, "There is a messen-

---

his Excellcy has done them in that matter of their land of which they complained." *NYCD,* IV, 565; Bonomi, *Factious People,* 298.

20. *NYCD,* IV, 589–590. For Dominie Dellius's exploitation of his Mohawk Valley lands and Governor Bellomont's similar plans, see *NYCD,* IV, 503–504; Rainbolt, "A 'great and usefull designe,'" 339. As early as January 22, 1699, Bellomont had discussed his naval stores project in a letter to Abraham de Peyster. He also included the subject in his correspondence with officials in England. Frederic de Peyster, *The Life and Administration of Richard, Earl of Bellomont, Governor of the Provinces of New York, Massachusetts, and New Hampshire, from 1697 to 1701* (New York, 1879), app., ii; *NYCD,* IV, 587–596, 671–672. For the 1698 instructions of the Lords of Trade to Bellomont regarding naval stores, see *NYCD,* IV, 298. The production of naval stores in New York had been considered as early as 1693. *Calendar of Council Minutes,* VI, 186. The development of a naval stores industry in the colonies was the subject of Edward Randolph's 1696 "Discourse how to render the Plantations more beneficiall & Advantageous to this Kingdom." Randolph, *Letters and Papers,* VII, 479–486. For the governor's visit to Albany in July 1698 and his correspondence at that time, see *NYCD,* IV, 362–367; Peter Wraxall, *An Abridgement of the Indian Affairs, 1678–1751,* ed. Charles H. McIlwain (New York, 1968), 28–30.

ger newly come from Albany who brings word the Undertakers for Masts were very forward with their work, that they had drawn several masts out of the woods to the side of the Mohack's River, ready to float down when the river is open, for at present 'tis froze up." The number of men who were employed in the felling and hauling of trees is not known, but at least some of the labor was provided by soldiers from the garrison at Albany, who were paid four shillings a week for their efforts. Directing the operations were Reyer Schermerhorn, the shipwright John Latham, and two other individuals identified only as Beekman and Taylor. The former was most likely Johannes Beekman of Albany, who is mentioned in contemporary documents and whose first wife was Schermerhorn's sister. The latter individual may have been the same John Taylor whose name appears in New Hampshire provincial records as receiving payment for supplying masts for the Royal Navy. Presumably, it was Taylor whom Bellomont encountered loading his ship of 450 tons at Piscataway during the governor's summer journey to New England in 1699.[21]

At New York City major participants in the venture included the governor and Abraham de Peyster, whose ship *Fortune* was intended to be loaded with the timber for delivery to Portsmouth, England. On December 30, 1699, Bellomont wrote de Peyster: "Sir. I desire you will immediately send for Mr. Latham, the ship Carpenter, and Ingage him to set about Cutting and Squaring such a quantity of Ship Timber as will load the Ship Fortune against the Spring." De Peyster's vessel did not in fact sail until October 1700, and both the ship and its cargo, the first installment of timber to go to England, were lost off the coast of Cornwall. Moreover, the *Fortune* departed without any timber from the Mohawk Valley lands. Its hold was filled instead with masts cut on the property of Captain John Evans, who had been granted land by Governor Fletcher both at Manhattan

---

21. *NYCD*, IV, 785, 825. For the participation of Schermerhorn and the others, the use of soldiers as laborers, and the first contract for masts, see *NYCD*, IV, 785, 833; De Peyster, *Life of Bellomont*, app., xi. On May 20, 1698, John Latham, "Ship Carpenter," became a freeman of the city of New York. *Burghers of New Amsterdam and the Freemen of New York, 1675–1866, NYHSC*, XVIII (1886), 61. Governor Bellomont's visit to Piscattaway had been intended, in part, as a means to learn about the production of naval stores. For this and for his meeting with John Taylor, see *NYCD*, IV, 587–588, 671; Sybil Noyes et al., *Genealogical Dictionary of Maine and New Hampshire* (Baltimore, 1972), 675; *Documents and Records Relating to the Province of New Hampshire*, ed. Nathaniel Bouton et al., 40 vols. (Concord, N.H., 1867–1941), II, 122, XVII, 647. For Johannes Beekman, see Munsell, ed., *Collections*, IV, 96.

and in Ulster County before falling from favor under the Bellomont administration. Although John Latham was issued a warrant "to cut ships timber for the public service" on March 14, 1700, and payment was forwarded to Reyer Schermerhorn on November 6, Governor Bellomont's letter of January 2, 1701, suggests that even at that date no Mohawk Valley timber had yet reached New York. Nevertheless, in correspondence to the Lords of Trade, Bellomont documented the precautions he had taken to see that the project not be subverted. To maintain secrecy he had drawn up the bond and instructions for Schermerhorn with his own hand: "Not a man of the Anti-Leisler party knew or dreamt of it, till it was actually concluded and the felling of the masts begun. . . . I am satisfyed had I employ'd Schuyler or any of his party to make the bargain with the Mohacks for their woods, they would not have done it without finding their account in it to the King's cost."[22]

Bellomont's characterization of his opponents as "the Anti-Leisler party" was only one of many indications that the political alliances of the preceding decade had not yet dissolved. At Schenectady, Sander Glen (now dead) had been succeeded as a justice of the peace and captain of the militia by his brother, Johannes. Bellomont also found it disadvantageous to ignore Albany's former mayor, Pieter Schuyler, who continued as a member of the governor's council even as Bellomont sought to strip him of his recent land acquisitions. The governor clearly anticipated difficulty from such individuals. Governor Fletcher's grant of land to Schuyler, Dellius, and the other patentees had been justified not only by their demonstrated political allegiance but as a reward for their influence with the Iroquois in matters of trade and war. Sensitive to this, Governor Bellomont, in instructions to Reyer Schermerhorn and Hendrick Hansen dated May 19, 1699, bound them to inform the Mohawks of the annulment of the Dellius grant and also to warn the tribe to "be watchful that they be not insnared by the further insinuations of Dellius and the interpretesse, for he is so inraged, that he will depart from truth to doe any thing." The woman interpreter mentioned by Bellomont was Hilletie van

22. De Peyster, *Life of Bellomont*, app. xi; *Calendar of Council Minutes*, VIII, 145; *NYCD*, IV, 833. De Peyster, a Leislerian favored by Governor Bellomont, had only recently acquired the *Fortune*. Kim, *Landlord and Tenant*, 73; *Calendar of Council Minutes*, VIII, 139; Ritchie, *Captain Kidd*, 170. For the sailing of the *Fortune* with its cargo of timber, see *NYCD*, IV, 710, 722, 780, 784, 841. For Captain John Evans, see Kim, *Landlord and Tenant*, 72–73; Ritchie, *Captain Kidd*, 69. For the November 6, 1700, payment to Reyer Schermerhorn, see *Calendar of Council Minutes*, VIII, 180.

Olinda of Schenectady, whom the governor called "a Mohack woman" and Dellius's "own convert." She was a vital asset to the minister, who taught the Mohawks "to pray and preach in their language by means of a woman Interpretres."[23]

Although Dominie Dellius left Albany to return to the Netherlands in 1699, Bellomont clearly perceived a need to counteract the influence he had had with the Mohawks. To this purpose, while at Albany in August 1700, the governor was instrumental in providing Schenectady with a new minister, Dominie Bernardus Freeman. Bellomont anticipated not only that Freeman would serve the needs of the village, which had been without a resident minister since 1690, but also that he would "be near the Mohacks" and would "take paines" to instruct the tribe. In this he was not disappointed. Freeman soon became fluent in the Mohawk language and proved to be both an able minister to the Indians and a useful auxiliary to the governor's designs for the production of naval stores. In 1701 Bellomont described him as "a very good sort of man, and is one of them that witness the writing or covenant with the Mohawks for their woods."[24]

In a January 16, 1701, letter to the Lords of Trade, Bellomont also praised Reyer Schermerhorn as "a very sensible man . . . [who] has managed this bargain with the Mohacks very skillfully." Participation in the naval stores project was only one indication of the favor with which Schermerhorn was now viewed by the governor. Beginning in 1699, he was one of those to whom payments were disbursed for provisioning the garrison at Schenectady and for other public services. On May 1, 1700, Bellomont appointed him an assistant judge of the court of common pleas at Albany, and when the governor journeyed to that city in August for a conference with the Five Nations, Schermerhorn was in attendance. Schermerhorn had already discovered the limits of his influence, however, when in August 1699 he and Hendrick Hansen petitioned the governor for a grant of land six miles long and two miles wide from which the ships masts were to be gathered. An angry Bellomont ordered a correspondent to "chide him

23. *NYCD*, IV, 364, 566. For Johannes Glen and Pieter Schuyler, see *NYCD*, IV, 170, 727; Bonomi, *Factious People*, 313; Kim, *Landlord and Tenant*, 72; "Muster Rolls of a Century from 1664 to 1760," Appendix H of *Second Annual Report of the State Historian of the State of New York* (Albany, 1897), 428. A summary of Dominie Dellius's career during this period is provided in Balmer, *Perfect Babel*, 48–49.

24. *NYCD*, IV, 727, 833. Dominie Dellius's departure from Albany and Dominie Freeman's fluency in the Indian language are noted in *ER*, II, 1336, 1341–1345, III, 1867. For the position of the Dutch clergy during and after Leisler's Rebellion, see Balmer, *Perfect Babel*, 7, 10–11, 30, 43–49, 104.

[Schermerhorn] and the Mayor of Albany [Hansen] for their disrespect to the King, and disingenueity to me."[25]

A greater check to Schermerhorn's ambition came with the governor's death on March 5, 1701, and the resulting shift of provincial political fortunes. Although Bellomont's policies were continued during the brief tenure of Lieutenant Governor John Nanfan, even before the arrival of his successor, Edward Hyde, Lord Cornbury, in 1702, the Leislerian and anti-Leislerian parties were once again exchanging places. Within Albany County, the divisive assembly elections of these years mark one of the clearest records of this transferral of power. At the beginning of 1701 the Albany city and county representatives remained Reyer Schermerhorn, Jan Jansen Bleecker, and Hendrick Hansen. But the dissolution of the assembly in June resulted in new elections that saw the return of Dirck Wessels Ten Broeck, Myndert Schuyler, and Johannes Abeel. At the August 19 opening of the subsequent assembly, Ten Broeck was declared disqualified because of nonresidence and ordered to withdraw. The candidate with the next highest number of votes, Reyer Schermerhorn, was admitted the following day. This reversal in turn precipitated the withdrawal of Schuyler and Abeel and their eventual expulsion for nonattendance. Further elections resulted in their replacement by Bleecker and Hansen. This was in any event to be Schermerhorn's final assembly. The arrival of Lord Cornbury in May 1702 prompted new elections at which Schuyler and Abeel were again returned, as was Evert Bancker—the son of one of Schenectady's proprietors, an early opponent of Jacob Leisler, and one of those who had participated in the Dellius grant during the Fletcher administration.[26]

As a figure closely associated with the previous administration,

25. *NYCD*, IV, 833; De Peyster, *Life of Bellomont*, app., viii. For the favors bestowed on Schermerhorn by Governor Bellomont, see *Calendar of Council Minutes*, VIII, 140, 150, 164, 182; *NYCD*, IV, 727. Bellomont's desire for land reform was expressed in his August 24, 1699, proposal to the Lords of Trade for the distribution of land to ex-soldiers who would be settled on New York's exposed northern frontier. The letter was written three days after the governor's rejection of Schermerhorn and Hansen's petition for a grant of land. *NYCD*, IV, 553.

26. Bellomont's death and Cornbury's arrival are noted in *Calendar of Council Minutes*, VIII, 211, 345. For the political reversal following the governor's death and the assembly elections of 1701 and 1702, see Bonomi, *Factious People*, 77–78, 298–299. Ten Broeck no longer lived at Albany but on Robert Livingston's manor. Kim, *Landlord and Tenant*, 100; *Albany Chronicles*, 140–141. For Ten Broeck's ouster and the withdrawal of Schuyler and Abeel, see *Journal of the General Assembly of New York*, I, 115–118. For Evert Bancker, see *DHNY*, II, 88–146; Kim, *Landlord and Tenant*, 80n; *FS*, 5. For New York's political divisions in the aftermath of Leisler's Rebellion, see Nash, *Urban Crucible*, 88–93.

Schermerhorn no longer received government payments and Governor Cornbury soon expressed dissatisfaction at his handling of the naval stores project. Although the correct number of masts had been cut, "they were not of the dimensions agreed for, nor were they brought to York as they ought to have been." Schermerhorn was commanded to appear before the governor in June to explain the situation.[27]

The resurgence of the anti-Leislerian party also may have contributed to Dominie Bernardus Freeman's decision to leave Schenectady at this time. Although lacking support from the Classis of Amsterdam, Freeman had sailed for New York in 1700, where his arrival in July at Manhattan coincided with that of Dominie Dellius's replacement, Johannes Lydius. Together they journeyed to Albany, where Lydius, evidently briefed by his predecessor on the state of provincial politics, associated himself with the city's anti-Leislerian party. Dominie Lydius later contended that Freeman was not invited to remain at Albany because of the party divisions that still existed there, "if the inhabitants, who for some time previously had been pretty well divided, were ever to be brought together in peace." Settled instead at Schenectady with Governor Bellomont's blessings, Freeman joined Reyer Schermerhorn not only in the naval stores project but also in an attempt to raise funds for the construction of a new church to replace the building destroyed in 1690. Governor Bellomont's death and Schermerhorn's deteriorating political position, however, may have determined Freeman to depart. By October 1702 he was being solicited by churches elsewhere in the colony. Initially, Governor Cornbury denied him permission to leave with the explanation that "Mr. Bernardus Freeman has not behaved well in the continuation and encouragement of the dissensions among the people of this province." Attempts by Schermerhorn and others to maintain Freeman at Schenectady were unsuccessful, and by 1705 he had removed to

---

27. Governor Cornbury supplied the following account of his dealings with Schermerhorn: "I sent for the Captain of the Jersey and the Captain of the Benjamine and ordered them to go to Albany along with Schermerhoorn to view those Masts. . . . And I told Schermerhoorn that if they were found serviceable I would appoint two persons to value them, and if he would do the like he should be paid according to that valuation, if not I would have nothing to do with his Masts. At last with some difficulty he consented to this proposal, the Carpenters went to view the Masts and reported them serviceable, Schermerhoorn brought them down to York where they have been viewed and valued." *NYCD*, IV, 976; Reyer Schermerhorn's last payment was dated May 7, 1702, and he appeared at New York on June 15 and 16. *Calendar of Council Minutes*, IX, 21, 50, 54.

Long Island, where he was installed as minister of the church at New Utrecht. This was near to where Arnout Cornelissen Viele had taken refuge in the 1690s and was a community that had supported Jacob Leisler on his seizure of power in 1689.[28]

Reyer Schermerhorn's increasingly difficult situation was only one indication of a more widespread remobilization of political forces now in effect. At New York, Nicholas Bayard (himself an early Leisler opponent) informed his correspondents: "Our former unhappy Breaches & Divisions . . . are of late broken out to a more violent Degree and Flame than ever—Occasioned by meanes of three addresses lately signed . . . by most all the . . . Principal Inhabitants that are in opposition against the Leislerian party." Of the three addresses, that of December 30, 1701, to King William III, styled "The humble Petition and address of Your Majesties Protestant subjects in your Plantation of New York in America," enables one to gain added insight into the divisions that continued at Schenectady. Moreover, the 1701 address provides significant evidence for a correspondence between the factions of that date and those at the time of the rebellion itself.[29]

Signed by numerous individuals throughout the colony, the document carried the names of nineteen persons from Schenectady. As had been the case a decade earlier, a majority of those persons "in opposition against the Leislerian party" were members of families who had been closely associated with the village's founding and early settlement (Table 15). They included the sole surviving proprietor at Schenectady, Pieter Danielsen van Olinda, his son Daniel, and five sons of other proprietors. The members of the anti-Leislerian party at Schenectady were united among themselves by ties of both family and politics. Johannes Sanders Glen, Adam Vrooman, Harmen van Slyck, and Daniel Jansen van Antwerpen all held civil or military

28. *ER*, II, 1373, III, 1507. For the recruitment of Dominie Lydius and the arrival of Dominie Freeman, see *ER*, II, 1317, 1336–1350. For Dominie Freeman's installation at Schenectady, his cooperation with Reyer Schermerhorn, and his eventual departure for Long Island, see *ER*, III, 1487, 1503–1507, 1539–1543, 1639–1645, 1762–1767; *NYCD*, IV, 727, 833; *DHNY*, III, 139–182; Birch, *Pioneering Church*, 30–39; David S. Sutphen, *Historical Discourse Delivered . . . at the Celebration of the Two-Hundredth Anniversary of the Reformed Dutch Church of New Utrecht, L.I.* (Brooklyn, 1877), 11–12, 15–16. In the years after Dominie Freeman's departure, children in several Schenectady families were named "Bernardus" in his honor, *FS*, 22, 161, 289.

29. *NYCD*, IV, 933, 946–947. For Nicholas Bayard, see Ritchie, *Captain Kidd*, 171; Balmer, "Traitors and Papists," 348. For the Schenectady signers of the 1701 address to King William III and for their affiliation with the anti-Leislerian party, see *NYCD*, IV, 939–941, 946–947.

Table 15. Schenectady signers of 1701 address to King William III

Surviving Proprietor	Sons of Early Settlers
Pieter Danielsen van Olinda	Jan Baptist van Eps
Sons of Proprietors	Evert van Eps
Johannes Sanders Glen	Arrived 1670–1690
Johannes Teller	Philip Philipsen (de Moor ?)
Daniel van Olinda	Jan Luycassen Wyngaerd
Harmen van Slyck	Adam Vrooman
Cornelis van Slyck	Hendrick Vrooman[a]
Martin van Slyck	Arrived after 1690
Early Settlers (before 1670)	Ahasuerus Marselis
Bent Bagge	Thomas Smith
Jacobus Peek	
Daniel Jansen van Antwerpen	
Harmen Vedder	

Sources: *NYCD*, IV, 939–941; *FS*; *SP*, 82–230.
[a]Hendrick Vrooman was the son of Adam Vrooman. In 1701 he was living in Albany but shortly thereafter returned to Schenectady.

office at the village. Moreover, at least twelve of the nineteen persons who endorsed the address were related to one or more of their fellow signers by birth or marriage.[30]

Schenectady began the eighteenth century as it concluded the seventeenth, a divided community. Several factors, including the death of Leisler supporters and opponents, the removal of individuals during the years of war, the arrival of numbers of English settlers, and the influx of new families after 1697, prevent one from too easily asserting that the village's factions at this later date merely reflected in composition and purpose those which had existed previously. Nevertheless, at the center of controversy was the most prominent surviving Leislerian, Reyer Schermerhorn, and his supporters included both original Leisler partisans, such as Douwe Aukes, Barent Wemp, and Isaac Cornelissen Swits, as well as members of several families

30. The most intricate relationships were among the van Slyck, van Olinda, and Vrooman families. By his marriage to Hilletie van Slyck, Pieter Danielsen van Olinda was the uncle of his wife's brother's children and his son Daniel was their cousin. After Jacques Cornelissen van Slyck's death in 1690, his widow, Gerritje Ryckman, took Adam Vrooman as her second husband. Vrooman, whose first wife had been killed in the 1690 French attack, thus gained a stepmother for his children, while the van Slyck offspring acquired Vrooman as their stepfather. For the family relations of the members of the anti-Leislerian party, see *SP*, 82–230; *FS*. For the offices held by Johannes Glen and the others, see *NYCD*, IV, 161, 727, 811; *FS*, 205–206. William Teller was dead by 1702, making Pieter Danielsen van Olinda the sole surviving proprietor. *FS*, 189. *Abstracts of Wills*, XXV, 102–103; *Calendar of Wills*, 449.

Table 16. Supporters of Reyer Schermerhorn at Schenectady

Family/Name	Family Relationship[a]
Schermerhorn	
Reyer	
Jan	s of Reyer Schermerhorn
Wemp	
Johannes	s of Myndert Wemp m/d of Reyer Schermerhorn
Ephriam	s of Myndert Wemp
Barent	b of Myndert Wemp
Jan	s of Barent Wemp
Symon	s of Barent Wemp
Veeder	
Volkert	s of Symon Veeder m/d of Reyer Schermerhorn
Gerrit	s of Symon Veeder m/sd of Reyer Schermerhorn
Pieter	s of Symon Veeder m/d of Claes Lourens Van der Volgen
Van der Volgen	
Claes Lourens	
Van Brakel	
Gysbert Gerritse	
Gerrit	s of Gysbert Gerritse m/d of Claes Lourens Van der Volgen
Viele	
Cornelis	n of Arnout Cornelissen Viele m/d of Claes Fredericksen van Petten
Lowis	c to Cornelis, Jr.
Douwe Aukes	m/d of Arnout Cornelissen Viele
Van Petten	
Arent	s of Claes Fredericksen van Petten
Andries	s of Claes Fredericksen van Petten
Nicolaas	s of Claes Fredericksen van Petten
Groot	
Symon	s of Symon Groot m/d of Jan Rinckhout
Philip	s of Symon Groot
Rinckhout	
Jan	
Van der Bogaert	
Tjerk Fransen	s of Frans Harmens van der Bogaert
Claes	s of Frans Harmens van der Bogaert
Swits	
Isaac Cornelissen	m/d of Symon Groot
Cornelis	s of Isaac Cornelissen
Symon	s of Isaac Cornelissen
Abraham	s of Isaac Cornelissen
Brouwer	
Hendrick	s of Willem Brouwer
Willem	s of Willem Brouwer
Jan	s (?) of Hendrick Brouwer
Others	
Arent Pootman	
Andries Bradt	

Table 16. Continued

Name	Family Relationship[a]
Arent (?) Bradt	
Goosen van Oort	
Johannes Teller	s of William Teller[b]
Teunis Swart	
Jillis Fonda	
Johannes Glen	
William Appel	
Jan Luycassen	
Wyngaerd	
Non-Dutch	
Philip Bosie	
Benjamin Lenyn	
Manasseh Sixberry	
Thomas Davie	
Jonathan Stevens	
William Bowin	
John Lench	
Thomas Noble	
Jonathan Dyer	
John McIntyre	
Jacobus Cromwell	

Sources: The list above has been compiled from the names of those individuals who signed the 1705 power of attorney in support of Reyer Schermerhorn. Fifty-three of the fifty-six persons who signed the document can be identified. For the 1705 document as well as for information on family relations, see *SP*, 32, 82–230; *FS*.

[a]s = son; m/ = married; d = daughter; b = brother; sd = stepdaughter; n = nephew; c = cousin.

[b]Schenectady proprietor.

(Wemp, van Petten, Swits, and Viele) linked to the Leisler axis during the years 1689–1691 (Table 16). Moreover, Schermerhorn's opponents, many of whom signed the December 1701 address to King William III, were among those persons identified by contemporaries as belonging to the colony's anti-Leislerian party. At Schenectady, however, the 1701 address to King William III served as the prelude for another petition to Governor Cornbury the following year.

Signed by many of the same individuals as the previous year's appeal, the 1702 document disputed Schermerhorn's authority to "dispose and sell the lands belonging to said Village and buy other as they then will, without Rendering any account of the same." At this time, Schermerhorn and his son-in-law Johannes Wemp controlled the distribution of all unpatented land surrounding the village, perhaps eighty thousand acres total. Their authority to do so rested on a 1684 patent from Governor Thomas Dongan. This challenge to Schermerhorn's authority and the resulting dispute over the village's common lands most clearly distinguished the Leislerian and anti-Leislerian parties at Schenectady as they were then constituted.[31]

Sung Bok Kim has argued that Leisler's Rebellion needs to be examined not only as a political phenomena but as "a social and economic conflict between the landed and landless merchants of New York." Attacks on the property holding of the rich, whether English or Dutch, were a prominent element of the rebellion at New York City. In addition, the acquisition of landed property marked a fundamental dividing line between the two factions that existed at Schenectady during the early eighteenth century. Moreover, available evidence suggests that the possession of or ability to acquire land had been a crucial element in the dissension that originally surrounded Leisler's Rebellion at the village.[32]

During the 1660s, Schenectady's proprietors and first settlers received properties distributed along the south bank of the Mohawk River, with the farm lands located on the low-lying flats to the west of the village itself. The ownership of this property was not static, however. As early as 1667 Sander Leendertsen Glen presented his sons with a portion of his lands. Moreover, as new settlers arrived, it was possible for them to purchase land from those who departed. In 1667, for example, Claes Fredericksen van Petten and Cornelis Cornelissen Viele combined to acquire the bouwery of Martin van Ysselsteyn for 330 beavers worth eight guilders each. The death of an original owner also provided a means for the acquisition of land by others. In April 1664 Philip Hendricksen Brouwer's estate was sold at auction, much of it passing to Jan van Eps and his stepfather, Cornelis van Ness. The death of Anthonia Slachboom, the widow of Arent van Curler, in 1676 resulted in the splitting up of her remaining property. Benjamin Roberts had already acquired a section of the original van Curler house lot, and now the final portions were purchased by Ludovicus Cobes, Symon Groot, and the widow of Jan Peek.[33]

31. *SP*, 24–25. The estimate of 80,000 acres is Jonathan Pearson's. For Johannes Wemp's June 15, 1700, marriage to the daughter of Reyer Schermerhorn, see *FS*, 289.

32. Kim, *Landlord and Tenant*, 51. For attacks on the property holding of the rich, see Nash, *Urban Crucible*, 48.

33. The Glen family had additional holdings opposite the community on the north side of the river. For the initial distribution of land at Schenectady and for the subse-

Disputes over the use of reedland and woodland may indicate that Schenectady's first settlers were already seeking to protect their right to exploit the village's resources against competition from later arrivals. In 1671, when Jan Jansen Jonckers (van Rotterdam) and Andries Albertsen (Bradt) attempted to acquire property near the village, a petition was presented at Albany "by those of Schaenhechtede praying that Jan van Rotterdam and Andries Aelberts may not enjoy [the exclusive use of] a certain parcel of land near Schaenhechtede, as it tends to the benefit of all." The court ruled "the gift of land invalid and, furthermore, that for the benefit of the inhabitants no land may be taken up within three miles of the place, the same to be reserved as pasture for those of Schaenhechtede and no other purpose." Similarly, complaints about individuals who had not fenced their land may indicate that some persons were seeking to exploit or appropriate more property than was rightfully theirs. A suit brought against William Teller, one of the original proprietors, claimed that he occupied "more ground at Schaenhechtede than belongs to him." The 1663 murder of Claes Cornelissen Swits suggested the potential for violence in such disputes. Swits, head farmer at William Teller's bouwery, was shot by Philip Hendricksen Brouwer while plowing land claimed by both men.[34]

By the second decade of Schenectady's settlement, a movement of population westward via the Mohawk River already was in progress. Directly opposite the village, the north bank of the river was occupied, first by Sander Leendertsen Glen, and later by Benjamin Roberts, Cornelis Cornelissen Viele, and Claes de Graaf. Above Schenectady, however, it was the flats on the less exposed south side of the river which attracted settlement and cultivation. As early as 1670 Jacobus Peek and Isaac Truax were in possession of the Second Flat about five miles from Schenectady, and Daniel Jansen van Antwerpen occupied the Third Flat at eight miles distance. At this time, the Schenectady authorities sought additional grants of land from the Mohawks which included the as yet unoccupied flats above the village. On May 28, 1670, a quantity of wampum, beer, and gun-

---

quent acquisitions and transferrals noted here, see *SP*, 58–81, 139, 168–171, 176–177; *ERAR*, I, 346–348, 423, 449–451. In 1669 Sander Glen made another gift of land to his sons. *NL*, 119.

34. *ARS*, I, 217, 264–265. For complaints about the fencing of lands and the use of reedland and woodland, see *ARS*, I, 138–139, 194–195. Claes Cornelissen Swits had arrived at Schenectady in 1662 and was killed in September 1663. *ERAR*, III, 200–201, 267–269. For van Rotterdam and Bradt, see *FS*, 19, 98.

powder was paid to two Mohawk sachems in return for an unspecified amount of land, and in July 1672 a more explicit deed was entered into by the Dutch and Mohawks. Although the magistrates failed to get Governor Edmund Andros to confirm this acquisition, the document was later to form the basis for the 1684 Dongan patent.[35]

Favored by their half-breed status, the members of the van Slyck family were among those persons who were most successful in obtaining lands from the Mohawks. Jacques Cornelissen van Slyck's possession of the First Flat above Schenectady was specifically provided for by the tribe in their 1672 deed with the Schenectady magistrates. His sister Hilletie, the wife of Pieter Danielsen van Olinda, also was the recipient of several properties from the Mohawks, as was Lea, the Indian wife of Claes Willemsen van Coppernol, and possibly another van Slyck sister. In addition, Schenectady's magistrates served as agents for persons seeking governmental acknowledgment of their possessions. In 1677 the Schenectady court recommended to Governor Andros that Jacobus Peek, Isaac Truax, and Daniel Jansen van Antwerpen be awarded patents for their lands. The following year, Sander Leendertsen Glen petitioned the governor to grant the Fourth Flat to Ludovicus Cobes, Schenectady's schout, and to Cobes's son-in-law, Johannes Kleyn. The Schenectady magistrates also sought permission to use the Fifth Flat to support a minister at the village.[36]

This movement of population upriver alarmed the Mohawks. At Fort James in New York on October 4, 1683, representatives of the tribe complained to Governor Thomas Dongan that they had never intended to relinquish full control of their lands to anyone other than Arent van Curler and the van Slycks:

> That one Arent Van Corlaer bought all Schannectade, & payed them for it, but now there be some who have bought only the Grasse, & pretend to the land Allso, they say Allso that they have bought the first

35. For the land holdings of Sander Glen and the rest, see *SP*, 69, 107, 136; *ARS*, I, 207. For the 1670 and 1672 deeds, see *SP*, 17–19; *NL*, 182–183. In December 1684 the five Schenectady trustees under the Dongan patent confirmed Isaac Truax's possession of the Second Flat. Schenectady Court Minutes, 1684.

36. For the van Slyck family's property, see *NL*, 182–183; *SP*, 167, 183–185, 188–191; Higgins, *Expansion in New York*, 18–19. In 1675 Governor Andros refused to grant a patent to the Schenectady magistrates for the lands acquired under the 1672 deed with the Mohawks. *SP*, 19–20. For petitions for land near Schenectady in 1677 and 1678, see *SP*, 72, 73; *Calendar of Council Minutes*, III, 182; *CHME*, XXVI, 139.

flatt, but that is not so, for it belongs to Acques Cornelissen . . . for he is of their people, & . . . that there are writeings made of a sale of land but It was never sold but only the Grasse tho it may be some drunken fellows may have made som Writeings without their knowledge. That they have only bought the grasse & are now going to live upon it, but they ought to pay for the land as well as the Grasse, & that they had given some to that woman (*Hillah* & another *Leah* who have the propirety of it) the other have only the grasse.

In their protest, the Mohawks referred to attempts to dispossess Jacques (Aukes) Cornelissen van Slyck of his ownership of the First Flat. Governor Dongan's reply is significant because it not only addressed the complaints of the Mohawks but also revealed the dissatisfaction of other persons at Schenectady. Evidently, the success of the van Slycks did not sit well with those who were less favored: "The people of Schannectady say they sent Acques to purchase the Land in the name of their Town, and that Acques bought it in his own name; & they sent allso one Kemel to purchase it for the Towne; the Indians told them that Acques had bought & paid some part of the payment." Most likely, the Kemel mentioned in this document was Cornelis Cornelissen Viele, who traded at Beverwyck (Albany) before removing to Schenectady in 1667. Like van Slyck, Viele was intimate with the natives, whose language he spoke and by whom he was known as Keeman.[37]

That Viele and van Slyck should confront each other over the acquisition of land from the Mohawks was not surprising given their previous record of dispute. In 1671 Viele, who had recently settled at Schenectady, had petitioned the court at Albany to "be granted permission to tap liquor at Schaenhechtede by the quart and the pint, to be taken out, and to provide good lodging and accommodation to strangers." This was a direct challenge to van Slyck, who was then acting as the sole village tapster. Although unsuccessful in maintaining this exclusive privilege, in its defense van Slyck presented the court with "a petition of some patentees complaining about the tapping done by Cornelis Cornelisz Vielen." The support van Slyck received from his fellow patentees is significant, partic-

---

37. *NYCD*, XIV, 773–774. The Schenectady community compensated van Slyck for the land. For Viele, see *ARS*, III, 80n; *ERAR*, I, 449–451, III, 283; *NL*, 182–183. In 1682 the Mohawks made grants of woodland at Niskayuna to Jan Mangelse and to Claes Jansen van Bockhoven. Under terms of the latter deed, they retained a right to "free wood and hunting there without contradiction." *ERAR*, II, 151–153.

ularly if one concludes that by this date Schenectady's founders and first settlers had determined to defend their exploitation of the community's resources against encroachment by later arrivals. It was also at this time that the village schout, Jan Gerritsen van Marcken, brought suit against William Teller for occupying more land at Schenectady than was his allowance. Van Marcken had moved from New Amstel on the Delaware River to Beverwyck about 1659 but, unlike Teller, was not included among Schenectady's proprietors or original settlers. Within a short time after this action, he was removed as schout and replaced by the proprietor Pieter Danielsen van Olinda. Finally, it was during these years (1672) that Schenectady's magistrates first sought, by deed from the Mohawks and patent from Governor Andros, to place the village's remaining common lands under their control.[38]

The development of a provincial export trade in wheat and other grains during this period heightened the economic advantage of land ownership. But opposition to the effort of Jan Jansen Jonckers (van Rotterdam) and Andries Albertsen (Bradt) to acquire property near the village (in 1671) had already indicated that some persons were to be more successful than others in exploiting the lands that surrounded the community. Indeed, it is notable that those individuals who were most fortunate in this regard associated themselves with the anti-Leislerian party, whereas the Leislerian partisans such as Reyer Schermerhorn and Arnout Cornelissen Viele were among those persons least favored in the acquisition of Mohawk Valley lands. Although the bouweries at and above Schenectady were not initially of great size, by the early 1700s the holdings of some individuals associated with the anti-Leislerian party were extensive. Harmen van Slyck possessed over 2,000 acres near present-day Canajoharie, and Adam Vrooman accumulated nearly 1,400 acres before his death in 1730.[39]

38. *ARS*, I, 283, 294–295. For Viele's dispute with van Slyck, see *ARS*, I, 289, 307; *Minutes of the Executive Council*, II, 667–669; *BGE*, I, 458–459, 479. Although not successfully, in 1668 van Marcken also challenged van Slyck's tapping rights. For van Marcken, see *SP*, 183; *NYCD*, XII, 314; *ARS*, I, 30, 44, 217, 273.

39. The alteration in the value of land is noted in Kim, *Landlord and Tenant*, 53–54. Contemporaries were aware of the increased value of land and agriculture. *CMVR*, 148. Among the anti-Leislerian figures who owned land above Schenectady were several members of the van Slyck and van Olinda families as well as Arent Vedder, Adam Vrooman, Jan Baptist van Eps, Jan Pietersen Mabie, Daniel Jansen van Antwerpen, Jacobus Peek, Philip Philipsen (de Moor?), and Jan Luycassen Wyngaerd. For the property holdings of these individuals, see *SP*, 82–230; Higgins, *Expansion in*

The employment of Cornelis Cornelissen Viele in 1683 by persons dissatisfied with Jacques Cornelissen van Slyck's handling of negotiations with the Mohawks may have been an expression of the divisions that separated Schenectady's first patentees and oldest and most successful settlers from later arrivals seeking a more equitable distribution of the village's resources. Such dissension may explain the selection of thirty-one-year-old Reyer Schermerhorn to be Schenectady's representative at the colony's first assembly (also in 1683). The choice of Schermerhorn is otherwise surprising, given that his family had not been among the village's founders and that he had settled at Schenectady only a few years previous. Significantly, although Schermerhorn owned land both at Schenectady and Albany, he had been unable to acquire any property above the village nearer than the Seventh Flat on the exposed north bank of the river. Meanwhile, Arnout Cornelissen Viele (Cornelis Cornelissen Viele's brother and a future Leisler adherent) was also frustrated in his attempt to take possession of the Fourth Flat. On September 26, 1683, the Mohawks presented Viele with "a certain piece of land, lyeing above Schinnechtady on the Northside of the river, covering about 16 to 17 morgens, over against the flat, where Jacobus Peek lives." The conveyance was made "to Aernout Cornelise, his heirs and successors, free an unencumbered." Viele, however, failed to patent the property, and the following year the land was transferred to Ludovicus Cobes and Johannes Kleyn under title received from the newly established trustees for Schenectady.[40]

The Dongan patent issued to Schenectady on November 1, 1684, gave legal form to the earlier transferal of land negotiated by the village magistrates and the Mohawks in 1672. For a yearly quitrent of "forty Bushels of Good Winter Wheat," Governor Thomas Dongan presented the community with a territorial bounty of over 120 square miles. Rather than place the distribution of the common lands at Schenectady in the hands of the local magistrates, Dongan commanded that an independent body of five trustees be established. His

---

New York, 18, 19, 47, 57; *Calendar of Council Minutes*, IX, 70; *CHME*, XXVI, 139; *FS*, 240, 277; *ERAR*, II, 393–394; *Calendar of New York Colonial Manuscripts Indorsed Land Papers in the Office of the Secretary of State of New York, 1643–1803* (Albany, 1864), II, 58, 221, III, 13, 73, 74, 98, IV, 27, 52 (hereafter cited as *Indorsed Land Papers*); Schenectady Court Minutes, 1684.

40. *NYCD*, XIII, 573. For property owned by Reyer Schermerhorn and Arnout Cornelissen Viele, see *SP*, 72, 103, 143–145, 211–212; Viele, *Viele Records*, 26; Higgins, *Expansion in New York*, 19; Schenectady Court Minutes, 1684."

motivation for creating and empowering such a separate, self-perpe-
tuating body with authority to grant the village's unpatented lands is
uncertain, but it was a procedure he also employed in March 1685 in
issuing a similar patent to the inhabitants of Flushing on Long Island.
The governor, certainly, was aware of the protests of both the Mohawks and various members of the Schenectady community expressed in conference at New York a year earlier. Subsequently, on
March 22, 1684, Dongan and his council had determined "Rules for
the purchase of land from the Indians," and that summer the governor acted to ensure full possession and proper title to lands acquired
from the Mohawks at Half Moon and Niskayuna near Albany. Dongan may have wished to settle matters concerning the Schenectady
lands in order to bolster his province's military and economic relations with the Mohawks. Traders from Pennsylvania were penetrat-
ing Iroquois territory by way of the Susquehanna River and siphon-
ing a part of the colony's annual export of furs. The governor was
eager to halt this practice, but he needed the willing cooperation of
the Mohawks and other tribes to do so. Additionally, it was at this
time that Anglo-French competition for control of the western fur
trade and the allegiance of the Iroquois was becoming increasingly
serious. Any unhappiness among the tribes was fertile ground for the
recruitment efforts of the French, who were courting the Mohawks
through their intermediary, the Indian leader Kryn.[41]

The trustees named in the 1684 Schenectady patent included William Teller, Reyer Schermerhorn, Sweer Teunissen van Velsen, Jan

41. The Dongan grant consisted of "A Certaine Tract . . . beginning at the Maquaes River, by the Towne of Schenectade, and from thence Runnes Westerly on
both sides up the River to a Certaine Place called by the Indians Canaquarioeny,
being Reputed three Dutch Miles or twelve English Miles; and . . . downe the River
one Dutch or four English miles to a kill or creeke called the Ael Place, and from the
said Maquaes River into the woods South Towards Albany to the Sandkill one Dutch
Mile and as much on the other side of the River North." SP, 21–23. For the March
24, 1685, patent issued to the community at Flushing, see Colonial Charters, Patents,
and Grants to the Communities comprising the City of New York, comp. Jerrold Seymann
(New York, 1939), 523–529. For the March 1684 council meeting, see Calendar of
Council Minutes, V, 60. On January 10, 1684, Dongan also granted the petition of
"Johannes Sanders Glen of Schenectady asking that no one but himself be allowed to
plow the Mohawk sachems' land." Calendar, V, 38. For Governor Dongan and the
lands at Half Moon and Niskayuna, see ARS, III, 470–471. For Dongan's concern
about the French and their Indians as well as the Pennsylvania traders, see ARS, III,
470–471; NYCD, XIV, 772–774; DHNY, I, 393–420; Gary B. Nash, "The Quest for
the Susquehanna Valley: New York, Pennsylvania, and the Seventeenth-Century Fur
Trade," NYH, 48 (1967), 3–27; John H. Kennedy, Thomas Dongan, Governor of New
York (1682–1688) (Washington, D.C., 1930), 25, 35–39, 54–59.

van Eps, and Myndert Wemp. To them was "Ratifyed and Confirmed . . . on the Behalfe of the Inhabitants of the Towne of Schenectade . . . there Associates, Heires, Successors and Assigns, all and
Singular the before recited Tract and Tracts, Parcell and Parcells of
Land, Meadow, Ground and Premises." Unfortunately, the method
of selection of the trustees is not known. Although several of the
village's original proprietors remained alive, only one (William Teller)
was included as a trustee. Sweer Teunissen van Velsen and Jan van
Eps, however, were early settlers at Schenectady, both had served as
magistrates, and, in that capacity, each had taken part in the initial
1672 negotiations with the Mohawks for their lands. Of the remaining trustees, Myndert Wemp was van Velsen's stepson and the son of
the late proprietor Jan Barentsen Wemp, and Reyer Schermerhorn
may have gained recognition from Dongan as the village's assembly
representative. The inclusion of Teller, van Velsen, and van Eps,
however, marked the trustees as from among the village's earliest
founders and established authorities.[42]

During 1690, both Schermerhorn and Wemp received commissions
from Jacob Leisler, while Teller, van Velsen and van Eps were all
confirmed Leisler opponents. It was less the shifting of political fortunes, however, than the attack of the French and Indians which
most altered the composition of power among the trustees. After February 8, 1690, only Schermerhorn and Teller remained alive. Teller,
now seventy years old, not only was elderly but soon removed to
New York City. As Sweer Teunissen van Velsen had died without
issue, Schermerhorn could be joined in his capacity as a trustee only
by the heirs of Jan van Eps and Myndert Wemp, both of whom had
been killed in the massacre. Van Eps's eldest son, Jan Baptist, married a daughter of Johannes Sanders Glen and refused to associate
himself with Schermerhorn; his brother Evert may have been too
young for such responsibility. Of Myndert Wemp's two sons,
Ephraim also may not have been of age, but the elder, Johannes, not

42. *SP*, 22. Both Jan van Eps and Reyer Schermerhorn were village magistrates in
1684. The court records for this year include examples of land distributed by the
trustees under the Dongan patent. Schenectady Court Minutes, 1684. Several trustees
were favored by the governor in other ways. On October 8, 1684, William Teller was
commissioned as a justice of the peace for Albany County. In December, Jan van Eps
was commissioned a lieutenant, Sander Glen, Jr., a captain, and Johannes Glen an
ensign in the Schenectady militia. It is surprising that no member of the Glen family
was chosen a trustee, as were none of the original proprietors, except William Teller.
BGE, II, 316, 327.

only acted with Schermerhorn as a trustee, in June 1700 he married Schermerhorn's daughter, Catalina.[43]

In 1700, the year before his death, William Teller returned briefly to Schenectady. At this time "many Inhabitants complained of ye Grievance they suffered by ye administration of said Ryer Schermerhorn and John Wemp." Not until 1702, however, was there a concerted effort to remove Schermerhorn as a trustee. The May 3, 1702, dissolution of the assembly by Governor Cornbury marked the end of Schermerhorn's career as a representative. No longer was he favored with payments for supplying the Schenectady garrison, and in June he was called to New York to explain his handling of the naval stores project. Cornbury himself was at Albany the following month and remained at Schenectady for two days in late July in order to meet with representatives of the Mohawks. It is likely that the governor also conferred with Schermerhorn's opponents at the village. Shortly after Cornbury's return to New York, Adam Vrooman and Jan Pietersen Mabie, members of the anti-Leislerian party who had been seeking patents for land near Schenectady for almost a decade, had their property holdings confirmed.[44]

With the collapse of Reyer Schermerhorn's political influence, on October 10, 1702, thirty-eight individuals at Schenectady addressed a petition to the governor and council complaining of Schermerhorn's and Wemp's trusteeship, "that yee Power of said Ryer Schermerhorn . . . may be annuld and made Void and to present a new patent Confirming the Land [and] other Priviledges . . . for ye Beehoofe of the Inhabitants of said Village." The petition may have been timed to arrive at New York coincident with the opening of the first assembly of Cornbury's administration. That body, which began its initial ses-

---

43. For the commissions issued by Leisler to Schermerhorn and Wemp, the anti-Leislerian stance of the other trustees, and the February 1690 deaths of all but Teller and Schermerhorn, see *DHNY*, I, 304–305, II, 110–112, 122, 149, 350. For William Teller's removal to New York City, see *ERAR*, II, 383; *CHME*, XL, 177. For the van Eps brothers, see *SP*, 24; *FS*, 221–222. For Johannes and Ephraim Wemp, see *FS*, 289; William Barent Wemple, "Wemple Genealogy," *New York Genealogical and Biographical Record*, 35 (1904), 192.

44. *SP*, 24. While at Schenectady in 1700, William Teller distributed his remaining property to his son Johannes, *ERAR*, II, 383. For the conclusion of Reyer Schermerhorn's assembly career, his final payment, and his appearance before Governor Cornbury, see Bonomi, *Factious People*, 298; *Calendar of Council Minutes*, IX, 21, 50. For Cornbury's Albany visit and his confirmation of the Vrooman and Mabie patents, see *Calendar*, IX, 70; *NYCD*, IV, 977–999; *Indorsed Land Papers*, III, 73, 74.

sion October 20, was clearly in the hands of the anti-Leislerian party. Expecting to be favored by the new governor, the petitioners were not disappointed. On February 17, 1703, a new patent was issued which, although maintaining Schermerhorn and Wemp as trustees, diluted their influence by the addition of Johannes Sanders Glen, Adam Vrooman, and Pieter Schuyler (of Albany). Schermerhorn disregarded this patent, though, and continued as before, so a second protest was lodged with the governor on April 21, 1704. Cornbury now solicited the advice of the provincial attorney general. His report, returned on May 18, declared Schermerhorn "guilty of very great mismanagements and breach of trust upon the Patent aforesaid and of Great disregard and Contempt of your Excellency." It recommended that "said Ryer Schermerhorn ought not to continue longer in the same trust but be Discharged from the same." To this end, on May 25, Schermerhorn and Wemp appeared before the governor and council, at which time both were suspended as trustees and a third patent was issued. Schuyler, Vrooman, and Glen were now joined as trustees by Daniel Jansen van Antwerpen and Glen's son-in-law, Jan Baptist van Eps.[45]

The dispute was as notable for its irresolution as for the issues and personalities involved. In 1705 and 1706 the new trustees were obliged to commence further suits against Schermerhorn in the provincial court of chancery. In response, in 1705 Schermerhorn filed a countersuit, executing a power of attorney to Jacob Reynier and Abraham Gouverneur of New York City "for us and In our Names . . . to file a bill In the Chancery Court of This Province against Such persons and according To such Instructions as You or Either of You Shall have from us . . . and To Prosecute the Same with all vigour and Effect." Fifty-five names were attached to this document, supplying the most detailed record available for the identity of Schermerhorn's supporters at Schenectady. When compared with the December 1701 address to King William III, the October 1702 complaint to Governor Cornbury, as well as with two existing assessment

<hr />

45. *SP*, 25, 29. The anti-Leislerian sentiments of Governor Cornbury were expressed in his speech before the assembly on October 20, 1702. That body indicated its similar political leanings in its October 22 reply. *Journal of the General Assembly of New York*, I, 145. For the 1703 patent and the April 1704 protest, see *Indorsed Land Papers*, III, 186; *SP*, 25–28. A third individual, Thomas Williams, also appeared with Schermerhorn and Wemp at New York in May 1704. Williams was the sheriff of Albany County and had been associated with Schermerhorn and Wemp since at least 1701. For this and for the May 1704 patent, see *SP*, 26–27; *Calendar of Council Minutes*, IX, 419; *ERAR*, II, 387; *NYCD*, IV, 693, 727.

rolls for Schenectady (from 1705 and 1708), the 1705 power of attorney enables one to project a profile of the opposing camps into which the village was then divided.[46]

Thirty-eight of the forty-four persons who signed either or both of the 1701 and 1702 documents can be identified. The petitioners hostile to Schermerhorn were overwhelmingly of Dutch origins, the exceptions being several members of the Glen family and Thomas Smith of New England, who had married the widowed daughter of Schenectady's former schout, Ludovicus Cobes. As had been the case more than a decade earlier, ties of family and marriage were a significant element binding together both opponents and supporters of Reyer Schermerhorn. The village's only surviving proprietor, Pieter Danielsen van Olinda, was counted among those opposed to Schermerhorn, as were the offspring of several other proprietors including van Olinda's son Daniel, Johannes Sanders Glen, and the three sons of Jacques Cornelissen van Slyck: Harmen, Martin, and Cornelis (Table 17). It was predominantly from among these persons that the Schenectady community drew its leaders. At this time Johannes Sanders Glen, Harmen van Slyck, Adam Vrooman, and Daniel Jansen van Antwerpen all held positions of civil or military authority at the village. Former Leislerians such as Douwe Aukes, Barent Wemp, and Isaac Cornelissen Swits backed Schermerhorn. But, Schermerhorn also received support from the village's non-Dutch residents, who included two Frenchmen, Philip Bosie and Benjamin Lenyn, as well as nine other individuals of English descent, only two of whom had been at Schenectady earlier than 1697 (see Table 16). Several, for example, Manasseh Sixberry, William Bowin, Jacobus Cromwell and Jonathan Dyer, could be found on contemporary military lists "at ye fronteers," suggesting that their arrival at Schenectady coincided with the French and Indian wars of the 1690s and early 1700s.[47]

Thomas Archdeacon and Gary Nash have highlighted Anglo-Dutch hostility and the role of "ethnic aggression" as a precipitant of Leisler's Rebellion at New York City. Archdeacon writes, "Jacob

---

46. *SP*, 31.

47. For Glen, Smith, Bosie, and Lenyn, see ibid., 82–230; *FS*. Bosie may have been the son of Peter Bosie, a Frenchman at Albany in the late 1600s. *ARS*, I, 32n, 35–36, 42, 114, III, 94, 474, 519. For the offices held by Glen and the others, see *FS*, 205–206, 240; *NYCD*, IV, 727; "Muster Rolls," 428. For the soldiers who settled at Schenectady, see "Colonial Muster Rolls from 1686 to 1775," Appendix M of *Third Annual Report of the State Historian of the State of New York* (Albany, 1898), 464–480.

Table 17. Opponents of Reyer Schermerhorn at Schenectady

Family/Name[a]	Family Relationship[b]
Van Slyck	
Cornelis	s of Jacques Cornelissen van Slyck[c]
Martin	s of Jacques Cornelissen van Slyck[c]
Harmen	s of Jacques Cornelissen van Slyck[c]
Samuel Bradt	m/d of Jacques Cornelissen van Slyck[c]
Johannes Mynderse	m/d of Jacques Cornelissen van Slyck[c]
Vrooman	
Adam	m/wd of Jacques Cornelissen van Slyck[c]
Jan	s of Adam Vrooman
Hendrick	s of Adam Vrooman
Barent	s of Adam Vrooman
Van Olinda	
Pieter Danielsen[c]	m Hilletie van Slyck
Daniel	s of Pieter Danielsen van Olinda[c]
Glen	
Johannes Sanders	s of Sander Leendertsen Glen[c] m/d of Jan Peek
Johannes	s of Johannes Sanders Glen
Johannes Jacobsen	n of Johannes Sanders Glen
Jacobus van Dyck	m/d of Johannes Sanders Glen
Peek	
Jan	
Van Eps	
Jan Baptist	s of Jan van Eps m/d of Johannes Sanders Glen
Evert	s of Jan van Eps
Gysbert Gerritse van Brakel	m/wd of Jan van Eps
Jillis Van de Vorst	m/d of Jan van Eps
Vedder	
Harmen	s of Harmen Vedder m/d of Jacques Cornelissen van Slyck[c]
Albert	s of Harmen Vedder m/d of Johannes Sanders Glen
Arent	s of Harmen Vedder m/d of Symon Groot
Tjerk Fransen Van der Bogaert	m/d of Harmen Vedder
Brouwer	
Hendrick	m/d of Pieter Jacobsen Borsboom[c]
Mabie	
Jan Pietersen	m/d of Pieter Jacobsen Borsboom[c]
Groot	
Symon	
Daniel Jansen van Antwerpen	m/d of Symon Groot
Isaac Cornelissen Swits	m/d of Symon Groot
Others	
Gysbert Marselis	
Ahasuerus Marselis	
Benjamin Robert	
Esasias Swart	
Martin (?) van Benthuysen	

Table 17. Continued

Name[a]	Family Relationship[b]
Johannes Teller	s of William Teller[c]
Barent Wemp	s of Jan Barentsen Wemp[c]
Jan Luycassen Wyngaerd	
Philip Philipsen (de Moor ?)	
Thomas Smith	

Sources: The names included have been compiled from those persons who signed either or both the December 1701 address to King William III and the October 1702 petition to Governor Cornbury concerning Reyer Schermerhorn's administration of the common lands. See *NYCD*, IV, 939–941; *SP*, 25. For family relationships, see *SP*, 82–230; *FS*.

[a]The list excludes five individuals who signed the 1702 petition to Governor Cornbury who cannot be identified. It does include eight persons who later signed the 1705 power of attorney as supporters of Reyer Schermerhorn: Johannes Glen, Gysbert Gerritsen van Brakel, Tjerk Fransen Van der Bogaert, Isaac Cornelissen Swits, Hendrick Brouwer, Johannes Teller, Barent Wemp, and Jan Luycassen Wyngaerd.

[b]s = son; m/ = married; d = daughter; wd = widow.

[c]Schenectady proprietor.

Leisler and his followers were the products of the societal dislocation caused by the transformation of New York into an English city." Nash concurs: "The feeling grew steadily in the 1670s and 1680s among ordinary Dutch families that they were being crowded out of an economic system which they had built." Whatever the revelance of this analysis to events at New York City, their conclusions appear to have less application to the frontier situation at Schenectady.[48]

Further investigation of the Schenectady records suggests that, as seems to have been the case in 1689–1691, not ethnic origins but differences in economic and social status helped to distinguish the two parties. Schenectady's population was growing during these years from 238 persons in 1697 to 591 by 1714. Like the Frenchmen Bosie and Lenyn, and like the soldier settlers of English descent, many of whom married local Dutch women (Table 20), several of Reyer Schermerhorn's Dutch supporters were also recent arrivals at the village. Some, such as Jillis Fonda, not only were newly established as Schenectady residents but had recently married and undertaken the process of providing for their growing families. Fonda was a maker of gunstocks at Albany who removed to Schenectady in

48. Archdeacon, "Age of Leisler," 70; Nash, *Urban Crucible*, 45, 88.

1700. Married in 1695, by 1705 he had four children aged seven or under. In all, dates of first marriage can be determined for thirty-one of the signers of the 1705 power of attorney in support of Reyer Schermerhorn. Eight persons had married before 1695, but eighteen others were married between 1695 and 1704, and five not until 1705 or later.[49]

Analysis of two Schenectady assessment rolls from 1705 and 1708 also suggests that Schermerhorn's supporters, while not the poorest members of the village, were as a whole less well off than their rivals. Only twenty-eight of Schermerhorn's backers appear on the 1705 assessment roll, whereas thirty-three of his opponents are represented (the same number who appear on the 1708 document). As a group, Schermerhorn's adversaries were better established than his supporters in terms of their status as heads of families and as property holders. In fact, almost two dozen of Schermerhorn's adherents in 1705 do not appear on the assessment list of that year. They include most of his non-Dutch followers and a number of individuals whose families lived at Schenectady but who had not yet themselves married and established independent households. Thus the 1708 document, although three years removed from the events under consideration, provides a more complete picture of the economic status of the opposing parties. While the average (mean) estate value in 1708 for the village as a whole was 25.2 pounds, that of the thirty-three opponents and thirty-eight backers of Schermerhorn who can be identified on the assessment list was 32.6 and 27.9 pounds respectively. The 1705 figures were 19.7 and 15.8. Presumably, the men who supported Reyer Schermerhorn in his position as a trustee did so as a means to advance their family fortunes or to begin new lives. Jillis Fonda, for example, had been conveyed an island in the Mohawk River by Schermerhorn acting as a trustee in 1702.[50]

Historians of colonial New York have noted a provincewide restoration of political harmony which followed the arrival of Governor Robert Hunter in 1710. But the history of Schenectady, where the

49. For Schenectady's population in 1697 and 1714, see *Annals*, IX, 88–89; *DHNY*, III, 905. For Jillis Fonda, see *FS*, 70; *SP*, 110–111. Marriage and family information on both the supporters and the opponents of Reyer Schermerhorn is contained in *SP*, 82–230; *FS*.

50. For the Schenectady assessments, see Livingston-Redmond Papers, roll 10. The 1708 figures for the value of estates are approximately double those which appear on the 1705 document. Additionally, one can note that Schermerhorn's non-Dutch supporters were among the poorest village inhabitants. The average (mean) estate for households headed by persons of English or French descent was less than ten pounds.

distribution of the village's common lands remained a point of dissension until the 1790s, suggests that, at least for this community, the divisive legacy of the Leisler years was long-lingering and only slowly healed. Leisler's Rebellion and its aftermath exposed the serious economic, social, and political divisions that existed at Schenectady. Moreover, the dispute remained an unresolved source of contention for many years after. Reyer Schermerhorn died in 1719, but the quarrel he helped to inaugurate long outlived him. In 1713 and 1744, the trusteeship of, first, Schermerhorn and, second, his son-in-law Johannes Wemp was the subject of further petitions of protest. Indeed, at the end of the eighteenth century, Schenectady became an incorporated community without having put to rest the controversy that surrounded the allocation of its remaining common lands.[51]

By the first years of the 1700s "all the arable lands on both sides and even beyond the western limits of the township of Schenectady were taken up and settled." The response of the village's inhabitants to the increasing constriction on the availability of land was varied. Some, such as Harmen van Slyck, used their influence with the Iroquois or connections with the provincial government to acquire land elsewhere. Others, such as Symon Danielsen van Antwerpen and Lowis Viele, left the village. Adam Vrooman did both, exploiting his contacts with Governor Hunter to gain land at Schoharie and then settling there with his sons. For those persons who stayed at Schenectady, only one recourse remained: to contest with one another for the lands that were the village's to dispose.[52]

51. For Robert Hunter's influence on New York's politics, see Bonomi, *Factious People*, 78–79; Mary Lou Lustig, *Robert Hunter 1666–1734, New York's Augustan Statesman* (Syracuse, 1983), chaps. 3–6. The dispute over Schenectady's common lands is noted in *SP*, 33–57.

52. Higgins, *Expansion in New York*, 18. The map of Schenectady drawn by Colonel Wolfgang Romer in 1698 depicted a village surrounded by land already under cultivation. Grassmann, *Mohawk Indians*, 527. For Adam Vrooman, see *DHNY*, III, 687–688; *ER*, III, 2170.

6

To "gain some little profit"

For nearly a decade, from 1689 to 1697, life in Albany County remained difficult and dangerous. Less than four months after the attack on Schenectady, in May 1690, several persons were killed by Indians at nearby Niskayuna, and another raid in 1691 resulted in two more deaths. In April 1692 Alida Schuyler informed her husband, Robert Livingston (then at New York City), that people were fleeing Albany by every available boat. Census figures from the period record this dramatic removal of population from the exposed frontier. In 1689 at least 2,016 persons (slaves were not counted) were living in Albany County. By 1698 this population had been reduced by over one-quarter to 1,453 (plus 23 slaves). Numerous persons had been killed, taken prisoner, or died of natural causes, but over 400 men, women, and children had chosen to leave the county.[1]

Among the massacre survivors who are known to have departed were Symon Schermerhorn and Johannes and Willem Appel. Both Appel brothers settled at New York City, although Johannes eventually returned to Albany. Until his death in about 1696, Symon Schermerhorn operated a sloop on the Hudson River between Manhattan and Albany. The Teller family (with the exception of Johannes) also relocated to New York during this decade. Remarriage could remove women survivors (and their children) well beyond

1. The attack at Niskayuna was reported to have "made the whole country in an alarm, and the people leave their plantations." *DHNY*, I, 311; II, 235–236. For the 1691 raid and 1692 flight of people from Albany, see *NYCD*, III, 783–784; *CHME*, XXXVII, 176; Alida Schuyler Livingston, "Business Letters of Alida Schuyler Livingston, 1680–1726," ed. Linda Biemer, *NYH*, 63 (1982), 190. The census data for 1689 and 1698 is included in *DHNY*, I, 689–690.

Table 18. Number of marriages performed in the New York Reformed Dutch church in which at least one member of the couple was from Albany County, 1680–1699

Year	Number	Year	Number
1680	1	1690	1
1681	1	1691	2
1682	3	1692	6
1683	7	1693	7
1684	1	1694	3
1685	3	1695	6
1686	6	1696	8
1687	3	1697	7
1688	4	1698	7
1689	1	1699	3
TOTAL	30	TOTAL	50

Source: *Marriages from 1693 to 1801 in the Reformed Dutch Church of New York*, ed. Samuel S. Purple, New York Genealogical and Biographical Society, *Collections*, I (New York, 1890), 46–91.

Note: For the years 1680 through 1689, no one from Schenectady was married at the New York Dutch Reformed church. On five occasions between 1690 and 1699, however, the bride or groom was from Schenectady. Those persons marrying at the New York church included Cornelis Viele (April 1693), Aeltje Jans (July 1693), Johannes Paulusen (June 1695), Lysbeth Valentyn (August 1696), and Johannes Clara (Ten ?) Eyck (September 1698).

the local community. Jacquemyn Swart's second husband, Bennony Arentsen van Hoeck, was killed February 8, 1690. Her next spouse, Cornelis Vynhout, was from Ulster County, where she lived in 1700. In 1697 her son Lowis Viele married at the Kingston Dutch church. Within two years he had returned to Schenectady where he stayed until 1709, after which he relocated to the newly established farming community at Schaghticoke north of Albany.[2]

2. For Symon Schermerhorn, see *DHNY*, II, 218; *SP*, 145; *Calendar of Council Minutes*, VII, 53, 94; *CHME*, XXXIX, 71. William Appel removed to New York City, but Johannes Appel may have been back at Albany by 1692. *FS*, 3; *SP*, 82–83; *Indorsed Land Papers*, IV, 119; *Annals*, IX, 84; *Calendar of Council Minutes*, VI, 149, VII, 115, 196. In 1696 William Teller was exporting foodstuffs from New York City to Boston. *CHME*, XL, 177. For the Appel brothers, Symon Schermerhorn, and the Teller family at New York, see *Tax Lists of the City of New York, December 1695–July 15th, 1699*, NYHSC, XLIII–XLIV (1911–1912). For Jacquemyn Swart, see *ERAR*, II, 385–386; *FS*, 180, 227–228; Viele, *Viele Records*, 156–158. Her first husband was Pieter Viele. For Lowis Viele, see Viele, 159–160; *ERAR*, II, 385–387; R. Beth Klopott, "The History of the Town of Schaghticoke, New York, 1676–1855" (Ph.D. diss., State University of New York at Albany, 1981), 48.

Like Symon Schermerhorn, the Appel brothers, and the Teller family, many persons who left Albany County removed to New York City. As early as May 1690, in fact, the Iroquois urged the Dutch to "send for your wifes and children from New York and encourage them that we shall be safe and fear not." An examination of the records of the Dutch Reformed church in New York provides additional evidence of this exodus. For the years 1680–1689, a total of 274 marriages were performed at the church. In each instance, the place of residence or origin of the bride and groom was recorded. Although no one from Schenectady was married at the church during this decade, thirty weddings, or 10.9 percent of the total, involved couples at least one of whom was from Albany County. For the decade 1690–1699, however, 15.2 percent of the marriages performed (50 of 330) fell into this category and included persons identified as from Albany, Rensselaerswyck, and Schenectady (Table 18). Persons resettled from Albany County presumably would use the New York Dutch church for their own or their children's weddings, and this indeed seems to be the case. During the 1690s, the annual number of such marriages both increased and was more constant, especially between 1692 and 1698. The abrupt decline in these marriages in 1699 may reflect a movement of population northward after the restoration of peace.[3]

Certainly, for most massacre survivors, the community at Albany provided the most immediate place of refuge. On March 31, 1690, Jacob Leisler made reference to "the remnant sheltering themselves at Albany, where is provision made for them from New Yorke." Already supplies, including clothes and material for clothing, had reached Albany and were distributed on March 28, 1690. Crowded with refugees, the city became even more congested with the arrival during May and June of troops from New England and other parts of New York for what proved to be an abortive attack against Canada commanded by Fitz-John Winthrop of Connecticut. Not surprisingly, with such a concentration of refugees and troops, disease, both smallpox and "the bloody flux," was prevalent at Albany throughout the spring and summer. Among those who may have succumbed to

3. *DHNY*, I, 311; *NYCD*, III, 714. During this period there also was an increase in the number of weddings of people from Albany County which took place at the Dutch Reformed church during the winter months from November to March when the Hudson River south from Albany was difficult or impossible to navigate—a further indication that these ceremonies involved persons then residing at or near New York City.

these maladies was Jacques Cornelissen van Slyck, who on May 18, 1690, was at Albany "lying . . . sick abed" and who died soon after.[4]

In spite of a joint plea to the Albany magistrates by Sander Glen and Douwe Aukes that the "inhabitants of Schenectady sojourning at Albany . . . be sent back," many of the village's residents remained there for some time. When Reyer Schermerhorn's stepdaughter (Tryntje Helmers) married Gerrit Symonsen Veeder on August 3, 1690, they were both identified as living at Albany. Indeed, for many the return to Schenectady could be long delayed. As late as 1697, the families of Reyer Schermerhorn, Pieter Danielsen van Olinda, and Johannes Teller still resided at the city. The return of survivors was hindered not only by the possibility of further attack but by the extensiveness of the destruction at Schenectady itself. A year after the massacre, Cathalyna de Vos's property was described only as "a lot lying within the village of Shinnechtady, where her dwelling was." Many like Johannes Teller had lost everything: "cattle, household goods, etc. at Schinnechtady were destroyed by the enemy from Canada and he was carried away captive, whereby his family was impoverished."[5]

4. *NYCD*, III, 700. The distribution of goods to the Schenectady inhabitants is noted in *DHNY*, II, 199–202. Although the Winthrop campaign proved abortive, several members of the Schenectady militia participated in the effort. The officers of the Schenectady militia at this time were Sander Glen (captain), Johannes Sanders Glen (lieutenant), and Douwe Aukes (ensign). On August 13, Captain Sander Glen was reported at Wood Creek (near today's Fort Edward) with "his company [of] 28 whites and 5 savages." At least some of these troops continued northward and carried out a small but successful foray against the French at La Prairie near Montreal. Whether Glen and the others participated in the raid or returned to Albany with Winthrop's retiring army is uncertain. Among those who did join the band of 29 whites and 120 Indians led by Johannes Schuyler of Albany were Barent Wemp and, most likely, Jan Luycassen Wyngaerd. On July 23 Wyngaerd composed his will at Albany "having fled from his lands lying at Schanechtede and at present maintaining himself in the aforesaid city, intending to go to war against the French nation and their Indians in Canada." *DHNY*, II, 285; *ERAR* , III, 602, IV, 119. For the 1690 campaign and the Schuyler raid against La Prairie, see *DHNY*, II, 212–216, 279–282, 285–288; *NYCD*, IV, 193–196; "Muster Rolls," 398–405; Fitz-John Winthrop, *Winthrop Papers*, Massachusetts Historical Society, *Collections*, 5th ser., VIII (Boston, 1882), 307–319. Not only was there disease among the Albany population, but the Mohawks also suffered from an outbreak of smallpox. *NYCD*, IV, 195; *DHNY*, II, 252–254. Jacques Cornelissen van Slyck was about fifty years old when he died. He may have been sick the previous fall, but was not noted to be in poor health when he testified against Robert Livingston on April 1, 1690. *DHNY*, II, 205–206; *FS*, 239; *ERAR*, IV, 119–121.

5. *ERAR*, II, 383, 404; *CHME*, XXXVI, 45. For the 1697 census of households at Albany, see *Annals*, IX, 81–85. For the marriage of Gerrit Symonsen Veeder and Tryntje Helmers, see *Records of the Reformed Dutch Church of Albany, New York, 1683–*

Recognition that Schenectady would not be abandoned had been
provided by Albany's magistrates as early as February 1690, when
they resolved to persuade the Mohawks "to come & live & Plant at
Shinnectady lately Destroyed . . . wh will be a means yt ye winter
Corn sowed there may be Reaped & ye Indians in Readinesse to joyn
with our forces . . . if ye enemy should come." The Leisler government at New York also evidenced its determination to maintain the
village in a April 1690 directive to its Albany agents: "mest riars
[Reyer Schermerhorn ?] desired som guns . . . for Schonectede with
wee Desiers ma not be desertet doo It shuld kost 50 soldiers to maen-
tain." The placement of troops at the village and the erection of new
defenses would serve little purpose, however, unless former settlers
were willing to return. In his May 1690 will, Jacques Cornelissen van
Slyck clearly expressed the intention that his wife and children
should reoccupy the family's Schenectady property. Jan Luycassen
Wyngaerd had a similar expectation when he made his wife, Catharyna, "the sole and universal heir to all his personal and real estate"
that summer before departing to fight the French. In February 1691,
when Cathalyna de Vos entered into a contract of marriage with her
third husband, Claes Jansen van Bockhoven, her property at Schenectady, although in ruins, was counted equally among their combined estate.[6]

The return of population to the village was facilitated by there
being at least a few houses and barns left standing and some horses,
cattle, hogs, and poultry remaining in the woods to be recaptured.
Most of the produce stored at the village had been consumed by fire,
but the French attack had left the snow-covered fields sown with
winter wheat untouched and ready to be harvested and replanted in
the spring. No fort would be completed at Schenectady until 1695,
but the blockhouse was rebuilt, and contemporary documents again

---

1809 (Baltimore, 1978), 24; Vreeland Y. Leonard, *The Genealogical Record of the Veeder
Family* (n.p., 1937), 1–6.

6. *ERAR*, III, 602; *DHNY*, II, 162, 238. Even the Iroquois signaled their concern
that the village be restored when, in conference at Albany, the Mohawks urged that it
be garrisoned and the blockhouse rebuilt. See *DHNY*, II, 166; *NYCD*, III, 714. As
early as May 1690, troops were present at what remained of the village. On May 13
Jacob Leisler's commissioners at Albany ordered "Capn Sander Glen . . . & Inhabitants belonging to ye said Schanechtede and adjacent Parts, with the Souldiers there
in Garrison, to build a substantial Fort of due magnitude and strength upon that part
. . . of ground (called by the name of Cleyn Isaacs)." *DHNY*, II, 224. For the van
Slyck and Wyngaerd wills and the 1691 marriage contract of Cathalyna de Vos and
Claes Jansen van Bockhoven, see *ERAR*, II, 403–405, III, 602, IV, 119–121.

refer to this structure as early as April 1692. Moreover, the Glen residence opposite the village could provide protection and refuge if needed. In May 1691 Governor Henry Sloughter visited the village and met briefly with its inhabitants. That same summer the surviving Wemp children took action to settle the estate of their late stepfather, Sweer Teunissen van Velsen. As weapons were distributed to the troops at Schenectady in October 1691, one can presume that this force remained quartered there throughout the following winter. When, on December 10, 1691, Harmanus Vedder married Grietje van Slyck, both were identified in the Albany church records as residing at Schenectady.[7]

During these same years (in fact as early as the summer of 1690), several of those persons who had been taken captive by the French and Indians returned to the village (Table 19). Isaac Cornelissen Swits was the first to do so. In separate efforts, Swits and one of the Connecticut soldiers escaped from their French captors at Montreal and reached Albany the same day—July 9. Next, in March 1691, four unidentified captives (possibly the sons of Symon Groot) were returned by "a party of Christians and maquase." That June the Mohawks restored two more captives, Joseph Marks, a soldier, and Symon, the eldest son of Symon Groot. In February 1693 Jan Baptist van Eps and Arnout Viele, Jr., both of whom were forced to act as guides for a party of French and Indians intent on attacking the Mohawks, fled as the invaders passed near to Schenectady. By 1693 at least ten captives were back. Eventually, of the twenty-seven inhabi-

---

7. The existing records disagree as to the number of buildings that remained at Schenectady after the French attack. The French claimed that only one house was spared, but Robert Livingston stated that "6 or 7 houses" had been left standing. Structures located outside the village may not have been destroyed. In June 1691 Governor Sloughter reprimanded the Iroquois for burning deserted houses and barns near Schenectady and for killing the settlers' animals that remained in the woods. *DHNY*, I, 301, 309; *NYCD*, III, 773–774, 779, 792. Both the Dutch and the Iroquois were concerned for the preservation of the village's harvest of winter wheat. *NYCD*, III, 714; *DHNY*, II, 162. For the French attack on the blockhouse, its subsequent restoration, and the building of a fort at Schenectady, see *DHNY*, I, 300; *ERAR*, II, 352; *Calendar of Council Minutes*, VII, 88, 136. Both Myndert and Barent Wemp received commissions from Jacob Leisler, but their sister was married to Sander Glen. On June 15, 1691, Johannes Sanders Glen married Myndert Wemp's widow. In August 1691 Lieutenant Governor Ingoldsby received a petition regarding the division of the van Velsen estate. *CHME*, XXXVII, 216; *FS*, 76–77, 289; *DHNY*, II, 350, 353. For the distribution of arms to the soldiers and the December 1691 Vedder marriage, see *Calendar of Council Minutes*, VI, 56; *Records of the Reformed Dutch Church of Albany*, 24. Grietje (Margarita) van Slyck was the daughter of the late Jacques Cornelissen van Slyck and the widow of Andries Arentsen Bradt. *FS*, 20, 239, 255.

Table 19. Return of captives to Schenectady

Name	Date of return[a]	Evidence of return
Inhabitants		
Isaac Cornelissen Swits	1690	
Symon Groot, Jr.	1691	
Abraham Groot	(1691)	married April 15, 1696
Philip Groot	(1691)	son baptized September 5, 1702
Dirck Groot	(1691)	son baptized October 16, 1707
Claes Groot	(1691)	
Johannes Teller	(1692)	daughter baptized February 19, 1693
Jan Baptist van Eps	1693	
Arnout Viele, Jr.	1693	
Barent Vrooman	1697	
Albert Vedder	?	married December 17, 1699
Claes Fransen		
Van der Bogaert	?	married December 31, 1699
Lourens Claesen		
Van der Volgen	(1699)	July 1700 paid by province for journey to Iroquois
Johannes Wemp	?	married June 15, 1700
Cornelis Swits	?	married October 9, 1702
Johannes Vedder	?	married July 8, 1705
Soldiers		
John Webb	?	one unnamed soldier reached Albany
David Burt	?	on July 9, 1690
Joseph Marks	1691	

Note: The names of the five slaves taken captive are not known and there is no evidence that any returned to Schenectady.

Sources: For the 1690 list of captives, see *DHNY*, I, 305–306. For information on the return of the captives, see *DHNY*, I, , 306, II, 162–163, 273; *NYCD*, III, 778, 781, 782, 815, 817, IV, 6, 16, 17, 574, IX, 551, 559; *CHME*, XLIII, 139, 140; *SP*, 82–230, 272–273; *FS*, 80.

[a]Parentheses indicate estimated year of return.

tants, soldiers, and slaves taken prisoner, eighteen can be identified as having returned. At least two of the three soldiers and all but three of the inhabitants escaped, were rescued, or were released at the conclusion of hostilities. It is not certain, however, if any of the five slaves taken away were ever restored.[8]

The return of so many of the Schenectady inhabitants appears surprising given the experience of English captives who chose to remain

8. *SP*, 273. Jonathan Pearson claimed that the five sons of Symon Groot returned in 1691. *FS*, 80–81. Prisoners other than the Schenectady captives also escaped from the French during these years. *Calendar of Council Minutes*, VI, 135.

among the Indians. A primary reason for taking captives was to secure new members for families and clans who had lost individuals
through death or in warfare. As such, white captives had to be edu-
cated into Indian society. The transformation was both physical and
cultural, clothes were provided, faces painted, and men and boys had
their hair shaved in native fashion. The prisoners were taught songs
and dances and, after an adoption ceremony, were distributed among
individual families for their further immersion into the native culture.
The effectiveness of these techniques was often demonstrated. At the
conclusion of King William's War, for example, according to the Jesuits, many of the English children held by the Abenakis in Maine
balked at being restored to their natural parents and families.[9]

In 1680 Jasper Danckaerts had commented on the distinctive behavior of those persons who lived "somewhat nearer the Indians." As
noted elsewhere, the village attracted as settlers half-breeds such as
Jacques and Hilletie van Slyck, their Mohawk nephew Wouter, and
Lea, the Indian wife of Claes Willemsen van Coppernol. That even
those captives who were most influenced by their stay with the Canadian Indians, such as Jan Baptist van Eps and Lourens Claesen Van
der Volgen, returned to and lived out the remainder of their lives at
or near Schenectady, suggests that the distinction between white and
native cultures which characterized community life in New England
was not as sharp a dividing line at the village on the Mohawk River.[10]

Word of the fate of the Schenectady captives was first provided by
three Frenchmen, themselves taken prisoner by the Mohawks and
examined at Schenectady March 3, 1690: "Being Inquired concerning
ye Prisoners they carried along with them, Said they were well
Treated by ye way, and within 4 or 5 days journey of Canida Some
of our Prisoners went with ye Indians and ye Remainder With ye
french, Butt yt we need not doubt of there good Entertainment at
Canida Since they will be delivered to ye Jesuits, to be instructed in

---

9. Axtell, *European and Indian*, chap. 7. *JR*, LXV, 91–93. Although I do not quote
it in the text, I am impressed by a statement made by Gary Nash: "But in colonial
America the half-Indian, half-white person, usually the product of a liaison between a
white fur trader and an Indian woman, remained in almost all cases within Indian
society." Nash, *Red, White, and Black*, 283. There seems to be something singular
about the community at Schenectady. Individuals of mixed European and native descent lived at Schenectady, as did full-blooded Mohawks such as Hilletie van Olinda's
nephew Wouter. Moreover, unlike the experience of English captives, not one of the
persons taken away in 1690 remained among the Indians or French: eventually, all
who survived returned to Schenectady.

10. *JD*, 196.

there Religeon." Existing evidence substantiates the Frenchmen's claims. Isaac Cornelissen Swits escaped from Montreal in June 1690 and one of Adam Vrooman's sons was said to have converted to Catholicism while in French hands. Meanwhile, other prisoners such as Symon Groot, Jr., were left with the Praying Indians. In June 1691 he was given over by them to a Mohawk named Taonnochreo and in this manner returned to Albany after a journey of less than two weeks. Finally, both Jan Baptist van Eps and Lourens Claesen Van der Volgen became so fluent in the Iroquois language as a result of their captivity that they were made provincial interpreters.[11]

For captives such as Symon Groot, Jr., and Jan Baptist van Eps, the date and means of their return are known, but for most others their release is documented only by the reappearance of their names in surviving community records. Johannes Teller, for example, had returned by mid-1692, if not earlier, for in February 1693 his wife gave birth to a daughter. A majority of captives were restored by some method, but two at least may have perished in the effort. This end befell "2 Christian boys that were taken at Schennectady." Both boys were rescued in December 1691 when a party of Mohawks and Oneidas ambushed a band of Praying Indians while the latter were hunting on the Richelieu River below the Chambly rapids. The Iroquois killed four men, losing one of their own. With sixteen prisoners, in addition to the two youths from Schenectady, they began their return down Lake Champlain. After traveling for five days, "they perceived the Enemeys tract being a deep snow and cutt trees like a penn for their security and sent out three Indians . . . who came back, and see none but many tracts they resolved to proceed on their march . . . 4 Indians in the Reere . . . about 9 oclock the French and Indians fall upon them . . . killd the whole party none escaping but the 4 that were in the reere." Although the identity of the two boys was not revealed, most likely they were Stephen, the son of Gysbert Gerritse van Brakel, Arnout, the son of Paulyn Jansen, or

---

11. *LIR*, 159. For Swits's escape from Montreal, see *DHNY*, II, 273. Jonathan Pearson claimed that as late as 1697 two sons of Adam Vrooman, Wouter and Barent, were still held by the French. Only Barent is listed among 1690 captives. *DHNY*, I, 306; *SP*, 213. For the captivity of Symon Groot, Jr., among the Praying Indians and for the abilities of van Eps and Van der Volgen as interpreters, see *NYCD*, III, 781, 782, IV, 539, 569, 727; *CHME*, XXXVII, 169. Their influence is suggested by the grant of five islands in the Mohawk River which the two received from the Iroquois in 1701. *Calendar of Council Minutes*, VIII, 265; *Indorsed Land Papers*, III, 13. For the return of captives in 1691, see *JR*, LXIV, 59–61.

Stephen, the adopted son of Gerritje Bonts, none of whom is again mentioned in the Schenectady records after their 1690 capture.[12]

Unsuccessful attempts were made to exchange French prisoners held at Albany for those who remained in Canada, but as late as 1697 at least one son and several relatives of Adam Vrooman were still held captive, and in that year Vrooman undertook an embassy to Canada to secure their release. Apparently, the final captive to return was Lourens Claesen Van der Volgen. At thirteen, one of the youngest of those taken in 1690, Van der Volgen was greatly influenced by his stay among the Canadian Indians and remained with them of his own volition after the restoration of peace. In 1699 Jean Rosie of Albany was at Montreal, where he made inquiries with the French authorities about Van der Volgen: "The said Jean Rosie asked why that Purmerent [Claes Lourens Van der Volgen] an inhabitant of Shonnectady's son [Lourens Claesen Van der Volgen] was not sent home, the Govr answered that he was free to goe when he pleased, he did not detain him." The younger Van der Volgen did not return with Rosie but may have departed soon after and was back at Schenectady before July 1700, in which month he was reimbursed by the provincial government for a journey undertaken to the Mohawks, Oneidas, and Onondagas. Family tradition would have it that he arrived at Schenectady in native garb, intending to rejoin his adopted Indian family. Only the cutting off of his scalplock by a sister while he slept prevented an immediate departure. This story may be fanciful, but Van der Volgen evidently did become reconciled to the Dutch community. He married twice and, until his death in about 1740, was employed as a provincial interpreter.[13]

The village to which the captives returned remained a struggling community throughout the 1690s. In May 1691, while at Albany, Governor Henry Sloughter rode to Schenectady to "see the ruines of that Towne occasioned by the French." He found the settlement "in

12. *NYCD*, III, 815. For the attack on Lake Champlain, see *NYCD*, III, 817; *DHNY*, I, 306, II, 162–163; *Calendar of Council Minutes*, VI, 66.

13. *NYCD*, IV, 574. For an attempted exchange of prisoners, see *JR*, LXIV, 61. For the 1697 Vrooman embassy, see *SP*, 213; *NYCD*, IV, 338. For Van der Volgen, see *FS*, 217–218; *CHME*, XLIII, 139, 140. Van der Volgen's name was included on a Schenectady tax list for 1738. His will was filed August 30, 1739, and proved October 21, 1741. Schenectady Tax List, 1738; *Calendar of Wills*, 63. The scalplock story may be fabrication, but it is consistent with existing ethnohistorical data concerning the veneration of scalplocks among the eastern woodland Indians. Having lost his, Van der Volgen presumably would have hesitated to return to his Indian family until his hair had regrown. Axtell, *European and Indian*, 30–34, 212–214.

a very sad and miserable condicon occasioned by the late Troubles."
When in October 1692 the inhabitants petitioned Governor Benjamin
Fletcher "that they may be released from their portion of taxes, on
account of their losses by the French," the request was quickly
granted. Indeed, neither the presence of troops nor the construction
of a fort by 1695 could make the community entirely safe. In September 1696 one man was killed and another wounded near the village, and French documents recorded that "some Regulars and Indians captured at the gate of Schenectady a very influential
Onnondaga Chief." Added to the disruptions of war were equally
upsetting, if more natural, calamities. A fire in October 1694 destroyed 1,000 schepels of wheat from that year's harvest. Nature too
proved unrewarding. The winter of 1691–1692 was difficult, and
that of 1697–1698 was described as "the severest that ever was known
in the memory of man." Also at least three years, 1695, 1698, and
1699, saw unfavorable weather conditions during the growing season
which resulted in poor harvests.[14]

   In spite of these tribulations, former inhabitants and families returned and new ones arrived. Many persons who had lost spouses at
the time of the massacre remarried, including Douwe Aukes, Cathalyna de Vos, Adam Vrooman, and Gerritje Ryckman (the last two to
each other). Several persons of English descent also married and settled at Schenectady during this period (Table 20). Many of these men

14. *SP*, 284; *CHME*, XXXVIII, 207; *NYCD*, III, 779, 792, IX, 666. At Albany, in
1694 it was reported that Canadian Indians threw "a warclub over the stockadoes,"
and chased the inhabitants. In 1696, Martin Gerritse, a justice of the peace for Albany County, was killed by the French and Indians. *Calendar of Council Minutes*, VII,
68, 189. The 1690s also was a troubled decade for the Mohawks. Many warriors were
killed and the Mohawk population was scattered for a time in February 1693 when a
force of French and Indians burned the three main tribal villages. *NYCD*, IV, 14–20,
37, 54, 648, 689. Hard times for the Mohawks created a security problem for the
Dutch. On February 24, 1693, the Albany magistrates informed Governor Fletcher
that "the Maquase nation is wholley dispersed by the enemyes late burning all their
three Castles & [as] our farmers live straggling up & down the country [they are] in
great danger to be cutt off by sculking Indians." *NYCD*, IV, 20. For the 1692 Schenectady petition regarding taxes, see *Calendar of Council Minutes*, VI, 135. In 1693
Governor Fletcher offered a bounty of fifty shillings for each enemy scalp taken
within three miles of Albany or Schenectady. *NYCD*, IV, 46. In July 1696 the Schenectady garrison numbered thirty-three men. For this and an account of the military
stores then at Schenectady, see *NYCD*, IV, 431. For the September 1696 killing near
Schenectady, see *NYCD*, IV, 198. For evidence that the fear of attack hindered agricultural activities, see *NYCD*, IV, 53; Livingston, "Business Letters," 190. For the
1694 fire at Schenectady and the harshness of the winters, see *Calendar of Council
Minutes*, VI, 63; *SP*, 284; *NYCD*, IV, 115. For the poor harvests of 1695, 1698, and
1699, see *NYCD*, IV, 575; Livingston, "Business Letters," 193.

Table 20. Englishmen at Schenectady, 1690–1705

Name	Year of marriage	Spouse[a]
William Bowin	1702	m/d of Jan Jansen Jonckers
Jacobus Cromwell	1703	m/ Maria Philipse
Thomas Davie	1701	m/d of Johannes Kleyn
Jonathan Dyer	1695	m/wd of Harmanus Hagedorn
William Hall	1695	m/wd of Elias van Guyseling (wd with c)
Philip Harris	1692	m/wd of Frans Harmensen Van der Bogaert (wd with c)
John McIntyer[b]	1704	m/wd of Jorges Rinckhout
Daniel Mascraft	1696	m/wd of Willem Noble
Thomas Nobel	1701	m/d of David Marinus
Mannaseh Sixberry	1699	m/d of Jan Jansen Jonckers
Thomas Smith	1696	m/wd of Gerrit Janse
Jonathan Stevens	1693	m/wd of Claes Willemsen van Coppernol (wd with c)
Jeremy Thickstone	1697	m/wd of David Willemse

Sources: FS; SP, 82–230.
[a]m/ = married; d = daughter; wd = widow; c = children.
[b]May have been of Scottish or Irish descent, not English.

were soldiers stationed on the frontier, and it may be that such individuals helped to fill a void created by the removal of population from Albany County after 1689. Jan Jansen Jonckers (van Rotterdam), for example, saw two of his unmarried daughters provided for in this manner. More often, these Englishmen married Dutch women who had recently been widowed. In most instances, their husbands had died of natural causes and not as a result of the 1690 French attack. Several had children and their remarriage was, presumably, a matter of convenience. A new husband, even an English one, may have been preferable to burdening one's relatives or shouldering sole responsibility for one's own providence and the rearing of children. Given the anti-English sentiments of the local Dutch population, it is possible that these women suffered a reduction in status within the community in order to be provided with a helpmate.[15]

15. For marriages, see FS, 3–4, 276–277; ERAR, II, 403. A Cornelis Viele of Schenectady also was married in New York. Marriages from 1639 to 1801 in the Reformed Dutch Church, 74. CHME, LIX, 15. Between 1689 and 1698, a total of 142 men, 68 women, and 209 children left Albany County. NYCD, IV, 420–421. The following Englishmen who settled at Schenectady between 1690 and 1705 can be identified in existing military records: William Bowin, Jonathan Stevens, Manasseh Sixberry,

Schenectady remained a community without a minister, but as early as 1691 the congregation was again electing elders and deacons. The performance of baptisms at the village by Dominie Godfridus Dellius beginning in 1694 was a further indication that a settled population was now in residence. The massacre and its aftermath retarded but never entirely halted the natural processes of marriage, conception, and birth. The wives of at least five Schenectady residents were pregnant at the time of the 1690 attack and delivered children during the succeeding months between March and July. Reyer Schermerhorn's stepdaughter, Tryntje Helmers, also may have been pregnant at this time and gave birth to a son less than three months after her August 3, 1690, marriage to Gerrit Symonsen Veeder. After these women brought their pregnancies to term, during the following year, 1691, only the wives of Isaac Cornelissen Swits and Barent Wemp are known to have given birth to children. The cycle of marriages, however, appears to have followed a reverse pattern, with a reduction immediately after the massacre and an increase the next year. The disruption of the period is evident. The Dutch church at Albany, which witnessed thirteen marriages in 1689, saw only four in 1690—and two of these occurred before the events of February. Records are available for only half a year in 1691, but ten Albany marriages were recorded between June and December.[16]

The restoration of a stable pattern of marriages and baptisms suggests that this cycle was among the most resilient elements of community life. Schenectady had been founded not by single individuals but by families—parents, siblings, and relatives. Throughout the period covered here, marriage was an expected status and preceded the responsibilities of adulthood. Most couples married for the first time during their early twenties. Although premarital pregnancy was not unknown, in almost all cases a wedding ceremony soon followed. Childbearing and rearing rapidly succeeded marriage for most women. Within two years a typical Schenectady wife had given birth to her first child. This infant would be followed by several others,

---

Jonathan Dyer, Jacobus Cromwell, and Jeremy Thickstone. The Frenchman Benjamin Lenyn also may have reached Schenectady in this manner. "Colonial Muster Rolls," 464–480.

16. For the election of church officials at Schenectady on November 20, 1691, and for the resumption of baptisms in 1694, see Records of the First Reformed Church at Schenectady, I, 68, 101. The birth of children to Schenectady women in 1690 and 1691 is recorded in *FS*, 185, 198, 206, 217, 231, 235, 264, 289. For the marriages at Albany, see *Records of the Reformed Dutch Church of Albany*, 22–24.

perhaps six or seven more offspring, during the next decade and a half.[17]

Any interruption in this sequence was, most likely, the result of a miscarriage, a baby born dead, or a child who died within days of birth. The birth of twins, for example, often ended with the death of one or both children. Existing church and family records are incomplete, however, and the evidence for such events often rests solely on a suspiciously long space of years between baptisms or, in the case of infant deaths, the reuse of a name first given to an earlier child. Children were born at home, with the attendance of one or more midwives. At Albany, midwives were sworn civic officials, a practice that presumably was also followed at Schenectady.[18]

17. Since 1982 I have established a community research file consisting of approximately ten thousand individual life histories for persons who were born at or resided at Schenectady before 1800. Such information has been gathered from Dutch, Anglican, and Presbyterian church records, tax lists (1705, 1708, 1719, 1738, 1751, 1779, 1799), lists of freeholders (1720, 1763), census records (1697, 1790, 1800), will abstracts, Bible records, midwives records, and the like.

The reconstitution work that will allow for a careful analysis of the demographic history of Schenectady for the years before 1710 remains incomplete. Dutch church records before 1690 are lacking, and in too many instances basic information regarding dates of birth, marriage, and death for the community's residents remain unknown or must be approximated from wills and other family records.

Although Jonathan Pearson's genealogy of Schenectady-area families (compiled more than a century ago from Dutch church records) is a standard reference used by many genealogists and an occasional historian, his work must be approached with caution as it includes many individuals and families whose names appear in the Schenectady church records but who actually lived at Albany, Niskayuna, Schoharie or elsewhere. Pearson's information is deficient, both for the years prior to 1690 (before extant Dutch church records) and for after 1760, when the Anglican church at Schenectady offered families an alternative setting for marriage, baptisms, and burials. An essay that depends heavily on Pearson's genealogy is Edward H. Tebbenhoff, "Tacit Rules and Hidden Family Structures: Naming Practices and Godparentage in Schenectady, New York, 1680–1800," *Journal of Social History*, 17 (1985), 567–585.

18. For the birth of twins and for infant deaths, see *FS*, 28, 70, 206, 218, 231. For midwives at Albany, see *ARS*, II, 160, 182. In most cases, a woman's cycle of pregnancy and childbirth was completed within two decades of her marriage. Deviations from this pattern were infrequent and served as variations that highlighted the standard practice. The death of a spouse and the survivor's remarriage sometimes produced families into which children were born beyond the span of two decades. Harmanus van Slyck, for example, was born about 1680, the son of Jacques Cornelissen van Slyck and Gerritje Ryckman. He married Jannetie Vrooman and between 1704 and 1724 the couple had at least eleven children. In 1726 he married a second time (Antje Shell) and fathered two more children. As a result of van Slyck's two marriages, children were born into this household over a twenty-five year span (1704–1729). *FS*, 240. Such households were more complex in their relations among parents, stepparents, children, and stepchildren. Not surprisingly, evidence exists for intergenera-

By 1697 Schenectady had a population of 238 persons, including
14 slaves. In July 1702, when Governor Cornbury visited the community, he found it an open village: "It was formerly stockadoed
round but since the peace no care having been taken to repair the
Stockadoes they are all down." The community's defenses consisted
of a stockaded fort, "more like a pound than a fort," with eight cannon (only three of which were fit for service), and a garrison of "but a
Serjeant and twelve men, no powder nor shot neither great nor small
nor no place to put it into." In spite of renewed conflict that same
year (Queen Anne's War, 1702–1713), Schenectady was not threatened as it had been during the previous decade. As a result, the village's population continued to grow, perhaps more than doubling by
1710. In that year, the Reverend Thomas Barclay estimated that 116
families resided at the village, both Dutch and English. The census
for 1714 recorded 591 inhabitants, including 276 white males of all
ages, 271 white females, and 17 male and 27 female slaves.[19]

At the opening of the eighteenth century, with their community's
strategic position enhanced by two decades of warfare, Schenectady's
settlers found themselves increasingly encompassed by the English
imperial system. The English garrison, which had amounted to only
thirteen men in 1702, had reached forty in number by 1710. Among
those who received payments for provisioning the troops and for
making repairs to the fort during this period were Johannes Sanders
Glen and Reyer Schermerhorn. In 1711 Governor Robert Hunter
determined to extend the English military and ecclesiastical presence
westward into the Mohawk Valley with the construction of a fort for
twenty men and a chapel for the Mohawks. These structures were to
be located on the south bank of the Mohawk River at the juncture
with the Schoharie River. Five carpenters from Schenectady, including two sons of Adam Vrooman, received the contract for their erection. During these same years, the Reverend Thomas Barclay of Albany began ministering at the village, teaching English to the Dutch

tional tension within these families. As noted in Chapter 5, during the 1680s, several
of the Wemp offspring squabbled with their stepfather, Sweer Teunissen van Velsen,
regarding the disposition of a bequest made to a recently deceased sister. For the
Wemp family, see *ARS*, III, 324–326, 344.

19. *NYCD*, IV, 968. For Schenectady's population in 1697 and 1714, and for Reverend Barclay's 1710 count of families, see *Annals*, IX, 88–89; *DHNY*, III, 905; *ER*,
III, 1866. The 1708 tax list counted 115 households at or near Schenectady. Livingston-Redmond Papers, roll 10.

children and hoping (prematurely) for the Anglicization of the village's religious and educational institutions.[20]

As early as 1680, Jasper Danckaerts remarked on the quantity and quality of the wheat grown at Schenectady. During the last decades of the seventeenth century, grain production emerged as the predominant economic activity at the village and remained so into the eighteenth century, a fact signaled by the maintenance of wheat procurement agents at Schenectady by Robert Livingston and his son Philip. Agricultural lands to the north and west of the community also began to be exploited even before the end of Queen Anne's War. After 1709 eight Dutch farmers settled at Schaghticoke on the east bank of the Hudson River north of Albany on land belonging to that city. Here they raised wheat with which to pay their rents due to the Albany Corporation. Among the first settlers were three individuals from Schenectady: Symon Danielsen van Antwerpen, Lowis Viele, and Daniel Ketelhuyn, Viele's uncle. There was even greater interest in the acquisition and settlement of land to the west. Among those seeking Mohawk Valley lands were Harmen van Slyck, Reyer Schermerhorn, Jan Pietersen Mabie, and Adam Vrooman. By the second decade of the eighteenth century, Schenectady was no longer the frontier settlement of New York. The opening of its attractive agricultural hinterland began in 1712 when fifty or sixty German Palatine families, refugees from an unsuccessful naval stores project sponsored by Governor Robert Hunter, cut a road from Schenectady to the Schoharie River and settled on lands about twenty miles from the river's mouth. By 1724, according to Cadwallader Colden, farming was being undertaken even fifty miles to the west of Schenectady.[21]

20. For the size of the Schenectady garrison in 1702 and 1710, see *ER*, III, 1866; *NYCD*, IV, 968. For the payments to Glen and Schermerhorn, see *Calendar of Council Minutes*, VIII, 30, 71, 140, 164. For information on Fort Hunter, see *NYCD*, V, 279–281; Norton, *Fur Trade in New York*, 157; Douglas E. Leach, *The Northern Colonial Frontier, 1607–1763* (New York, 1966), 127–129. Reverend Barclay's hope of converting the Schenectady population to the Anglican religion and the English tongue are expressed in *ER*, III, 1866–1867.

21. The increased production of grain in New York after 1670 and the Livingstons' interest in acquiring wheat at Schenectady are noted in Kim, *Landlord and Tenant*, 53–54, 158. In 1707 Robert Livingston acquired title to an island and an additional twenty acres of land at Schenectady. *SP*, 77; *FS*, 39. Danckaerts's comments are included in *JD*, 213. For Albany's control of the Schaghticoke lands, see *Colonial Laws of New York*, I, 199. For the 1709 settlement of Schaghticoke, see Klopott, "Schaghti-

The early 1700s witnessed both a continuation and an accentuation of economic developments rooted in the previous century. Grain production flourished, and in 1705 Governor Cornbury reported to the Lords of Trade: "The Trade of this Province consists chiefly in flower and biskett, which is sent to the islands in the West Indies." The simultaneous decline of the fur trade, however, resulted in alterations that were as much social and cultural as economic. Not only was the yearly number of furs traded much reduced, but the locale for their exchange now moved decisively westward. Some trading still took place at Schenectady and delegations of Indians were ferried by wagon to and from Albany for conferences, but the arrival of large numbers of western Indians in the early 1720s caused much surprise and comment. Ironically, it was at the moment that Albany's monopoly of the fur trade was broken (1727) and Schenectady's participation given legal sanction that the trade in furs moved beyond the village to Oswego and Lake Ontario.[22]

Some persons from Schenectady remained among the hundred or more traders who journeyed to the new post each year, while others found employment as bateau men in the subsidiary activities of hauling supplies and pelts up and down the Mohawk River. But as wheat

coke," 47–48. Van Antwerpen was the son of Daniel Jansen van Antwerpen. In 1695 Daniel Ketelhuyn married Debora Viele at Schenectady. She was Lowis Viele's aunt. *FS*, 99, 205–206, 271–272; Munsell, ed., *Collections*, IV, 137. For the failure of Governor Hunter's naval stores project and the removal of the Palatines to Schoharie, see *NYCD*, V, 347, 364, 418; *DHNY*, III, 541–607; Leach, *Northern Colonial Frontier*, 127–129; Walter A. Knittle, *Early Eighteenth-Century Palatine Emigration* (Baltimore, 1965), 188–195. For the interest in Mohawk Valley lands, see Higgins, *Expansion in New York*, 19, 60; *SP*, 190–191; *DHNY*, III, 687; *Indorsed Land Papers*, VI, 12, 34, 94, 110, 138, 153. In 1724, Cadwallader Colden wrote: "The Mohawks . . . live . . . forty Miles directly West from Albany, and within the English Settlements, some of the English Farms . . . being thirty Miles further West." Colden, *History of the Five Nations*, II, 15–16.

22. *NYCD*, IV, 1150. For the decline of the fur trade and growth of agriculture, see Kim, *Landlord and Tenant*, 53–54; Norton, *Fur Trade in New York*, 100–103. In November 1700, Governor Bellomont reported to the Lords of Trade: "The Beaver trade here and at Boston is sunk to nothing." Bellomont calculated the total export of beavers from New York for the period June 1699 to June 1700 as only 15,241 skins. *NYCD*, IV, 789. For evidence that some trading still occurred at Schenectady and for the transporting of Indians to and from Albany, see *NYCD*, V, 217, 591, 867, VI, 633. In 1724 Governor Burnet stated that between 1716 and 1720 thirty canoes of "far Indians" had arrived at Schenectady, but that between 1720 and 1724 the number was over three hundred. *NYCD*, V, 739; Colden, *History of the Five Nations*, II, 26–27. For the establishment of a trading post at Oswego, see *DHNY*, I, 443–463; Norton, *Fur Trade in New York*, 94, 170–171. For the end of Albany's monopoly, see Norton, 57–59.

replaced furs as the colony's export staple, there was a contraction of the community's economic horizon, which previously had extended north and west to the peltry-producing regions of Canada, the Iroquois Confederacy, and beyond. Moreover, as the transactions that surrounded the exchange of furs no longer occurred at Schenectady, there was a severing of the once intimate economic, social, and cultural relations that had transpired at the village between the settlers and the Indians. The worlds of both grew increasingly separate with the new century. Only during the brief tenure of Dominie Bernardus Freeman were numbers of Indians baptized or married at the Dutch church. In addition, the liaison of red and white was a seventeenth-century phenomenon, not to be repeated at Schenectady during the eighteenth century. By 1707 both Jacques Cornelissen van Slyck and his sister Hilletie were dead. Although the children of a Dutch father and an Iroquois mother, they had married Dutch spouses and their sons and daughters did likewise. Surviving them by only a few years was Lea, now the wife of an Englishman, Jonathan Stevens. It is not certain, however, whether she was a Mohawk woman or another sister to the van Slycks.[23]

Analysis of the assessment roll for Schenectady from 1708 reveals that most community residents possessed estates valued at only a modest amount. Three individuals with estates worth over one hundred pounds—Johannes Sanders Glen, Reyer Schermerhorn, and Robert Livingston—far outdistanced their neighbors, two-thirds (64.0 percent) of whom had estates valued at less than thirty pounds and four-fifths (80.7 percent) below forty pounds. Only two persons were so poor that they had no assessment, but the average (mean) for the community as a whole was only twenty-five pounds. The wealthiest few, those with estates of fifty pounds or more, constituted one-eighth (12.3 percent) of the persons whose names appeared on the

23. For the hauling of supplies and pelts between Schenectady and Oswego, see Howell and Munsell, *History of the County of Schenectady*, 46–47; Smith, *Tour of Four Rivers*, 22. In 1727 Governor Burnet estimated that 200 traders were at Oswego. Three years later, Jacob Brouwer of Schenectady was killed by Indians while at Oswego. *DHNY*, I, 447; *NYCD*, IX, 1019; *FS*, 28. As regards the interest in the fur trade at Schenectady during the seventeenth century, one might note Arent van Curler's 1667 journey to Canada as well as Arnout Cornelissen Viele's involvement in the Macgregory expedition during the 1680s and his own 1692–1694 journey to the Ohio. Van Laer, ed., "Documents Relating to Arent van Curler's Death," 30–34; Broshar, "The First Push Westward of the Albany Traders," *MVHR*, 7 (1920–1921), 233–235, 239. For Jacques Cornelissen van Slyck, his sister Hilletie, and Lea, see *SP*, 188–191; *FS*, 50, 177, 229–230, 239–240.

list, while nearly one-third (31.6 percent) had assessments of less than ten pounds. Those in the poorest category controlled only 6.3 percent of the village's assessed wealth compared with 37.6 percent for the most well-to-do. Among the thirty-six least wealthy individuals was the proprietor Pieter Danielsen van Olinda, now an elderly widower. The others included at least fifteen persons who were sons of seventeenth-century settlers, but many had ties to Schenectady which were less substantive in time or family connections. Several, including Ahasuerus Marselis, Isaac van Valkenburgh, and Caleb Beck, were new men whose residence at the village dated back no further than the preceding decade. This also was the case with the ten individuals of English or French descent who made up over one-quarter of the village's poorest inhabitants. That almost two-thirds (22 of 36) of these men were either not yet married or had married for the first time during the previous decade (1699–1708) reinforces the impression that these were individuals just then establishing themselves at Schenectady both as residents and as heads of families. Finally, the 1708 assessment roll provides a measure of quantitative evidence that Schenectady was still predominantly a Dutch community. With the significant exception of two of the village's three wealthiest men, Johannes Sanders Glen and Robert Livingston, both of whom were of Scottish origins (but only the former a Schenectady resident), no non-Dutch household was assessed at over thirty pounds. The average (mean) estate for the village's households headed by persons of English or French descent was less than ten pounds.[24]

Only two of Schenectady's original proprietors lived into the eighteenth century. William Teller died in 1701, and Pieter Danielsen van Olinda in 1716. Van Olinda's wife, Hilletie, had died in 1707, as did Isaac Cornelissen Swits. Douwe Aukes last appears in existing records in 1720, and Reyer Schermerhorn had died one year before.

---

24. For the 1708 assessment, see Livingston-Redmond Papers, roll 10. Robert Livingston may have appeared on this list as a result of his purchase of an island in the Mohawk River from Johannes Clute in 1707. Livingston also received twenty acres of land on the mainland. *SP*, 77; *FS*, 39. Pieter Danielsen van Olinda's wife, Hilletie, died in 1707, and he died in 1716. *FS*, 229. For Marselis, van Valkenburgh, and Beck, see *SP*, 89, 129, 191. On February 4, 1699, "Caleb Beck, Mariner," was listed among the New York City freemen. *Burghers and Freemen of New York*, 73. Thomas J. Archdeacon has analyzed the distribution of wealth at New York City in 1703–1704. New York was a more economically stratified community than Schenectady. Ten percent of New York's families owned forty-seven percent of the city's wealth. Moreover, the Dutch were no longer so prominent a part of New York's population as they remained at Schenectady. Archdeacon, "Age of Leisler," 64–68; Archdeacon, *New York City*.

Schermerhorn's opponents were more long-lived; Adam Vrooman died in 1730 and Johannes Sanders Glen the following year, 1731. Glen was survived by Harmen van Slyck, the son of Jacques Cornelissen van Slyck, but they were both among the last remaining offspring of Schenectady's original proprietors. Memories of the founding and founders of the village must have faded rapidly with their passing. Until the middle of the eighteenth century, however, there were still persons alive at Schenectady who could recount the events that culminated in death or captivity for so many at the village in 1690. The interpreter Lourens Claesen Van der Volgen died about 1740, but other former captives including Jan Baptist van Eps and the sons of Symon Groot continued to live at or near to Schenectady. Indeed, as late as 1751, Albert Vedder (1671–1753) still resided at the village.[25]

The conclusion of Queen Anne's War in 1713 inaugurated three decades of peace. These were prosperous years for the community on the Mohawk River. In 1739 Schenectady was described as "a large village like a city, with several streets built house to house, very delightfully located on a plain, along a pleasant running stream, provided with a very attractive large stone church." The settled character of Schenectady's domestic institutions at this date belied the village's initial frontier setting. Moreover, a review of the community's development suggests that the classic statements of frontier evolution have little validity for deciphering the experience of Schenectady's early inhabitants. Such analyses often posit that the pioneering process contributed to the democratizing of political institutions and the heightening of economic mobility. During the first half-century of the village's existence, however, innovations, such as the use of juries, were imposed from without by the colony's English rulers. Similarly, the influx of new figures into the political arena after 1689 was less a result of an increasingly democratic or broadly based system of representation than the outcome of bitter community factionalism—one response to the unequal distribution of and access to landed property.[26]

In contrast to a hypothesized reality in which "Indian and alien

25. For information on the longevity of Schenectady's early settlers, see *FS*; *SP*, 82–230; *DHNY*, I, 371; *Abstracts of Wills*, XXV (1892), 102–103, XXVII (1894), 67–68; *Calendar of Wills*, 449; Schenectady Tax List, 1738; Schenectady Tax List, 1751.

26. *ER*, IV, 2730; Ray Allen Billington, "The American Frontier," in Paul Bohannan and Fred Plog, eds., *Beyond the Frontier: Social Process and Cultural Change* (Garden City, N.Y., 1967), 10.

enemies . . . [and] commonly-shared problems created a bond among frontiersmen," relations with surrounding native tribes were as frequently characterized by economic and cultural exchange as by mutual hostility. And, too, Schenectady's residents were as likely to consider the English soldiers and settlers who appeared at their gates as foreign and dangerous as the French in Canada—perhaps more so. Certainly, there was no bond of "commonly-shared problems" cementing the community's inhabitants to one another. Rather, family rivalry and competition for economic success divided and split the village residents.[27]

A majority of Schenectady's first settlers were the offspring of one of the most economically mature societies in Europe. Indeed, it may be that the individualism and rivalry displayed by Schenectady's farmers and traders reflected both the cultural baggage of the community's first arrivals and the material possibilities offered by their Mohawk Valley setting. The interaction of values and environment in early America has been noted by such writers as T. H. Breen and Jack Greene. Of the profit-motivated, exploitative, tobacco-growing settlers in Virginia, Breen has written, "The attitudes, beliefs, and the ideas that the founders brought with them to the New World interacted with specific environmental conditions." In particular, "the discovery of a lucrative export preserved the founders' privatistic orientation." If one substitutes furs for tobacco, Breen's portrait of Virginia's early settlers sounds suspiciously like that offered for the inhabitants of the Hudson-Mohawk region by Father Isaac Jogues as early as the 1640s.[28]

Schenectady remained a community in which property (land, buildings, slaves, crops, and the like) were bought and sold, deeded and leased. In time, land and produce supplanted furs as a vehicle for wealth. At Schenectady, however, neither increasing prosperity nor the passing of prior generations enabled the village's residents to find release from their former disputes. Schenectady was seemingly a community trapped by the divisions of the past. From 1700 to 1714, Reyer Schermerhorn, with the aid of his son-in-law Johannes Wemp, sought to manage the Schenectady common lands as sole surviving

27. Billington, "American Frontier," 13.
28. T. H. Breen, *Puritans and Adventurers: Change and Persistence in Early America* (New York, 1980), 110. Jack P. Greene, *Pursuits of Happiness: The Social Development of Early Modern British Colonies and the Formation of American Culture* (Chapel Hill, N.C., 1988), 169. For Father Jogues, see *NNN*, 262.

trustee under the patent of 1684. A subsequent patent of 1714 enabled Wemp to remain a trustee until his death in 1749, at which time administration of the common lands again rested in the hands of one individual, Arent Bradt. As late as 1744, however, forty-two persons at the village formally protested Wemp's and Bradt's trusteeship, and the entire dispute was reincarnated and given further impetus by Reyer Schermerhorn's grandson and namesake, Reyer Schermerhorn III. For over forty years, from 1754 until his death in 1795, Schermerhorn sought to regain control of the village's remaining common lands, which now amounted to about 50,000 acres.[29]

That the roots of such prolonged dissension lay deeply embedded in Schenectady's origins and first development must be given serious consideration. From its earliest days, Schenectady was a village that suffered from a severe structural atrophy, lacking the autonomous political, economic, and even religious institutions of community. Although provided with its own subcourt during the 1670s, Schenectady remained subject to the ordinances of the Albany magistrates. Even a century after its founding, when the number of freeholders at Albany and Schenectady was almost identical, the latter community had not yet achieved political emancipation. Only in 1765 did Lieutenant Governor Cadwallader Colden grant Schenectady a borough charter, and not until 1798 was it fully incorporated. Not only was Schenectady's political development circumscribed, Albany's monopolization of the fur trade represented an equally fundamental intrusion into and limitation on the village's economic life. In the area of religion, too, the community matured slowly. Although a majority of the population adhered to the Dutch Reformed religion, no church was built or minister settled at the village for over twenty years after its founding. Even then the Schenectady community proved unfortunate both in the recruitment and maintenance of a minister. Because of a lack of available candidates, the church accepted ministers who had not been properly certified by the Classis of Amsterdam. Dominie Petrus Tesschenmaeker, the first, was killed in 1690. His successor, Dominie Bernardus Freeman, was an active participant in the factionalism of the early eighteenth century and departed soon after

29. The Schenectady situation should be contrasted with that of traditional societies in which "production . . . is almost wholly for direct consumption, for use, rather than exchange in the market." Alan Macfarlane, *The Origins of English Individualism* (New York, 1979), 21–22, 163, 165, 171. The continuation of the dispute over Schenectady's common lands is noted in *SP*, 33–57.

his arrival. Not until 1714 and after would an orderly and proper succession of ministers be achieved.[30]

In its economic and political subordination to Albany, Schenectady's experience resembled the relationship that existed between certain New England towns and their surrounding hinterlands. Albany's efforts at maintaining Schenectady as a noncommercial, agricultural satellite were paralleled by communities such as Dedham and Salem, Massachusetts. At Dedham, by the early eighteenth century, the centrifugal forces of population dispersal and the granting of lands ever more distant from the original village center gave rise to a series of separate communities complete with their own churches and town meetings. Such autonomy, however, was resisted by Dedham proper and was achieved only after years of dissension that fractured the village's political and religious institutions. The depressed economic and social status of Salem's agricultural hinterland fostered a schism between that region and the more prosperous and commercial Salem port. The resulting tensions and bitterness played a dramatic role in the witchcraft accusations and trials of the 1690s. Similarly, the contentious relationship of Schenectady and Albany served as a backdrop to the village's adherence to the Leislerian cause in 1689 and after. Indeed, in the fall of 1689, Leisler's lieutenant, Jacob Milborne, had promised that "the gentlemen of Shennechtady will be preferred to those of Albany in the approaching New Government. . . . you shall have no less Privileges than those of Albany."[31]

However, it is by no means certain that either autonomous or long-established community institutions would have provided a successful forum for the resolution of Schenectady's divisions. As historians of

30. For Schenectady's political and economic subjection to Albany, see Norton, *Fur Trade in New York*, 45. For the number of freeholders at Albany and Schenectady in 1763, see Kenneth Scott, "The Freeholders of the City and County of Albany, 1763," *National Genealogical Society Quarterly*, 48 (1960), 171–182. For the 1765 borough charter and Schenectady's later incorporation, see *SP*, 430–432; Cadwallader Colden, *The Letters and Papers of Cadwallader Colden*, NYHSC, LVI (New York, 1923), 13–16. The 1678 petition by the Schenectady magistrates to Governor Andros seeking permission to use land above Schenectady for the support of a minister is the first indication of any attempt to recruit one for the village. *Calendar of Council Minutes*, III, 182. During these years, the Schenectady community was served by the Dutch minister at Albany. Balmer, *Perfect Babel*, 4–5. For the early church at Schenectady, see Birch, *Pioneering Church*, 1–47.

31. *DHNY*, II, 118. For Salem and Dedham, see Paul Boyer and Stephen Nissenbaum, *Salem Possessed: The Social Origins of Witchcraft* (Cambridge, Mass., 1974), chap. 4; Kenneth A. Lockridge, *A New England Town: The First Hundred Years, Dedham, Massachusetts, 1636–1736* (New York, 1970), chap. 6.

colonial New England have discerned, local institutions, whether political or religious, could be subverted by dissension if not sustained
by a community ethos favoring harmony and the prevention of dis-
cord. At least momentarily, many New England villages were able to
promote the shared values and behaviors that resulted from a harmo-
nious, often utopian "other-oriented communalism." In contrast, as
Jasper Danckaerts discovered in 1680, the inhabitants of the upper
Hudson and Mohawk region were "wild and untamed, reckless, unrestrained, haughty . . . addicted to misusing the blessed name of
God and to cursing and swearing." Danckaerts considered such behavior a result of the influence of the nearby Indians. His own account, however, suggests that what he described was equally a mani-
festation of behavior associated with the pursuit of self-profit—an
orientation to economic individualism and acquisitiveness of which
Danckaerts disapproved. Indeed, his character sketches are invariably
favorable or unflattering to the extent that his subjects embraced a
pietistic moralism similar to his own or the more questionable ethics
of the trader. At Schenectady, the half-breed convert Hilletie van
Olinda received praise, but her brother, Jacques Cornelissen van
Slyck, was "covetous" and concerned only for "the devilish profit of
the world." The Labadist Danckaerts may be dismissed for his over-
great sensitivity to the workings of the economic world, but even
such committed traders as the Mohawks found the acquisitive instincts of their Dutch counterparts disconcerting.[32]

Donna Merwick and the late Alice Kenney emphasize in their
work the urban, bourgeois values and behavior of the colonial Dutch.
As a result, the colonists' motivation and actions have been viewed as
a consequence of the Netherlands-derived experience of one class.
David Steven Cohen, however, suggests that both authors take too
restricted a view of the geographic and social background of those

---

32. Michael Zuckerman, *Peaceable Kingdoms: New England Towns in the Eighteenth
Century* (New York, 1970), vii; *JD*, 196, 206. Zuckerman argues that during the eigh-
teenth century there was little if any diminution in the values and behaviors that
exemplified the communal ethos of the seventeenth-century New England Puritans.
Other historians, however, have noted a decline in the early communal instincts of
New England's settlers. Zuckerman, *Peaceable Kingdoms*; Lockridge, *New England
Town*; Boyer and Nissenbaum, *Salem Possessed*; Darrett B. Rutman, *Winthrop's Boston:
Portrait of a Puritan Town, 1630–1649* (New York, 1965). For Jasper Danckaerts, see
JD, 189, 201–212, 215. In 1660 the Mohawks protested the actions of Dutch traders
at Beverwyck: "We have requested that the Dutch would not beat us any more. . . .
The Dutch are sending so many brokers into the woods . . . that they [the Mohawk]
do not know where to go with their beavers." *FOB*, II, 285.

persons who settled in New Netherland: "The emphasis of both American and European historians on the middle class, burgher tradition in the Netherlands does not explain the Dutch experience in New Netherland. Most of the immigrants were farmers, soldiers, or craftsmen." Cohen further notes that many immigrants came not from Holland but from other Dutch provinces and that "almost half the immigrants to New Netherland were not from the Netherlands, but from places adjacent to the Netherlands." If Merwick and Kenney overemphasize the Holland-like, urban heritage of Dutch life in New Netherland, Thomas Condon presents the opposite extreme, asserting that the history of New Netherland "is not the story of the gradual development of a distinctively Dutch society in the New World but rather the story of why such a society did not take shape."[33]

The historian Louis Hartz once wrote, "When a part of a European nation is detached from the whole of it, and hurled outward onto new soil, it loses the stimulus toward change that the whole provides. It lapses into a kind of immobility." Each from their own perspective, Merwick, Kenney, and Condon picture a Dutch society in the New World immobilized either by a clonelike repetition of the traditions of the homeland or by the failure to create any singular society at all. Yet, as Jasper Danckaerts discerned, by the end of the seventeenth century the Dutch in New York had indeed created a unique society, distinctive in its ethnic diversity, its contact with the local natives, and from day-to-day opportunities for profit from trade. This society responded to the active stimulus of cultural pluralism and economic individualism. At Schenectady, the end product was a unique, but divisive, community.[34]

No covenant such as that which pledged the English Puritan founders of Dedham, Massachusetts, to the creation of a "loveing and comfortable Societie" ever united the Schenectady proprietors. The only document that they or their representatives joined in signing was a baldly economic petition to Director-General Petrus Stuyves-

---

33. Cohen, "How Dutch Were the Dutch of New Netherland?" 60; Condon, *New York Beginnings*, 120. For Kenney and Merwick, see Alice P. Kenney, *Stubborn for Liberty: The Dutch in New York* (Syracuse, 1975), chap. 4; Merwick, "Dutch Townsmen and Land Use," 58–68, 71, 77. Professor Merwick's premise is well expressed in a 1989 article on Leisler's Rebellion. Of Jacob Leisler's conduct and motivation, she writes: "Jacob Leisler consistently acted as though his defense of New York on behalf of William III was a North American version of the Low Countries' stand against the Spanish: It was a *burgeroorlog*, literally a townspeoples' war." Merwick, "Being Dutch," 378.

34. Louis Hartz et al., *The Founding of New Societies* (New York, 1964), 3.

ant regarding the fur trade. Schenectady's founders and settlers sought not flight from but active participation in the colonial commercial world as it then existed. This motivation accounted both for their years'-long effort to abridge the Albany fur trade monopoly and for the contempt of authority and ready resort to violence which surrounded the smuggling of peltry and trade goods to and from Albany. It also explains their divisive attempts to accumulate landed property as profits from the production of grain crops increased. Schenectady's founders viewed the village less as a new home and community than as a profit-seeking investment. This attitude was consistent with the behavior of proprietors such as William Teller and Gerrit Bancker, who chose to maintain their domiciles not at Schenectady but at Albany. In such manner were they able to legally trade at Albany, to smuggle furs from Schenectady to Albany, and at the same time to derive an income in produce from lands at Schenectady worked by tenant farmers or slaves. It also corresponded with the actions of the proprietors Martin Cornelissen van Ysselsteyn and Symon Volkertsen Veeder, who departed to take up land elsewhere when it became evident that no privilege of trading would be extended to the village.[35]

Even Arent van Curler, Schenectady's chief protagonist, was a man divided in his loyalties to a community that must have proven a personal disappointment. Van Curler never completely severed his long-established ties to the van Rensselaer estate and could be found acting in the capacity of a colony official even after his settlement at Schenectady. Van Curler's influence with Petrus Stuyvesant had not proven sufficient to secure the right to trade at the village. As such, his cultivation of relations with the French, so worrisome to the English authorities, may have been the prelude to one final attempt to promote Schenectady's strategic position as a trading community—within the orbit of New France. Tragically, van Curler's summer 1667 journey to Canada ended in death when, during a storm on Lake Champlain, he refused to abandon his trade goods and high waves swamped his overloaded canoe.[36]

The history of Schenectady for the years 1661–1710 incorporates

35. Frank Smith, *A History of Dedham, Massachusetts* (Dedham, 1936), 8. For the May 18, 1663, petition to Governor Stuyvesant, see *ARS*, III, 493–494. For Bancker and Teller, see *ARS*, II, 129; *ERAR*, III, 242–243, 285–287. Van Ysselsteyn went to Claverack and Veeder acquired land on the Normanskill. *ERAR*, I, 449–451, III, 545; *SP*, 180–181, 203.

36. For van Curler, see *ERAR*, III, 198–199, 221–222, 263–264, 283–285, 303–305; van Laer, ed., "Documents Relating to Arent van Curler's Death," 31.

much of the experience of New Netherland and New York during this same period. The pursuit of trade in furs and the prevention of English usurpation, two overriding concerns of New Netherland's promoters, intertwined equally to give impetus to the establishment of a village on the Mohawk River. Similarly, Schenectady's location on New York's northern frontier destined it to be among the first communities to bear the brunt of conflict between England and France in the years after 1689. As did farmers elsewhere in the colony, Schenectady's husbandmen bent their efforts to the production of wheat, which became a crucial element in the province's export economy during the late 1600s and early 1700s. Factious, economically individualistic, and acquisitive, Schenectady's population reflected that of a colony more this-worldly and pluralistic than its New England neighbors. Finally, as much as any community in New York, Schenectady experienced the divisions of the Leisler years and after.[37]

Perhaps it is this legacy of division which is particularly significant for an understanding of the seventeenth-century Dutch who settled New Netherland and who remained such an important element in the population of post-conquest New York. That the pursuit of profit was poorly attuned to the creation of a cohesive community had been implicit in the description of the scattered settlement at Rensselaerswyck provided by Father Isaac Jogues in the 1640s, "each of the Hollanders outbidding his neighbor, and being satisfied provided he can gain some little profit." The history of Schenectady is an expression of the motives of its founders and settlers. That its own communal legacy, itself an outgrowth of the competition and dissension that existed among the upper Hudson traders during the 1650s, should also be one of division is not surprising. Not withstanding the contention of one historian of New York's colonial communities—that "there is little evidence that [they] were ever paralyzed by dissension, except in New York City and King's County during Leisler's Rebellion"—Schenectady not only was a community fatally paralyzed in 1690, it was to remain a village divided by the conflicting economic and political motives of its inhabitants for long after.[38]

37. For colonial New York, see Milton M. Klein, "New York in the American Colonies: A New Look," in Judd and Polishook, eds., *Aspects of Early New York*, 8–28.
38. *NNN*, 262; Langdon G. Wright, "In Search of Peace and Harmony: New York Communities in the Seventeenth Century," *NYH*, 61 (1980), 20. At Schaghticoke, north of Albany, the Dutch settlers failed to create a compact or cohesive village community during the eighteenth century. Klopott, "Schaghticoke."

Bibliography

PRIMARY SOURCES

Unpublished Material

New York State Library
Livingston-Redmond Papers. Microfilm.
Gerrit Y. Lansing Papers. Microfilm.
Records of the First Reformed Church at Schenectady, N.Y., 1683–1852. 3 vols.
Photostat copy. Albany, N.Y., 1942.

New-York Historical Society
Schenectady Tax List, 1738.

Schenectady County Historical Society
Schenectady Tax Lists, 1719 and 1751.

Albany Institute of History and Art
Schenectady Court Minutes, 1684. Caldwell Family Papers. Trans. Charles T.
Gehring.

Published Material

Official Documents
Abstracts of Wills on File in the Surrogate's Office, City of New York, 1665–1800.
New-York Historical Society, *Collections*, XXV–XLI, 1892–1908. New York:
Printed for the Society, 1893–1909.
Administrative Papers of Governors Richard Nicolls and Francis Lovelace, 1664–1673.
Ed. Peter R. Christoph. Baltimore: Genealogical Publishing, 1980.
*The Andros Papers: Files of the Provincial Secretary of New York during the Administra-
tion of Governor Sir Edmund Andros, 1674–1680.* Ed. Peter R. and Florence A.
Christoph. Trans. Charles T. Gehring. 3 vols. Syracuse: Syracuse University
Press, 1989–1991.

Books of General Entries of the Colony of New York, 1664–1688. Ed. Peter R. and Florence A. Christoph. 2 vols. Baltimore: Genealogical Publishing, 1982.

Burghers of New Amsterdam and the Freemen of New York, 1675–1866. New-York Historical Society, *Collections*, XVIII, 1885. New York: Printed for the Society, 1886.

Calendar of Council Minutes, 1668–1783. Ed. Berthold Fernow. Albany, 1902; reprint, Harrison, N.Y.: Harbor Hill Books, 1987.

Calendar of Historical Manuscripts in the Office of the Secretary of State, Albany, N.Y. Dutch Manuscripts, 1630–1664. Ed. Edmund B. O'Callaghan. Albany: Weed, Parsons, 1865.

Calendar of Historical Manuscripts in the Office of the Secretary of State, Albany, N.Y. English Manuscripts, 1664–1776. Ed. Edmund B. O'Callaghan. Albany: Weed, Parsons, 1866.

Calendar of New York Colonial Manuscripts Indorsed Land Papers in the Office of the Secretary of State of New York, 1643–1803. Albany: Weed, Parsons, 1864.

Calendar of Wills on File and Recorded in the Offices of the Clerk of the Court of Appeals, of the County Clerk at Albany, and that of the Secretary of State, 1626–1836. Comp. Berthold Fernow. New York, 1896; reprint, Baltimore: Genealogical Publishing, 1967.

Colonial Charters, Patents, and Grants to the Communities Comprising the City of New York. Comp. Jerrold Seymann. New York: Board of Statutory Consolidation, 1939.

The Colonial Laws of New York from the Year 1664 to the Revolution. 5 vols. Albany: James B. Lyon, 1894.

"Colonial Muster Rolls from 1686 to 1775." Appendix M of *Third Annual Report of the State Historian of the State of New York.* Albany: Wynkoop, Hallenbeck, Crawford, 1898.

"Colonial Records of the State [1664–1673]." Appendix G of *Second Annual Report of the State Historian of the State of New York.* Albany: Wynkoop, Hallenbeck, Crawford, 1897.

Documentary History of the State of New York. Ed. Edmund B. O'Callaghan. 4 vols. Albany: Weed, Parsons, 1849–1851.

Documents and Records Relating to the Province of New Hampshire. Ed. Nathaniel Bouton et al. 40 vols. Concord, N.H.: George E. Jencks et al., 1867–1941.

Documents Relating to the Administration of Jacob Leisler. New-York Historical Society, *Collections*, I, 1868. New York: Printed for the Society, 1868.

Documents Relative to the Colonial History of the State of New York. Ed. Edmund B. O'Callaghan and Berthold Fernow. 15 vols. Albany: Weed, Parsons, 1856–1887.

Early Records of the City and County of Albany and Colony of Rensselaerswyck. Ed. A. J. F. van Laer. Trans. Jonathan Pearson. 4 vols. Albany: University of the State of New York, 1869–1919.

Ecclesiastical Records of the State of New York. Ed. Edward T. Corwin. 7 vols. Albany: James B. Lyon, 1901–1916.

Historical Collections: Consisting of State Papers and Other Authentic Documents. Ed. Ebenezer Hazard. 2 vols. Philadelphia: T. Dobson, 1792–1794.

The Jesuit Relations and Allied Documents: Travels and Explorations of the Jesuit Mission-aries in New France, 1619–1791. Ed. Reuben G. Thwaites. 73 vols. Cleveland, 1896–1901; reprint, New York: Pageant Book, 1959.

Journal of the Votes and Proceedings of the General Assembly of the Colony of New York, 1691–1765. 2 vols. New York: Hugh Gaine, 1764–1766.

Kingston Papers. Ed. Peter R. Christoph et al. Trans. Dingman Veersteeg. 2 vols. Baltimore: Genealogical Publishing, 1976.

Laws and Ordinances of New Netherlands, 1636–1674. Ed. Edmund B. O'Callaghan. Albany: Weed, Parsons, 1868.

The Livingston Indian Records, 1666–1723. Ed. Lawrence H. Leder. Gettysburg, Pa.: Pennsylvania Historical Association, 1956.

Minutes of the Court of Albany, Rensselaerswyck, and Schenectady, 1668–1685. Ed. A. J. F. van Laer. 3 vols. Albany: University of the State of New York, 1926–1932.

Minutes of the Court of Fort Orange and Beverwyck, 1652–1660. Ed. A. J. F. van Laer. 2 vols. Albany: University of the State of New York, 1920–1923.

Minutes of the Executive Council of the Province of New York: Administration of Francis Lovelace, 1668–1673. Ed. Victor H. Paltsits. 2 vols. Albany: State of New York, 1910.

Minutes of the Supreme Court of Judicature, 1693 to 1701. New-York Historical Society, *Collections*, XLV, 1912. New York: Printed for the Society, 1913.

"Muster Rolls of a Century from 1664 to 1760." Appendix H of *Second Annual Report of the State Historian of the State of New York.* Albany: Wynkoop, Hallen-beck, Crawford, 1897.

New York Historical Manuscripts: Dutch, Council Minutes, 1638–1649. Ed. Kenneth Scott and Ken Stryker-Rodda. Trans. A. J. F. van Laer. Baltimore: Ge-nealogical Publishing, 1974.

New York Historical Manuscripts: Dutch, Delaware Papers, 1648–1664. Ed. Charles T. Gehring. Vols. XVIII–XIX. Baltimore: Genealogical Publishing, 1981.

New York Historical Manuscripts: Dutch, Land Papers. Ed. Charles T. Gehring. Vols. GG, HH, and II. Baltimore: Genealogical Publishing, 1980.

New York Historical Manuscripts: Dutch, Register of the Provincial Secretary, 1638–1660. Ed. Kenneth Scott and Ken Stryker-Rodda. Trans. A. J. F. van Laer. 3 vols. Baltimore: Genealogical Publishing, 1974.

Pennsylvania Archives. Ed. Samuel Hazard et al., 138 vols. Philadelphia: Joseph Severens et al., 1852–1949.

Public Records of the Colony of Connecticut (1636–1776). Ed. James H. Trum-bell and C. J. Hoadly. 15 vols. Hartford: Brown & Pearson et al., 1850–1890.

Quinn, David B., ed., *New American World: A Documentary History of North Amer-ica to 1612.* 5 vols. New York: Arno Press, 1979.

The Records of New Amsterdam from 1653 to 1674. Ed. Berthold Fernow. 7 vols. New York, 1897; reprint, Baltimore: Genealogical Publishing, 1976.

Tax Lists of the City of New York, December 1695–July 15th, 1699. New-York His-torical Society, *Collections*, XLIII–XLIV, 1910–1911. New York: Printed for the Society, 1911–1912.

Wraxall, Peter. *An Abridgement of the Indian Affairs, 1678–1751.* Ed. Charles H. McIlwain. New York: Benjamin Blom, 1968.

Letters, Papers, Chronicles

Albany Chronicles: A History of the City Arranged Chronologically. Ed. Cuyler Reynolds. Albany: J. Lyons, 1906.

Andros, Edmund. *The Andros Tracts.* Ed. W. H. Whitmore. 3 vols. Boston: Prince Society, 1868–1874.

The Annals of Albany. Ed. Joel Munsell. 10 vols. Albany: Joel Munsell, 1850–1859.

Champlain, Samuel de. *The Works of Samuel de Champlain.* Ed. H. P. Biggar. 6 vols. Toronto: Champlain Society, 1922–1936.

Church, Benjamin. *The History of King Philip's War.* Ed. Henry Martyn Dexter. Boston: John Kimball Wiggin, 1865.

Colden, Cadwallader. *The History of the Five Indian Nations.* 2 vols. New York: New Amsterdam, 1902.

———. *The Letters and Papers of Cadwallader Colden.* New-York Historical Society. *Collections*, LVI, 1923. New York: Printed for the Society, 1923.

Collections on the History of Albany, from Its Discovery to the Present Time. Ed. Joel Munsell. 4 vols. Albany: J. Munsell, 1865–1871.

Danckaerts, Jasper. *Journal of Jasper Danckaerts, 1679–1680.* Ed. Bartlett Burleigh James and J. Franklin Jameson. New York: Charles Scribner's Sons, 1913.

Gookin, Daniel. *Historical Collections of the Indians in New England.* Massachusetts Historical Society, *Collections*, 1st ser., I, 1792. Boston: Published by the Society, 1792.

Livingston, Alida Schuyler. "Business Letters of Alida Schuyler Livingston, 1680–1726." Ed. Linda Biemer. *New York History*, 63 (1982).

Mather, Increase. *The History of King Philip's War.* Albany: Joel Munsell, 1862.

The Moravian Journals Relating to Central New York, 1745–1766. Ed. William M. Beauchamp. Syracuse: Dehler Press, 1916.

Morton, Thomas. *The New English Canaan.* Ed. Charles Francis Adams, Jr. Boston: Prince Society, 1883.

Narratives of the Indian Wars, 1675–1699. Ed. Charles H. Lincoln. New York: Charles Scribner's Sons, 1913.

Narratives of the Insurrections, 1675–1690. Ed. Charles M. Andrews. New York: Charles Scribner's Sons, 1915.

Narratives of New Netherland, 1609–1664. Ed. J. Franklin Jameson. New York: Charles Scribner's Sons, 1909.

Papers concerning the Attack on Hatfield and Deerfield by a Party of Indians from Canada September 19, 1677. Ed. Franklin Benjamin Hough. New York: Privately printed by the author, 1859.

"Passengers to New Netherland, 1654–1664." Holland Society of New York, *Year Book*, 15 (1902).

Pynchon, John. *Letters of John Pynchon, 1654–1700.* Ed. Carl Bridenbaugh. Publications of the Colonial Society of Massachusetts, *Collections*, 60 (1982). Boston: Colonial Society, 1982.

———. *Pynchon Papers.* Massachusetts Historical Society, *Collections*, 2d ser., VIII (1826). Boston: Nathaniel Hale, 1826.

———. *Selections from the Account Books of John Pynchon, 1651–1697.* Ed. Carl Bridenbaugh and Juliette Tomlinson. Publications of the Colonial Society of Massachusetts, *Collections*, 61 (1985). Boston: Colonial Society, 1985.

Randolph, Edward. *His Letters and Official Papers, 1676–1703*. Ed. Robert N. Toppan and Alfred T. S. Goodrick. 7 vols. Boston: Prince Society, 1898–1909.

Scott, Kenneth. "The Freeholders of the City and County of Albany, 1763," *National Genealogical Society Quarterly*, 48 (1960).

Sewall, Samuel. *The Diary of Samuel Sewall*. Ed. M. Halsey Thomas. 2 vols. New York: Farrar, Straus & Giroux, 1973.

Smith, John. *The Complete Works of Captain John Smith (1580–1631)*. Ed. Philip L. Barbour. 3 vols. Chapel Hill: University of North Carolina Press, 1986.

Smith, Richard. *A Tour of Four Great Rivers. The Hudson, Mohawk, Susquehanna, and Delaware in 1769, Being the Journal of Richard Smith*. Ed. Francis W. Halsey. Port Washington, N.Y.: Ira J. Friedman, 1964.

Smith, William, Jr. *The History of the Province of New York*. Ed. Michael Kammen. 2 vols. Cambridge: Harvard University Press, 1972.

Strickland, William. *Journal of a Tour in the United States of America, 1794–1795*. Ed. J. E. Strickland. New-York Historical Society, *Collections*, LXXXIII, 1971. New York: Printed for the Society, 1971.

Van den Bogaert, Harmen Meyndertsz. *A Journey into Mohawk and Oneida Country, 1634–1635: The Journal of Harmen Meyndertsz van den Bogaert*. Ed. Charles T. Gehring and William A. Starna. Syracuse: Syracuse University Press, 1988.

Van der Donck, Adriaen. *A Description of New Netherland*. Ed. Thomas F. O'Donnell. Syracuse: Syracuse University Press, 1968.

Van Laer, A. J. F., ed., "Albany Notarial Papers, 1666–1693," Dutch Settlers Society of Albany, *Yearbook*, 13 (1937–1938).

——, ed. "Albany Notarial Papers, 1667–1687." Dutch Settlers Society of Albany, *Yearbook*, 14 (1938–1939).

——, ed. "Albany Wills and Other Documents, 1665–1695." Dutch Settlers Society of Albany, *Yearbook*, 6 (1930–1931).

——, ed. "Albany Wills and Other Documents, 1668–1687." Dutch Settlers Society of Albany, *Yearbook*, 10 (1934–1935).

——, ed. "Arent van Curler and His Historic Letter to the Patroon." Dutch Settlers Society of Albany, *Yearbook*, 3 (1927–1928).

——, ed. "Documents Relating to Arent van Curler's Death." Dutch Settlers Society of Albany, *Yearbook*, 3 (1927–1928).

——, ed. *Documents Relating to New Netherland, 1624–1626, in the Henry E. Huntington Library*. San Marino, Calif.: Henry E. Huntington Library, 1924.

——, ed. "The Dutch Grants along the South Side of State Street. A Contribution toward the Early Topography of the City of Albany." Dutch Settlers Society of Albany, *Yearbook*, 2 (1926–1927).

——, ed. "Settlers of Rensselaerswyck, 1659–1664." Dutch Settlers Society of Albany, *Yearbook*, 5 (1929–1930).

——, ed. *Van Rensselaer Bowier Manuscripts*. Albany: University of the State of New York, 1908.

Van Rensselaer, Jeremias. *Correspondence of Jeremias van Rensselaer, 1651–1674*. Ed. A. J. F. van Laer. Albany: University of the State of New York, 1932.

Van Rensselaer, Maria. *Correspondence of Maria van Rensselaer, 1669–1689.* Ed. A. J. F. van Laer. Albany: University of the State of New York, 1935.

Winthrop, Fitz-John. *Winthrop Papers.* Massachusetts Historical Society, *Collections*, 5th ser., VIII (1882). Boston: Published by the Society, 1882.

Winthrop, John. *Winthrop's Journal, 1630–1649.* Ed. James K. Hosmer. 2 vols. New York: Charles Scribner's Sons, 1908.

Genealogies

Knittle, Walter A. *Early Eighteenth-Century Palatine Emigration.* Baltimore: Genealogical Publishing, 1965.

Leonard, Vreeland Y. *The Genealogical Record of the Veeder Family.* N.p., 1937.

Noyes, Sybil, et al. *Genealogical Dictionary of Maine and New Hampshire.* Baltimore: Genealogical Publishing, 1972.

Pearson, Jonathan. *Contributions for the Genealogies of the Descendants of the First Settlers of the Patent and City of Schenectady.* Albany: 1873; reprint, Baltimore: Genealogical Publishing, 1976.

Schermerhorn, Richard. *Schermerhorn Genealogy and Family Chronicles.* New York: Tobias A. Wright, 1914.

Vedder, Edwin Henry. *The Vedder Family in America, 1657–1973.* N.p., 1974.

Viele, Kathlyne Knickerbacker. *Viele Records, 1613–1913.* New York: Tobias A. Wright, 1913.

Wemple, William Barent. "Wemple Genealogy," *New York Genealogical and Biographical Record,* 35 (1904).

Church Records and Histories

Birch, John J. *The Pioneering Church of the Mohawk Valley.* Schenectady: Consistory First Reformed Church, 1955.

Hannay, William Vanderpoel, comp. "Burial Records, First Dutch Reformed Church, Albany, N.Y., 1654–1862." Dutch Settlers Society of Albany, *Yearbook,* 8–9 (1932–1934).

Marriages from 1639 to 1801 in the Reformed Dutch Church, New York. Ed. Samuel S. Purple. New York Genealogical and Biographical Society, *Collections,* I. New York: Printed for the Society, 1890.

Records of the Reformed Dutch Church of Albany, New York, 1683–1809. Baltimore: Genealogical Publishing, 1978.

Sutphen, David S. *Historical Discourse Delivered . . . at the Celebration of the Two-Hundredth Anniversary of the Reformed Dutch Church of New Utrecht, L.I.* Brooklyn: Union-Argus Printing, 1877.

Three Centuries, The History of the First Reformed Church of Schenectady, 1680–1980. 2 vols. Schenectady: First Reformed Church of Schenectady, 1980.

Two-Hundredth Anniversary of the First Reformed Protestant Dutch Church of Schenectady, N.Y. Schenectady: Daily and Weekly Union, 1880.

SECONDARY SOURCES

Books

Allen, David Grayson. *In English Ways: The Movement of Societies and the Transferal of English Local Law and Custom to Massachusetts Bay in the Seventeenth Century.* Chapel Hill: University of North Carolina Press, 1981.

Andrews, Charles M. *The Colonial Period of American History.* 4 vols. New Haven: Yale University Press, 1934–1938.

Aquila, Richard. *The Iroquois Restoration: Iroquois Diplomacy on the Colonial Frontier, 1701–1754.* Detroit: Wayne State University Press, 1983.

Archdeacon, Thomas J. *New York City, 1664–1710: Conquest and Change.* Ithaca: Cornell University Press, 1976.

Armour, David A. *The Merchants of Albany, New York, 1686–1760.* New York: Garland Publishing, 1986.

Axtell, James. *The European and the Indian: Essays in the Ethnohistory of Colonial North America.* New York: Oxford University Press, 1981.

———. *The Invasion Within: The Contest of Cultures in Colonial North America.* New York: Oxford University Press, 1985.

Bachman, Van Cleaf. *Peltries or Plantations: The Economic Policies of the Dutch West India Company in New Netherland, 1623–1639.* Baltimore: Johns Hopkins University Press, 1969.

Bailey, Rosalie Fellows. *Pre-Revolutionary Dutch Houses and Families in Northern New Jersey and Southern New York.* New York: William Morrow, 1936.

Baker, C. Alice. *True Stories of New England Captives.* Greenfield, Mass.: E. A. Hall, 1897.

Balmer, Randall. *A Perfect Babel of Confusion: Dutch Religion and English Culture in the Middle Colonies.* New York: Oxford University Press, 1989.

Barbour, Violet. *Capitalism in Amsterdam in the 17th Century.* Ann Arbor: University of Michigan Press, 1966.

Berkhofer, Robert F., Jr. *The White Man's Indian: Images of the American Indian from Columbus to the Present.* New York: Alfred A. Knopf, 1978.

Biemer, Linda B. *Women and Property in Colonial New York: The Transition from Dutch to English Law, 1643–1727.* Ann Arbor: University of Michigan Press, 1983.

Boerderijen Bekijken: Historisch Boerderij-Onderzoek in Nederland. Amersfoort: De Horstink, 1985.

Bonomi, Patricia U. *A Factious People: Politics and Society in Colonial New York.* New York: Columbia University Press, 1971.

Boxer, Charles R. *The Dutch Seaborne Empire, 1600–1800.* New York: Alfred A. Knopf, 1965.

Boyer, Paul, and Stephen Nissenbaum. *Salem Possessed: The Social Origins of Witchcraft.* Cambridge: Harvard University Press, 1974.

Bradley, James W. *Evolution of the Onondaga Iroquois: Accommodating Change, 1500–1655.* Syracuse: Syracuse University Press, 1987.

Brasser, T. J. *Riding on the Frontier's Crest: Mahican Indian Culture and Culture Change.* Ottawa: National Museums of Canada, 1974.

Breen, T. H. *Puritans and Adventurers: Change and Persistence in Early America.* New York: Oxford University Press, 1980.

Brodhead, John R. *History of the State of New York.* 2 vols. New York: Harper & Brothers, 1853–1871.

Condon, Thomas J. *New York Beginnings: The Commercial Origins of New Netherland.* New York: New York University Press, 1968.

Crosby, Alfred W. *The Columbian Exchange: Biological and Cultural Consequences of 1492.* Westport, Conn.: Greenwood Press, 1972.

Crouse, Nellis M. *Lemoyne d'Iberville: Soldier of New France.* Ithaca: Cornell University Press, 1954.

Davis, Thomas J. *A Rumor of Revolt: The "Great Negro Plot" in Colonial New York.* New York: Free Press, 1985.

De Peyster, Frederic. *The Life and Administration of Richard, Earl of Bellomont, Governor of the Provinces of New York, Massachusetts, and New Hampshire, from 1697 to 1701.* New York: Published for the Society, 1879.

De Vries, Jan. *The Dutch Rural Economy in the Golden Age, 1500–1700.* New Haven: Yale University Press, 1974.

Dillard, Maud Esther. *An Album of New Netherland.* New York: Twayne Publishers, 1963.

Eccles, W. J. *Canada under Louis XIV, 1663–1701.* New York: Oxford University Press, 1964.

——. *The Canadian Frontier, 1534–1760.* New York: Holt, Rinehart & Winston, 1969.

Fitchen, John. *The New World Dutch Barn.* Syracuse: Syracuse University Press, 1968.

Foster, Michael K., Jack Campisi, and Marianne Mithun, eds. *Extending the Rafters: Interdisciplinary Approaches to Iroquoian Studies.* Albany: State University of New York Press, 1984.

Geyl, Pieter. *The Netherlands in the Seventeenth Century, 1609–1648.* New York: Barnes & Noble, 1961.

——. *The Revolt of the Netherlands, 1555–1609.* New York: Barnes & Noble, 1958.

Grant, Anne. *Memoirs of an American Lady.* 2 vols. New York: Dodd, Mead, 1901.

Grassmann, Reverend Thomas. *The Mohawk Indians and Their Valley, Being a Chronological Documentary Record to the End of 1693.* Schenectady: Eric Hugo, 1969.

Greene, Jack P. *Pursuits of Happiness: The Social Development of Early Modern British Colonies and the Formation of American Culture.* Chapel Hill: University of North Carolina Press, 1988.

Hanna, Charles A. *The Wilderness Trail or the Ventures and Adventures of the Pennsylvania Traders on the Allegheny Path.* 2 vols. New York: G. P. Putnam's Sons, 1911.

Hart, Larry. *Tales of Old Schenectady.* Vol. I: *The Formative Years.* Scotia, N.Y.: Old Dorp Books, 1975.

Hartz, Louis, et al. *The Founding of New Societies.* New York: Harcourt, Brace & World, 1964.

Hendrick, Ulysses P. *A History of Agriculture in the State of New York.* Albany: New York State Agricultural Society, 1933.

Higgins, Ruth L. *Expansion in New York with Especial Reference to the Eighteenth Century.* Columbus: Ohio State University, 1931.

Howell, George R., and Joel Munsell. *History of the County of Schenectady, N.Y., from 1662 to 1886.* New York: W. W. Munsell, 1886.

Howell, George R., and Jonathan Tenney. *History of the County of Albany, N.Y., from 1609 to 1886.* New York: W. W. Munsell, 1886.

Hunt, George T. *The Wars of the Iroquois: A Study in Intertribal Trade Relations.* Madison: University of Wisconsin Press, 1940.

Innes, Stephen. *Labor in a New Land: Economy and Society in Seventeenth-Century Springfield.* Princeton: Princeton University Press, 1983.

Jennings, Francis. *The Invasion of America: Indians, Colonialism, and the Cant of Conquest.* New York: W. W. Norton, 1976.

Jordan, Winthrop D. *White over Black: American Attitudes toward the Negro, 1550–1812.* Baltimore: Penguin Books, 1968.

Kammen, Michael. *Colonial New York: A History.* New York: KTO Press, 1975.

Kennedy, John H. *Thomas Dongan, Governor of New York (1682–1688).* Washington, D.C.: Catholic University of America, 1930.

Kenney, Alice P. *Stubborn for Liberty: The Dutch in New York.* Syracuse: Syracuse University Press, 1975.

Kim, Sung Bok. *Landlord and Tenant in Colonial New York: Manorial Society, 1664–1775.* Chapel Hill: University of North Carolina Press, 1978.

Kupperman, Karen Ordahl. *Settling with The Indians: The Meeting of English and Indian Cultures in America, 1580–1640.* Totowa, N.J.: Rowman and Littlefield, 1980.

Lambert, Audrey M. *The Making of the Dutch Landscape: An Historical Geography of the Netherlands.* New York: Seminar Press, 1971.

Lanctot, Gustave. *A History of Canada.* 3 vols. Cambridge: Harvard University Press, 1963–1965.

Lauber, Almon W. *Indian Slavery in Colonial Times within the Present Limits of the United States.* Williamstown, Mass.: Corner House Publishers, 1970.

Leach, Douglas E. *Flintlock and Tomahawk: New England in King Philip's War.* New York: Macmillan, 1958.

———. *The Northern Colonial Frontier, 1607–1763.* New York: Holt, Rinehart & Winston, 1966.

Leder, Lawrence H. *Robert Livingston, 1654–1728, and the Politics of Colonial New York.* Chapel Hill: University of North Carolina Press, 1961.

Lockridge, Kenneth A. *A New England Town: The First Hundred Years, Dedham, Massachusetts, 1636–1736.* New York: W. W. Norton, 1970.

Lovejoy, David S. *The Glorious Revolution in America.* New York: Harper & Row, 1972.

Lustig, Mary Lou. *Robert Hunter, 1666–1734, New York's Augustan Statesman.* Syracuse: Syracuse University Press, 1983.

Lydekker, John W. *The Faithful Mohawks.* New York: Macmillan, 1938.

Macfarlane, Alan, *The Origins of English Individualism.* New York: Cambridge University Press, 1979.

McManus, Edgar J. *A History of Negro Slavery in New York*. Syracuse: Syracuse University Press, 1966.

Morgan, Lewis Henry. *League of the Iroquois*. Rochester, 1851, reprint, Secaucus, N.J.: Citadel Press, 1962.

Morison, Samuel E. *Samuel de Champlain, Father of New France*. Boston: Little, Brown, 1972.

Mullin, Gerald W. *Flight and Rebellion: Slave Resistance in Eighteenth-Century Virginia*. New York: Oxford University Press, 1972.

Nash, Gary B. *Red, White, and Black: The Peoples of Early America*. Englewood Cliffs, N.J.: Prentice-Hall, 1974.

——. *The Urban Crucible: Social Change, Political Consciousness, and the Origins of the American Revolution*. Cambridge: Harvard University Press, 1979.

Nissenson, Samuel G. *The Patroon's Domain*. New York: Columbia University Press, 1937.

Northrop, A. Judd. *Slavery in New York, A Historical Sketch*. State Library Bulletin, History No. 4. Albany: University of the State of New York, 1900.

Norton, Thomas E. *The Fur Trade in Colonial New York, 1686–1776*. Madison: University of Wisconsin Press, 1974.

O'Callaghan, Edmund B. *History of New Netherland*. 2 vols. Spartanburg, S.C.: Reprint Company, 1966.

Osgood, Herbert L. *The American Colonies in the Seventeenth Century*. 3 vols. New York, 1904–1907; reprint, Gloucester, Mass.: Peter Smith, 1957.

Parry, J. H. *The Establishment of European Hegemony: 1415–1715*. New York: Harper & Row, 1961.

Pearson, Jonathan. *A History of the Schenectady Patent in the Dutch and English Times*. Ed. J. W. MacMurray. Albany: Joel Munsell's Sons, 1883.

Peckham, Howard H. *The Colonial Wars, 1689–1762*. Chicago: University of Chicago Press, 1964.

Quinn, David B. *North America from Earliest Discovery to First Settlements*. New York: Harper & Row, 1977.

Reich, Jerome R. *Leisler's Rebellion: A Study of Democracy in New York, 1664–1720*. Chicago: University of Chicago Press, 1953.

Richter, Daniel K., and James H. Merrell, eds. *Beyond the Covenant Chain: The Iroquois and Their Neighbors in Indian North America, 1600–1800*. Syracuse: Syracuse University Press, 1987.

Rink, Oliver A. *Holland on the Hudson: An Economic and Social History of Dutch New York*. Ithaca: Cornell University Press, 1986.

Ritchie, Robert C. *Captain Kidd and the War against the Pirates*. Cambridge: Harvard University Press, 1986.

——. *The Duke's Province: A Study of New York Politics and Society, 1664–1691*. Chapel Hill: University of North Carolina Press, 1977.

Ritchie, William A. *The Archeology of New York State*. Harrison, N.Y.: Harbor Hill Books, 1980.

Rutman, Darrett B. *Husbandmen of Plymouth: Farmers and Villages in the Old Colony, 1620–1692*. Boston: Beacon Press, 1967.

——. *Winthrop's Boston: Portrait of a Puritan Town, 1630–1649*. New York: W. W. Norton, 1965.

Salisbury, Neal. *Manitou and Providence: Indians, Europeans, and the Making of New England, 1500–1643*. New York: Oxford University Press, 1982.

Sanders, John. *Centennial Address Relating to the Early History of Schenectady*. Albany: Van Benthuysen Printing House, 1879.

Schoonmaker, Marius. *The History of Kingston, New York, from Its Early Settlement to the Year 1820*. New York: Burr Printing House, 1888.

Schuyler, George W. *Colonial New York: Philip Schuyler and His Family*. 2 vols. New York: Charles Scribner's Sons, 1885.

Smith, Frank. *A History of Dedham, Massachusetts*. Dedham: Transcript Press, 1936.

Trelease, Allen. *Indian Affairs in Colonial New York: The Seventeenth Century*. Ithaca: Cornell University Press, 1960.

Trigger, Bruce G. *The Children of Aataentsic*. 2 vols. Montreal: McGill-Queen's University Press, 1976.

———. *The Huron, Farmers of the North*. New York: Holt, Rinehart & Winston, 1969.

Trigger, Bruce G., and James F. Pendergast. *Cartier's Hochelaga and the Dawson Site*. Montreal: McGill-Queen's University Press, 1972.

Tuck, James A. *Onondaga Iroquois Prehistory: A Study in Settlement Archaeology*. Syracuse: Syracuse University Press, 1971.

Ulrich, Laurel Thatcher. *Good Wives: Image and Reality in the Lives of Women in Northern New England, 1650–1750*. New York: Oxford University Press, 1983.

Van der Kloot Meijburg, Hermanus. *Onze Oude Boerenhuizen: Tachtig Schetsen van Boerenhuizen in Nederland*. Rotterdam: W. L. & J. Brusse, 1912.

Wallace, Anthony F. C. *The Death and Rebirth of the Seneca*. New York: Vintage Books, 1969.

Ward, Christopher. *The Dutch and Swedes on the Delaware, 1609–1664*. Philadelphia: University of Pennsylvania Press, 1930.

Weise, Arthur James. *The History of the City of Albany, New York*. Albany: E. H. Bender, 1884.

Werner, Edgar A. *Civil List and Constitutional History of the Colony and State of New York*. Albany: Weed, Parsons, 1888.

Weslager, C. A. *The English on the Delaware, 1610–1682*. New Brunswick, N.J.: Rutgers University Press, 1967.

Wood, Peter H. *Black Majority: Negroes in Colonial South Carolina from 1670 through the Stono Rebellion*. New York: W. W. Norton, 1975.

Wright, James Leitch. *The Only Land They Knew: The Tragic Story of the American Indians in the Old South*. New York: Free Press, 1981.

Wroth, Lawrence C. *The Voyages of Giovanni da Verrazzano, 1524–1528*. New Haven: Yale University Press, 1970.

Yates, Austin. *Schenectady County, New York, Its History to the Close of the Nineteenth Century*. New York: New York History Company, 1902.

Zuckerman, Michael. *Peaceable Kingdoms: New England Towns in the Eighteenth Century*. New York: Vintage Books, 1970.

Zwierlein, Frederick J. *Religion in New Netherland: A History of the Development of the Religious Conditions in the Province of New Netherland, 1623–1664*. Rochester: J. P. Smith, 1910.

Articles

Anderson, P. M., et al. "Climatic Changes of the Last 18,000 Years: Observations and Model Simulations." *Science*, 241 (August 1988).

Archdeacon, Thomas J. "The Age of Leisler—New York City, 1689–1710: A Social and Demographic Interpretation." In *Aspects of Early New York Society and Politics*. Ed. Jacob Judd and Irwin H. Polishook. Tarrytown, N.Y.: Sleepy Hollow Restorations, 1974.

Axtell, James. "The Ethnohistory of Early America: A Review Essay." *William and Mary Quarterly*, 3d ser., 35 (1978).

Baart, Jan M. "Dutch Material Civilization: Daily Life between 1650–1776, Evidence from Archaeology." In *New World Dutch Studies: Dutch Arts and Culture in Colonial America, 1609–1776*. Ed. Roderic H. Blackburn and Nancy A. Kelley. Albany: Albany Institute of History and Art, 1987.

Balmer, Randall. "Traitors and Papists: The Religious Dimensions of Leisler's Rebellion." *New York History*, 70 (1989).

Béchard, Henri. "Joseph Togouiroui." In *Dictionary of Canadian Biography*. Vol. I. Toronto: University of Toronto Press, 1966.

Billington, Ray Allen. "The American Frontier." In *Beyond the Frontier: Social Process and Cultural Change*. Ed. Paul Bohannan and Fred Plog. Garden City, N.Y.: Natural History Press, 1967.

"Blacks in New Netherland and Colonial New York." Proceedings of the sixth annual Rensselaerswyck Seminar. *Journal of the Afro-American Historical and Genealogical Society*, 5 (1984).

Blain, Jean. "Jacques Le Moyne De Sainte-Hélène." In *Dictionary of Canadian Biography*. Vol. I. Toronto: University of Toronto Press, 1966.

———. "Nicolas D'Ailleboust De Manthet." In *Dictionary of Canadian Biography*. Vol. II. Toronto: University of Toronto Press, 1969.

Bourque, Bruce J., and Ruth Holmes Whitehead. "Tarrentines and the Introduction of European Trade Goods in the Gulf of Maine." *Ethnohistory*, 32 (1985).

Brasser, T. J. "Mahican." In *Handbook of North American Indians*. William C. Sturtevant, gen. ed. Vol. XV, *Northeast*. Ed. Bruce G. Trigger. Washington, D.C.: Smithsonian Institution, 1978.

Broshar, Helen. "The First Push Westward of the Albany Traders." *Mississippi Valley Historical Review*, 7 (1920–1921).

Bryson, R. "A Perspective on Climate Change." *Science*, 184 (May 1974).

Buffington, Arthur H. "New England and the Western Fur Trade, 1629–1675." Publications of the Colonial Society of Massachusetts, *Transactions*, 18 (1915–1916).

Burke, Thomas E., Jr. "Arent van Curler and the Fur Trade at Early Schenectady." Dutch Settlers Society of Albany, *Yearbook*, 49 (1984–1987).

———. "Leisler's Rebellion at Schenectady, New York, 1689–1710." *New York History*, 70 (1989).

———. "The New Netherland Fur Trade, 1657–1661: Response to Crisis." *De Halve Maen*, 59 (1986).

Cohen, David Steven. "Dutch-American Farming: Crops, Livestock, and Equipment, 1623–1900." In *New World Dutch Studies: Dutch Arts and Culture in Colonial America, 1609–1776*. Ed. Roderic H. Blackburn and Nancy A. Kelley. Albany: Albany Institute of History and Art, 1987.

——. "How Dutch Were the Dutch of New Netherland?" *New York History*, 62 (1981).

Cohen, Ronald D. "The Hartford Treaty of 1650: Anglo-Dutch Cooperation in the Seventeenth Century." *New-York Historical Society Quarterly*, 53 (1969).

Eccles, W. J. "The Social, Economic, and Political Significance of the Military Establishment in New France." *Canadian Historical Review*, 52 (1971).

Feister, Lois M. "Archaeology in Rensselaerswyck, Dutch 17th–Century Domestic Sites." In *New Netherland Studies: An Inventory of Current Research and Approaches*. Ed. Boudewijn Bakker. Utrecht: Bohn, Scheltma, Holkema, 1985.

Fenton, William N., and Elisabeth Tooker. "Mohawk." In *Handbook of North American Indians*. William C. Sturtevant, gen. ed. Vol. XV, *Northeast*. Ed. Bruce G. Trigger. Washington, D.C.: Smithsonian Institution, 1978.

Gehring, Charles T. "Material Culture in Seventeenth-Century Dutch Colonial Manuscripts." In *New World Dutch Studies: Dutch Arts and Culture in Colonial America, 1609–1776*. Ed. Roderic H. Blackburn and Nancy A. Kelley. Albany: Albany Institute of History and Art, 1987.

Gehring, Charles T., and Robert S. Grumet. "Observations of the Indians from Jasper Danckaerts's Journal, 1679–1680." *William and Mary Quarterly*, 3d ser., 44 (1987).

Gehring, Charles T., and William A. Starna. "A Case of Fraud: The Dela Croix Letter and Map of 1634." *New York History*, 66 (1985).

Gehring, Charles T., William A. Starna, and William N. Fenton. "The Tawagonshi Treaty of 1613: The Final Chapter." *New York History*, 68 (1987).

Goodfriend, Joyce D. "Burghers and Blacks: The Evolution of a Slave Society at New Amsterdam." *New York History*, 59 (1978).

——. "The Social Dimensions of Congregational Life in Colonial New York City." *William and Mary Quarterly*, 3d ser., 46 (1989).

Grassmann, Thomas. "Flemish Bastard." In *Dictionary of Canadian Biography*. Vol. I. Toronto: University of Toronto Press, 1966.

Hagedorn, Nancy L. "'A Friend to Go between Them': The Interpreter as Cultural Broker during Anglo-Iroquois Councils, 1740–1770." *Ethnohistory*, 35 (1988).

Howe, Adrian. "The Bayard Treason Trial: Dramatizing Anglo-Dutch Politics in Early Eighteenth-Century New York City." *William and Mary Quarterly*, 3d ser., 47 (1990).

Huey, Paul. "Archaeological Excavations in the Site of Fort Orange, a Dutch West India Company Trading Fort Built in 1624." In *New Netherland Studies: An Inventory of Current Research and Approaches*. Ed. Boudewijn Bakker. Utrecht: Bohn, Scheltma, Holkema, 1985.

Jaenen, Cornelis J. "Amerindian Views of French Culture in the Seventeenth Century." *Canadian Historical Review*, 55 (1974).

Jennings, Francis. "Susquehannock." In *Handbook of North American Indians*. Wil-

Bibliography

liam C. Sturtevant, gen. ed. Vol. XV, *Northeast*. Ed. Bruce G. Trigger. Washington, D.C.: Smithsonian Institution, 1978.

Klein, Milton M. "New York in the American Colonies: A New Look." In *Aspects of Early New York Society and Politics*. Ed. Jacob Judd and Irwin H. Polishook. Tarrytown, N.Y.: Sleepy Hollow Restorations, 1974.

Kulikoff, Allan. "The Origins of Afro-American Society in Tidewater Maryland and Virginia, 1700 to 1790." *William and Mary Quarterly*, 3d ser., 35 (1978).

——. "A 'Prolifick' People: Black Population Growth in the Chesapeake Colonies, 1700–1790." *Southern Studies*, 16 (1977).

Leder, Lawrence H. "The Politics of Upheaval in New York, 1689–1709." *New-York Historical Society Quarterly*, 44 (1960).

Lee, Jean Butenhoff. "The Problem of Slave Community in the Eighteenth-Century Chesapeake." *William and Mary Quarterly*, 3d ser., 43 (1986).

Lenig, Donald. "Of Dutchmen, Beaver Hats, and Iroquois." In *Current Perspectives in Northeastern Archeology*. Ed. Robert E. Funk and Charles F. Hayes, III. Albany: New York State Archeological Association, 1977.

Lyndon, James G. "New York and the Slave Trade, 1700 to 1774." *William and Mary Quarterly*, 3d ser., 35 (1978).

Menard, Russell R. "The Maryland Slave Population, 1658 to 1730: A Demographic Profile of Blacks in Four Counties." *William and Mary Quarterly*, 3d ser., 32 (1975).

Merwick, Donna. "Becoming English: Anglo-Dutch Conflict in the 1670s in Albany, New York." *New York History*, 62 (1981).

——. "Being Dutch: An Interpretation of Why Jacob Leisler Died." *New York History*, 70 (1989).

——. "Dutch Townsmen and Land Use: A Spatial Perspective on Seventeenth-Century Albany, New York." *William and Mary Quarterly*, 3d ser., 37 (1980).

Miller, Christopher L., and George R. Hamell. "A New Perspective on Indian-White Contact: Cultural Symbols and Colonial Trade." *Journal of American History*, 73 (1986).

Nash, Gary B. "The Image of the Indian in the Southern Colonial Mind." *William and Mary Quarterly*, 3d ser., 29 (1972).

——. "The Quest for the Susquehanna Valley: New York, Pennsylvania, and the Seventeenth-Century Fur Trade." *New York History*, 48 (1967).

Penney, Sherry, and Roberta Willenkin. "Dutch Women in Colonial Albany: Liberation and Retreat." *De Halve Maen*, 52 (1977).

Pothier, Bernard. "Le Moyne D'Iberville." In *Dictionary of Canadian Biography*. Vol. II. Toronto: University of Toronto Press, 1969.

Rainbolt, John C. "A 'great and usefull designe': Bellomont's Proposal for New York, 1698–1701." *New-York Historical Society Quarterly*, 53, 1969.

Richter, Daniel K. "Cultural Brokers and Intercultural Politics: New York–Iroquois Relations, 1664–1701." *Journal of American History*, 75(1988).

——. "War and Culture: The Iroquois Experience." *William and Mary Quarterly*, 3d ser., 40 (1983).

Rink, Oliver A. "Company Management or Private Trade: The Two Patroonship Plans for New Netherland." *New York History*, 59 (1978).

——. "The People of New Netherland: Notes on Non-English Immigration to New York in the Seventeenth Century." *New York History*, 62 (1981).

Salwen, Bert. "Indians of Southern New England and Long Island: Early Period." In *Handbook of North American Indians*. William C. Sturtevant, gen. ed. Vol. XV, *Northeast*. Ed. Bruce G. Trigger. Washington, D.C.: Smithsonian Institution, 1978.

Smith, Elizur Yale. "Captain Thomas Willett, First Mayor of New York." *New York History*, 21 (1940).

Starna, William A. "Seventeenth Century Dutch-Indian Trade: A Perspective from Iroquoia." *De Halve Maen*, 59 (1986).

Tebbenhoff, Edward H. "Tacit Rules and Hidden Family Structures: Naming Practices and Godparentage in Schenectady, New York, 1680–1800." *Journal of Social History*, 17 (1985).

Tooker, Elisabeth. "The League of the Iroquois: Its History, Politics, and Ritual." In *Handbook of North American Indians*. William C. Sturtevant, gen. ed. Vol. XV, *Northeast*. Ed. Bruce G. Trigger. Washington, D.C.: Smithsonian Institution, 1978.

Trigger, Bruce G. "The Mohawk-Mahican War (1624–1628): The Establishment of a Pattern." *Canadian Historical Review*, 52 (1971).

——. "Ontario Native People and the Epidemics of 1634–1640." In *Indians, Animals, and the Fur Trade*. Ed. Shepard Krech. Athens: University of Georgia Press, 1981.

Van Alstyne, W. Scott, Jr. "The Schout: Precursor of Our District Attorney." *De Halve Maen*, 42 (1967).

Van Wijk, Piet. "Form and Function in the Netherlands' Dutch Agricultural Architecture." In *New World Dutch Studies: Dutch Arts and Culture in Colonial America, 1609–1776*. Ed. Roderic H. Blackburn and Nancy A. Kelley. Albany: Albany Institute of History and Art, 1987.

Wagman, Morton. "Corporate Slavery in New Netherland." *Journal of Negro History*, 65 (1980).

——. "The Rise of Pieter Claessen Wyckoff: Social Mobility on the Colonial Frontier." *New York History*, 53 (1972).

Wheeler, Robert G. "The House of Jeremias van Rensselaer, 1658–1666." *New-York Historical Society Quarterly*, 45 (1961).

Wright, Langdon G. "In Search of Peace and Harmony: New York Communities in the Seventeenth Century." *New York History*, 61 (1980).

Zantkuyl, Henk J. "The Netherlands Town House: How and Why It Works." In *New World Dutch Studies: Dutch Arts and Culture in Colonial America, 1609–1776*. Ed. Roderic H. Blackburn and Nancy A. Kelley. Albany: Albany Institute of History and Art, 1987.

Dissertations

Ceci, Lynn. "The Effect of European Contact and Trade on the Settlement Patterns of Indians in Coastal New York, 1524–1665: The Archeological and Documentary Evidence." Ph.D. dissertation, City University of New York, 1977.

Goodfriend, Joyce D. "'Too Great A Mixture of Nations': The Development of New York City Society in the Seventeenth Century." Ph.D. dissertation, University of California, Los Angeles, 1975.

Haan, Richard L. "The Covenant Chain: Iroquois Diplomacy on the Niagara Frontier, 1697–1730." Ph.D. dissertation, University of California, Santa Barbara, 1976.

Hardcastle, David P. "The Defense of Canada Under Louis XIV, 1643–1701." Ph.D. dissertation, Ohio State University, 1970.

Klopott, R. Beth. "The History of the Town of Schaghticoke, New York, 1676–1855." Ph.D. dissertation, State University of New York at Albany, 1981.

Kruger, Vivienne L. "Born to Run: The Slave Family in Early New York, 1626 to 1827." Ph.D. dissertation, Columbia University, 1985.

Peña, Elizabeth Shapiro. "Wampum Production in New Netherland and Colonial New York: The Historical and Archaeological Context." Ph.D. dissertation, Boston University, 1990.

Voorhees, David William. "'In behalf of the true Protestants religion': The Glorious Revolution in New York." Ph.D. dissertation, New York University, 1988.

Index

Abeel, Johannes, 175
Abenaki Indians, 85, 97, 98n, 203
Africa, 76
Agriculture
  farm buildings and other structures:
    barns, 38–41, 43–44, 55, 108; build-
    ing materials and techniques, 44, 47;
    fences, 40, 43, 47, 53, 55; grist mill,
    63, 162; hay rick, 40, 44, 55; stable,
    53; wagon shed, 55
  farm implements, 40, 57
  farm work: cutting wood, 59, 60; har-
    rowing, 58; harvest, 48, 59, 61, 127,
    128, 134, 139; haying, 39, 58; mow-
    ing, 60; plowing, 39, 48, 49, 55, 58,
    60, 182; seeding, 39, 58; threshing,
    59, 60; winnowing, 60
  interrupted by warfare, 88, 206n
  need for farmers in New Netherland, 7
  at Schenectady, 18, 33, 55, 154, 211
  See also Crops; Land; Livestock
Albany, city of, 3, 39, 41, 43, 46, 47, 50,
  51, 52, 59, 66, 67, 110, 111, 112, 119,
  121, 128, 150, 154, 155n, 162, 166,
  190, 210
  anti-English sentiment among Dutch at,
    78–79, 113–114, 113n
  anti-Leislerians at, 101–103, 157, 164,
    168, 173, 175–176
  comparison of with Schenectady, 33
  council of war at, 84, 86
  disease at, 198–199
  English military at, 78, 79–80, 82, 85,
    111, 111n, 115
  farming near, 39n, 57, 58n
  French at, 80n, 90, 120, 122, 130n

French attack of expected, 78, 83–84,
    88, 89, 94, 95, 96, 98, 98n, 99–100,
    104, 106–108
French prisoners at, 205
and fur trade, 13, 21, 30, 68–74, 92,
    116, 169, 184
Governor Bellomont at, 171, 172
Governor Cornbury at, 189
Governor Dongan at, 95, 117
Governor Sloughter at, 168, 205
harassment of by Canadian Indians,
    206n
Indians at, 72n, 142–147, 151–153,
    212
King Philip near, 85–87, 86n
Leisler supporters at, 158, 158n, 168,
    170
magistrates of and Schenectady, 48, 53,
    182
marriages at, 208
midwives at, 209
Mohawks attacked near, 75, 75–76n
people flee, 196
residents of acquire Schenectady prop-
    erty, 38, 193
and Schaghticoke, 197, 211
and Schenectady, 217–218, 221
Schenectady proprietors at, 23, 60
Schenectady refugees at, 198–199, 200,
    201, 204
Schermerhorn family at, 64, 118, 174,
    186
slavery at, 127–128, 130, 132–135, 137,
    139–140
van Rensselaer family claims at, 71
See also Beverwyck; Fort Orange

239

Albany County
  assembly elections in, 168, 175
  census of, 137, 141, 196
  French attack of expected, 98–99
  militia defend, 85, 115
  New York marriages of couples from,
    198
  population removal from, 98n, 196, 198,
    207
  slave population in, 137, 141, 142, 196
  status of Schenectady within, 69
Algonquians. *See* Mahican Indians
Amsterdam, city of, 16, 22
Andastes. *See* Susquehannock Indians
Andros, Edmund (governor of New York),
    71, 86n, 93, 94, 97, 101, 114, 126–
    127, 157, 183, 185
Anglicans. *See* Church of England
Anglicization, 110–111, 117–119, 154
Anglo-Dutch wars, 9, 76, 81
Anna (slave), 128, 140
Anniehronons. *See* Mohawk Indians
Appel, Adriaen, 65
Appel, Johannes, 84, 196, 197n, 198
Appel, Willem, 196, 197n, 198
Archdeacon, Thomas J., 191, 193, 214n
Arentsen, Hendrick, 60, 61
Arnhem (in Netherlands), 63
Assembly, 118, 169–170, 170n, 175, 186,
    188–190
Aukes. *See* Van Slyck, Jacques Cornelissen
Aukes, Douwe, 61, 64, 71, 102, 123, 131,
    135, 158, 159, 161, 178, 191, 199,
    206, 214
Axtell, James, 155

Bagge, Bent, 38–39. *See also* Roberts, Ben-
    jamin
Baker, Capt. John, 79–81, 113, 113n, 115
Bancker, Evert, 166n, 175
Bancker, Gerrit, 22, 22n, 23, 40, 60, 73,
    131–134, 159, 164, 221
Barclay, Rev. Thomas (Anglican minister),
    110–111, 116, 118–119, 121, 153–
    154, 210
Barentsz, Pieter, 5
Barrois family, 130n
Bayard, Nicholas, 177
Beck, Caleb, 214, 214n
Beekman, Johannes, 172
Beekman, William, 128, 140
Bellomont, Richard Coote, earl of (gover
    nor of New York), 115–116, 144, 174,
    175, 176, 212n

and Leislerians, 166–170, 173
opposition of to land grants to anti-
    Leislerians, 166–167, 169n, 170, 173
and Reyer Schermerhorn, 118, 145, 146,
    170–175
Benjamin, 176n
Beverwyck, 6, 35, 42, 43, 47, 62, 150, 161
  English at, 111, 113, 115
  fur trade at, 7, 8–13, 20–21, 30, 30n,
    68, 70
  Iroquois at, 8–11, 17, 24, 27, 31
  and John Pynchon, 14
  population growth at, 18
  Schenectady settlers from, 19, 21, 32,
    61, 64–66, 162, 184–185
  See also Albany, city of; Fort Orange
Binne Kill, 38, 48
Bishop of London, 98
Black Barent (slave), 132–133, 135
Bleecker, Jan Jansen, 144, 168–170, 175
Block, Adriaen, 3
Board of Trade, 55, 169, 170, 170n, 173,
    174, 212, 212n
Boffie (Bovie), Matthys, 121–122, 127,
    130–131
Bogardus, Cornelius, 80n
Bontekoe, 109
Bonts, Gerritje, 205
Bonts, Stephen, 205
Borsboom, Grietje, 72, 72n
Borsboom, Pieter Jacobsen, 22n, 62n,
    72
Bos, Cornelis Teunissen, 12, 12n
Bosie, Peter, 120
Bosie, Philip, 120, 191, 193
Boston, 98, 101, 108n, 112, 114, 155,
    197n, 212n
Bounties, 51, 206n
Bowin, William, 191
Bradt, Andries Albertsen, 47, 182, 185
Bradt, Andries Arentsen, 201n
Bradt, Arent, 217
Bradt, Arent Andriessen, 23n, 65
Bradt, Arriantje, 118
Bradt family, 23, 120n, 164–165
Brazil, 2, 125
Breen, T. H., 216
Bronck, Jonas, 65
Brooklyn, 129
Brouwer, Dominie Thomas, 119
Brouwer, Jacob, 213n
Brouwer, Philip Hendricksen, 19n, 21–22,
    22n, 23n, 35, 36, 39, 40, 43, 44, 49–
    50, 54, 58, 65, 161–162, 181, 182
Bruyas, Jacques (Jesuit), 89, 94, 121, 151
Bull, Capt. Jonathan, 103, 142

Burnet, William (governor of New York), 212n, 213n

Callières, Louis Hector, Chevalier de, 97, 99–101
Canada. *See* New France
Canajoharie, N.Y., 3, 185
Canaqueese (Dutch [Flemish] Bastard, Smith John), 79–80, 82, 149–150
Cape of Africa, 1
Carignan-Salières regiment, 77
Cartier, Jacques, 25, 77
Cartwright, Col. George, 115
Casco Bay, 25n
Catholicism, 122, 157, 204
Catskill, settlement at, 3, 44, 147
Caughnawaga (Mohawk village), 10, 17, 24, 74–75
Cayuga Indians, 29, 91n, 95, 144
Chaleur Bay, 25
Chambly, 90, 204
Champlain, Samuel de, 4, 77
Charles II (king of England), 76
Charles V (Habsburg ruler), 1
Chesapeake Bay, 26n
Chickwallop (Pocumtuck leader), 74, 75n
Children
    birth of to Schenectady women, 208–209, 209n
    as a burden, 66
    as captives, 114, 201–205
    of Dutch father and Indian mother, 147–149
    employment of at harvest, 58n
    land distributed to, 36, 181
    murdered, 134
    as refugees, 87, 98n, 110n, 196, 207n
    of slaves, 128–130, 135, 139–141
    and stepparents, 102, 165, 181, 188, 201
    widows with, marry Englishmen, 207
    See also Education; Families
Christiaensen, Hendrick, 3
Christoffelsen, David, 102, 111, 158–159, 165n. *See also* Davids, Christoffel
Church, Benjamin, 86n
Church of England, 112, 118–119, 146, 153–154, 210
Claes (slave), 131–135
Classis of Amsterdam, 153, 176, 217. *See also* Reformed Church
Claverack, settlement at, 66, 107
Clute, Johannes, 127–129
Cobes, Ludovicus, 48, 49, 61, 62, 67, 88, 117, 181, 183, 186, 191
Cohen, David Steven, 219–220
Cohoes Falls, 3, 23, 150, 171

Colbert, Jean Baptiste (adviser to Louis XIV), 77
Colden, Cadwallader, 60n, 144n, 211, 212n, 217
Colve, Anthony (Dutch governor), 70–73
Commissioners of Indian Affairs, 143
Condon, Thomas, 220
Confederation of New England, 15
Connecticut colony, 103, 105, 110, 142, 157, 198, 201
Connecticut River, 2, 13, 14, 76, 114, 125
Convention (government at Albany), 101–103, 157, 164
Cooper, Timothy, 112n
Cornbury, Edward Hyde, Lord (governor of New York), 56, 143, 175, 176, 176n, 180, 189–190, 210, 212
Cornwall, Eng., 172
Cortelyou, Jacques, 20–21
Council of War. *See* Albany, city of
Courcelle. *See* Rémy, Daniel, de Courcelle
Coureurs de bois, 92, 121–122, 130
Cromwell, Jacobus, 191
Crops
    export of to New England, 117
    gardens, 38, 40, 43, 48, 55
    individual: buckwheat, 41, 58; maize, 38, 56, 59–60, 87; oats, 38, 41, 43, 53, 58; peas, 18, 41, 55, 58; rye, 58; tobacco, 56, 56–57n; wheat, 40–41, 43, 48, 53, 55–59, 73, 87, 112, 185–186, 200, 206, 211–212, 222
    native agriculture, 56, 57n, 60
    orchards, 48, 54
    production of, 55, 55n, 56–58, 59, 60n, 206
    supplanting of fur trade by grain, 55–56, 185, 211–212
    See also Agriculture
Curaçao, 2, 50, 125

Damen, Maritie, 64, 133
Danckaerts, Jasper, 33n, 39, 44, 46, 52, 55, 56n, 57, 73, 88, 93, 148–150, 152, 155, 203, 211, 219–220
Danskamer, 66
Davids, Christoffel, 111, 120. *See also* Christoffelsen, David
De Bruyn, Johannes, 158n
Dedham, Mass., 218, 220
Deerfield, Mass., 106, 114
De Graaf, Claes, 46, 182
De Hinsse, Jacob, 80n
De Laet, Johannes, 3
Delavall, Capt. Thomas, 84, 128

Delaware River, 2, 16, 18, 22, 65, 76–77, 125, 185
Dellius, Dominie Godfridus, 152–153, 166–171, 173–174, 176, 208
Dellius grant, 166–167, 169–171, 173, 175
De Manthet, Nicolas d'Ailleboust, 103, 105
De Meyer, Nicholas, 73n
Denonville, Marquis de (governor of New France), 90, 92, 93, 95, 96, 103, 130
De Peyster, Abraham, 172
De Rasiere, Isaac, 6
De Tallie, Monsieur, 104
De Vos, Andries, 165n
De Vos, Cathalyna, 64, 135, 140, 164, 165n, 199–200, 206
De Willigen, near Schenectady, 135
De Wolff family, 22
Dina (slave), 128, 135
Disease, 28n, 52, 52n, 154, 198, 199n
Dongan, Thomas (governor of New York), 32, 47, 67, 89, 92–96, 113, 115, 117, 130, 145, 181, 183–184, 186–188
Douw, Volkert Jansen, 66
Duke's Laws, 125
Duplicee (*coureur de bois*), 122
Du Trieux. *See* Truax, Marie
Dutch
  unsuccessful Anglicization of, 119
  anti-English sentiment of, 79, 85, 113–115
  competition of with English for furs, 13–14, 111
  control of New Netherland by, 70, 76
  in Delaware Valley, 16, 18
  exploration and trade by, 1, 3–4
  and Governor Dongan, 95, 113
  intermarriage of with English, 119, 207
  and Leisler's Rebellion, 158–159, 161, 191, 193
  and natives, 145, 147–154, 202–203, 203n, 213, 219
  political practices of during English rule, 116, 116n
  population of in New Netherland and at Schenectady, 109–110, 210
  relations of with French, 80–81, 120–122
  relations of with Mohawks, 10, 24, 26–32
  trade of with New England, 112
  transmission of culture of to New World, 219–220
  See also Netherlands
Dutch East India Company, 1
Dutch West India Company, 2, 3, 5–6, 7, 15–16, 17n, 22, 125

Dyer, Jonathan, 191

Earthquake, 59
East Indies, 1, 148
Eccles, William J., 143n
Education (literacy, schools), 19n, 62, 64, 65n, 119, 122, 149
Eliot, Rev. John (Mass. missionary), 74
England, 76, 78, 81, 90, 96, 97, 99. 101
English
  and Albany fur trade monopoly, 21, 32, 68–70
  attack on settlements of by King Philip, 85
  competition of with French for furs and influence with Iroquois, 77, 89, 92, 97–98, 103, 146, 154
  conquest of New Netherland by, 116
  Dutch hostility toward, 79, 113–115, 216
  experience of Schenectady captives compared with, 202–203
  garrisons of, 78, 85, 111n, 114–116, 118, 206n, 210
  and Leisler's Rebellion, 158–159, 161, 191, 193
  and Schenectady, 110–112, 117–120, 178, 191, 206–207, 210–211, 214–215
  slavery under, 125, 131
  suspicions of about Dutch loyalty, 80, 83, 113
  threat of to Dutch fur trade, 13–16, 18, 28, 111–112
Esopus, village of, 18–19, 20, 35, 38, 47, 56, 56n, 66, 107, 113, 132, 197
Evans, Capt. John, 172

Families
  dispersal of after Schenectady massacre, 196, 198–199
  marriage patterns among at Schenectady, 64–65, 118, 161n, 178n, 193–194, 196, 206, 208, 209n
  mixed Dutch and English, 110–111, 119, 206–207
  number at and relations among at Schenectady, 19, 22, 61, 65, 102, 110, 119, 162, 164–165, 177–180, 183, 191, 193–194
  among settlers to New Netherland, 109
  slave-owning at Schenectady, 126, 136–137
  of slaves, 128–130, 135, 139–141
  of traders at Beverwyck, 13
  See also Women
Flatbush (L. I.), 154

Fletcher, Benjamin (governor of New York), 166, 168, 169, 172, 173, 175, 206, 206n
Flushing (L. I.), 187
Fonda, Jillis, 193–194
Fonda, N.Y., 24
Fort Albany, 73
Fort Amsterdam, 27
Fort Edward, 199n
Fort Frontenac, 91–92, 93, 95
Fort Hunter, 118, 146, 155n
Fort James, 183
Fort Nassau, 3
Fort Orange
  and Dutch West India Company, 3
  fur trade at, 5–6, 7, 10, 13, 15, 16, 24, 29–30n
  and Mohawks, 4–5, 26–27, 31
  slaves at, 125
  Walloons at, 120
  See also Albany, city of; Beverwyck
Fort St. Louis, 91
Fortune, 172
France, 77, 78, 81, 90, 96, 99
Francyn (slave), 123–124
Freeman, Dominie Bernardus, 151–154, 174, 176–177, 213, 217
Frémin, Jacques (Jesuit), 89
French
  at Albany, Schenectady, and vicinity, 120–122, 130, 130n, 191, 193, 214
  army of at Schenectady, 78
  attack on Schenectady by, 62, 88, 106, 124, 103–108, 110n
  invasion of New York by, 96–97, 99–101
  and Iroquois, 24, 29–30, 79, 82, 82n, 89, 91n, 93, 150, 152, 154–155, 169, 187
  as prisoners at Schenectady, 94
  at Quebec compared with Fort Orange, 4
  relations of with Dutch at Albany and Schenectady, 76, 79–81, 83
  rivalry of with English for furs and influence with Iroquois, 77, 90–92
  rumors of attack on Albany by, 78, 83–85, 95, 98, 117
  Schenectady captives among, 143, 144, 201–205
Fresh River. *See* Connecticut River
Fronde, 77
Frontenac, Comte de (governor of New France), 90, 91, 99–101, 104
Frontier
  concept of and community at Schenectady, 215–216

plan of Governor Bellomont for defense of, 115–116, 167, 175n
removal of population from, 196
location of Schenectady on, 62, 73–74, 74n, 76, 88–89, 155, 159, 193, 206–207, 222
See also Schenectady
Fur trade
  at Albany and Schenectady, 20–22, 30–32, 68–74, 76, 80–84, 112, 116, 121–122, 143–145, 169, 212–213, 220–221
  Anglo-French rivalry for, 77, 89–97, 100–101, 154, 187
  early evidence for, 24–26, 26n
  English threat to Dutch, 13–15
  at Fort Orange and Beverwyck, 5–13, 29–30n, 111
  and Mohawks, 8n, 24–32, 28–29n
  in New Netherland, 2–3, 7, 7n
Fuyck. *See* Beverwyck

Gandaouague. *See* Caughnawaga
Garoga (Mohawk village), 25
General Court of Massachusetts. *See* Massachusetts: General Court of
Gerritse, Martin, 206n
Glen, Helena, 144n
Glen, Jacob, 66, 73n, 84n, 127, 130, 144n
Glen, Johannes
  as anti-Leislerian and opponent of Reyer Schermerhorn, 101–102, 159, 161, 177, 188, 191
  death of, 215
  and government payments, 210
  marriage of, 161, 161n
  and Mohawk land, 118, 187n
  as officeholder, 102, 173, 188n, 191, 199n
  as slave owner, 136–137, 141
  as trustee for Schenectady patent, 190
  wealth of, 213–214
Glen, Sander Leendertsen, 127, 130, 183
  debts owed by, 22, 65–66, 73n
  property holdings of, 34, 36, 46, 48n, 113, 181–182, 182n
  as Schenectady proprietor, 21n, 23
  Scottish origins of, 113
  as slave owner, 126
  sons of at Schenectady and Albany, 66
  as trader, 22n, 61, 70
  and William Teller, 22, 64
Glen, Sander, Jr.
  as anti-Leislerian, 101–102, 103, 159, 161, 164, 165, 168
  death of, 168, 169n, 173
  and debt of father, 73n
  marriage of, 161, 161n

Glen, Sander, Jr. (*cont.*)
  as officeholder, 102, 173, 188n, 199n
  and order to build fort at Schenectady,
    200n
  and Schenectady massacre, 105–106, 199
  and 1690 raid against La Prairie, 199n
  as slave owner, 124, 135–136
Glen family, 118, 121, 135, 141, 164, 191,
  201
Goa, 1
Gookin, Daniel, 74–75
Gouverneur, Abraham, 166, 190
Great Lakes, 90
Greene, Jack P., 216
Greenhalgh, Wentworth, 112
Groot, Abraham, 137
Groot, Symon, 8n, 40, 66, 181, 201
Groot, Symon, Jr., 201, 204
Groot family, 215
Gulf of Mexico, 90

Half Moon, 17n, 187
Halve Maen, 2
Hansen, Hendrick, 144, 170, 170n, 173–
  175
Hartz, Louis, 220
Hatfield, Mass., 114
Hawthorne, William, 14–15, 111
Heerman, Augustine, 16
Helmers, Tryntje, 199, 208
Henry (Mohawk), 168, 169n
Hertel, François, 8on
Hesselingh, Dirck, 73
Hiawatha, 24
History of the Schenectady Patent. See Pear-
  son, Jonathan
Hochelaga, 25. *See also* Montreal
Hoop, 65n
Hoosick River, 87, 111
Houses, 48, 55
  at Albany, 41
  fire hazards of, 42, 48n, 66, 68, 69
  for Indians, 72n
  at Schenectady, 38–40, 47, 48n, 88,
    108, 164, 181, 201n
  uses for and construction of, 42–43, 47
  value of, 48, 54, 62
  Van Antwerpen/Mabie house, 42
Hudson, Henry, 2
Hudson Bay, 92, 103
Hudson River, 3–4, 14–16, 23, 24, 26, 59,
  60n, 111
Hudson Valley, 18–19
Hunt, George T., 8n, 24

Hunter, Robert (governor of New York),
  143, 145, 146, 158, 194, 195, 210–211
Huron Indians, 29, 89

Illinois Indians, 29, 90–92
Indians
  at Albany, 72n, 143, 143n
  children of by Dutch father, 23, 147–
    150
  contrasted to slaves by Dutch, 129, 147
  and Indianization of Dutch, 145, 150–
    151, 202–203, 213, 219
  and promotion of fur trade at Bever-
    wyck, 9–11
  as slaves, 141–142, 142n
  trade with Europeans, 24–26, 29
  See also individual tribes
Ingoldsby, Richard (lieutenant govenor of
  New York), 74n, 166
Ipswich, Mass., 14
Ireland, 99
Iroquois Indians
  agriculture of, 56, 57n, 60
  and Anglo-French military power, 95–
    96
  confederacy of, 24
  Dutch missionary efforts among, 151–
    153, 213
  and Dutch refugees in New York City,
    198
  European impact on culture and society
    of, 154–155
  and French, 29, 77, 82, 88–93, 95, 97–
    100, 121
  and fur trade, 4–8, 25–26, 187
  land of acquired by Governor Dongan,
    67
  in Mohawk Valley, 23, 26
  and Schenectady Dutch, 94, 143–144
  slaves of, 142n
  war parties of, 91, 91n, 96, 99, 103,
    106, 145
  and Wentworth Greenhalgh, 112
  See also Indians; Cayuga Indians; Mohawk
    Indians; Oneida Indians; Onondaga
    Indians; Seneca Indians
Isaabelle (slave), 135, 140
Itinerario, 1

Jack (slave), 135, 140
Jacob (slave), 64, 126, 127, 131–134
Jacques (Frenchman), 121
James II. *See* York, James, duke of
Jan (slave), 162n
Jansen, Arnout, 204
Jansen, Paulyn, 204

Jenning, Stephen, 114
Jennings, Francis, 29
Jersey, 176n
Jesuit Relation, 29, 82, 85, 89, 149
Jesuits, 89, 91, 121, 122, 151–153, 155,
    203–204
Jogues, Isaac (Jesuit), 6–7, 7n, 17, 18, 42,
    49, 121, 144, 216, 222
Johnson, Sir William, 19
Jolliet, Louis, 90
Jonckers, Jan Jansen. *See* Van Rotterdam,
    Jan Jansen Jonckers
Joseph (Mohawk), 168, 169n
Juet, Robert, 2

Kanagaro (Mohawk village), 24
Keeman. *See* Viele, Cornelis Cornelissen
Kenney, Alice P., 219–220
Ketelhuyn, Daniel, 211, 212n
Kieft, William (Dutch governor of New
    Netherland), 147
Kieft's War, 149
Kim, Sung Bok, 181
Kinaquariones, 75, 75n
Kinderhook, settlement at, 43, 53n, 58,
    107
King Philip's War, 85–86, 86n, 91, 97. *See
    also* Philip, King
Kingston. *See* Esopus, village of
King William's War, 114, 154, 203
Kleyn, Johannes, 183, 186
Kregier, Capt. Martin, 58n
Kryn (Mohawk leader), 89, 90, 93, 103–
    104, 106, 187

Labadists, 39, 219
La Barre, Joseph-Antoine Lefebvre de
    (governor of New France), 91–92
Labatie, Jean, 80n, 120
La Chesnaye, 99, 101
Lachine, 99, 101, 103, 106, 108
Lake Champlain, 81, 82n, 90, 95, 96, 104,
    204, 221
Lake Erie, 92
Lake George, 82n, 104
Lake Huron, 92
Lake Ontario, 92, 93, 115, 144n, 154, 212
Lake St. Sacrament. *See* Lake George
Lake of Two Mountains, 103
La Montagne, Johannes, 10–12, 80n
Land
    acquisition and distribution of, 17, 30,
        33–36, 38, 40, 54, 60, 63–64, 66–67,
        118, 122, 135, 144, 147–148, 162,
        164, 166, 173–174, 181–187, 211, 221

disputes over, 159, 180–182, 184, 186,
    189–191, 194–195, 216–217
use of, 20, 33–35, 38–42, 46–47, 53,
    55–58, 118, 182
See also Agriculture
La Prairie, 199n
La Salle, Robert, 83, 90
Latham, John, 170, 172–173
Lea (Mohawk), 183–184, 203, 213. *See also*
    Van Slyck family
Leiden, 111
Leisler, Jacob
    and Albany magistrates, 102, 103, 175
    assumption of power in New York by,
        101
    execution of, 166
    rebellion of characterized, 191
    and Schenectady massacre, 108, 109,
        157, 157n, 158, 198, 200
    supporters and opponents of at Schenec-
        tady, 101, 102, 159–165, 167–168,
        186, 188
    See also Leisler's Rebellion
Leisler, Jacob, Jr., 166
Leisler's Rebellion, 115, 158–159, 161,
    181, 191, 195, 222
Le Moyne, Charles, 103
Le Moyne, Jacques, de Sainte-Hélène,
    103, 105
Le Moyne, Pierre, d'Iberville, 103, 105
Le Moyne, Simon (Jesuit), 30
Lenyn, Benjamin, 191, 193, 208n
Lespinard, Anthony, 90, 91n, 120, 122–
    123, 123n, 130
Livestock
    killing of by Mohawks at Rensselaers-
        wyck, 9
    individual species: cattle, 20, 39–40, 46,
        48–55, 55n, 62, 108, 112, 112n, 128,
        200; hogs, 50–52, 53n, 54, 55n, 57n,
        58, 112n, 200; horses, 20, 39–40, 46,
        48–55, 62, 64, 106, 112, 121, 128,
        200; oxen, 49; poultry, 200
    owned by Dutch, 48–55
    trade in from New England, 55n, 112
    value of lost to French, 62, 106, 108,
        199
    See also Agriculture
Livingston, Philip, 211
Livingston, Robert, 102, 157–158, 164,
    196, 201, 211, 213–214
London, 108
Long Island, 18, 44, 52, 111, 158, 167,
    168, 177, 187
Long Lake. *See* Saratoga Lake
Lords of Trade. *See* Board of Trade

Louis XIV (king of France), 77, 99
Lovelace, Francis (governor of New York),
    51, 64, 68–70, 74n, 76n, 83–84, 112,
    113
Lutherans, 23
Lydius, Dominie Johannes, 176

Mabie, Jan Pietersen, 42, 185n, 189, 211
Macgregory, Maj. Patrick, 92
Maelwyck (near Schenectady), 66
Magellan's Strait, 1
Mahican Indians, 3–4, 13, 24, 26, 30–31,
    86
Manhattan, 6, 17, 70, 81, 124, 147, 172,
    176, 196
Mangelse, Jan, 184n
Marks, Joseph, 201
Marselis, Ahasuerus, 214
Maryland, 2, 16, 108
Massachusetts, 2, 14, 15, 85, 108, 111–
    112, 114, 218, 220
    General Court of, 14, 15n
Mazarin, Cardinal, 77
Megapolënsis, Dominie Johannes, 147, 151
Merwick, Donna, 219–220, 220n
Miami Indians, 90
Michaëlius, Dominie Jonas, 147, 150
Milborne, Jacob, 101–102, 158n, 162–164,
    166, 218
Miller, Rev. John (Anglican minister), 112
Mississippi Valley, 90
Mohawk Flats, 22, 23, 31, 39, 76
Mohawk Indians, 96, 134, 189, 204
    and Arent van Curler, 17, 19, 30–32,
        121
    attack of by Massachusetts Indians, 74–
        76, 134
    attack on King Philip's warriors by, 85–
        86, 86n, 91
    children of by Dutch father, 148–150
    and French, 29–30, 77–79, 81–82, 82n,
        83, 89, 96–98, 103–104, 154, 169
    and Governor Dongan, 89, 183–184,
        187
    impact of disease and war on, 28n, 154,
        199n, 206n, 212n
    land grants to Dutch by, 144, 168, 173,
        182–185, 187–188
    missionary work among, 6, 82, 89, 121,
        146, 151–154, 173–174, 210
    and Schenectady, 93–96, 104, 107–109,
        118, 144–146, 148–149, 173, 182–
        185, 200–201, 203–205, 219
    trade and relations with Dutch, 4–8, 8n,
        10–11, 13, 26–28, 27n, 29–30n, 219

    villages of, 3–4, 23–24, 26
    war of with Mahicans, 4
Mohawk River, 23, 26, 34, 38, 46, 46n,
    113, 118, 144n, 181–182
Mohawk Valley, 26, 94–95, 115–116, 146,
    154, 166, 173–174, 183–185, 210
Montigny, Monsieur, 105
Montreal, 30, 89–93, 97, 99, 101, 103,
    105–106, 108, 122, 144n, 201, 204–
    205. *See also* Hochelaga
Morton, Thomas, 13–14
Mullin, Gerald W., 132–133
Myndertse, Maritie, 65n

Nanfan, John (lieutenant governor of New
    York), 175
Narragansett Bay, 24
Narragansett Indians, 74
Nash, Gary B., 143, 151n, 191, 193, 203n
Navigation Acts (1651 and 1660), 76
Netherlands, 1, 9, 35, 43–46, 56, 78, 120,
    129, 155, 174, 219–220. *See also* Dutch
New Amstel, 16, 18, 22, 185
New Amsterdam, 7, 8, 18, 65, 76, 111,
    125, 149, 151. *See also* New York City
New English Canaan, 13–14
New France, 77, 80–81, 89–92, 94, 95,
    97–101, 103, 106, 114, 130–131, 143,
    150, 198, 203–205. *See also* French; Je-
    suits
New Hampshire, 172
New Netherland, 18, 64
    and English, 9, 16, 76, 113, 116
    fur trade in, 2, 5–7
    natives in, 28, 143, 148, 151
    population growth in, 2, 18–19, 109,
        120
    Schenectady on the frontier of, 62, 155,
        222
    slavery in, 124–125, 129, 131
    transfer of Dutch culture and population
        to, 219–220
New Utrecht (L. I.), 177
New York Bay, 2
New York City, 49, 56, 73, 94, 100, 114,
    132, 150, 157, 158, 159, 161, 165,
    172, 181, 188, 190, 191, 193, 196,
    198, 222. *See also* New Amsterdam
Niagara, 90, 95
Nicolls, Richard (governor of New York),
    69–70, 76, 78, 80–81, 85, 96, 113,
    116, 117, 121
*Nieuwe Wereldt ofte beschrijvinghe van West-
    Indien*, 3
Niskayuna, 184n, 187, 196, 196n

Normanskill, 50, 63, 64, 66
North River. *See* Hudson River
North Sea, 76
Norton, Thomas E., 8n, 69
Norway, 120n
Notre Dame de Foy, 89

Occupations
apprenticeship and servitude, 50, 60, 63, 65, 161
specific: armorer, 27, 147; baker, 61, 122; bateau men, 212; blacksmith, 147, 147n; brewer, 21, 61, 162; brickmaker, 61; carpenter, 61, 146–147, 147n, 162, 210; cattle herder, 53; confectioner, 61; farmhand, 60, 61; gunstock maker, 43, 193; mason, 147; miller, 61, 63, 162; saw mill operator, 63; ship carpenter, 170, 172; silversmith, 133; sloop operator, 61, 196; surveyor, 20; tailor, 61; tapster, 61, 117, 184
See also Agriculture
Officeholders, 116, 116–117n, 164–165, 177–178
Ohio River, 145, 168
Oneida Indians, 29, 82, 89, 95, 145, 150, 204, 205
Onnongonges. *See* Abenaki Indians
Onondaga Indians, 29–30, 92, 95, 144–146, 205–206
Oswego, 154, 212
Ottawa Indians, 91n, 92
Otten, Helmer, 64, 118

Paine, John, 75n, 111–112, 112n
Paine, William, 14, 111
Palatines, 211
Pearson, Jonathan, 30n, 38, 209n
Peek, Annatie, 161n
Peek, Jacobus, 67, 182–183, 185n, 186
Peek, Jan, 181
Pennequids. *See* Abenaki Indians
Pennsylvania, 91, 168, 187
Pey (slave), 130–131
Philip II (king of Spain), 1
Philip, King (Metacom), 85–86, 86n, 91
Philipsen, Philip, the Moor, 134, 135, 185n
Pierron, Jean (Jesuit), 74–75, 84, 89, 121
Pieters, Bastiaen (slave?), 134
Pinhorne, William, 166n
Piscataway, N.H., 172, 172n
Plymouth Colony, 14, 111
Pocumtuck Indians, 74

Poestenkill, 63, 64
Pootman, Johannes, 65, 102, 158, 161–162, 162n, 164–165
Portsmouth, Eng., 172
Portugal, 2
Praying Indians, 74, 74n, 103, 154, 204
Pretty, Sheriff Richard, 69, 72–73
Prevoost, Johannes, 158n
Prouville, Alexandre de, Seigneur de Tracy (governor of New France), 79–82, 150
Provoost, Johannes, 117
Pynchon, John, 14–15, 74, 78–80, 108, 111, 112n
Pynchon, William, 14

Quebec, 4, 30, 77, 80, 82, 89, 90, 91, 92, 96, 99, 101, 103, 149
Queen Anne's chapel, 146, 154, 210
Queen Anne's War, 210, 211, 215

Rachel (slave), 135, 140
Randolph, Edward, 98, 145n, 171n
Reformed Church, 64, 119, 121, 129, 130n, 133n, 141, 153, 164, 198, 208.
See also Classis of Amsterdam
"Refugio." *See* Narragansett Bay
Rémy, Daniel, de Courcelle (governor of New France), 77–79, 100n
Rensselaerswyck, 4, 9, 42, 84, 85, 87, 107, 147–148, 151, 198
agriculture at, 17–18, 35–36, 49–52, 56–58, 63
description of by Isaac Jogues, 6–7, 7n, 17–18, 42, 49, 222
fur trade at, 6–7, 21
population at, 18, 109, 120
Schenectady proprietors from, 19, 21–23, 48, 63–64, 66
slavery at, 137, 139
Reynier, Jacob, 190
Rhode (Mohawk sachem), 96
Richelieu River, 96, 204
Rinckhout, Daniel, 82, 83n
Rinckhout, Jan, 38
River Indians, 30, 150
Roads/trails/waterways, 23, 31, 39, 47, 48n, 75, 75n, 104, 104n, 105, 134, 144, 144n, 145, 211
Roberts, Benjamin, 46, 66, 113, 181–182
Rome, N.Y., 23
Romer, Col. Wolfgang William, 85n, 166–169
Roseboom, Hendrick, 43
Rosie, Jean, 83, 120, 123n, 205

Rotterdam Junction, 42
Round Lake, 104
Russia, 3
Ryckman, Gerritje, 148, 178n, 206

St. Lawrence River, 4, 24, 25, 90, 92, 97, 99
Salem, Mass., 218
Salisbury, Neal, 28n
Sam (slave), 135, 140
Sanders, Robert, 87
Sara (slave), 127
Saratoga, 67, 88, 122
Saratoga Lake, 104
Scandinavia, 23
Schaats, Dominie Gideon, 132, 151
Schaats, Reynier, 102, 158–159
Schaghticoke, 85–87, 86n, 91, 107, 122, 142, 197, 211, 222n
Schenectady, 30n, 38, 41–48, 48n, 55n, 61, 65
  and Albany, 69–73, 72n, 217–218
  and Arent van Curler, 19–21, 31, 76, 78–82, 221
  conception, birth, and marriage at, 208–209, 209n
  defense of, 83–88, 112–113, 115–116, 200n, 206n
  descriptions of, 33, 33n, 112–113, 215
  and English rule, 113–119, 210–211
  farming at, 33–36, 38–41, 48–61, 181–185, 211–212
  French army at, 77–78
  French attack of and aftermath, 88n, 93–108, 110n, 196–206
  as frontier community, 73–74, 74n, 155–156, 215–216
  and fur trade, 20–22, 23n, 68–74, 76, 82, 212–213
  half-breeds at, 79, 147–150, 155, 183
  historical significance of, 221–222
  incentive for settlement at, 16–18, 31–32
  Indianization of Dutch culture and behavior at, 150–151, 151n, 202–203, 203n
  Indian relations with, 143–146, 151–154
  and Leisler's Rebellion, 101–103, 157–195
  and Mohawks, 23–24, 26, 30–31, 30n, 74–75, 75–76n, 89
  movement of population from, 66–67, 88, 182, 196–199, 211
  and naval stores gathered near, 170–173
  non-Dutch settlers at, 111, 113, 120, 121–122, 206–207, 207n, 210
  patent, 180, 186–195
  population of, 87, 87n, 88, 88n, 109, 110n, 119, 120n, 137, 139, 141, 193, 210, 209–210n
  settlers of, 22–23, 63–65, 213–222
  slavery at, 123–141
  wealth of residents of, 63, 160–161, 194, 194n, 213–214
  See also Agriculture; Crops; Families; Frontier; Land; Livestock; Reformed Church; Women
Schermerhorn, Catalina, 189
Schermerhorn, Jacob Jansen, 27, 118, 161
Schermerhorn, Reyer
  arrest of, 168
  assessed wealth of, 213
  death of, 195, 214–215
  and Dominie Bernardus Freeman, 176
  family relations of, 64, 118, 161, 165, 199, 208
  and Governor Bellomont, 118, 145, 146, 170, 172–175, 210
  and Governor Cornbury, 176, 176n
  as Leislerian leader, 101, 102, 158, 167, 177–178, 180, 191, 193–194, 200
  as magistrate and assemblyman, 164, 168–170, 175, 186, 188n
  as member of Commissioners of Indian Affairs, 143
  property owned by, 39n, 164, 185–186, 211
  at Schenectady, 159
  as slave owner, 161, 162n
  as trustee for Schenectady patent, 180–181, 187–190, 195, 216
  visit of to Mohawks, 145–146, 170n, 173
Schermerhorn, Reyer (grandson of Reyer Schermerhorn), 217
Schermerhorn, Symon, 93, 107, 135, 158, 161, 196, 198
Schoharie River, 118, 195, 210–211
Schuyler, Alida, 196
Schuyler, Johannes, 199n
Schuyler, Myndert, 175
Schuyler, Philip Pietersen, 9, 16n
Schuyler, Pieter, 108, 145, 153n, 166, 173, 190
Scotia, near Schenectady, 42, 113
Seneca Indians, 8, 29, 57n, 60n, 90, 91n, 93–96, 103, 143–144, 144n, 146–147, 147n
Shattuck, Martha, 13n
Shell, Antje, 209n
Sixberry, Manasseh, 191

Slachboom, Anthonia, 53, 65, 68, 75, 118, 126, 128, 128–129n, 134–135, 140, 149, 181
Slavery
  and Duke's Laws, 125
  Dutch slave trade, 76, 109, 125, 125n
  in New Netherlands, 124–125, 131
  in New York compared with in other colonies, 132–133
Slaves
  within Albany County, 137–139, 141, 196
  and *coureurs de bois*, 130
  family relations of, 139–141
  freed, 134–135
  Indian, 141–142, 142n
  killing or capture of in 1690, 123–124, 202
  purchase of, 64, 126–128, 128–129n
  and Reformed Church, 129, 130n, 133n
  runaway, 130–131
  at Schenectady, 126, 130n, 131–137, 210
Sloughter, Henry (governor of New York), 153, 166, 168, 201, 201n, 205
Sluyter, Pieter, 44, 150
Smallpox. *See* Disease
Smith, Capt. John, 26n
Smith, Richard, 55n, 58n
Smith, Thomas, 191
Smith, William, Jr., 33n, 55
Society for the Propagation of the Gospel in Foreign Parts, 119
South Carolina, 132, 133, 141, 142
South River. *See* Delaware River
Spain, 2
Spoor, Antje, 128
Spoor, Jan, 128
Springfield, Mass., 14, 74, 108
Staats, Abraham, 13
Statyn, 64
Stevens, Jonathan, 207n, 213
Stockade Area (Schenectady), 42
Strickland, William, 46n, 55n, 58, 59n
Stuart government, 71
Stuyvesant, Petrus (governor of New Netherland), 2, 18, 18n, 27, 38, 111
  and Arent van Curler, 17, 81
  and English threat, 15–16, 18n
  and fur trade, 7, 8, 10–11
  and Schenectady, 17, 17n, 19, 20–21, 30, 32, 37, 39–40, 48, 71, 73–74, 220–221
  and Swedes on Delaware, 16
Susanna (slave), 141
"Sussanna" (slave), 135, 140

Susquehanna River, 187
Susquehannock Indians, 91
Swart, Jacquemyn, 196–197, 197n
Swart, Teunis Cornelissen, 22n, 35
Swits, Claes Cornelissen, 182
Swits, Isaac Cornelissen, 40–41, 65, 120, 159, 161, 178, 180, 191, 201, 204, 208, 214
Symon (slave), 141

Tadoussac, 26
Talmadge, Lt. Enos, 103
Taonnochreo (Mohawk), 204
Tardivett (*coureur de bois*), 122
Taylor, John, 172
Taylor, Rev. John, 39
Teller, Johannes, 36, 66, 124, 135, 196, 199, 204
Teller, William, 12, 21n, 84n, 130, 146
  as anti-Leislerian, 159, 164n, 188–189
  death of, 178n, 214
  move to New York City of, 188, 196, 197n, 198
  and Sander Leendertsen Glen, 22, 64
  as Schenectady proprietor, 22n, 23, 36, 38n, 40–42, 48, 50, 54–57, 60, 65, 66, 70, 88, 120, 161, 182, 187–188, 221
Ten Broeck, Dirck Wessels, 166, 168, 175
Tenotoge. *See* Tionnontoguen
Tesschenmaeker, Dominie Petrus, 106, 130–131, 151–153, 153n, 217
Thickstone, Jeremy, 208n
Thirty Years' War, 77
Tionnontoguen (Mohawk village), 24, 27, 84, 153n
Tonty, Henri, de, 92
Tracy. *See* Prouville, Alexandre de, Seigneur de Tracy
Trails. *See* Roads/trails/waterways
Treat, Robert (governor of Connecticut), 103
Trelease, Allen W., 11n, 24, 29n
Trico, Catelyn, 27n
Trigger, Bruce G., 8n
Trois Rivières, 103
Troupes de la Marine, 93
Truax, Isaac, 182–183, 183n
Truax, Marie, 122
Truax family, 120n

Ulster County, 173, 197
United Provinces. *See* Netherlands

Van Antwerpen, Daniel Jansen, 42, 46, 65, 67, 117, 177, 182–183, 185n, 190–191
Van Antwerpen, Symon Danielsen, 195, 211
Van Bael, Jan Hendricksen, 162n
Van Bockhoven, Claes Jansen, 135, 137, 140, 184n, 200
Van Brakel, Gysbert Gerritse, 204
Van Brakel, Stephen, 204
Van Bremen, Jan, 13
Van Coppernol, Claes Willemsen, 88, 119, 183, 203
Van Curler, Arent, 64, 126
  and Anthonia Slachboom, 65, 68, 120n
  death of, 23n, 81, 81–82n
  and French, 76, 78–83, 83n, 113, 150
  and Governor Nicolls, 80–81
  and Mohawks, 19, 120, 121, 144, 149
  and Petrus Stuyvesant, 17, 19–21
  and Philip Hendricksen Brouwer, 54, 162
  at Rensselaerswyck, 7, 7n, 21, 22n, 36, 43, 48, 48n, 56–57n, 66
  at Schenectady, 17, 19, 22–23, 30, 31, 33–34, 39–40, 47–49, 54, 148, 181, 183, 221
Van Curler, Jacob, 79n
Van den Bogaert, Harmen Meyndertsz, 27
Van den Bogaert, Myndert Harmensen, 158
Van der Baest, Joris Aertsen, 84
Van der Burgh, Cornelis Willemsen, 162
Van der Donck, Adriaen, 7, 17n, 50–51, 52n, 56–58
Van der Heyden, Jacob Tyssen, 12, 12n
Van der Volgen, Claes Lourens, 205
Van der Volgen, Lourens Claesen, 117, 143–145, 203–205, 215
Van Ditmars, Barent Jansen, 52
Van Eps, Evert, 188
Van Eps, Jan, 49, 64, 66, 69, 101–102, 116, 136, 162, 181, 187–188
Van Eps, Jan Baptist, 117, 136, 144–145, 185n, 188, 190, 201, 203, 204, 204n, 215
Van Eps, Jan Baptist (son of Jan Baptist van Eps), 144n
Van Eps family, 165
Van Gyseling, Elias, 122
Van Hoeck, Bennony Arentsen, 197
Van Krieckenbeeck, Daniel, 4–5
Van Linschoten, Jan Huighen, 1
Van Marcken, Jan Gerritsen, 53, 70, 71, 75, 185
Van Ness, Cornelis, 36, 40, 46, 49, 181

Van Nieukerck, Gerrit, 60–61
Van Olinda, Daniel, 177, 191
Van Olinda, Hilletie
  as cultural broker, 148–149, 152, 155
  death of, 213, 214
  and Dominie Dellius, 174, 219
  family relations of, 61, 117, 148–149, 152, 178n, 203
  as interpreter, 168, 173–174
  property of, 39n, 183–184
Van Olinda, Pieter Danielsen, 23, 61, 64, 148–149, 159, 177, 178n, 183, 185, 191, 199, 214
Van Petten, Arent, 147n
Van Petten, Claes Fredericksen, 40, 62, 65, 159, 161, 162n, 165, 180, 181
Van Ravesteyn, Elias, 43
Van Rensselaer family, 71–72, 139
Van Rensselaer, Jan Baptist, 127
Van Rensselaer, Jeremias, 12, 17, 18, 49, 51–52, 57n, 63, 80n, 83, 85, 112, 127n, 149
Van Rensselaer, Kiliaen, 4, 6, 13, 48, 58, 149
Van Rensselaer, Maria, 86
Van Rensselaer, Rev. Nicholas, 71
Van Rotterdam, Jan Jansen Jonckers, 47, 182, 185, 207
Van Sice, Joseph, 147n
Van Slyck, Cornelis (son of Jacques Cornelissen van Slyck), 191
Van Slyck, Cornelis Anthonisz, 147–149
Van Slyck, Grietje, 201, 201n
Van Slyck, Harmen, 177, 185, 191, 195, 209n, 211, 215
Van Slyck, Hilletie. *See* Van Olinda, Hilletie
Van Slyck, Jacques (Aukes) Cornelissen
  acquisition of land from Mohawks by, 183–184, 186
  as anti-Leislerian, 159
  as cultural broker, 148, 155, 203, 219
  death of, 199, 213
  as interpreter, 73, 93, 117
  marriage of daughter of, 164–165
  Mohawk nephew of, 152
  at Schenectady, 23, 48n, 50–51, 58, 60–61, 117, 184
  as trader, 22n, 70
  will of, 200
Van Slyck, Martin, 34, 60, 148
Van Slyck, Martin (son of Jacques Cornelissen van Slyck), 191
Van Slyck family, 23, 118, 178n
Van Tienhoven, Cornelis, 27, 39, 47
Van Valkenburgh, Isaac, 214

Van Vechten, Dirck Teunissen, 51–52
Van Velsen, Sweer Teunissen
  as anti-Leislerian, 101
  dealth of in 1690, 103, 128
  as magistrate, 64, 116
  at Schenectady, 48n, 50, 52, 63, 64, 70
  as servant of Jan Barentsen Wemp, 63–65, 65n
  as slave owner, 63, 64, 126–127, 131–132, 134, 136
  and stepchildren, 102, 165, 201
  as trustee for Schenectady patent, 187–188
Van Wassenaer, Nicolaes, 4
Van Woggelum, Pieter Adriaensen, 22n, 23n, 137
Van Ysselsteyn, Martin Cornelissen, 54, 66, 181, 221
Vedder, Albert, 215
Vedder, Harmanus (son of Harmen Vedder), 137, 201
Vedder, Harmen, 21n, 22, 40, 46, 73
Veeder, Gerrit Symonsen, 147n, 199, 208
Veeder, Symon Volkertsen, 22n, 53, 62n, 66, 221
Velsen (in Netherlands), 63
Venezuela, 2
Verrazzano, Giovanni da, 24–25, 25n
Viele, Arnout Cornelissen, 87, 94
  journeys of to Senecas, 94, 144, 144n
  as interpreter, 117, 169n
  lease of slave by, 127, 129
  as Leislerian, 165, 167–168, 177, 186
  property owned by, 66–67, 88, 185–186
  as trader, 92–93, 145, 168
Viele, Arnout, Jr., 67, 201
Viele, Cornelis Cornelissen
  and French, 83, 121–122, 184
  as interpreter, 94, 117, 184, 186
  at Schenectady, 46, 46n, 61–62, 73, 85, 117, 181–182
Viele, Cornelis, 46n
Viele, Debora, 212n
Viele, Lowis, 195, 197, 211, 212n
Viele, Pieter Cornelissen, 122, 197n
Viele family, 118, 180
Virginia, 91, 132, 133, 216
Volkje (slave), 141
Vrooman, Adam
  as anti-Leislerian, 162–164, 164n, 177, 191
  as carpenter and miller, 50, 61, 112n, 162
  death of, 215
  marriage of to Gerritje Ryckman, 178n, 206

  at Schenectady, 66, 185, 189–190, 195, 211
  as slave owner, 135, 137
  sons of, 204–205, 210
Vrooman, Barent, 147n, 204n
Vrooman, Hendrick, 39n, 66, 135, 162
Vrooman, Hendrick (son of Adam Vrooman), 147n
Vrooman, Jan, 66
Vrooman, Jannetie, 209n
Vrooman, Wouter, 204n
Vynhout, Cornelis, 197

Wabash River, 145
Waite, Benjamin, 114
Walloons, 120, 122
Wampanoag Indians, 85
Wappengers, 15
Water supply, 46–47
Waterways. *See* Roads/trails/waterways
Wemp, Antje, 165
Wemp, Barent, 136–137, 165, 178, 191, 199n, 201n, 208
Wemp, Ephraim, 188
Wemp, Hendrick, 147n
Wemp, Jan Barentsen, 23n, 34, 60–61, 63–64, 65n, 70, 148, 165
Wemp, Johannes, 147n, 180, 188–190, 195, 216–217
Wemp, Myndert, 63, 102, 136, 158, 161, 161n, 164–165, 188
Wemp, Myndert (son of Barent Wemp), 147n
Wemp family, 165, 201, 201n
Wendel, Diwer, 161n
Western Indians, 144, 212
West Indies, 2, 127, 142, 212
Willett, Thomas, 111
William III (king of England), 153, 177, 180, 190
Williams, Thomas, 190n
Wiltwyck (near Esopus) 19, 38
Winthrop, Fitz-John, 198, 199n
Winthrop, John (governor of Massachusetts), 13
Winthrop, John, Jr. (governor of Connecticut), 75n, 76n, 79
Witte Paert, 109
Women
  and childbirth, 208–209, 209–210n
  control of property and slaves at Schenectady by, 60, 126, 128, 135, 137, 140, 181, 199, 200
  Dutch relations with native, 147–150
  and fur trade, 68, 72
  as interpreters, 168, 173–174

Women (*cont.*)
  and marriage, 64–65, 119, 161, 193, 197, 206, 207
  slave, 123–124, 127, 130, 139–142
  status of, 61n
  as refugees, 87, 98n, 110n, 196, 198, 207n
  See also Families
Wood, Peter H., 132–133

Wood resources, 39, 44, 45–47, 59, 170–173
Wouter (Mohawk), 152, 155, 203
Wyngaerd, Catharyna, 200
Wyngaerd, Jan Luycassen, 185n, 199n, 200

York, James, duke of (James II), 76–77, 99, 158

Library of Congress Cataloging-in-Publication Data

Burke, Thomas E., 1951–
  Mohawk frontier : the Dutch community of Schenectady, New York, 1661–1710 / Thomas E. Burke, Jr.
    p. cm.
  Includes bibliographical references and index.
  ISBN 0-8014-2541-7 (cloth : alk. paper)
  1. Dutch Americans—New York (State)—Schenectady—History. 2. Schenectady (N.Y.)—History. I. Title.
F129.S5B87 1991
974.7′44—dc20
                                                  91-55237